Handbook of Educational Reform Through Blended Learning

Ming Li · Xibin Han · Jiangang Cheng
Editors

Handbook of Educational Reform Through Blended Learning

Editors
Ming Li
The International Centre for Higher
Education Innovation under the auspices
of UNESCO
Southern University of Science
and Technology
Shenzhen, Guangdong, China

Xibin Han
Institute of Education
Tsinghua University
Beijing, China

Jiangang Cheng
Institute of Education
Tsinghua University
Beijing, China

Preface

With the increasing popularity of digital technologies in daily life and work, such as big data, artificial intelligence, blockchain, and 5G, our lifestyles and work styles have undergone profound changes. The accelerated development of digital industrialization and industrial digitization has created new requirements (i.e., knowledge, skills, and abilities) for the global workforce. The development of the Internet has given rise to digital thinking, distributed cognition, knowledge dissemination in virtual space, and interpersonal communication, which will lead to systematic changes in workforce training. These changes require a digital transformation of higher education, where the workforce will be trained.

Many countries and organizations have announced policies and regulations to promote digital transformation of higher education and vocational training. For example, the International Telecommunication Union, UNESCO (United Nations Educational, Scientific and Cultural Organization), and UNICEF (United Nations International Children's Emergency Fund) in 2020 jointly published "Digital Transformation of Education: Connecting Schools and Empowering Students", which first proposed the concept and initiative of digital transformation in education. The European Union released the Digital Education Action Plan (2021–2027), which advocates the need to promote the two strategic plans: promoting the development of a high-performance digital education ecosystem and improving digital skills and competencies to achieve digital transformation. The American Higher Education Information Association released the Top 10 IT Issues of 2018—Driving Digital Transformation, which describes the key issues driving the digital transformation of higher education. In addition, China's Ministry of Education has proposed the implementation of a National Education Digitalization Strategy in early 2022. However, as UNESCO noted in 2021 in Reimagining Our Future Together: A New Social Contract for Education, the changing nature of knowledge (e.g., knowledge construction, acquisition, dissemination, validation, and use) resulting from computers and the Internet makes information more accessible, opens up new avenues for education, and has enormous transformative potential for education, but we have yet to find the way to turn this potential into reality.

To this end, the UNESCO Center for Higher Education Innovation (Shenzhen, China) and the Institute of Education of Tsinghua University jointly launched the "3+1" project (3 handbooks and 1 research report), which explores the digital transformation of higher education. The three handbooks include *Handbook of Educational Reform through Blended Learning, Handbook of Teaching Competency Development in Higher Education*, and *Handbook of Technical and Vocational Teacher Professional Development in the Digital Age*. The research report, *Research Report on Digital Transformation of Higher Education Teaching and Learning*, was officially released in four language versions (Chinese, English, French, and Spanish) at the *3rd World Conference on Higher Education* held by UNESCO in Barcelona, Spain in May 2022. The research report aims to provide international organizations, governments, universities, enterprises, and other stakeholders with ideas and methods for implementing digital transformation in higher education. The report has analyzed the background and current situation of digital transformation in higher education, clarified the related implementation framework, elaborated the characteristics and strategies of digital transformation in higher education, and discussed the challenges and suggestions for digital transformation implementation. The three handbooks have provided related theories, standards, methods, and strategies for the implementation of blended learning. In addition, the three handbooks aim to help all countries and districts around the world, especially developing countries, to use digital technology to achieve the goal of developing sustainable education by 2030, as advocated by UNESCO, and to build inclusive, resilient, open, and high-quality higher education and vocational education systems. The "3+1" project must not only meet the challenges of digital transformation in higher education, but also solve the problems proposed in the "last mile problem" of IT integrated in education. The "3+1" project was sponsored by the UNESCO Center for Higher Education Innovation (Shenzhen, China) and supported by Dr. Ming Li, Director of the UNESCO Center for Higher Education Innovation. Fifteen domestic and foreign research teams actively participated and cooperated, including Xibin Han, Meifeng Liu, Yuping Wang, Jihua Song, Tiedao Zhang, Li Chen, Shuyan Wang, Mingxuan Chen, Zhixian Zhong, Qingtang Liu, Shusheng Shen, Shuyu Yu, Mei Cao, Jieyuan Sun, and Hao Yang. Special thanks!

This *Handbook of Educational Reform through Blended Learning* summarizes the research and practice of blended learning in our research teams over the past 20 years, involving more than 50 experts from educational technology, higher education, vocational education, and education management around the world. The purpose of this handbook is to recommend relevant policies of blended learning for international organizations and governments of various countries, provide systematic solutions for administrators in higher education institutions to implement blended learning, provide blended learning methods for teachers, and serve as a reference for researchers and relevant enterprise practitioners. The Chinese version of this handbook is published by Tsinghua University Press and the English version is published by Springer.

This handbook first systematically discussed the theoretical foundations of blended learning, including theories of blended learning, models of blended learning, and design and practice models of blended learning (Chap. 1). It then elaborated on the core components and implementation of blended learning, as well as implementation suggestions for different modes (Chap. 2). Next, the handbook highlights China's recent approaches to developing academic programs in the digital age (Chap. 3). The next chapter elaborated on the core elements, implementation framework, and development strategies for higher education institutions to implement blended learning (Chap. 4). After that, the handbook explained the necessary support for implementing blended learning, including the core elements of support, and how to support students and instructors in blended learning (Chap. 5). Next, the handbook presented 16 practical cases from 11 countries, explaining the background, key issues, solutions, impacts, and implications of the cases (Chap. 6). Finally, the handbook provided future trends and development of education reform through blended learning from various aspects, such as space for blended learning, open educational resources, ubiquitous learning to support blended learning, and building an educational ecosystem (Chap. 7).

The entire book was edited by Ming Li, Jiangang Cheng, and Xibin Han. The Chinese version of Chap. 1 was edited by Meifeng Liu (Beijing Normal University), Guoqing Zhao (Beijing Normal University), Zhixian Zhong (Jiangxi Normal University), Jing Ma (Zhengzhou University), and Wen Wang (National Institute of Education Sciences of China). The Chinese version of Chap. 2 was edited by Xibin Han (Tsinghua University), Yiran Cui (Tsinghua University), Wen Wang, Shuyan Wang (University of Southern Mississippi), and Xiaoying Feng (Beijing Normal University). The Chinese version of Chap. 3 was edited by Shusheng Shen (Nanjing Normal University), Hao Yang (SUNY Oswego, USA) and Qian Zhou (Tsinghua University). The Chinese version of Chap. 4 was edited by Qian Zhou, Yue Huang (Beijing University of Posts and Telecommunications), Yangyang Luo (Lanzhou University), Xiaojing Bai (Beijing Open University), Yuping Wang (Griffith University, Australia), and Nan Chen (Beijing Academy of Educational Sciences). The Chinese version of Chap. 5 was edited by Qingtang Liu (Central China Normal University), Li Chen (Beijing Normal University), Xiaoying Feng, Xiaojing Bai (Beijing Open University), and Zhiqiang Ma (Jiangnan University). The Chinese version of Chap. 6 was edited by Mingxuan Chen (Jiangnan University), Zhuli Wang (Sun Yat-sen University), Linmei Liang (Henan University), Zhiqiang Ma, and Yingqun Liu (Tsinghua University). The Chinese version of Chap. 7 was edited by Shuyu Yu (Northwest Normal University), Li Chen, and Zhuli Wang.

Qingyu Jiang from UNESCO Higher Education Innovation Center (Shenzhen, China), Kaiyu Yi, Rifa Guo, Wanruo Shi, Jinjing Liu, and Hao Huang from Tsinghua University, Wenhui Liu, Min Liu, Tong Sun, Xiumiao Zhang, Zhiyan Zhang, Linlin Hu, Haixi Sheng, Gang Liu, and Cunchi Wang from Beijing Normal University, Xiaowei Zhao and Jiayu Zhou from Nanjing Normal University, Fuhong Ge, Fengjuan Chen, Zhiqiang Sang, Tiansheng Cao, Enhui Miao, Shiyao Gou, Liang Chen, Xinghan Yin, and Lei Sun from Central China Normal University, Huanhao Zhu, Zhenyu Deng, Niu He, Yiling Liang, Jing Wang, and Xiaoyan Chen from Jiangxi Normal University, Liang Zhou and Linfeng Guo from Jiangnan University, Yanli Wang, and Minjun Cai from Northwest Normal University provided support for the compilation of this handbook. Administrators and instructors from many higher education institutions provided practice cases.

Our sincere gratitude goes to the scholars who have provided support to improve the English version of the handbook. Lin Zhong from Southern Illinois University translated the preface and reviewed and revised Chap. 2 and part of Chap. 6. Jing Lei and Qiu Wang from Syracuse University reviewed and revised Chap. 1 and Chap. 4. Hao Yang from the State University of New York at Oswego reviewed and revised Chap. 3. Jingjing Zhang from Beijing Normal University reviewed and revised Chap. 5. Wenli Chen from Nanyang Technological University reviewed and revised Chap. 7. Taralynn Hartsell from Valdosta State University proofread the full English version.

cheng Jiangang

Jiangang Cheng
Director of Institute of Higher
Education Digital Transformation
of UNESCO-ICHEI
Professor at Institute of Education
Tsinghua University
Beijing, China

Contents

Contributors

Xiaojing Bai Beijing Open University, Beijing, China

Li Chen School of Educational Technology, Beijing Normal University, Beijing, China

Mingxuan Chen School of Humanities, Jiangnan University, Wuxi, China

Nan Chen Beijing Academy of Educational Sciences, Beijing, China

Yiran Cui School of International Education, Shandong University, Jinan, Shandong, China

Xiaoying Feng School of Educational Technology, Beijing Normal University, Beijing, China

Xibin Han Institute of Education, Tsinghua University, Beijing, China

Yue Huang School of Online Education, Beijing University of Posts and Telecommunications, Beijing, China

Linmei Liang Faculty of Education, Henan University, Kaifeng, China

Meifeng Liu School of Educational Technology, Beijing Normal University, Beijing, China

Qingtang Liu Faculty of Artificial Intelligence in Education, Central China Normal University, Wuhan, China

Yingqun Liu Institute of Education, Tsinghua University, Beijing, China

Yangyang Luo Institute of Higher Education, Lanzhou University, Lanzhou, China

Jing Ma School of Education, Zhengzhou University, Zhengzhou, China

Zhiqiang Ma School of Humanities, Jiangnan University, Wuxi, China

Shusheng Shen School of Education Science, Nanjing Normal University, Nanjing, China

Shuyan Wang School of Leadership, The University of Southern Miss Gulfport, Long Beach, MS, USA

Wen Wang National Institute of Education Sciences of China, Beijing, China

Yuping Wang School of Humanities, Languages and Social Science, Griffith University, Brisbane, Australia

Zhuli Wang Center for Faculty Development, Sun Yat-sen University, Guangzhou, China

Hao Yang School of Education at the State University of New York at Oswego, New York, USA

Shuyu Yu School of Educational Technology, Northwest Normal University, Lanzhou, China

Guoqing Zhao School of Educational Technology, Beijing Normal University, Beijing, China

Zhixian Zhong Institute of Teacher Education for Advanced Study, Jiangxi Normal University, Nanchang, China

Qian Zhou Institute of Education, Tsinghua University, Beijing, China

Chapter 1
Theoretical Foundations for Blended Learning

Meifeng Liu, Guoqing Zhao, Zhixian Zhong, Jing Ma, and Wen Wang

The practice of blended learning needs to be guided by blended learning theories and other related theories. The emergence and development of blended learning is the product of learning psychology and pedagogy in the information age. Therefore, the implementation of blended learning needs to be guided by systems theories, educational communication theories, learning theories, teaching theories, and curriculum theories. Certain learning modes, as well as related design and practice models, have emerged from blended learning research and practice. In this chapter, Sect. 1.1 briefly reviews the connotation and development of blended learning; Sect. 1.2 introduces the theoretical basis for the emergence and development of blended learning, pointing out that the increasing prevalence of blended learning is based on the development of teaching and learning in the information age; Sect. 1.3 explains the theoretical basis of blended learning and its guiding role for blended learning; Sect. 1.4 introduces several modes of blended learning and describes how these modes can seamlessly connect online and offline learning; Sect. 1.5 introduces the design models and implementation models of blended learning. As a systematic summary of relevant theories and research on blended learning, this chapter shows the connotations and characteristics of the theories and highlights their guiding significance and value for blended learning. This chapter can be used as a reference by teachers, instructional designers, educational technology personnel, educational administrators, and researchers.

M. Liu (✉) · G. Zhao
School of Educational Technology, Beijing Normal University, Beijing, China
e-mail: mfliu@263.net

Z. Zhong
Institute of Teacher Education for Advanced Study, Jiangxi Normal University, Nanchang, China

J. Ma
School of Education, Zhengzhou University, Zhengzhou, China

W. Wang
National Institute of Education Sciences of China, Beijing, China

M. Li et al. (eds.), *Handbook of Educational Reform Through Blended Learning*,
https://doi.org/10.1007/978-981-99-6269-3_1

1.1 The Concept of Blended Learning

Blended learning was first introduced in the field of corporate human resources training, aiming to overcome the limitations of time and space in face-to-face teaching, including small class size, poor timeliness, and high training cost. Since the 1960s, some large international companies, such as IBM and Boeing, have attempted to make it possible to train hundreds or even thousands of employees at the same time with the support of communication technology. Communication technology has been developing rapidly, evolving from the original mainframe computers and mini-computers to television media in the 1970s, CD-ROMs in the 1980s, and to various communication methods based on the Internet in this century. No matter how the technology has changed, the purpose of blended learning in corporations remains the same, that is to overcome the human resource constraints and maximize training effectiveness (Bersin 2004). The face-to-face learning component plays a vital role in training work skills and the inheritance of corporate culture. Therefore, integration of the technology-based learning mode and the advantages of the face-to-face mode has been adopted by corporate human resources training.

In the 1990s, Internet-based E-Learning had gradually become popular with the development of information technology. Due to the differences in the media, the approaches, and the target audience's needs between face-to-face learning and E-Learning, the two learning methods, to a large extent, were separated during that period. The E-Learning mode provided learners with a richer technical environment and a more convenient way to obtain resources. However, the E-Learning mode also had some disadvantages, such as low engagement and a poor real-time interactive experience. It is recognized that students have difficulties in completing learning tasks independently in the unsupervised network environment. As a result, a more effective and flexible blended learning method has been applied in teaching and learning by education researchers and practitioners. "Blended learning" has been proposed as a proper term. Initially, blended learning was considered as a simple combination of E-Learning and face-to-face learning, as moving classroom teaching to the Internet via information technology, or as supplementary extra-curricular learning tasks. Perceptions about blended learning have gradually changed; now it is seen as a learning mode that can improve classroom learning. An increasing number of researchers have begun to realize that the word "blended" should be considered as "integration" and "fusion", instead of simply referring to "combination". Blended learning is not limited to merely integrating face-to-face and online learning environments, but is a systematic reconstruction of multiple elements including learning resources, teaching strategies, learning environments, learning tools, and teaching and learning models.

From a historical perspective, as a social activity, education is certainly affected by social productivity, particularly technological advancement. Communication technology is the most important technology that affects education. Its development has revolutionized education. In primitive society, education was combined with life and labor without the distinction between formal and informal. Body language, as the dominant means of communication, aimed to maintain livelihoods. In an agricultural society, the dominant communication means used in education were word of mouth and hand-compiled books. Due to different needs in the society, formal and informal education was distinguished. Formal education was mainly in government and private schools, where teaching was conducted in either a centralized or a decentralized manner. Moreover, personalized learning was adopted without distinction among classes and school years. Informal education referred to the development of labor skills by using scenario-based learning for agriculture, and apprenticeship, etc. In industrialized society, word-of-mouth as the means of communication was adopted in education, though the bulk-printing of books and basic computer technology were also included. Due to the need for a large amount of standardized manpower, formal education shifted from the elite to the public, with classroom teaching as the main teaching mode. As a result, standardization and large-scale education came into being, such as schools, school years, curriculum, and courses. At the same time, the focus of informal education changed from labor skills in agricultural society to work skills, while the teaching strategy changed from scenario-based learning for agriculture to factory apprenticeship.

In the information society, information and communication technology are the foundation of the society; information resources are the major development resources; and digital industries are the leading field in the society. Information, together with matter and energy, constitutes the three key indispensable resources. Multimedia technology and Internet technology are widely integrated in education. Formal education has changed from popularization in industrial society to universalization in the digital society. In addition, with the learner-centered perspective, formal education has maintained its scalability and added the personalization. The teaching strategy has changed from face-to-face classroom teaching in the industrial society to the integration of scheduled face-to-face learning and flexible technology-enabled learning, such as a hybrid form that merges physical space and virtual cyberspace. With the development of emerging information technologies, such as cloud computing, Internet of Things, artificial intelligence, and biological computer technology, physical space and virtual cyberspace will be integrated more deeply. As a result, education has the potential to satisfy the learning need for everyone and can happen anytime and anywhere, allowing the seamless integration between formal and informal education, supporting personalized and lifelong learning. In this way, learning can move towards a new ecology of ubiquitous learning.

1.2 The Rationale for the Emergence and Development of Blended Learning

Blended learning is a learning mode that integrates face-to-face learning and technology-enabled learning. In order to achieve optimal learning effect under specific conditions, blended learning reconstructs the core elements of education, including goals, content (resources), media, methods, evaluation, and teaching teams, based on the nature of education, the laws of education and learning, and required future manpower. As a product of societal, economic, and technological development, it is certain that blended learning will become the new norm of education. Blended learning can not only meet the needs of societal development for education, but also meet the requirements of individual development. The emergence and development of blended learning has a solid theoretical foundation in psychology and pedagogy.

1.2.1 Psychological Rationale

Blended learning attends to both the commonality and individuality of students

Psychological research points out that people have common and individual traits, some highly relevant to teaching, while some not very relevant. Within the common and individual traits related to student learning, those that are not related to the content of a particular discipline are commonly referred to as common traits and individual traits of student learning in psychology.

The fact that students have learning-related common traits provides foundations for face-to-face teaching and online synchronous teaching, while students' learning-related individual traits demonstrates the role that E-Learning can play. Therefore, the emergence and development of blended learning is historically inevitable. In the following part, the common features, and individual characteristics of student learning in a general sense will be briefly described so as to gain a clearer understanding of how to design good blended learning accordingly.

Characteristics of common traits

The psychological development of an individual is sequential and phased, therefore students in different age ranges will show corresponding and common general characteristics, including stage characteristics of cognitive development, psychosocial development, and moral development.

Concerning the characteristics of cognitive development, the well-known psychologist Jean Piaget proposed the four Piagetian stages of cognitive development, namely Sensorimotor Stage (0–2 years old), Preoperational Stage (2–7 years old), Concrete Operations Stage (7–11 years old), and Formal Operations Stage (11 years old and later). Identifying learner characteristics of cognitive development at each stage is the key foundation to instructional design.

Regarding the characteristics of psycho-social development, Erik H. Erikson developed his eight stages of personality development that integrate self-development and environmental influences (Erikson 1964). Trust and Mistrust (birth to 18 months): at this stage, children feel secure if they receive love and affection in a stable and predictable environment. This security allows them to trust others, otherwise babies will mistrust. Autonomy and Doubt (18 months to 3 years old): at this stage, children who are allowed freedom to explore, within limits, learn self-confidence, otherwise they may become discouraged and begin to feel worthless. Initiative and Guilt (3 to 6/7 years old): at this stage, children are bundles of energy, full of imagination and initiative. They begin to master peer relationships and language. If they are not encouraged to participate, they may feel guilty about the extent of their own ambitions and fail to develop the skills to play and work with others. Industry and Inferiority (6/7 to 12 years old): children at this stage begin to undertake some tasks independently and work together with others. If teachers can encourage and praise them, it is more likely that children will develop a sense of diligence and a proactive personality, otherwise, they are prone to develop a sense of inferiority. Identity and Identity Confusion (12 to 18 years old): children in this period start to develop self-identity. In other words, individuals try to establish a coherent sense of self (including his/her physical appearance, previous situations, status-quo, the limitations of environment and conditions, and the prospect of his/her future) as a whole. If children are provided with the right guidance from teachers and parents, they will successfully construct their self-identity, otherwise confusion of self-identity may appear. Intimacy and Isolation (18 to 30 years old): this period is the stage of love, marriage, and early family life. Youths seek to develop intimate personal relationships with others without losing their self-identity. If they fail to do that, they will develop a sense of loneliness. Generativity and Stagnation (30 to 60 years old): this is the challenge of the middle years of life. Raising children, creative activities, and community service are ways people give to others in this stage. Being unable to contribute in these ways can bring about boredom, restlessness, stagnation, and a feeling that life is meaningless. Integrity and Despair (after age 60): being able to look back on life with contentment and few regrets is the main task of Stage 8. Integrity involves having a good perspective on life in one's final years. People who struggled through life without feeling a part of it may end up facing death in despair.

According to Erickson, there are corresponding key influencers in each of the above stages, namely: mother, father, family members, neighbors, as well as school teachers and students, peers and small group members, friends, colleagues, spouses, and the whole human race (Erikson 1964). Characteristics of psycho-social development influence the establishment of personality. How people interact with others and things affects the development of their personalities.

Regarding the characteristics of moral development, Lawrence Kohlberg proposed three moral levels and six stages of moral reasoning. The three levels are pre-conventional morality, conventional morality, and post-conventional morality. Each level has two stages. These stages can serve as reference for the development of students' morality (Shaffer and Kipp 2012).

The characteristics of cognitive development affect the design of the difficulty level of learning objectives, the abstraction of the content, the format of learning resources, and the design of learning activities. The characteristics of psycho-social development may constrain the design of emotional interaction between teacher-student, student–student, teams, activities, as well as feedback and assessment; while the characteristics of moral development affect the design of learning activity guidelines.

In a society that promotes lifelong learning, learners can range from primary to middle school students, college students to the elderly. All learners have the above-mentioned characteristics of cognitive, psycho-social, and moral development related to learning as common features. For learners of the same age, such common features can serve as the basic guidelines for designing learning objectives, content, resources, activities, collaboration, interaction, feedback, and assessment in face-to-face or real-time online learning. Yet, for the learners of different age groups, self-paced online learning might work better. Therefore, it is necessary to develop blended learning.

Individual traits

Human development involves not only common features, but also individual characteristics. In other words, people have individual differences which are influenced by genetics, social living conditions, education, and other factors in their process of socialization. Some are related to learning, including differentiated traits like learning interests and learning styles.

Learning interest demonstrates learners' willingness to learn. Psychologists divide learning interests into personal interests and situational interests. Personal interests are idiosyncratic and relatively stable, referring to a person's tendency to pay attention to specific stimuli, objects, and topics. Situational interests, on the other hand, are responsive. When situational interests are "triggered", they can attract learners' attention in a short period of time. If situational interests are "maintained", they can promote students to stay focused on the same task or topic over a long period of time (Ormrod 1999).

Generally, interests can facilitate information processing more efficiently (Ormrod 1999). In addition, to some extent, interests and learning mutually reinforce each other. When students experience a sense of competence, their learning interest may increase. Even if students are not initially interested in some learning content or an activity, they may develop an interest after experiencing success. Therefore, it is necessary to understand interests of learners, to trigger and maintain learners' personal and situational interests, to have a variety of teaching modes, and an autonomous learning atmosphere. All of these key elements can be included in blended learning.

Learning style refers to the psychological characteristics indicating learners' perception of stimuli and their responses to the stimuli. In other words, learners tend to choose special strategies in their learning process. The following section mainly discusses learners' different needs for learning environments and their different cognitive styles.

Learners' different needs for learning environments

Affective needs refer to learners' need for encouragement and comfort in their learning process. Social needs refer to learners' need for peer discussion. Environmental and emotional needs refer to learners' preference towards environment and emotions when learning, such as studying in a quiet environment, having snacks when reading, walking back and forth when thinking, or having a certain efficient learning period.

Differences in cognitive styles

Cognitive style refers to the strategies learners are used to adopting when they perceive, recall, and reflect. It shows the individual differences of learners in the process of organizing and processing information and reflects the different characteristics of learners in perception, memory, reflection, and problem-solving abilities. Each learner can have a variety of cognitive styles at the same time and utilize different combinations of them in the process of learning. Mainly, four types of cognitive styles have an impact on instructional design: the preferred sensory channel for perceiving or receiving stimuli, field-independent and field-dependent, holistic and sequential, and reflective and impulsive.

The preferred sensory channel for perceiving or receiving stimuli refers to the sensory channels that learners prefer in learning, including visual, auditory, and tactile/ kinesthetic.

Field-dependent and field-independent. The concept of the field dependence–independence cognitive style emerged as a result of the work of Witkin. A relatively field-independent person is likely to overcome the organization of the field, or to restructure it, when presented with a field having a dominant organization, whereas the relatively field-dependent person tends to adhere to the organization of the field as given (Witkin et al. 1977). Witkin et al. (1977) claimed that field independent individuals rely on an internal frame of reference, while field dependent individuals rely on an external frame of reference. Whilst field dependent individuals have a preference to learn in groups and to interact frequently with one another as well as the teacher, field independent learners may respond better to more independent and more individualized approaches. Also, field independent learners are more likely to have self-defined goals and to respond to intrinsic reinforcement, whilst field dependent learners require more extrinsic reinforcement and more structured work by the teacher. Whereas the field independent learners prefer to structure their own learning and to develop their own learning strategies, field dependent learners may need more assistance in problem-solving strategies or more exact definitions of performance outcomes (Witkin et al. 1977). Field independent individuals are more capable of dealing with situations requiring impersonal analysis, whilst field dependent individuals are better equipped to deal with situations requiring social perceptiveness and interpersonal skills.

Holistic and sequential. When dealing with learning tasks, individuals have two tendencies: one is a holistic, hypothesis-oriented strategy, which deals with tasks as a whole and tests relatively more complex hypotheses at the same time; the other is a sequential, fact-oriented, step-by-step strategy, which tests only one limited hypothesis at a time. Holistic learners are good at solving problems from a comprehensive and holistic perspective. They prefer to grasp the overall situation, and then find a breakthrough to solve problems, or solve complex problems first. They have high intuition and ambiguity, but low accuracy and profundity. In contrast, sequential learners use the "operational" method to learn. They are used to dividing problems into details to understand them and solving problems step by step, according to a logical sequence. They are also good at discovering the differences between different entities.

Reflective and impulsive. The concept was originally introduced by Kagan et al. (1964) to describe the individual differences in the speed with which decisions are made under conditions of uncertainty to employ impulsive or reflective cognitive tempos.

Impulsive children respond quickly with short latencies and numerous errors, while reflective children tend to inhibit their initial responses and to reflect upon the correctness of their responses, thereby exhibiting longer latencies and fewer errors.

Reflective children tend to analyze stimuli and organize them into detail components and, accordingly, perform better on tasks requiring attention to details. Impulsive children, on the other hand, tend to focus more on the stimulus as a whole and thus perform better on tasks requiring a more global analysis.

Since different learning activities require different psychological characteristics, it can only be said that a certain tendency is more suitable for a certain learning context, rather than that a learner with a certain tendency is necessarily smarter than one with another tendency.

In a relatively flexible and autonomous learning mode, blended learning can provide students with more choices in terms of the learning environment and learning partners, giving feedback via the system, resources via various media (such as visual, audio and text media), and allowing students to follow at their own pace. Thus, blended learning can meet the needs of students with different learning styles.

Blended learning provides personalized learning paths or pacing for students with different potential. The previous subsection discussed the common features and individual characteristics related to learning in general. To account for these characteristics simultaneously, a flexible learning mode like blended learning is needed and will become more prevalent. In fact, in psychology, some individual characteristics of learners, such as the disciplinary learning potential, learning needs, and learning competence of different students, are closely related to subject learning, but are difficult to be taken into consideration by face-to-face teaching alone; thus they would benefit from online teaching.

Multiple intelligence structure

Howard Gardner, a professor of psychology at Harvard University, proposed the Multiple Intelligences Theory after years of research. He defined intelligence as a "biopsychological potential to process information that can be activated in a cultural setting to solve problems or create products that are of value in a culture". On this basis, he proposed nine different types of intelligence, namely, linguistic intelligence, logical/mathematical intelligence, spatial intelligence, bodily-kinesthetic intelligence, musical intelligence, interpersonal intelligence, naturalist intelligence, intrapersonal intelligence, and existential intelligence. Everyone was born with more than eight types of intelligence that are both independent and interrelated and has different strengths and weaknesses in intelligence. When solving problems and creating products, people combine and use these intelligences differently, which gives rise to each person's different and individualized multiple intelligence structure. For students, each subject may tap multiple intelligences and involve their various combinations, which explains why they are talented and full of potential in one subject but lacking in potential in another subject.

Gardner's "Multiple Intelligences Theory" helps educators to be aware of the multiple differences among students, and explains why some students can learn subjects they are good at easily and fast, but relatively hard and slowly when they learn the subjects that they are not good at. Online learning has the advantage to make full use of "multiple intelligences" to teach, to enable students to have their individualized learning paths, and to help students learn at their own pace (Zhang 2002).

Learning needs

Learning needs refer to the gap between what the learner wants to get out of the learning experience and their current state of learning and development. Due to learners' differences in terms of their living environments, future jobs and positions, and their development potential, differences can be found in learners' learning expectations.

Meanwhile, since the current learning levels of learners are also different, their learning needs vary too. Due to the large number of people in traditional classrooms, teaching is at the same pace and teachers cannot take into account the learning needs of different students. However, blended learning, which adopts a learning mode that combines "online and offline", can expand the time and space of learning and thus meet the learning needs of different students. With a variety of learning resources, students can not only review and relearn, but also learn more content more deeply.

Learning competence

Learning competence refers to people's ability to acquire knowledge, work on tasks, and seek development (Liu et al. 2018). Learning competence includes general abilities and specific abilities (Gao 1989; Zeng and Cao 2005). General ability is a comprehensive ability that is applicable to all or most studies. Although it is not discipline-specific, it has an impact on discipline learning and has the characteristics of transferability, universality, wide application, and stability. Yin and Bi (2000) categorized general learning abilities into basic abilities and comprehensive abilities, and proposed that the basic abilities of learners include observation ability, memory ability, thinking ability, and expression ability, while comprehensive abilities include self-learning ability, problem-solving ability, experimental ability, and creativity. It is also proposed that learners' basic abilities and comprehensive abilities are cultivated through the learning of professional knowledge of a discipline, and can be applied to new learning, serving not only as the basis, but also the purpose of learning.

Special abilities are the abilities demonstrated in professional activities, such as disciplinary abilities. Lin (1997) believes that the intelligence and ability of learners should be organically combined with general abilities of the discipline, such as listening, speaking, reading, and writing in language subjects. The combination of discipline-related intelligence and competencies, strategies, and methods should also be included. Gardner's (1993) multiple intelligence structure links disciplines to the intellectual structure of learners. He stated that everyone has a different match from the eight or nine types of intelligence, which explains why people perform differently in different subject areas.

There are differences in general learning abilities and the disciplinary competence of leaners, which directly affect the way, the efficiency, and the quality of their completion of disciplinary learning activities. Blended learning can not only provide a variety of learning paths and various learning support methods, but also enable learners to review, repeat, or learn more things, helping them to exercise and develop their own learning ability. Therefore, blended learning can resolve learners' differences in learning ability and facilitate learners to better complete their learning tasks.

1.2.2   Pedagogical Rationale

Blended learning takes into account common features and individual characteristics of learners and enables learners with potential in different disciplines to learn through different learning paths at their own pace. Meanwhile, the information society requires education to promote the holistic and personalized development among students, which serves as an important pedagogical basis for the emergence and development of blended learning.

Blended learning realizes the essence of education—to promote "the development of each student". Education is a social activity in which educators should have a positive impact on students. Having an accurate perspective on students is very important to systematically develop education. Likewise, such a perspective is crucial to realize the essence of education—"to promote the development of each student and improve the life quality and value of each one". According to Gardner's theory of multiple intelligences, although students' intellectual structures vary, they all have unique potentials, which means that there are no students that cannot learn, only different students. At the same time, there are differences among students in terms of learning foundation, learning speed, learning interest, learning motivation, learning needs, and learning ability. Therefore, if schools can provide multiple development approaches for each student, it is possible to further develop each student's superior intelligence, thus encouraging their learning motivation and facilitating the development of their weaker intelligence area to a certain extent. In this way, each student can enjoy a successful learning experience at school and contribute to the achievement of the educational purpose, which is to promote the development of every student.

Promoting the development of each student requires schools to carry out customized and individualized teaching and learning. Teaching and learning needs to be tailored to the unique needs of students. However, the realization of real personalized teaching and learning is a huge challenge for schools. It is not feasible to equip each student with a tutor, yet the development of technology enables the possibility to promote the personalized development of students. Learning analysis based on big data, adaptive systems, and Massive Open Online Courses (MOOC), has created conditions for providing students with suitable learning content and learning methods. "In the age of technology, people are more likely to pursue learning on their own and will not feel the sense of failure that comes when everyone is supposed to learn the same thing at the same time" (Collins and Halverson 2009, p. 110). Moreover, the development of information technology facilitates a variety of learning methods, from E-Learning to U-learning, which enable students to have more space to learn outside the classroom.

In recent years, scholars have examined how technology can facilitate personalized teaching and learning. For instance, Wei et al. (2019) identified seven behaviors of students in the classroom by using intelligent learning analysis technology, namely, listening to class, looking around, raising hands, sleeping, standing, reading, and writing. This technology can offer timely and accurate feedback on the learning of each student in the classroom, which can help teachers enhance teaching strategies, and optimize classroom learning and management. This will improve the efficiency of teaching and learning and contribute to the reform of personalized teaching and learning.

Since 2016, Tsinghua University has launched a smart teaching and learning tool—Rain Classroom. The tool covers every data collection session, from "before class" to "during class" to after class". The back-end of the tool records detailed data of teaching and learning behavior, such as the number of students participating in the classroom, the timeslot that students enter the classroom, the slides they fail to understand, the questions that are answered incorrectly, the frequency that a preview video is watched before the class, and the completion and correct rate of the after-class homework. Such data can clearly restore most of the teaching and learning process in the real classroom. Using such data for data analysis and mining can support teachers to enhance the teaching process and help students to enhance the learning process. By adopting machine learning and artificial intelligence, the panoramic recording of big data will provide the foundation for teachers and students to make decisions in a scientific fashion, including individually analyzing past teaching and learning processes, objectively reflecting on the current teaching and learning situation, and proactively arranging future teaching and learning (Wang 2017).

Blended learning is one of the important approaches for schools to achieve student-centered personalized teaching and learning. On the one hand, blended learning allows teachers to implement various student-centered offline learning modes so that they can have interaction and communication with students. On the other hand, with the advantages of promoting personalized development among students, blended learning can take advantage of emerging technologies to break the limitations of time and space for providing students with personalized learning. By integrating online and offline learning, blended learning aims to "deliver 'appropriate' skills to 'appropriate' learners at 'appropriate' times by applying 'appropriate' learning techniques that fit 'appropriate' learning styles" (Singh and Reed 2001). In this way, learners will be able to have a personalized learning experience rather than learning in a one-size-fits-all classroom (Horn and Staker 2017).

Therefore, blended learning meets the essential requirements of education, follows the fundamental principles of education, and will become increasingly more common in education.

Blended learning helps to cultivate talents with twenty-first century core competences. So far, human beings have witnessed hunter-gatherer society, agricultural society, industrial society, and the move towards an information society (Toffler 1990). In the agricultural society, education was through apprenticeship or one-to-one tutoring, generally with only one room as the school building. In the industrial society, in order to meet the needs of large-scale teaching and learning, modern schools emerged and the education system transformed into "Factory Models of Schools" (Duan et al. 2009). In the twenty-first century, with the fast knowledge update and the diverse ways of knowledge acquisition, traditional teaching and learning are unable to adapt to the increasingly complex living and working environments. This is because society has put forward higher requirements for talents in terms of creativity, diversity, and individualization.

In the era of rapid change, the education field has been changing in order to cope with the development of the new era. Countries and international educational organizations have a common challenge to understand what kinds of talents to be trained for the new century. According to the Organization for Economic Cooperation and Development (OECD), the talents to be cultivated should have the following characteristics. The first is reflection, a relatively complex mental process including metacognition, creativity, and critical thinking. The second is the ability to cope with complex problems and unpredictable scenarios. According to the EU, the expectation is to cultivate talents with competences including critical thinking, problem-solving, teamwork, communication and negotiation skills, creativity, cross-cultural communication, and life-long learning (European Commission 2018). Regarding the development of core competences in Chinese students, it is expected that students will have six core competences, namely, humanity, scientific spirit, ability to learn, healthy life, responsibility, and innovation (Research Group on Core Literacy 2016).

By comparing the eight frameworks for core competences in the world, Dutch scholar Voogt and others came to the following conclusions: ① Four core competences are advocated by all the frameworks, namely collaboration, communication, ICT-related competences, and social and/or cultural awareness (including citizenship); ② The other four core competences advocated by most frameworks are creativity, critical thinking, problem-solving, and the capacity to develop high-quality products or productivity. These eight competences are the common pursuit of human beings in the information age and are called "the world common core competences" (Voogt and Roblin 2012). The above-mentioned competences can be further refined into the following four, namely, collaboration, communication, creativity, and critical thinking, which are the "twenty-first century 4Cs". The world common core competences are the common pursuits of human development goals in the information age, which reflect educational trends in the world.

Blended learning has the advantages of offline, face-to-face classroom teaching and the advantages of online learning, such as various learning models, self-paced learning, idea sharing, resource sharing, and collaborative, inquiry-based problem solving. Blended learning can promote the development of students' autonomous learning ability, identification ability, critical thinking skills, and creativity, which are the talents needed in an information society.

Researchers advocate that blended learning can contribute to the cultivation of twenty-first century core competences in students. Zhang et al. (2019) used the Wisdom Tree platform to establish a blended learning model based on the Small Private Online Course (SPOC), and found that students' autonomous learning ability and learning efficiency were enhanced by adopting this model. Wang et al. (2018) conducted a survey on college students who participated in blended learning courses based on Massive Open Online Courses (MOOC). Their study found that this model improved students' language expression, autonomy, and teamwork, strengthened the teacher-student and student–student communication, and thus improved learning effectiveness. These studies suggest that blended learning plays an important role in enhancing students' problem-solving skills, teamwork, and other higher-order thinking skills.

Apparently, blended learning can help to cultivate talents with twenty-first century skills. To achieve this goal, blended learning needs to utilize the teacher-led and student-centered learning model to promote students' autonomy and provide authentic problems to cultivate students' problem solving skills. Also, blended learning needs to integrate the advantages of various teaching modes to provide students with appropriate learning paths and focus on collaborative learning to cultivate their collaboration and communication skills. Moreover, students should be offered a variety of learning tools and sufficient technical resources for self-paced learning so that students can become lifelong learners. The cultivation of students' critical thinking and innovation skills should be integrated in the teaching and learning process. Nowadays, with rich online resources, students should be exposed to different ideas and be offered with more opportunities for hands-on practice and expression of their opinions with proper guidance.

All colleges and universities in China now consider blended learning as a development direction of educational reform. Colleges have started to use the established online resources, such as Chinese University MOOC, Chaoxing, and Zhihui Shu (Wisdom Tree) to support blended learning. More importantly, colleges need to choose or establish their own learning management systems, develop online resources, and implement multi-modal blended learning, so that blended learning can be widely adopted in all fields and disciplines of higher education, thus contributing to the reform of teaching and learning. The sixth part of this handbook provides helpful examples of blended learning in colleges and universities.

According to the theoretical foundations in psychology and pedagogy, blended learning should have face-to-face and online learning closely coordinated and seamlessly connected, considering the common features and the individual characteristics of students. Additionally, blended learning should respect the common development principles of learners at different stages and meet their individual learning needs.

Therefore, blended learning requires a diversified design of learning activities and a hierarchical design of learning resources to allow different learning paces and paths, as well as personalized guidance for learners, according to their learning effectiveness, so that their learning potential can be fully developed. Meanwhile, blended learning can adopt more teaching strategies, such as independent learning, collaboration, and inquiry, to cultivate students' core competences in the information age.

1.3   The Theoretical Basis of Blended Learning

To sum up, blended learning conforms to the laws of psychology, the nature of education, and its future trends. Blended learning is beneficial to cultivating individualized talents required by social development. The next question is how to design ideal blended learning. This section will illustrate the theoretical basis for identifying the ideal instructional design of blended learning, including systems theory, educational communication theory, learning and teaching theory, and curriculum theory.

1.3.1   Systems Theory and the Guidance for Blended Learning

Systems thinking was introduced by the Austrian American theoretical biologist, L. Von. Bertalanffy, in 1932. By using the concept of system as the focus, systems thinking explores the basic framework and methods that can tackle the complexity and dynamics of a system in a more appropriate and effective way. It emphasizes considering issues as a system. In other words, the components and the interrelationships and interactions among these components and their interactions with the environment should be considered, and the system should be processed as a whole to generate an overall effect of "$1 + 1 > 2$".

The basic viewpoints of systems thinking are as follows: problems should be addressed as a whole; the emphasis is on the interconnection and interaction among systems, components and environments; the structure of the system is the internal basis for the system to maintain integrity and certain functionality; systems are hierarchical—a system itself is also a component part of a larger system, while a component is a subsystem made up of components of a lower layer; systems are dynamic, purposeful, and open; and exchange with the environment on matter, energy and information (Dou 1988).

Systems thinking is an important guiding ideology of blended learning. Blended learning considers online and offline learning as a whole. In other words, it is a process of design, development, implementation, evaluation, feedback, and refinement of online and offline learning. This process needs good planning and seamless connection between online and offline learning. Meanwhile, a good instructional design of blended learning requires systems thinking to involve the participation of several parties (such as content experts, technicians, graphic designers, instructional design experts, teachers, and students); the variety of teaching and learning modes and process (such as learning objectives, learning content, the composition of learners and their characteristics, online and offline learning activities, learning space, other teaching strategies, assessment and evaluation, teachers, learning support staff, the teaching and learning environment, and community). Moreover, the implementation of blended learning needs to consider learning support, online and offline learning activities, communication with peers and communities, the tracking of the learning process, and according personalized adjustment based on data analytics. In addition, the evaluation of blended learning needs to integrate online learning data and offline classroom performance to consider the relationship between students' overall development and personality development. Several factors need to be balanced when focusing on learning outcomes and the learning process.

Systems Approach and the implications for blended learning

The scientific systems approach, or a systems approach, is a method according to the systematisms of things. It examines the research object as a whole with organization, structure, and function (Li et al. 2007). To be specific, it comprehensively examines research objects from the aspects of mutual relationship between the system and the components, between components and components, and between the system and the external environment. The general process of applying a systems approach to solve problems includes five basic steps: define the problem and set the goal, identify solutions, select the strategies, implement the solution, and evaluate the effectiveness. This problem-solving approach focuses on situational analysis and a holistic view, as well as relationship analysis. It is the general approach to support the whole process and the sub-processes of design, implementation, evaluation, feedback, and improvement in blended learning. Further, the application of the systems approach in blended learning can ensure optimal learning effectiveness.

The Theory of Complex Systems and the implications for blended learning

The Theory of Complex Systems is a series of theories about complex systems and is the further development of the Theory of General Systems. The Theory of General Systems refers to human-made established systems with central control mechanisms, stable structures, and predictable changes, while the Theory of Complex Systems focuses on complex systems without central control mechanisms and stable structures. Such systems are not designed, but evolve from the interactions between many dynamic components at the group level. The evolving process is a bottom-up process, as a self-organized process from messy to organized at the group level with numerous unpredictable possibilities. Along with the bottom-up process, the system will develop a top-down regulation process. Thus there is tension between the bottom-up process and the top-down process of the system. When this tension is directed toward adaptation to the environment, it not only generates many possible changes, but also filters the possibilities according to adaptability requirement, thus guiding the system to evolve and finally develop a system structure and operation mechanism that is adaptive to the environment.

In fact, teaching and learning is a complex system in itself. Blended learning is more complex than pure face-to-face or online learning. The goal of blended learning is to integrate the advantages of various teaching modes to achieve optimal learning effectiveness. How to integrate various teaching modes to develop an optimal teaching and learning system is particularly important because such teaching and learning systems include various elements, complex relationships, and unpredictable evolution processes. Students and teachers who pursue personalized teaching and learning play an active role. The required complex teaching system can be self-formed through the self-adaptation of the bottom-up generative process to the top-down environmental requirement and can result in the integration of various teaching modes. For blended learning, it is essential to provide teachers and students with freedom to choose teaching and learning modes independently so as to encourage their enthusiasm, but also to regulate the teaching and learning environment according to expected learning outcomes. By maintaining a reasonable tension, it is possible to integrate a variety of teaching modes and develop an optimal teaching and learning system, thus achieving optimal learning effectiveness.

1.3.2 Educational Communication Theory and Its Implications for Blended Learning

Educational communication is a communication activity between educators and learners in which educators select appropriate content according to the learning objectives and transmit knowledge, skills, ideas, and concepts to specific learners through effective media channels. The essence is to make communication and interaction more effective. Therefore, the theoretical framework of educational communication, which appeared before educational technology, can be used to interpret blended learning, as they both pursue the optimal effectiveness of teaching and learning interaction. With the development of psychology and the increasing recognition of constructivist epistemology, it is gradually realized that educational communication is a multi-directional interactive activity in which ideas and meanings are constructed by learners as subjects instead of being transmitted, thus adding new meaning to educational communication theories.

Communication channel selection and blended learning

Educational communication is a system mainly consisting of four components: educators, educational information, educational media, and learners. The four components interact and develop the following six relationships: educators and learners, educators and educational information, educators and educational media, learners and educational information, learners and educational media, and educational information and educational media (Nan and Li 2005). Dealing well with these six relationships is very important to ensure and improve the effectiveness of educational communication.

When educators and learners are identified in the system, the educational information will be provided accordingly. Among all the components, educational media is the most active and abundant, because most forms of media can store and transmit plenty of information, though the effectiveness of different communication channels may vary. This leads to the issue of the choice of communication channels, or even the simultaneous use of multiple channels. On the one hand, some specific content needs to use the most suitable transmission channel to achieve better communication effectiveness. On the other hand, according to constructivism and connectivism (see the Learning Theory section), there are meanings distributed across the connections among different nodes. For learners, they can adopt different educational media to gain information, support their scaffolding, and develop their own cognitive framework and understanding.

There are a variety of communication channels in blended learning that can meet different needs, including different subject matter, students' learning styles, and students' meaning construction, and thus enhance communication effectiveness. The relationship of educational media channels with educators, learners, and educational information respectively needs to be well aligned in order to achieve high-quality educational communication effectiveness.

Educational communication model and blended learning

The educational communication model is a theoretically simplified version that replicates the reality of educational communication. It briefly outlines the phenomenon of educational communication and the composition and relationship of various components in the process of educational communication. This model reveals the essential characteristics of educational communication.

The basic model of educational communication

The basic model of educational communication is developed according to the four components of the educational communication system and the important influences of feedback and environment on communication effectiveness. These four components are educators, educational information, educational media, and learners. This model reveals that the effectiveness of educational communication is the result of the interaction and interconnection of all components involved in the communication process instead of being determined by one component. Therefore, the various components in the communication process and the relationships among them should be considered in a holistic manner.

The typical model of educational communication

Based on the basic model of educational communication, whether educators and learners are physically together determines the development of a communication model of face-to-face education or distance education (Wei and Zhong 1992).

With the development of technology, the communication model of distance education based on the Internet has gradually become the mainstream. Information suppliers, i.e., information sources, are more diverse. It is more convenient to identify the characteristics of information recipients through big data. According to those relatively accurate data, information or content will be encoded more appropriately.

Means of transmission will be more abundant. Information recipients also have the right to choose. Given various decoding methods, and the different decoding of groups and individuals, interaction, communication and feedback can happen in a timely and multi-directional manner, making the meaning constructed by information recipients more diverse. Accordingly, the communication model of distance education based on the Internet is becoming increasingly diversified.

Blended learning involves face-to-face communication modes and distance, particularly Internet-based communication modes. Its communication processes, such as design, implementation, evaluation, feedback, and improvement, as well as functional elements, should not only follow the steps of these communication models and involve all elements, but also conform to all the principles of communication.

1.3.3 Learning Theories and Their Guidance on Blended Learning

Since the emergence of psychology in 1879, learning theories have gradually developed and resulted in many representative genres. Although the genres have distinctive viewpoints, all of them mainly explore three fundamental aspects: the essence of learning, the learning process, and the principles and conditions of learning (Chen and Liu 2019). An in-depth understanding of these theories and the application will help us fully understand the definition, nature, functions, and conditions of learning, thus providing a suitable theoretical basis for different blended learning scenarios.

Behaviorism and its applicable teaching scenarios

In the first half of the twentieth century, behaviorism became dominant in psychology. The core idea of behaviorism is that learning is the result of connections between stimuli and responses through repetitive attempts (Watson and Kimble 2017). If the desired response is reinforced in time, it is easier to develop stimulus–response connections and result in learning. The connections between stimuli and responses are emphasized by not only the classical conditioning theory by Ivan Pavlov and John Broadus Watson and the connectionism learning theory by Edward Thorndike, but also the operant conditioning theory by Burrhus Frederic Skinner. Later, some behaviorists began to absorb the ideas of the cognitive school and Albert Bandura's social learning theory is an example. He believed that learning in essence refers to the process in which individuals obtain some new behavioral responses or amend existing behavioral responses by observing the behaviors of others and their reinforcement results.

Regarding the teaching content of each discipline, there is always something that does not require much thinking but needs to be remembered by students (such as English vocabulary, mathematical symbols, etc.), or something that has been approved by thinking but requires skilled memory and fast responses, or some motor skills. This is the teaching scenario where behaviorist learning theory can come into play. Behaviorism has been playing an important role in all teaching processes, including blended learning.

Cognitivism and its educational applications

In the 1960s and 1970s, behaviorist learning theories showed more and more limitations and could not explain how people learn through internal psychological mechanisms. More and more psychologists began to adopt a cognitivist approach, focusing on learners' internal processing of knowledge. Based on behaviorist theories of stimulus–response connections, cognitivism emphasizes that the stimulus–response connections are resulted from the formation of cognitive structures, and claims that learning, in essence, is the process in which learners actively form cognitive structures in their minds through understanding. Cognitive learning theories mainly include Jerome Seymour Bruner's discovery theory, David Ausubel's assimilation theory, and Robert Mills Gagné's information processing theory.

The philosophical basis of the cognitivist learning theory is objective epistemology, which recognizes the existence of objective truth or absolute knowledge. The theory determines that teaching, with students' cognitive structure as the basis, is to persuade students to accept the newly taught knowledge and to incorporate it into their original knowledge structure, which then either expands or changes into a new one. This is how learning occurs.

Blended learning can take advantage of dual or multiple channels to gain a better understanding of students' cognitive structures. It does so by adopting advanced learning analytics technology, such as big data or data mining, and analyzing the online learning trajectory of learners and the dialogue texts of activities, together with scales and questionnaires. This serves as the basis for the design of blended learning. At the same time, cognitivism emphasizes that learning is a meaningful process in which organisms actively form new cognitive structures. Therefore, the instructional plans of blended learning should be designed to meet the needs of different students so as to arouse students' learning enthusiasm and enable them to internalize external objective stimuli into their internal cognitive structures through autonomous learning and teacher guidance. Cognitivism emphasizes the need to adopt flexible teaching procedures and instructional modes according to students' age and experience as well as the nature of the discipline. Thus, in blended learning, appropriate arrangements should be based on learners' mental development level and cognitive representation, so that they can make connections between their prior knowledge and experience and their new knowledge.

Learning perspective from constructivism and its applications to teaching

Constructivism is a further development of cognitivism and its essence is in direct contrast to the philosophical epistemology of objectivism. Specifically, extreme constructivist epistemology does not recognize the existence of objective truth, while moderate constructivist epistemology believes that the objective truth can be put aside first and the cognition of things is formed through the interaction of an individual's prior experience with existing things. Different from the view of behaviorism and cognitivism, which regards learning as the individual activity of the learner, constructivism regards learning as a process in which an individual builds knowledge on prior understanding through interactions with social environments.

The pioneer of modern constructivism is Jean Piaget, who believed that knowledge neither comes from the subject nor the object but is constructed in the process of interaction between the subject and the object. The enrichment process of the cognitive structure of the organism is the process of the progressive construction of the cognitive structure of the subject from equilibrium to imbalance and back to equilibrium (Piaget 1997). Piaget's view of cognitive learning is mainly to explain how to internalize the objective knowledge structure into a learner's cognitive structure through their interaction with it (Piaget 1976). Therefore, his constructivist view belongs to cognitive constructivism.

As one of the representatives of social constructivism, Vygotsky emphasized the role of socio-cultural history in psychological development, especially the prominent position of activities and social interactions in the development of people's higher psychological functions. He believed that higher psychological functions come from the internalization of external actions, which is achieved not only through teaching, but also through daily life, games, and labor (Vygotsky 1980). In addition, the inner intellectual action is also externalized into the external actual action, so that the subjective can be seen in the objective. The bridge between internalization and externalization is human activity.

Constructivists emphasize the dynamic nature of knowledge, the richness and diversity of learners' empirical world, active construction, social interaction, and the situational nature of learning. That learners are builders of their own knowledge is an important theoretical basis for blended learning. It is convenient to use various mediated tools in blended learning. Thus teaching can be placed in a certain context, which can stimulate students' learning interest and allow them to actively construct meaning (Hung 2001). Blended learning can not only promote in-depth, face-to-face communication of all parties through offline teaching, but also promote broader and longer in-depth discussions through the establishment of online virtual communities, in which participants can have multilateral collaboration and even cross-cultural communication to achieve corresponding learning outcomes (Lam 2015). Blended learning is more likely to provide a way for students to learn independently, pay attention to the construction of an autonomous learning environment, and then enhance the dominant status of students (Gharacheh et al. 2016). Due to the seamless connection between online and offline teaching, more activities can be carried out from class to out-of-class.

The guiding role of humanism in teaching and learning

Humanistic psychology was first proposed in the 1960s and prevailed in the 1970s. It is grounded in the belief that people are innately good and will grow and develop if provided with suitable conditions. Humanism advocates respect for human values and self-actualization and proposes that education should meet the actual needs for learners' development of human nature. The typical representatives of humanism are Maslow and Rogers.

Abraham Harold Maslow (1908–1970) proposed the hierarchy of needs theory, based on which he further proposed the motivational theory of student learning and development.

The hierarchy of needs theory believes that people's needs are diverse, and these needs can be divided into 7 levels arranged in a ladder according to their nature (Maslow 1970).

The hierarchy of needs has the following relationships: first, after the needs of the lower layer are satisfied, the needs of the higher layer will appear and dominate the individual's behavior. Second, all needs can be divided into two categories: basic needs and growth needs. Basic needs include the first four levels of needs, all of which are directly related to human instincts, and the satisfaction of which is beneficial to one's physical and mental health. The last three levels of needs are growth needs, which are driven by the development of one's self-potential, and the satisfaction of which will bring the greatest degree of happiness to the individual.

Human needs determine their motivation, which means that the nature of needs affects the nature of motivation and the intensity of needs affects the intensity of motivation. Among all the needs, self-actualization is the central idea of Maslow's motivation theory. Self-actualization means that all organisms are born with special potential, which is also an internal need of the organism. The desire to satisfy such a need drives the organism to realize its full potential.

Carl Ransom Rogers (1902–1987) pioneered "client-centered therapy", believing that each individual has the potential for healthy growth. As long as a friendly, supportive, and sincere atmosphere is created for patients, the patient will recover on their own with no need for treatment.

During psychotherapy, Rogers developed the theory of personality, in which the notion of self or self-concept becomes the central focus. Self-concept believes that people are innately motivated by "self-enhancement", which is manifested as the individual's tendency to maximize their potential. This is the most basic motive and purpose of man and is the same as the Maslow motivation theory.

In addition, Rogers unequivocally proposed to cultivate a "whole person". It is believed that traditional education only emphasizes cognition, but abandons any emotion associated with learning activities and denies the most important part of itself, which leads to the separation of knowledge and emotion in education. He believed that the ideal education is to cultivate a "whole person" who is "integrated in body, mind, feelings, spirit, and intellect" (Rogers, 1982). "Educated people only refer to those who have grasped how to learn and how to adapt to changes, and realized that no knowledge, only the process of seeking knowledge, is reliable." To achieve this teaching objective, the autonomous learning of learners and the sincere attitudes that teachers show to learners are indispensable. Rogers believed that the key to teaching is not lesson plans, teaching skills, teaching resources, or teaching methods, but the relationship between teachers and students. To this end, teachers should fully trust students to develop their potential, respect learners' feelings and personal experiences, treat learners with their "true" self, and have empathy. With leaners at the center of teaching, both schools and teachers should work for this learner-centered education (Rogers et al. 2012).

Rogers believed that learning is "meaningful" and "self-initiated" and he valued the relationship between learning materials and learners' real life (such as learning interests, expectations, and needs). It is proposed that teachers should be facilitators and adopt a "nondirective" approach. Teachers and learners must gain mutual trust and follow eight principles: first, teachers and students jointly formulate curriculum plans and management methods and share responsibilities. Secondly, teachers provide students with various learning materials, including their own learning experience, books, reference materials, etc. Thirdly, learners' exploration of their own interests should be taken as an important teaching resource and learners should be required to make a learning plan independently or with peers. Fourth, a good atmosphere for learning should be established. Fifth, the focus of learning is not on the content, but on the continuity of the learning process; the goal of teaching is not to have students master "what they need to know", but to *know how* to master "what they need to know". Sixth, learning objectives should be set by learners themselves and the realization of this goal should be promoted through the "self-training" of learners. Seventh, the learning results should be evaluated by students. Eighth, learners should be encouraged to display immersive emotions and reasoning in the learning process from the beginning to the end, so that learning can become an integral part of their lives and behaviors.

Both Maslow and Rogers pointed out that education, instead of being received from outside, should be self-initiated by students. Schools and teachers should create a good educational environment and a friendly, supportive, and sincere atmosphere for students. In this way they can have their basic needs satisfied and in turn spontaneously pursue self-actualization out of growth needs, fully tapping into their potential and achieving their value.

As a powerful supplement to behaviorism and cognitivism, the philosophical thoughts and learning theory of humanism have important guiding significance for teaching, especially in blended learning.

Connectivism and blended learning

Connectivism learning theory was proposed by George Simmons and Stephen Downes in 2005 (Siemens 2005; Downes 2005). The theory was born at a time when human society, with the challenges brought by rapid changes in and emergence of knowledge, tended to be digitalized, networked, and intelligent. It is an important theory to explain how learning occurs in the network age. This theory believes that knowledge is constantly changing and is a network phenomenon (Downes 2012); learning is not only a process in which connections are established and networks are formed, but also one that promotes the formation and connection of internal cognitive neural networks, conceptual networks, and social networks (Siemens 2005). In order to maintain the continuous flow and growth of knowledge, it is necessary to continuously establish, maintain and update connections in complex environments. This theory provides a new perspective for interpreting the learning mechanism in the Internet age and developing instructional designs in cyberspace more effectively.

Siemens proposed eight principles in his paper "Connectivism: A Learning Theory for the Digital Age" (Siemens 2005), which was further supplemented several years later, constituting of the 13 basic principles of connectivism.

- Learning and knowledge rests in diversity of opinions.
- Learning is a process of connecting specialized nodes or information sources.
- Learning may reside in non-human appliances.
- Learning is more critical than knowing.
- Maintaining and nurturing connections is needed to facilitate continuous learning.
- Perceiving connections between fields, ideas, and concepts is a core skill.
- Currency (accurate, up-to-date knowledge) is the intent of learning activities.
- Decision-making is itself a learning process.
- The integration of cognition and emotions in meaning-making is important.
- Learning has an end goal—namely the increased ability to "do something".
- Organizational and personal learning are integrated tasks.
- Learning happens in many different ways. Courses are not the primary conduit for learning.
- Learning is a knowledge creation process, not only knowledge consumption.

The connectivism learning theory provides new teaching ideas that adapt to complex network environments and new knowledge concepts, thus it can best reflect the normality of social learning in the current and future network environments (Duke et al. 2013). It is conducive to not only promoting innovations in complex and rapidly changing fields, but also training and developing learners' learning ability and literacy in the digital age, providing them with a broader perspective to grasp the ever-changing growth of knowledge and to adapt to the development of society (Cabrero and Román 2018).

Connectivism learning involves both the consumption and production of content. The contribution of learners can expand in the network, such as reflection, critical comments, linked resources, the creation and communication of other digital knowledge, and problem solving (Anderson and Dron 2011). The continuous expansion, maintenance, and development of learning networks are the key to maintaining the timeliness and effectiveness of learning among individuals and groups. This point of view also affects the focus of the instructional design in blended learning under the guidance of connectivism, which has shifted to building an ecological environment that is conductive to network development and knowledge growth (Carreño 2014).

1.3.4 Curriculum Theory and Blended Learning

Curriculum is related and subject to educational goals and objectives, serving as the concrete embodiment of objectives and as the basis for achieving educational goals. In the meantime, it also constrains teaching and learning modes and strategies. As a theory and method system for curriculum design, the curriculum theory is established on different cognition and value orientations of the disciplines, individual psychological characteristics, and social needs. After the middle of the twentieth century, different curriculum theory genres emerged, such as the knowledge-centered theory, learner-centered theory, and social-centered curriculum theory, all of which are the theoretical basis for the curriculum design of blended learning.

Knowledge-Centered curriculum theory

The development of knowledge-centered curriculum theory involved Herbert Spencer's substantive curriculum theory and Johann Friedrich Herbart's intellectualism theory in the nineteenth century, plus the essentialism proposed by Johann Friedrich Herbart and Michael John Demiashkevich, Robert Maynard Hutchins' perennialism, and Jerome Bruner Seymour Bruner's subject curriculum theory in the twentieth century.

Intellectualism mainly refers to the genre represented by Johann Friedrich Herbart (Strozier 2002). It emphasizes knowledge and its associated intellectual and rational values and advocates knowledge transmission and intelligence development as the basis and purpose of education and teaching and learning processes. It is also emphasized that imparting knowledge is also education, edification, and training, and is the basic approach to provide moral, aesthetic, and religious education.

The main representative of substantive curriculum theory is Herbert Spencer. He defined the purpose and task of education as teaching individuals how to live. Since only science can prepare people for a full life, the knowledge of science is of most value, and thus curricula should be composed of practical scientific knowledge.

The main representatives of essentialist curriculum theory at the early stage include William Chandler Bagley, Michael John Demiashkevich, and F. Alden Shaw. This genre believes that the ultimate purpose of education is to promote social progress and improve the level of democracy. The key factors that determine whether society will advance and develop are personal morality and wisdom, which can be found in excellent cultural heritage from history. Therefore, course content should include common and unchanged cultural elements in cultural heritage, which are the fundamental core of social knowledge.

The main representatives of perennialism curriculum theory include Hutchins of the United States, Alain of France, and L Stone of the United Kingdom (Otiende and Sifuna 1994). This genre believes that the nature and purpose of education and curriculum content are eternal; traditional "eternal disciplines" that involve intellectual training are more valuable than practical disciplines. Those "eternal disciplines" with the most valuable knowledge are the most appropriate for schools to include.

Subject curriculum theory, developed in another wave of American education reform led by the noted American psychologist Jerome Seymour Bruner, focuses on satisfying the needs of developing the intellectual resources of modern human beings. The basic ideas of this reform are included in Bruner's book, *The Process of Education*, which expounds the four key ideas of this curriculum reform. First, to learn any discipline is mainly to master its basic structure and to master the basic attitude or method of learning the discipline; second, the fundamentals of any discipline can be taught in some form to students of any age; third, teaching in the past only paid attention to the development of learners' analytical thinking, but in the future, attention should be paid to the development of learners' intuitive thinking; fourth, the best motivation for learning is to be interested in the learning resources themselves, instead of overemphasizing external stimuli such as rewards and competitions. Among these four key ideas, the core is the basic structure of disciplines.

Knowledge-centered curriculum theory is based on discipline knowledge to explain the curriculum. All knowledge-centered curriculum theories focus on which knowledge is most valuable.

Learner-Centered curriculum theory

The learner-centered curriculum theories originated in the twentieth century, and now mainly include the humanistic curriculum theory represented by Abraham H. Maslow and Carl Ransom Rogers, the empirical curriculum theory represented by John Dewey, and the existential curriculum theory represented by William Morris. With students as the focus, the learner-centered curriculum theories believe that curriculum content should change as students change during the teaching and learning process.

The founders of humanistic curriculum theory are Maslow and Rogers. The theory advocates considering people as a whole, rather than dismembering people's psychology into several parts that cannot be integrated. It is believed that the fundamental value of education is to help people realize their potential and meet their needs. The purpose of education is to cultivate "a whole person" with good personalities, harmonious development, and freedom. Such a "whole person" can fulfil their potential. In other words, their needs at all levels are met. Also, the harmonious unity of emotional development and cognitive development is achieved. These should be unveiled throughout the entire process of curriculum development, implementation, and evaluation. Humanistic curriculum theory overemphasizes the importance of the "individual" and the values of individualism, which can be considered as its limitations.

Dewey is the representative of the empirical curriculum theory. In the past, curriculum theory witnessed a long-term battle between subject-centered and child-centered instruction. At the beginning of the twentieth century, Dewey resolved this conflict with his unique concept of experience and established the unique empirical curriculum based on naturalistic empiricism (Dewey 1963). Dewey (2001) shared four key ideas about the empirical curriculum theory in his book, *Democracy and Education*. First, education is continuous reconstruction or reorganization of experience, which adds to the meaning of experience, and which increases ability to direct the course of subsequent experience (p. 81–85). Second, "education as growth" (p. 46). Growth is a natural process, in which people's habits, minds, and capacities continually grow and improve. Third, "Education as a Necessity of Life"(p. 5). Education itself is the process of life instead of preparation for future life." Fourth, "Education as a Social Function" (p. 14). If school education is organized according to the form of social life, as a tool and a means to promote social progress and realize the democratic ideal, schools become a form of social organization and social life.

Existential curriculum theory is an educational trend based on existentialism. Existential educational philosophy emphasizes that the main purpose of education is to serve individuals. Education should guide people to become aware of their own environmental conditions, teach individuals to live spontaneously and authentically, and facilitate their smooth engagement in their meaningful existence. The whole emphasis of curriculum for schools must shift from the things to personality. It is advocated that the ideal curriculum should recognize individual differences in experience and take the interests of learners as the basis for learning plans and activities. It advocates activity-based learning starting from learners' needs. It emphasizes that students have freedom in group and individual activities and recommends the use of a "dialogue" style for individualized learning. Also, it emphasizes reflection and enlightenment in the learning process, against subject-centered learning.

Social-Centered curriculum theory

Social-centered curriculum theory is also known as "social reconstructionist curriculum theory" and its main representatives are George Counts, Harold Rugg, Theodore Brameld, and Paulo Freire. This curriculum theory believes that the fundamental value of education is for social development, emphasizing social problems, and social transformation. It is believed that schools should focus on social transformation rather than personal development. The purpose of education is to "transform society", according to the subjective blueprint. Schools are the main tools for forming a "new social order". To this end, school curricula should be organized around the "central issue" of social transformation. The value of the curriculum is social value. The curriculum is the means for realizing the future ideal society. The four key ideas of this theory are as follows: first, the goal of the curriculum is to transform society. Second, the curriculum is centered on a wide range of social issues, which is decided by educators, according to the needs of the society. Third, the curriculum should be organized based on solving practical social problems, rather than subject knowledge. Fourth, in terms of learning strategies, students should be involved in social life as much as possible to enhance their adaptability to social life.

Curriculum theory and blended learning

Knowledge-centered curriculum theory, learner-centered curriculum theory, and society-centered curriculum theory all have different emphases, each of which is important to the current society. Therefore, the design, implementation, and evaluation of the curriculum of blended learning should integrate the above three theories. It is advocated that a curriculum of blended learning should be based on learners' own needs, interests, development, and self-realization and pay attention to social problems and social needs. Through systematic learning and practice of disciplinary or interdisciplinary knowledge, such a curriculum should be able to meet the needs of social development.

From the perspective of the relationship between the system and the environment, blended learning takes social needs and problems as the input of the environment to the system so that the learning objectives and content can meet the social requirement to students. Blended learning has reshaped the existing form and organization of knowledge, broken down the exclusive nature of disciplinary knowledge in traditional teaching, and thus blurred the boundaries among disciplines. In blended learning, knowledge is identified and selected according to the learning objectives. The learning and application of knowledge are strengthened so that the ability of learners can be improved to meet the needs of social development. Blended learning provides content, resources, and learning paths that suit students' characteristics to promote students' self-realization, which represents the concept of learner-centered curriculum. In short, many curricular practices of blended learning are based on project-based learning or problem-based learning. The content of blended learning has focused more on solving specific problems, such as social problems. In the online environment, the learner-centered approach enables learners to set up personalized learning goals, have the autonomy to work on their learning progress, and select the curriculum according to their own needs. In this way, learners can enhance their capabilities of knowledge building and autonomous problem-solving skills.

1.3.5 Instructional Theory and Blended Learning

The design, implementation, and evaluation of curriculum and instruction of blended learning should follow the foundational principles of learning and teaching. In the following section, several major pedagogical theories for guiding blended learning will be introduced.

The theory of Mastery Learning and its implications for blended learning

The theory of mastery learning was founded by Benjamin Bloom and his colleagues. The so-called "mastery of learning" refers to supplementing classroom teaching and learning with frequent and timely "feedback-correction" sessions, in which students can have sufficient study time and receive individual help, so that they can master a unit and continue on a more advanced one, and thereby meet the standards set by the curriculum objectives. The theory of mastery learning contains two implications: first, it is an optimistic theory of teaching and learning; second, it is a set of effective individualized teaching and learning practices that can help most students learn. The core idea is to allow each student to have enough study time. As long as each student is provided enough study time that suits them, they should be able to achieve their learning objectives.

Bloom further pointed out that there are three variables that affect academic achievement: firstly, cognitive entry behaviors include learner's aptitude and cognitive structure level. They account for 50% of learning. Secondly, affective entry characteristics refer to the integration of non-intellectual factors, such as the learner's affection, attitude, interest, or confidence. They account for 25% of learning. Thirdly, the quality of instruction refers to whether the presentation, explanation, and arrangement of each element of learning tasks are suitable for learners. It accounts for 25% of learning.

Blended learning can facilitate the realization of mastery learning theory. First, for blended learning, it is more convenient to understand learners' cognitive level in advance and use online learning resources to enable students to acquire knowledge required at an early stage. Moreover, designing blended learning activities in which students are interested and encouraging students through various ways can facilitate learners' emotional engagement. Additionally, the online learning space can be fully utilized to provide personalized help and allow an individualized pace, thereby ensuring every learner to achieve their learning objectives.

First Principles of Instruction and their implications for blended learning

Professor M. David Merrill of Utah State University in the United States studied the common basic principles underlying instructional design theories and models. He summarized five principles (Merrill 2002). First, problem-centered: Learners learn more when they acquire concepts and principles in the context of real-world tasks. Second, activation: learners learn more when they activate relevant previous knowledge. Third, learners learn more when they observe a demonstration of the skills to be learned. Fourth, application: learners learn more when they apply their newly acquired knowledge and skills. Fifth, integration: learners learn more when they reflect, discuss and integrate their new skills in their everyday life.

Merrill believed that if the First Principles of Instruction can be applied, the effectiveness of teaching strategies will gradually improve. If the principle of "demonstration" is applied, effectiveness will reach the first level; if the principle of "application" is implemented, effectiveness will reach the second level; if the principle of "problem-centered" is implemented, the effectiveness level will reach the third level; if both of the principles of "activation" and "integration" are applied, the level of teaching effectiveness will be improved to a higher level.

The First Principles of Instruction can be used directly to guide the instructional design of blended learning and its implementation.

Scaffolding instruction

"Scaffolding", originally referring to temporary platforms used to assist construction, is used as a metaphor for the conceptual framework that assists students in problem solving and meaning construction.

The theoretical basis of "scaffolding instruction" originated from the social constructivism founded by the noted psychologist Lev Vygotsky of the former Soviet Union. There are two related basic viewpoints. One, the sociocultural theory, holds that higher mental functions are social by their origin. Higher mental functions, including judgment, reasoning, imagination, intentional recall, will, higher emotion, and language, initially exist as an activity content or form among people. They are internalized by students, as students' mental ability or inner mental process. Therefore, learning activities serve as important approaches for students to promote the development of their higher mental functions in the context of social interaction with teachers and peers. Second is the Zone of Proximal Development (ZPD) theory, which is "the distance between the current level of development and the level of their potential development" (Vygotsky 1980). The former refers to the ability to solve problems independently, while the latter refers the ability to solve problems under the guidance of an adult or in collaboration with more capable peers.

Instruction makes ZPD a reality and creates a new ZPD. The distance between the two levels is dynamic. Everyone's ZPD is different. In terms of instruction, it is necessary for teachers to fully consider learners' current level of development, set higher developmental requirements for students according to their proximal development zones, and provide personalized scaffolding.

The instructional design of blended learning can refer to the design of scaffolding instruction theory, namely to build a scaffolding according to the requirement of the zone of proximal development; to create a problem solving scenario to generate a cognitive gap; to guide students to independently explore knowledge construction with the help of the scaffolding built by the teacher; to strengthen knowledge construction through the communication between student–student and teacher–student; and to adopt multi-dimensional evaluation for diagnostic and reflective learning.

Activity Theory and its implications for blended learning

Activity Theory was proposed by Lev Vygotsky and enhanced by former Soviet Union psychologists Alexei Nikolaevich Leontyev and Alexander Romanovich Luria. It is the product of sociocultural activity and sociohistorical research. Activity theory emphasizes the bridging role of activities in the process of internalization of knowledge and skills. Activities are the basis of psychology, particularly for the occurrence and development of human consciousness, while human activities are objective and social.

In instructional design, the subjects are the students and the object is learning objectives, which are affected and changed by the subjects through certain activities. The community refers to other common learners except the students themselves, such as teachers, classmates, other personnel, etc. The tools can be understood as part of the instructional environment, including the design of hardware and software used in the instructional process. The rules are used to coordinate subject and community, as restrictions or agreement in teaching and learning activities. The division of labor means that different members must complete different tasks in the teaching and learning process.

According to activity theory, blended learning should fully utilize technology as a "tool" to help students to achieve their learning goals. At the same time, the rules that need to be followed should be fully designed in the learning activities involving community and individuals; if there are tasks, the division of labor should be well designed to ensure the effectiveness of blended learning.

Community of Inquiry

In 1999, the theoretical framework of the Community of Inquiry for the online learning environment was proposed by Randy Garrison, Terry Anderson, and Walter Archer of the University of Alberta in Canada (Garrison et al. 1999).

There are three core elements of teaching and learning in the Community of Inquiry theory proposed by Garrison et al.: cognitive presence (Garrison et al. 2001), social presence (Rourke et al. 1999) and teaching presence (Anderson et al. 2001). Garrison specified the categories and indicators of the three presences (Garrison and Arbaugh 2007).

The focus of the community of inquiry is the creation of educational experiences, which need to adhere to the following eight principles: first, establish purposeful and active inquiry activities. Second, plan for preparing critical thinking through critical reflection and discourse. Third, plan for building trust and creating an atmosphere that supports open communication. Fourth, establish a learning community and form cohesion. Fifth, establish mutual respect and responsibility. Sixth, plan the curriculum content, learning method, and learning time, and effectively monitor and manage critical dialogues and collaborative reflection activities. Seventh, sustain inquiry that moves to a resolution. Eighth, ensure assessment is congruent with intended processes and outcomes.

The following section elaborates on the three community of inquiry presences. Cognitive presence refers to the learners' ability to construct and confirm meaning on their own through continuous reflection and discourse (Anderson et al. 2001). It includes four phases, namely triggering events, exploration, integration, and resolution (Garrison and Arbaugh 2007). Specifically, the process consists of a problem or task designed to trigger students for further inquiry; exploration for relevant information or knowledge, analysis, and integration of different perspectives and understandings; and solutions to the problems (Garrison et al. 2000).

Teaching presence refers to the design, facilitation, and guidance of cognitive and social process so that learners can achieve personally and educationally meaningful learning outcomes. According to Anderson et al. (2001), there are three categories in teaching presence, namely, instructional design and organization, discourse facilitation, and direct instruction. The main tasks of teaching presence are to create curriculum content; design learning activities and methods; set learning activity sequences; effectively use communication media; organize, accommodate, and manage purposeful critical dialogues and collaborative reflection activities; and provide students with timely feedback. Teaching presence encourages learners to become investigators with metacognitive awareness and metacognitive strategies in collaborative inquiry.

Social presence refers to the learners' ability to project themselves socially and emotionally, thereby being perceived as "real people" in mediated communication (Short et al. 1976). Social presence consists of three components: affective expression, open communication, and group cohesion.

According to the theoretical model of the Community of Inquiry, the three elements are interrelated and reciprocally influence each other. Partially overlapping the three elements will generate meaningful educational experiences.

The revised CoI framework introduced three external factors apart from communication medium, namely educational context, discipline standards, and applications (Garrison, 2016).

Critical thinking is one of the ultimate goals of higher education. The CoI framework can play an important role in the development of students' critical thinking skills in blended learning. Teachers need to understand and make full use of the three elements of CoI, facilitate in-depth and meaningful learning through collaborative learning activities and reflective dialogues involving critical thinking, and help to achieve student development goals.

1.4 Models of Blended Learning

The previous sections have first discussed the psychological and pedagogical basis for the emergence and development of blended learning, then elaborated on the theoretical foundations (system theory, educational communication theory, learning theory, and curriculum theory) for designing ideal blended learning. In this section, the theory of blended learning will be illustrated, including the blended learning model (namely the plan of blended learning based on theoretical foundations), the instructional design process model of blended learning (namely the process of designing blended learning), and the practice model of blended learning, which explains how to blend in practice. This section will first elaborate on the blended learning model.

A instructional model refers to a relatively stable interaction relationship among various instructional elements designed and gradually developed through practice and guided by educational philosophy that aims to achieve specific learning objectives. Such a model includes the integration of various elements of instructional process, instructional procedures, and corresponding strategies and evaluation methods.

Next, several commonly used instructional models and their applications in blended learning will be introduced. Designers can adopt a model according to their own instructional scenarios (such as learning objectives, learning content, and learners). It should be noted that the following instructional models can be applied in face-to-face, online learning, as well as online and offline learning.

1.4.1 Cognitive Apprenticeship Instruction

Before formal schooling, apprenticeship used to be the most common learning approach. In the ancient apprenticeship system, the apprentice observed the master's work, communicated with the master, and tried to do the work. After having feedback from the master, the apprentice reflected and gradually developed skills that were as good as the master's. This method enables learners to put into practice what they have learned because learning occurs in the real world. After the establishment of schools, and as learning has gradually been separated from real-life situations, it is difficult to develop learners' higher-order cognitive abilities, such as applying knowledge to problem solving. To remedy the defects of traditional education, Collins et al. first proposed Cognitive Apprenticeship Instruction in 1989 (Collins et al. 1988). "Apprenticeship" indicates its inheritance or similarity with the traditional apprenticeship system, emphasizing that learning should take place in application scenarios, and knowledge and skills are acquired through the integration of observation of expert work and practice; "cognition" reflects a relatively strong practical significance, emphasizing that learning of generalized knowledge occurs in application scenarios to facilitate the application of knowledge in various scenarios. Cognitive apprenticeship aims to develop learners' higher-order cognitive skills, such as problem-solving and reflective skills.

Six operational strategies for Cognitive Apprenticeship Instruction are recommended as follows: modeling, coaching, scaffolding, articulation, reflection, and exploration. Five socialization strategies are also recommended: situational learning, simulation, community of practice, intrinsic motivation, and cooperation.

Cognitive apprenticeship can be implemented in face-to-face learning. However, when the class size is relatively large, learning effectiveness will be compromised. Therefore, blended learning has more advantages in terms of providing scenarios, demonstrating through technical means, providing scaffolding, individual tutoring, and showing students' practice.

1.4.2 Resources-Based Learning

Resources-based learning refers to an instructional model in which learners learn by interacting with a wide range of learning resources instead of attending classes. The learning resources refer to all available print and non-print media, including books and articles, audio-visual materials, electronic databases, and other computer-based, multimedia, and Internet-based resources. This instructional model aims to develop learners' ability to learn or explore independently. At the same time, resources-based learning allows learners to choose the methods and pace they prefer to solve the same problem, with the flexibly to make adjustments according to their learning styles, interests, and competences. Therefore, the learning style with this instructional model is individualized or personalized. Resources-based learning usually involves the following steps:

- Identify the problem. Key points of courses need to be changed to questions and learning objectives that students can explore.

- Identify methods for collecting information. Students need instruction and guidance on information collection and the exploration of potential sources of information.
- Collect information. During the process of information collection, students are required to be able to identify and select important information or facts relevant to research questions and to classify the information collected.
- Use information. Students need to be instructed on how to use the information they have collected, and how to take note of sources of information.
- Synthesize information for solving problems and present. Students are guided to organize information into a systematic, logical synthesis in order to solve the problem. Afterwards, students are required to present in oral, written, or other forms to demonstrate how they synthesized information to solve problems.
- Evaluate. Students need to be provided the opportunity for evaluation and understanding on how to evaluate what they have completed. Evaluation and self-reflection are the highlights of resources-based learning (Awaludin 2019).

It can be argued that blended learning has advantages in implementing resources-based learning.

1.4.3 Project-Based Learning

Project-based learning (PBL) is a situational learning method based on constructivist theory (Lave and Wenger 1991). To be specific, when students actively build understanding by fully grasping concepts and applying them to real-world situations, they are able to acquire a deeper understanding of the learning materials. PBL is usually project-driven and requires students to integrate their understanding across disciplines. PBL projects must integrate fragmented discipline problems to address practical challenges and complex problems.

PBL is mainly composed of four core components, namely content, activity, context, and result. The implementation process is generally divided into six steps, namely learning relevant knowledge, selecting projects that comprehensively apply knowledge to create products (e.g., artifacts, schemes, etc.), forming groups, working in groups to complete projects guided by teachers, sharing project results, and conducting project evaluation. Steps can be added or deleted according to the implementation status of the projects. Blended learning can provide a better learning environment for the implementation of project-based learning.

1.4.4 Problem-Based Learning

Problem-based learning (PBL) emphasizes setting learning in complex and meaningful problem contexts. Students can collaboratively address real-world problems to acquire scientific knowledge, develop problem-solving skills, and become autonomous learners (Hmelo and Ferrari 1997). The steps of the PBL process are as follows (Chang et al. 2020):

- Students are introduced to an ill-structured problem related to their real life.
- Students collaboratively analyze the problem and discuss what they need to learn to solve the problem.
- Students work on their own to find resources.
- Students meet and discuss with group members regarding whether they can have a feasible solution based on the resources they found, which may need several rounds of attempts.
- Students report the process of learning and problem solving in front of the whole class.
- Students reflect and evaluate the whole process with their teacher and peers.

When it comes to blended learning, problem-based learning has the following benefits for students:

- the construction of a more authentic problem context
- timely communication and collaboration anytime, anywhere
- autonomous learning based on resources
- online Q&A areas for questioning and feedback
- timely feedback for supporting their inquiry process.

1.4.5 Distributed Learning

Distributed learning, as an instructional model, allows teachers, students, and teaching content to be distributed in a decentralized way, so that teaching and learning can take place at different times and locations. The characteristics are:

- distributed learning resources, which enable students to access good instructional resources everywhere
- learner-centered, which means students can choose instruction resources suitable for themselves
- collaboration and communication through interactive community, which enables students to acquire learning skills and social skills
- knowledge construction through learning experience in the virtual environment (Li et al. 2007; Zhong and Zhang 2005)

Distributed learning can overcome the time and space limitations of traditional classrooms and expand the circle of teachers and peers. In other words, students can access instructional resources and resource persons on the Internet so that students can have cognitive views and experiences that are different from those locally to support their knowledge and meaning construction. Students can learn anytime, anywhere based on their needs. A blended learning environment is more conducive to the implementation of a distributed learning model.

1.4.6 Random Access Learning

Random access learning is an instructional model in which complex (or advanced) knowledge and skills are taught. Students can learn the same content several times for different purposes, through different channels, from different aspects, and with different methods, so as to gain a multi-faceted understanding (Spiro et al. 1995).

Due to the complexity and multi-faceted nature of problems in some fields, it is difficult to have a comprehensive understanding of the inherent nature of these complex problems and the interrelationships between things from one perspective or at one time. Therefore, random access learning advocates multiple attempts at the learning content for different purposes and from different perspectives. As a result, learners can have a qualitative leap in gaining a comprehensive understanding of the problem. In other words, learners will be able to improve their ability to understand complex interrelationships between things and flexibly apply the knowledge and skills acquired.

Random access learning, based on constructivist theory, helps to develop learners' creativity and encourages their communication and cooperation. It is applicable in learning contexts including ill-structured and complex problem-solving scenarios, which focus on knowledge application and transfer.

Blended learning makes it more convenient to implement random access learning. Face-to-face learning is suitable for learners to share opinions about one issue from different angles, while online learning enables students to approach the same content from multiple angles by providing learning resources that involve different viewpoints of the same content. At the same time, students can take advantage of the discussion area on the platform to present and share their own opinions with others, which can promote the effective implementation of random access learning.

1.4.7 Flipped Classroom

The educational philosophy behind the flipped classroom is active learning, the core of which is to reverse the activities that take place inside and outside the classroom. That is, "the events that have traditionally taken place inside the classroom now take place outside the classroom and vice versa" (Lage and Treglia 2000).

Alten et al. (2019) summarized five advantages of flipped classrooms by reviewing the existing literature:

- It requires students to have strong self-regulation learning ability and in turn helps to develop students' self-regulation ability.
- Students take the initiative to complete assignments in class with the help of teachers, avoiding cognitive overload when completing homework alone.
- Students have more time for learning activities, which is an active, constructive, and interactive mode of participation.
- Students have more opportunities to receive effective feedback and differentiated instruction from their teachers.
- Finally, FTC is often assumed to be a promising pedagogical approach that increases student satisfaction about the learning environment.

Criticisms of flipped classroom include:

- Video production is too time- and energy-consuming for teachers and places an excessive demand on learners' abilities.
- It takes up too much time after class and causes too much pressure on students.

The design framework of flipped classrooms should consist of 9 principles (Kim et al. 2014), specifically:

- provide an opportunity for students to gain first exposure prior to class
- provide an incentive for students to prepare for class
- provide a mechanism to assess student understanding
- provide clear connections between in-class and out-of-class activities
- provide clearly defined and well-structured guidance
- provide enough time for students to complete assignments
- provide facilitation for building a learning community
- provide prompt/adaptive feedback on individual or group works
- provide technologies that are familiar and easy to access.

Teachers can refer to this framework to design flipped courses. The flipped classroom is a typical model of blended learning, which aims to establish an organic systematic integration between online and face-to-face learning activities.

1.5 Blended Learning Models and Blended Learning Practice Models

To realize the above-mentioned instructional models of blended learning and their learning objectives, the implementation process needs to be designed. From this design process is formed the design process model of blended learning (simply named the blended learning design model). The blended learning design model follows the common characteristics of general instructional design models and has its own uniqueness. This section first discusses the general learning design model to be followed during blended learning, then examines the special characteristics of blended learning design, discusses the blended learning design models that are based on these specific characteristic, and introduces some practice models of blended learning i.e., how to blend in practice.

1.5.1 Blended Learning Design Model

According to the levels of the system, the instructional design can be divided into three levels: "system centered" (such as professional program plans, curriculum, etc.), "product centered" (such as instructional software and resources, etc.) and "classroom centered" (from a unit that takes several hours of classroom teaching). The instructional design at the three levels share common elements of design, but the emphasis at different levels varies.

By summarizing thousands of models of instructional design, Wu (1994) formed the general model of classic instructional design. This model is designed based on learning theories, instructional theories, communication theories, and systems theories, including all elements of the instructional design process in a relatively systematic and holistic manner.

The general learning design model should be followed for blended learning design. In terms of different levels, blended learning has the design of a blended learning platform and blended courses for system-focused level, as well as a blended instruction process (several hours of classroom teaching) that is at a classroom-focused level. The development of a variety of instructional resources is required in blended learning, at the product-focused level. All elements of the general learning design model are also involved in blended instructional design.

At the same time, the particularity of blended learning also needs to be considered, compared with pure offline or online instruction, which should be the most important difference between the blended instructional design model and the general model of instructional design.

Compared with traditional face-to-face learning, blended learning extends and widens the teaching and learning time and space. Students can learn independently or cooperatively at anytime and anywhere at their own pace. At the same time, instructors are more likely to obtain a variety of relevant information about student learning and provide a personalized learning environment that is more appropriate for them by tracking their online learning traces with the support of big data and learning analytics. Compared with online learning, blended learning would dissolve the sense of alienation between teachers and students and the sense of isolation of students, offer a more flexible organization of teacher-student meetings, allow for group teaching of content suitable for face-to-face instruction, and thus increase the effectiveness of teaching and learning.

Stein/Graham's design model of blended learning

Jared Stein and Charles R. Graham co-authored a book on blended learning, *Essentials for blended learning: a standards-based guide*, in 2014. They proposed the blended course design model when conducting research on blended learning in colleges and universities. Blended course design is a cyclic process consisting of three activities: designing, engaging, and evaluating. Stein and Graham emphasized that blended classrooms need iterative development and pointed out that the design of individual learning activities, courses, or units can be supported through continuous improvement of the three activities.

The design part of the model includes four components: designing learning goals and objectives, designing evaluation and feedback, describing learning activities that can achieve teaching goals, and adding online elements to the learning process. The process starts with learning outcomes, then designs corresponding assessment tasks, and finally creates activities for achieving learning outcomes. Teachers are encouraged to design a small part (such as a single course or unit) at a time, and further optimize the design after students have participated in blended learning activities and evaluated online and offline learning effectiveness. In order to support the implementation of instructional design, Stein and Graham (2014) provided a blended course design template in the book *Essentials for blended learning: a standards-based guide.*

Eagleton's design model of blended learning

Eagleton (2017) proposed a blended learning intervention design model for the teaching of psychology in higher education, including three parts: identifying learning task needs (through pre-tests, learning outcomes, and student profile analysis), designing learning interventions (including developing and disseminating instructional strategies, learning strategies, and evaluation strategy) and evaluation.

- Determining learning task requirements is divided into three sub-tasks: obtaining students' personal profiles, pre-testing students, and specifying learning outcomes, i.e., learning objectives
- Finalizing learning task needs based on basic student learning information and learning objectives, followed by learning intervention design (teachers' teaching strategies, students' learning strategies, forms of instructional content development and dissemination, and design of instructional evaluation); and
- Evaluation (mainly feedback and slight adjustment of instructional programs in the implementation process).

In addition, Eagleton et al. argued that creating a blended learning program is a process that needs to take into account the ability of teachers, the infrastructure of the institution, and the learners' acceptance of the new learning mode. The blended learning design can be integrated into the whole-brain learning model (Eagleton and Muller 2011). It is necessary to consider the differences in students' information processing of the left brain and the right brain when learning different materials, and integrate the whole-brain learning model to design the learning content and learning form.

1.5.2 Blended Learning Practice Models

In blended learning, one problem to be faced is when to implement online learning and when to implement offline learning. Through blended learning and teaching practices, scholars have summarized some blended learning practice models. These models can help teachers to increase their knowledge and experiences of how to blend online and offline learning.

Zhu Zhiting's three models of blended learning practice

Zhu and Hu (2021) summarized three models of blended learning practice, namely O2O, OAO, and OMO, and pointed out that blended learning would inevitably move towards OMO in the future.

O2O (Online to Offline) model refers to a learning environment based on online, offline, or online-to-offline practice. The teaching process mainly takes place offline, while an online learning environment serves as the triage. In a flipped classroom, the 'students' online learning determines offline teaching' model is an embodiment of this type of triage. Another example is maker learning, in which tasks are provided online and explored offline. Learning in this model is mainly a one-way flow from online to offline. There are clear boundaries between online and offline.

OAO (Online and Offline) model refers to the integrated 'dual store' form that integrates online and offline practice organically. It is a model based on the integration of online and offline practice, with two-way online and offline intercommunication, interconnection, and mutual appreciation. There are clear boundaries between online and offline.

OMO (Online Merge Offline) model refers to a student-centered learning environment based on the comprehensive integration of online and offline practice, synchronously and asynchronously. Technical methods are used to bridge various structures, levels, and types of data online and offline; establish an ecology of online and offline merging through virtual and real learning scenarios; and realize a new teaching style of personalized teaching and service. This kind of environment is developing in the direction toward the 'physicalizing of online space and virtualization of offline space'. There are two important changes in the development direction of the learning environment constructed by OMO: 1. the interface boundaries between online and offline is weakening and disappearing; 2. the learner has changed from "marching with heavy burdens" to "walking with ease".

Michael Horn's six blended learning models

Micaeal Horn of the *Innosight Institute* in the United States has identified six blended learning models (Horn and Staker 2011).

Face to face driven model is a blended learning model mainly based on face-to-face learning. Teachers deliver course content through traditional classroom teaching, supplemented by online course resources or review materials, so that students can learn independently at home, in the classroom, or the laboratory. Another approach to this model is for teachers to allow students to learn online course content at their own pace in the classroom. The role of the teacher in the process is to provide individualized instruction.

Online driven model is mainly based on online learning. Students primarily study online at a distance, with the option to attend face-to-face instruction. This model provides all learning content through dynamic management of online courses and uses remote synchronous interactive systems (such as video conferencing systems) or asynchronous interactive systems (such as BBS discussion areas) to conduct Q&A discussions with individual students and groups. This model can provide students with learning opportunities at any time and any place and provides more choices for students' extracurricular activities.

Face-to-face and online rotation model: alternating between face-to-face and online instruction, students alternate between a period of face-to-face instruction and a period of online learning outside of the classroom. A flipped classroom is a form of this model, where students learn online course content in advance, at home and then come to the classroom to receive face-to-face instruction from teachers.

In the **flex model**, learning content happens online or face-to-face in groups/ individual tutorials. Most students learn in an online environment. They can receive face-to-face instruction in the classroom, but the face-to-face instruction is only for group or individual tutoring. Students decide how to arrange the learning content and construct their knowledge at their own pace. While students can access course resources through mobile devices at home and in school or anywhere, teachers play a key role in facilitating learning with individuals and groups of students in a brick-and-mortar school. This model requires obtaining information through the Internet, no matter where the students are located.

Online lab model refers to learning in the computer lab and completing the interactions online. All course materials and teaching activities are completed in the computer lab. Students are supposed to learn independently by watching multimedia learning materials and interacting synchronously or asynchronously with teachers or classmates through video conferencing systems, forums, and e-mails. Although this model sets up a complete online course for students to learn at their own pace, the learning process is in the space of a brick-and-mortar school. Most course units are completed by students on their own, while some units require the collaboration of study groups of three to four students.

The **self-blended model** allows students to choose between online and offline learning. This is a personalized instructional model. Students can choose learning content online and learn based on their learning needs. Most of the learning is completed online, but students can participate in face-to-face classroom instruction. In the implementation of this model, to support students on the acquisition of relevant knowledge and learning tools, teachers need to prepare corresponding online courses in advance as necessary resources for students to complete learning tasks.

References

Alten, D. V., Phielix, C., Janssen, J., & Kester, L. (2019). Effects of flipping the classroom on learning outcomes and satisfaction: a meta-analysis. *Educational Research Review, 28*, 1-18.

Anderson, T., & Dron, J. (2011). Three generations of distance education pedagogy. *International Review of Research in Open and Distance Learning, 12(3)*, 80-97.

Anderson, T., Rourke, L., Garrison, D. R, & Archer, W. (2001). Assessing teaching presence in a computer conferencing context. *Online Learning, 5(2)*.

Awaludin, A. (2019). Resource based learning for teaching Arabic. *Ijaz Arabi Journal of Arabic Learning, 2(1)*.

Bersin, J. (2004). How Did We Get Here? The History of Blended Learning. Chapter one of The Blended Learning Book: *Best Practices, Proven Methodologies, and Lessons Learned*. New Jersey: Wiley.

Cabrero, R. S., & Román, O. C. (2018). Psycho-pedagogical Predecessors of Connectivism as a New Paradigm of Learning. *International Journal of Educational Excellence, 4(2)*, 29-45.

Carreño, I. (2014). Theory of connectivity as an emergent solution to innovative learning strategies. *American Journal of Educational Research, 2(2)*, 107-116.

Chang, N., Wang, Z., & Hsu, S. H. (2020). A Comparison of the Learning Outcomes for a PBL-based Information Literacy Course in Three Different Innovative Teaching Environments. *Libri, 70(3)*, 213–225.

Chen Q., & Liu R. (2019). *Contemporary Educational Psychology (in Chinese)*. 3rd Edition. Beijing: Beijing Normal University Press.

Collins, A., Brown, J. S., & Newman, S. E. (1988). Cognitive apprenticeship: Teaching the craft of reading, writing and mathematics. *Thinking: The journal of philosophy for children, 8(1)*, 2–10.

Collins, A., & Halverson, R. (2009). *Rethinking Education in the Age of Technology: The Digital Revolution and Schooling in America*. Technology, Education--Connections (TEC) Series. New York: Teachers College Press.

Dewey, John. (1963). *Experience and Education*. New York: Collier Books, Print.

Dewey, John. (2001). *Democracy and Education*. Penn State Electronic Classics Series Publication.

Dou X. (1988). Introduction to System Theory (in Chinese). *Ningxia Education, (4)*, 10-11.

Duan M., Pei X., & Li X.(2009). The Paradigm Shift of Educational System——A Dialogue with Prof. Charles M. Reigeluth, an International Instructional Design Expert (in Chinese). *China Educational Technology, (5)*,1-6.

Duke, B., Harper, G., & Johnston, M. (2013). Connectivism as a Digital Age Learning Theory. *The International HETL Review*, Special Issue: 4–13.

Downes, S. (2005). Feature: E-learning 2.0. *E-learning magazine, (10)*, 1.

Downes, S. (2012). Connectivism and Connective Knowledge: essays on meaning and learning networks. *National Research Council Canada*.

Eagleton S, Muller A. (2011). Development of a model for whole brain learning of physiology. *Adv Physiol Educ, 35*, 421–426.

Eagleton S. (2017). Designing blended learning interventions for the 21st century student. *Adv Physiol Educ, 41(2)*, 203-11.

European commission. (2018). Proposal for a Council Recommendation on Key Competences for Lifelong Learning.

Erikson, Erik H. *Childhood and society, 2nd ed.,* 1964. W.W. Norton & Co. New York: Cambridge. University Press.

Gardner, H. (1993). *Multiple intelligences*. Basic books.

Garrison D R. (2016). *Thinking collaboratively: Learning in a community of inquiry*. New York: Routledge.

Garrison, D. R., & Arbaugh, J. B. (2007). Researching the community of inquiry framework: Review, issues, and future directions. *The Internet and higher education, 10(3)*, 157-172.

Garrison, D. R., Anderson, T., & Archer, W. (1999). Critical Inquiry in a Text-Based Environment: Computer Conferencing in Higher Education. *The Internet and higher education, 2(2)*, 87-105.

Garrison, D. R., Anderson, T., & Archer, W. (2000). Critical inquiry in a text-based environment: Computer conferencing in higher education. *The Internet and Higher Education, 2(2-3)*, 87–105.

Garrison, D. R., Anderson, T., & Archer, W. (2001). Critical thinking, cognitive presence, and computer conferencing in distance education. *American Journal of Distance Education, 15(1)*, 7-23.

Gao Y.X. (1989). *Personality Psychology (in Chinese)*. Beijing: Beijing Normal University Press.

Gharacheh, A., Esmaeili, Z., Farajollahi, M., & Jamaizadeh, M. (2016). Presentation of blended learning conceptual pattern based on individual and social constructivism theory. *Int., J. of Humanities and Cultural Stud.*, 1.

Horn, M. B., & Staker, H. (2017). Blended: Using disruptive innovation to improve schools. John Wiley & Sons.

Horn, M. B., & Staker, H. (2011). The rise of K-12 blended learning. *Innosight institute, 5(1)*, 1-17.

Hmelo, C. E. & Ferrari (1997). The problem-based learning tutorial: Cultivating higher order thinking skills. *Journal of the education of the gifted, 20 (4)*, 401- 422.

Hung, D. (2001). Design principles for web-based learning: Implications from Vygotskian thought. *Educational Technology, 41 (3)*, 33-41.

Kagan, J., Rosman, B., Day, D., & Albert, J. (1964). Information processing in the child: Significance of analytic and reflective attitudes. *Psychological Monographs,78(1)*,1-37.

Kim, M. K., Kim, S. M., Khera, O., & Getman, J. (2014). The experience of three flipped classrooms in an urban university: An exploration of design principles. *The Internet and Higher Education, 22*, 37-50.

Lage, M. J., Platt, G. J., & Treglia, M. (2000). Inverting the Classroom: A Gateway to Creating an Inclusive Learning Environment. *The Journal of Economic Education, 31(1)*, 30.

Lam, J. (2015). Collaborative learning using social media tools in a blended learning course. *In International conference on hybrid learning and continuing education (pp. 187–198)*. Springer, Cham.

Lave, J., & Wenger, E. (1991). *Situated learning: legitimate peripheral participation*. Li L.(2010). *Instructional Design (in Chinese)*. Beijing: Higher Education Press.

Li Y., Jiang W. & Yao Q.(2007). A Brief Discussion on Distributed Learning (in Chines(e). *Modern Educational Technology, (1)*, 52–54, 14.

Lin C. (1997). On the Construction of Subject Competence (in Chinese). *Journal of Beijing Normal University (Social Science Edition), (1)*, 5-12.

Liu M., Kang C., Dong L. (2018). Instructional design research: A disciplinary perspective (in Chinese). Beijing: Beijing Normal University Press.

Nan G., Li Y. (2005). *Educational Communication (Second Edition) (in Chinese)*. Beijing: Higher Education Press.

Maslow, A. H. (1970). *Motivation and personality (2nd ed.)*. New York: Harper & Row.

Merrill, M. D. (2002). First principles of instruction. *Educational technology research and development, 50*, 43-59.

Ormrod, J. E. (1999). *Human learning*. Pearson Education.

Otiende, J. E., & Sifuna, D. N. (1994). *An introductory history of education*. Nairobi: University of Nairobi Press.

Piaget, J. (1976). Piaget's Theory. In B. Inhelder, H. H. Chipman, & C. Zwingmann (Eds.), *Piaget and His School: A Reader in Developmental Psychology (11-23)*. Springer Berlin Heidelberg.

Piaget, J. (1997). *The principles of genetic epistemology (Vol. 7)*. Psychology Press.

Research Group on Core Literacy. (2016). Core Competencies and Values for Chinese Students (in Chinese). *Journal of The Chinese Society of Education, (10)*, 1-3.

Rogers, C. R. (1982). *Freedom to learn (2nd ed.)*. Ohio: Merrill.

Rogers, C. R., Lyon, H. C., & Tausch, R. (2012). *On becoming an effective teacher: Person-centered teaching, psychology, philosophy, and dialogues with Carl R. Rogers and Harold Lyon*. London: Routledge.

Rourke, L., Anderson, T., Garrison, D.R. & Archer, W. (1999). Assessing Social Presence in Asynchronous Text-based Computer Conferencing. *The Journal of Distance Education / Revue de l'ducation Distance, 14(2)*, 50-71.

Shaffer, D. R. & Kipp, K. (2012). Developmental psychology: Childhood and adolescence (9th ed). Wadsworth Cengage Learning.

Short, J., Williams, E., & Christie, B. (1976). *The social psychology of telecommunications*: London; New York: Wiley.

Siemens, G. (2005). Connectivism: A learning theory for the digital age. *International Journal of Instructional Technology & Distance Learning, 2(1)*, 3-10.

Singh, H., & Reed, C. (2001). A white paper: Achieving success with blended learning. *Centra software, 1*, 1-11.

Spiro, R. J., Feltovich, P. J., Jacobson, M. J., & Coulson, R. L. (1995). Cognitive flexibility, constructivism, and hypertext: Random access instruction for advanced knowledge acquisition in ill-structured domains. *Constructivism, Hillsdale, NJ: Erlbaum, 9*.

Steffe, & J. E. Gale (Eds.), *Constructivism in education; Constructivism in education* (pp. 85–107, Chapter xvii, 575 Pages). Lawrence Erlbaum Associates, Inc, Hillsdale, NJ.

Stein, J., & Graham, C.R. (2014). *Essentials for blended learning: a standards-based guide*. New York: Routledge.

Strozier, R. M. (2002). *Foucault, subjectivity, and identity: Historical constructions of subject and self*. Wayne State University Press.

Toffler A. (1990). *Powershift: Knowledge, wealth, and violence at the edge of the 21st century*. Bantam Books.

Voogt, J, Roblin N. (2012). A comparative analysis of international frameworks for 21st century competences: *Implications for national curriculum policies. Journal of Curriculum Studies, 4(3)*, 299-321.

Vygotsky, L. S. (1980). *Mind in society: The development of higher psychological processes*. Cambridge, MA: Harvard University Press.

Wang J., Yuan S. & Zhao G.(2018). The impact of blended teaching on college students' learning effectiveness: An empirical study based on the application effect of MOOC in first-class universities in China (in Chinese). *Modern Distance Education, (5)*, 39-47.

Wang S. (2017). Rain Classroom: Smart Teaching Tools in the Background of Mobile Internet and Big Data (in Chinese). *Modern Educational Technology, (5)*, 26-32.

Watson, J. B., & Kimble, G. A. (2017). *Behaviorism*. Routledge.

Wei Q., & Zhong Z.(1992). *Educational Communication (in Chinese)*. Nan Chang: Jiangxi Education Press.

Wei Y., Qin D., Hu J., Yao H. & Shi Y.(2019). Classroom action recognition of students based on deep learning (in Chinese). *Modern Educational Technology, (7)*, 87-91.

Witkin, H. A., Moore, C. A., Goodenough, D. R., & Cox, P. W. (1977). Field-dependent and field-independent cognitive styles and their educational implications. *Review of educational research, 47(1)*, 1-64.

Wu M.(1994). *Instructional Design*. Beijing: Higher Education Press.

Yin H., & Bi H.(2000). *Learning Ability (in Chinese)*. Qingdao: Qingdao Ocean University Press.

Zhang Xiaofeng. (2002). Curriculum Development under the consideration of multiple intelligences theory (in Chinese) . Journal of Educational Development, (1), 20-23.

Zhang Y., Yi D., Liu L., Wu Y., Liu X., Zhao Z. & Cao Y.(2019). Construction and practice of blended teaching mode based on SPOC (in Chinese). *Chongqing Medicine, (21)*, 3766-3769.

Zeng W., & Cao R. (2005). *Analysis of Learning Subjects (in Chinese)*. Beijing: Chinese Cultural and Historical Press.

Zhong Z., & Zhang Q.(2005). On Distributed Learning (in Chinese). *Studies In Foreign Education, (7)*, 28-33.

Zhu Z. & Hu J. (2021). Technology empowers educational innovation in the later stage of the epidemic: a new form of online and offline integrated teaching (in Chinese). *Open Education Research, (1)*, 13-23.

Chapter 2
Implementation of Blended Learning at the Course Level

Xibin Han, Yiran Cui, Wen Wang, Shuyan Wang, and Xiaoying Feng

Curriculum is a vessel that provides directions for instruction. With the popularization and application of various Internet-based information technologies in instruction, blended learning has increasingly become popular. This chapter first discusses core components of blended learning as well as relationships among the components (Sect. 2.1). The chapter then elaborates on the implementation process of blended learning process (as shown in Fig. 2.1). The first phase of the process is analysis (Sect. 2.2), which is the foundation for all other phases of implementing blended learning. This section analyzes the learning tasks, characteristics of learners, and the contexts of implementing blended learning.

The second phase is design (Sect. 2.3), development, and implementation (Sect. 2.4). Design involves using the outputs from the analysis phase to plan a strategy for developing the instruction. Design phase (Sect. 2.3) includes writing course learning objectives, determining learning units, writing unit learning objectives, and selecting learning content and delivery media. Development and implementation are to generate learning activities and assessment instruments. Development, implementation and evaluation phases (Sect. 2.4) include developing course activities, developing unit activities and evaluates whether students have acquired the

X. Han (✉)
Institute of Education, Tsinghua University, Beijing, China
e-mail: hanxb@tsinghua.edu.cn

Y. Cui
School of International Education, Shandong University, Jinan, Shandong, China

W. Wang
National Institute of Education Sciences of China, Beijing, China

S. Wang
School of Leadership, The University of Southern Miss Gulfport, Long Beach, MS 39560, USA

X. Feng
School of Educational Technology, Beijing Normal University, Beijing, China

© The Author(s) 2024
M. Li et al. (eds.), *Handbook of Educational Reform Through Blended Learning*,
https://doi.org/10.1007/978-981-99-6269-3_2

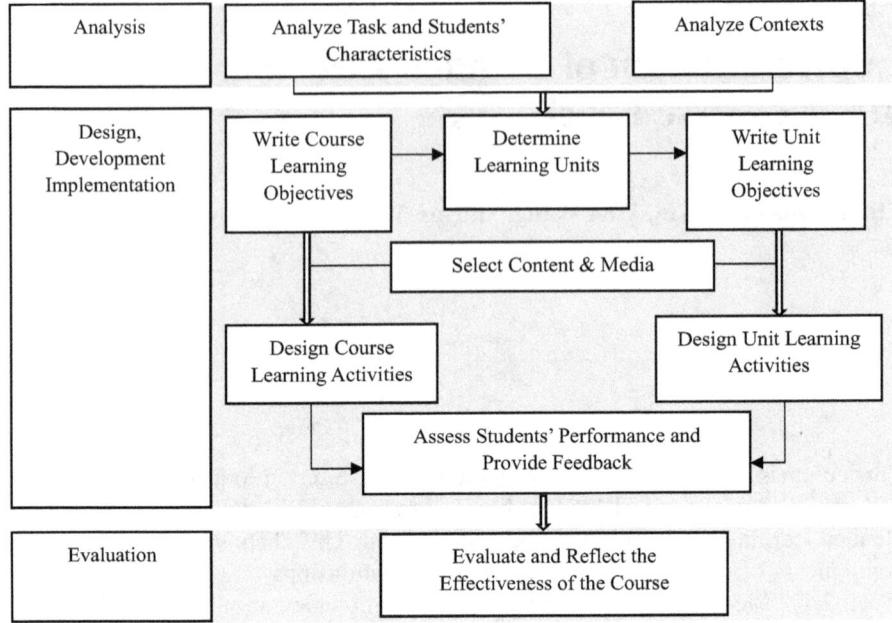

Fig. 2.1 The implementation process of blended learning

knowledge, performed the skills, and exhibited changes in attitudes as required by the learning objectives of the course. Implementation strategies of blended learning and analyzes effectiveness of blended course design are provided to conclude this section.

Section 2.5 provides suggestions of implementing blended learning for different modes, such as different learning objectives, different time and space, and different teaching environment.

This chapter not only explains how to implement blended learning, but also highlights related supporting theories. Additionally, this chapter provides contemporary design examples that help teachers, instructional designers, educational technicians, and business personnel link current theoretical concepts to practical applications.

2.1 Core Components of Blended Learning and Related Relationships

The components of instruction include learning objectives, students, teachers, learning content, learning activities, evaluation and feedback, and learning environment (Li 1991). These components also apply to blended learning, but the definitions have been expanded in blended learning. Figure 2.2 shows the core components of blended learning and related relationships.

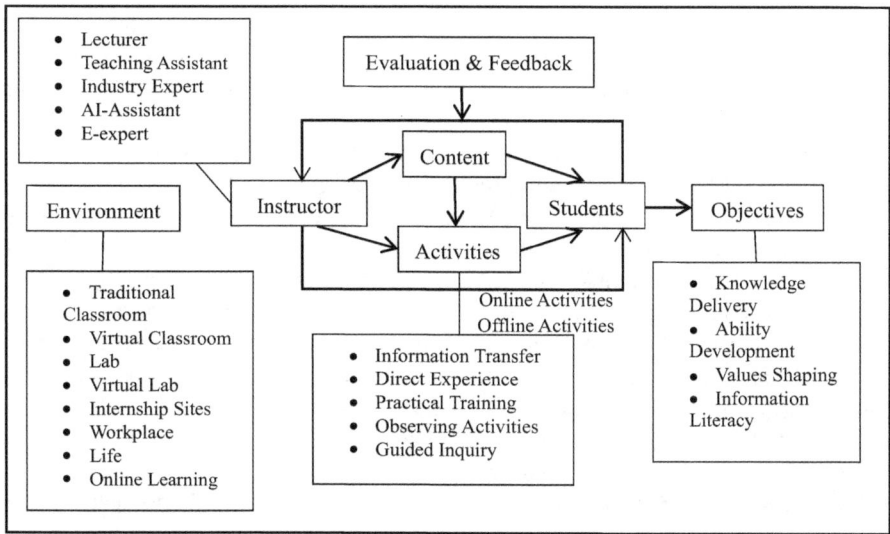

Fig. 2.2 The seven core components of blended learning and related relationships (Han et al. 2016)

2.1.1 Definitions of the Core Components

Learning Objectives. The learning objectives in blended learning emphasizes the overall cultivation of knowledge, skills, comprehensive abilities, and qualities required in the information age, as well as the development of attitudes, emotions, and values in the e-learning. The "Framework for 21st Century Learning" published by Battelle for Kids (2019)[3] in the United States explains that besides the 3Rs (reading, writing, and arithmetic), the core competencies that students in the information age need to master are (a) learning and innovation skills, (b) information, media, and technology skills, and (c) life and career skills. Among them, learning and innovation skills are the key to promoting creative work and lifelong learning. Learning and innovation skills include 4Cs: critical thinking and problem solving, communication, collaboration, and creativity and innovation. Information, media, and technology skills include information literacy, media literacy, and ICT (Information, Communication, and Technology) literacy. Life and career skills are essential for learning, working, and living in the twenty-first century. They include flexibility and adaptability, initiative, and self-direction, social and cross-cultural skills, productivity and accountability, and leadership and responsibility (Binkley et al. 2012). The goal of blended learning should point to the skills and abilities required in the information age. Blended learning should embody these goals in specific learning content and instructional activities to cultivate students who are adaptable to the twenty-first century.

Students. Students are indigenous learners in the information age. They have changed from being passive information receptors, receivers, and dominated learners, to active subjects who control their own behaviors, methods, and preferences that even participate in the construction of learning content. The transformation of the role requires blended learning to pay attention to students' learning behaviors, learning styles, learning outcomes, and social characteristics in the digital environment. Doing so can lead to a better understanding of the learning patterns and to help promote student engagement, thus enhancing the learning outcomes.

Teachers. In the information age, teachers have changed from individual operators to team collaborators, from individual lecturers to instructional teams including teaching assistants, and industry experts. In the meantime, artificial-intelligent (AI) teaching assistants and e-Experts can also enhance instruction. Therefore, teachers of blended learning should not only be equipped with information-based teaching ability, but demonstrate leadership skills in the teaching team. To adapt to the new characteristics of indigenous students in the information age, the role of teachers must change from the traditional knowledge holders and dispensers to the designers, instructors, and facilitators of learning activities.

Learning Content. In the information age, the sources of students' learning are more abundant and diverse than before. The presentation of knowledge reflects the integration of various media. The knowledge structure has also changed from a fixed, structured knowledge to a dynamically unstructured knowledge. These changes have provided both opportunities and challenges for the implementation of blended learning. On one hand, the explosive growth of knowledge not only creates opportunities for students' self-directed learning, but also provides rich instructional resources for teachers' instructional design. On the other hand, the massive amount of information can easily force students into making choices and cause cognitive load (Clark et al. 2010). Thus, teachers need to be equipped with the capabilities of selecting, developing, and applying different forms of instruction when designing and implementing blended learning.

Learning Activities. In the context of blended learning, learning activities expand from the face-to-face instruction limited to the physical space to more diverse instruction that combine both physical and virtual spaces. Diversified electronic equipment and technological systems such as smartphones, tablets, e-schoolbags, learning management systems, and video conferencing systems enable teachers to direct students to various forms of learning activities. The format of class expands from fixed in-person sessions to hybrid sessions, which combine face-to-face and online session and consist of pre-class, in-class, and after-class activities. For example, students outside the classroom participate via the Internet. Large-scale online teaching is combined with small-scale offline discussions.

Evaluation and Feedback. Emerging technologies such as mobile Internet, cloud computing, large databases, data mining, learning analytics, and artificial intelligence, provide innovative methods for learning evaluation and feedback. In blended learning, the learning analysis, evaluation, and dynamic feedback are conducted from multiple dimensions with the help of large amounts of data generated in learning. The data sources include not only information on learning behaviors, but also physiological signals, psychological awareness activities, facial expressions, and more. In addition to the regular academic performance, the generated data can also reveal students' satisfaction and students' learning process. The data-driven approach makes evaluation and feedback more convenient so that teachers could provide feedback to students in a timely manner. The various presentation formats of the evaluation results (e.g., automatically generated visual presentation) can help teachers analyze students' learning behaviors and learning effects from both horizontal and vertical aspects, thereby promoting the timely improvement of teaching and learning.

Learning Environment. Information technology has had a profound impact on social and economic environments, forming a blended environment in which physical and virtual spaces coexist. The physical teaching environment has also changed accordingly. Extending from traditional classrooms, laboratories, training sites, and workplaces to the online learning space, virtual simulation laboratories, virtual practice/training base, and virtual space supported by IoT (Internet of Things) work scenarios learners can now fully control.

2.1.2 Relationships Among the Components

The seven components of blended learning interrelate, and at the same time constrain each other. Learning objectives guide the whole process of instruction. The other six components are designed to achieve the learning objectives. The other six components affect achievement of the learning objectives. An example is the impact of COVID-19 on learning. Teachers and students were forced to teach and learn at home due to COVID-19. For example, experiments, internships, and practical training courses were suspended or replaced with experimental videos. The change of the learning environment has tremendous impact on the achievement of learning objectives.

Students play a central role in blended learning as they directly influence the learning activities and learning environment. Students are members of the classroom community where they create a culture of learning.

Learning content aligns with the learning objectives. The quality of the learning content affects achievement of the learning objectives. Learning content is grouped within subject area under knowledge, skills, values, and attitudes that are expected to be learned. Learning content forms the basis of teaching and learning. Teachers' beliefs, values, competency, and even learning environment affect the presentation of learning content.

Learning activities reflect the learning content as well as the venues of achieving the learning objectives. They are flexible in course design and depend on the teachers' preferences. Learning environment also impact the learning activities as some activities can only be performed in certain environments.

Evaluation is to measure the degree to which learners have acquired the knowledge, can perform the skills, and exhibit changes in attitudes as required by the learning objectives. Learning evaluations verify whether the learning content and activities support students to achieve the learning objectives. Feedback provides formative information to learners regarding how to improve learning performance.

In blended learning, the learning environment impacts the implementation of evaluation and feedback environment, as it needs support from various technologies. The advancement of technologies in education provides more opportunities such as assisting teachers collect students' online and offline data. Yet, teachers' technical skills in how teachers use this data for conducting evaluation and providing feedback is impacted.

Schools construct the learning environment, especially the digital learning environment affected by the planning and construction of the entire digital campus. Teachers' digital literacy determines whether these learning environments can be fully utilized to maximize the potentials. This also affects the presentation of learning content (e.g., digital resources selection and production), the possibility and suitability of learning activities (e.g., design of VR simulation training activities), and ultimately affect the achievement of learning objectives.

Whether teachers can coordinate the above seven components into instruction reflects their competencies in designing and delivering blended learning. In digital age, the emerging of new technologies (e.g., virtual reality) brings unprecedented possibilities to blended learning. This also poses unprecedented challenges to teachers as they need to adapt to digital native students whose cognitive styles have changed from individual cognition to Internet-based group cognition and distributed cognition. At the same time, the learning environment is changing dynamically in blended learning such as temporary network disruption, failure of technology tools, and more. The dynamic learning environment requires teachers to coordinate the seven components (including teachers themselves) throughout the instruction process. The key of improving the quality of blended learning is the rational deployment of the seven components and their relationships in a specific situation. This is also essential for teachers to implement blended learning successfully.

2.2 Analysis

Analysis phase is the foundation for all other phases of blended learning design. Tasks completed in the analysis phase include task analysis, learner analysis, and contextual analysis.

2.2.1 Task Analysis

Task analysis is the most crucial part of designing blended learning. It defines the content required to solve the performance problem. It also identifies whether and how blended learning is the best way to solve problems. Task analysis in blended learning usually follows three types of questions:

Q1: What are the problems with the current curriculum? It can be analyzed from seven dimensions: objectives, students, contents, activities, evaluation, environment, and teachers (as shown in Table 2.1). Worth noting is that the curriculum instruction needs to be consistent. The content (resources) and instructional activities should align with learning objectives measured in evaluation.

Q2: What problems can be solved by blended learning? Blended learning cannot solve all teaching problems. Thus, necessary is determining whether the blended learning is suitable for the problems. Systematic consideration of the problems will help with the design of blended learning.

Q3: How can blended learning address the problems? After identifying the problems addressed, further considerations to identify ways of addressing these problems using blended learning are needed. An example of task analysis is shown in Table 2.2.

2.2.2 Learner Analysis

Facilitating student learning effectively is the purpose of blended learning, so it is necessary to have a clear understanding of students' characteristics. As the subjects of learning activities, students' cognitive, emotional, and social characteristics impact the learning process and outcomes (He et al. 2002). Studies have found that students' age, gender differences, class size, prior knowledge, skills, and attitudes, learning

Table 2.1 List of problems in curriculum instruction

Dimension	Issues to consider
Objectives	• Are the course objectives measurable? Are the intended objectives achieved in terms of knowledge, skills, values, social competence, information literacy, motivation, etc.?
Students	• Does the instruction match students' characteristics? Do students' learning abilities vary much? Do students join both online and face-to-face lessons?
Contents	• Is the learning content designed around objectives? Is it out of date? Is the choice of resource appropriate?
Activities	• Do the learning activities support the achievement of the objectives? Do they support active/cooperative learning? Are they appropriate for the class size?
Evaluation	• Can learning evaluation measure the achievement of the objectives? Is it simple and easy to administer the evidence across multiple sources? Can it be used to explicitly guide student learning?
Environment	• Does the teaching environment support the implementation of blended learning? Can the classroom environment and cyberspace integrate seamlessly? Is it easy to use?
Teachers	• Are teachers in control of blended learning? Is there assistance and support provided from relevant personnel such as teaching assistants, educational technicians, etc.?

Consistency guidelines: objective-content (resources)-activity-evaluation (Feedback)

Table 2.2 Example of task analysis

Existing problems	Can it be solved by blended learning?	Solution
There are many concepts and formulas in the course, which are difficult for students to understand and remember, resulting in students' fear of difficulties and affecting students' knowledge and skill training	Yes	Putting concepts and formulas into online learning before class and presenting them in visual forms such as short videos can help students with different foundations for self-regulated learning. According to the pre-class learning, teachers will answer and explain questions in class to deepen students' understanding of concepts. At the same time, the concept structure diagram is used to show the relationship between concepts and emphasize the logical connection and the primary and secondary relationship between concepts, which is easy for students to remember and recall, thus reducing the difficulty of learning caused by a large number of concepts

styles, and technology access can lead to different learning outcomes in blended learning (Lim and Morris 2009; Woltering et al. 2009).

Age. Students in different ages vary in their psychological states and cognitive levels such as attitudes, perceptions, and commitment (Rodríguez-Ariza 2011). According to a survey of Chinese college students, college students' learning experience, emotional perceptions, learning motivation, and time management vary in different age and grades. Freshmen have significantly better psychological perception than sophomores and juniors. But, it has increased among senior students (Shi 2015). Another survey in China for higher vocational students showed that the learning concentration of freshmen is higher than that of sophomores. It may be because freshmen have just entered the university, and their emotional states are high. When they come to junior level, their commitment to learning (e.g., vigor, dedication, and absorption) begin to recover (Xu and Xu 2012).

Accordingly, blended learning designed for sophomore needs more attention on the decline of students' learning interests and the rise of fatigue. In classroom, teachers need to provide more support, assign continuous tasks, and scaffold questions to enhance classroom learning. In students' online self-learning, teachers need to provide timely feedback and even provide one on one tutoring opportunities for students. Teachers also need to adjust the content of assignments, pay attention to difficulty levels of assignments, and make them as interesting as possible to engage students in blended learning.

Gender differences. Smaldino et al. (2005) found that gender differences may affect the students' willingness to participate in some activities. Research found that female students' perceptions of entertainment in blended learning significantly affect their attitudes toward using blended learning while male students' attitudes toward using blended learning were impacted only when they perceived the usefulness of blended learning (Padilla-Meléndez et al. 2013). Therefore, teachers need to consider different gender groups when implementing blended learning and focus on assisting students adopt blended learning. According to Zhang and Jiao (2015), male students are more interested in electronic products and more likely to be influenced by games, social media, and social networking tools. They are more likely to adopt blended learning than female students. Some researchers have summarized nearly 1,500 studies on gender differences and found that there are significant differences between male and female students in intelligence, interests, and personality (Maccoby and Jacklin 1974). For example, female students are less likely to get frustrated and more likely to face failure. Thus, at the beginning of the class, teachers can decrease difficulty of using technology to attract female students' interest and engage them in blended learning. In the teaching process, teachers also need to pay attention to students who are more vulnerable and less psychologically resilient, provide guidance, and be mindful of the impact of teachers' behaviors on the students' perception (Conroy 2001).

Class size. Teachers need to consider the class size and consider learning activities that are more flexible. For example, large class size (e.g., 70 students in one class) is more suitable for group activities. Students can collaborate in groups and teachers can provide personalized support for each group. Small class size (e.g., 15 students in one class) is more appropriate for teacher-student discussions and interaction. Providing students with sufficient and balanced learning opportunities for collaboration and interactions is suggested.

Prior knowledge, skills, and attitudes. Prior knowledge refers to students' basic knowledge of a specific subject or task, including knowledge, skills, and attitudes. It is the starting point for the design of instructional content. Students' prior knowledge skills and attitudes can affect their learning outcomes in blended learning (Ausburn 2004). Grover et al. (2015) investigated American computer science students' learning in blended learning and found that prior knowledge was one of the most significant factors influencing their algorithmic thinking skills and promoting deep learning. Additionally, Wu's (2010) study focused on physical education courses for Chinese college students and found that blended learning was more appropriate for college students who had intermediate or above-average motor skills. Thus, instructional design should first identify students' prior knowledge (e.g., facts, concepts, propositions, theories) and take these as the starting point of the instructional design. Teachers also need to consider students' differences in prior knowledge when making instructional decisions.

In summary, understanding students' prior knowledge, skills, and attitudes via surveys can improve the effectiveness of blended learning by adjusting the instructional strategies that support students' Zone of Proximal Development (Note: For a theoretical explanation of the Zone of Proximal Development, see Part 1, "Basic Theory"). In this regard, the following instructional strategies are proposed to assist the design of blended learning: (a) developing instruction that matches students' abilities, (b) using the same elements in learning and application settings, and (c) selecting appropriate teaching methods to facilitate learning transfer (Lim and Morris 2009).

Learning styles. Differences in learning styles among students affect how students learn such as students' behavior in group learning, performance in different learning activities inside and outside of the classroom, ways of interacting with others, and problem-solving styles (Lim and Morris 2009).

Active and Reflective. Active learners tend to have active discussions, and teachers should design group work, discussions, role-playing, and other activities that require students to work collaboratively. Reflective learners prefer to work on the assigned problems quietly. Thus, teachers can assign individual assignments accordingly.

Sensing and Intuitive. Sensing learners are good at memorizing facts and learning explicit knowledge. In the teaching process, teachers can relate to everyday phenomena and use case studies to help sense if learners understand. Intuitive learners like to work innovatively and understand abstract information. Pre-tests can give them sufficient time and space for independent exploration. However, if learning content requires memorization and formulation, intuitive learners need reminders to spend time reading the questions and check the results to avoid mistakes caused by repeated activities.

Visual and Verbal. Visual learners prefer visual information such as pictures, audio, video, and images. Teachers can use more multimedia resources, and especially for the abstract knowledge difficult to understand. This way the media can enhance students' understanding of the content. Verbal learners prefer abstract information such as words, texts, and discourse. Thus, lectures, handouts, and text-based materials will be more appropriate for them.

Sequential and Global. Sequential learners like to follow logical steps. When designing instructional activities, teachers need to provide more specific "scaffolding" to assist sequential learners establish logical orders. Global learners are more inclined to use a more divergent approach to solve problems. When designing instructional activities, teachers can moderately increase the distance between each "scaffold" and encourage self-exploration of the problems guided by the questions provided by teachers. In other words, critical is to provide students with sufficient space for thinking and understanding, independent exploration, and divergent thinking.

Assimilator and Diverger. Assimilator learners pay more attention to the logic and rationality of the theory than to the practical value. Thus, more attention is needed for teaching courses for engineers, technicians, and other positions. Diverger learners are better at observation and divergent thinking. More attention is needed for teaching courses for artists and service personnel such as conducting "brainstorming," group discussions, and other activities that need interaction, ideas, and creativity. In blended learning, divergent learners have significantly higher scores in terms of ease of web environment usage, perception of the face-to-face teaching environment, online environment, and evaluation (Akkoyu & Soylu, 2008). Therefore, teachers may need to provide more assistance for assimilated learners.

 **Extended Reading 2.1**

Some researchers have created different divisions and introductions from learners' sensory preferences, personality types, desired degree of generality, and biological differences. Teachers interested in this can further read the article, Language Learning Styles and Strategies: An Overview (Oxford 2003) or can access the online resource space on different learning styles at: https://www.engr.ncsu.edu/stem-resources/legacy-site/. Special scales can also be used to measure learners' learning preferences. Reid's (1984) Perceptual Learning Style Preference Questionnaire is used to measure the participants' preferences in six learning style preferences: visual, auditory, kinesthetic, tactile, individual learning, and group learning (Chen 2009).

 **Extended Reading 2.2**

Gardner (1999) believed that there were eight kinds of intelligence that exist relatively independently and related to specific cognitive fields or knowledge categories.

Table Eight Intelligences and Descriptions.

Intelligences	Description
Linguistic	• An ability to analyze information and create products involving oral and written language such as speeches, books, and memos
Logical-mathematical	• An ability to develop equations and proofs, make calculations, and solve abstract problems
Spatial	• An ability to recognize and manipulate large-scale and fine-grained spatial images
Musical	• An ability to produce, remember, and make meaning of different patterns of sound
Naturalist	• An ability to identify and distinguish among different types of plants, animals, and weather formations that are found in the natural world
Bodily-Kinesthetic	• An ability to use one's own body to create products or solve problems
Interpersonal	• An ability to recognize and understand other people's moods, desires, motivations, and intentions
Intrapersonal	• An ability to recognize and understand his or her own moods, desires, motivations, and intentions

Different people have different combinations of intelligence. For example, architects and sculptors have a stronger sense of space (spatial intelligence), athletes and ballet dancers have a stronger physical strength (physical/kinetic intelligence), publicists have a stronger sense of interpersonal intelligence, and writers have a stronger sense of self-reflection intelligence. Based on this theory, teachers need to recognize the characteristics of different learners, accept their different learning styles, and provide corresponding instructional designs and activity arrangements suitable for their tailored blended learning.

Technology access. Before implementing blended learning, teachers need to know the technology tool available to students including hardware equipment such as notebooks, mobile phones, and tablets, and software such as WIFI, live broadcasting software, learning platforms, and professional software. Teachers need to adjust instructional activities according to students' technology access. For example, if students only have mobile phones, the instructional materials should be opened via mobile phones. Certain formats such as compressed packages or files do need specific software that may not be available on mobile phones. Additionally, if after class activities require specific software, teachers need to ensure students can access software after class such as providing lab hours after class.

2.2.3 Contextual Analysis

The teaching environment is a necessary condition for the development of instructional activities. The teaching environment in the information age has extended from physical environments such as classrooms and laboratories to online learning spaces equipped with affluent digital teaching resources and diverse technological tools. At the same time, the physical teaching environment is also equipped with a variety of technical equipment, emphasizing the connection with the online learning space to support the effective integration between online and offline instructional activities (Ferreira-Meyers 2019).

Selection of physical space. When designing blended learning, teachers need to obtain sufficient information of the physical space where learning occurs to make instructional decisions. The types of physical learning spaces and learning objectives and content that fit into these spaces are shown in Table 2.3. For detailed characteristics of these physical learning spaces, please refer to the section "blended learning environment and resources support" in Chap. 5.

Selection of online learning platform. When designing blended learning, teachers also need to choose appropriate online learning platforms. There are three types of online learning platforms: (1) learning management systems, (2) video conferencing systems, and (3) special online teaching tools.

Table 2.3 Types of physical learning spaces and fitting learning objectives and content

Types of physical learning Spaces	Fitting learning objectives and learning content
Multimedia classroom	It is applicable to general teaching objectives. When the course teaching objectives are mainly to teach declarative knowledge, multimedia classrooms can be selected as the information-based physical environment
Physical experiment training room	The courses that adopt skill practice as the main teaching goal. At the same time, when the school has the physical experimental training room required for the course teaching, it can be used as an information-based physical environment
Workplace	It is suitable for high-level skills training. Teachers can choose factories as the information-based physical environment when making post-training, internship, and other teaching arrangements
Smart classroom	When schools have intelligent classrooms, teachers who originally chose multimedia classrooms as the teaching environment could choose intelligent classrooms as information-based physical environment to improve students' learning experience and teaching interaction effect
Intelligent interaction classroom	Teachers have high requirements for students' group cooperative learning activities. If the school has an intelligent interactive classroom, teachers should choose it as the information-based physical environment
Network interaction classroom	Teachers need to connect many places to carry out course teaching. At the same time, when the school has the network interactive classroom required for the teaching of the course, it can be selected as the information-based physical environment
Digital skills room	The courses taught by teachers adopt digital skills as the main teaching goal. At the same time, when the school has the digital skills room required for teaching the course, it can be used as the information-based physical environment
Virtual simulation experiment training room	The courses taught by teachers take skill training as the main teaching goal, but when there is no physical experimental training room or students have not yet reached the level of practical operation, the virtual simulation experiment training room can be used as the information-based physical environment
Large scale virtual simulation training room	The course instructional activities taught by teachers are mainly based on large-scale observation training, teaching, or multi-person skill training. At the same time, when the school has a large-scale virtual simulation training room required for the teaching of the course, it can be used as the information-based physical environment

(continued)

Table 2.3 (continued)

Types of physical learning Spaces	Fitting learning objectives and learning content
Virtual-real integration experimental training room	The teaching goal of the courses taught by teachers is skill training, which requires students to perform both simulation training and practical skills. At the same time, when the school has the virtual-real integration experimental training room required for the teaching of the course, the virtual-real integration laboratory can be used as the information-based physical environment
Multi-functional laboratory	The teaching objectives of the courses taught by teachers include knowledge imparting and skill training (including simulation and practical operation). At the same time, when the school has the multi-functional integration laboratory required for the teaching of the course, it can also be used as the information-based physical environment
Situational interactive laboratory	The teaching objectives of the courses taught by teachers are mainly expressive skills, and the teaching method mainly consists of role-playing. At the same time, when the school has the situational interactive laboratory required for teaching the course, it can also be selected as the information-based physical environment
Strong interactive virtual experiment training room	Teachers' teaching goals based on sensory and perceptual skills training. At the same time, when the school has the strong interactive virtual experiment training room required for the teaching of the course, it can also be used as the information-based physical environment

Learning management systems aim to provide asynchronous instructional activities, deliver course materials, and support the whole learning process. There are hundreds of learning management systems that mainly fall into three categories: general platforms, specific platforms, and MOOC platforms. General platforms include commercial platforms (Blackboard, Canvas, THEOL) and open-source platforms (Moodle, Sakai, Drupal). Specific platforms are usually developed for institutions or certain types of courses such as WISE (web-based inquiry science environment). Examples of MOOC platforms are Coursera, Udacity, and edX (US), FutureLearn (UK), OpenupEd (Europe), OpenCourseWorld and Iversity (Germany), Miriada X (Spain), Alison (Ireland), Open2Study (Australia), XuetangX (China), and more. The Edutools has developed an online learning platform from users' perspectives that consist of learning management tools, system support tools, and system technical features (see Table 2.4).

A video conferencing system mainly provides live broadcasting services. It incorporates interactive whiteboard, screen sharing, instant messaging, live recording, in-class evaluation, and educational administration management. It can support a variety of synchronous teaching modes such as large class, small class, one on one, and in-class test. In video conferencing systems, learners can interact with teachers

Table 2.4 EDUTOOLS course management system features and criteria

First category	Secondary category	Tertiary category
Learning management tools	Productivity tools	Bookmarks; Calendar/Progress Review; Searching Within Course; Work Offline/Synchronize; Orientation/Help
	Communication tools	Discussion Forum; Discussion Management; File Exchange; Internal Email; Online Journal/Notes; Real-time Chat; Whiteboard
	Student involvement tools	Group Work; Community Networking; Student Portfolios
System support tools	Content development tools	Accessibility Compliance; Content Sharing/Reuse; Course Templates; Customized Look and Feel; Instructional Design Tools; Instructional Standards Compliance
	Course delivery tools	Test Types; Automated Testing Management; Automated Testing Support; Online Marking Tools; Online Gradebook; Course Management; Student Tracking
	Administration tools	Authentication; Course Authorization; Registration Integration; Hosted Services
	Hardware/software	Client Browser Required; Database Requirements; UNIX Server; Windows Server
System technical features	Compatibility/ integration	Internationalization/localization, API, third-party software integration, digital campus compatibility
	Company Details/ licensing	Company Profile; Costs/Licensing; Open Source; Optional Extras;

or peers through messages, bullet screens, and comments. Examples include Zoom, Tencent Meeting, Skype, and DingTalk.

Special online teaching tools include, but not limited to, computing tools (e.g., MATLAB), cognitive-enhancement tools (e.g., Xmind and CoSpaces), presentation enhancing tools (e.g., Buncee), translation tools (e.g., Google Translator and IFLYTEK), subject teaching tools (e.g., FCS Biology and NOBOOK), simulation software (e.g., CNC simulation system Machining), simulation training software, and simulation practice software (Ministry of Education of the People's Republic of China 2020).

2.3 Design

Design phase involves using the outputs from the Analysis phase to plan a strategy for developing the instruction. In this phase, designers need to outline how to reach the instructional goals determined during the Analysis phase. Tasks completed in design phase include writing learning goal and objectives, determining learning units, writing unit objectives, and selecting learning content and delivery media.

2.3.1 Learning Goals

Learning goals are broad ideas about where you want to go. Learning objectives are concrete steps toward achieving goals. Goals are the higher-order ambitions set for students, whereas objectives are the specific, measurable competencies used to assess whether goals were met. (https://bokcenter.harvard.edu/learning-goals-and-learning-objectives).

Learning goals provide a means to select and organize instructional activities and resources that facilitate effective learning (Cui, 2004). The overall course goal is determined first, and then broken down into smaller learning objectives for each unit of learning. Learning goals in blended learning are typically grouped into three categories: cognition, skills, and attitudes. Blended learning also emphasizes technology literacy in digital age. Thus, learning goals in blended learning also include proficiency in using technology in learning and profession. Learning goals in blended learning can be established through three questions: (1) What is the core/critical content of the course? (2) What are students' expectations? and (3) What are key points for learning?

 **Case 2.1**

"IT Project Management" course (Associate Professor Zhengzhou Zhu, School of Software and Microelectronics, Peking University).

The core content of this course is software development and practice. Students will acquire software development and software project management methods and skills related to the field, that are also the key point for learning. Therefore, the goal of this course is to equip students with the **methodological skills in software development and software project management.**

The goals are decomposed and transformed into three learning objectives of knowledge, skills and attitudes. Teachers need to consider students' learning outcomes related to the objectives. Learning objectives should be student-centered and specific, precise, and measurable. They should also clearly describe what students should know or be able to do at the end of the course.

 **Case 2.2**

"IT Project Management" course (Associate Professor Zhengzhou Zhu, School of Software and Microelectronics, Peking University).

The goal of the "IT Project Management course" is further broken down into learning objectives at two different levels of competency. For outstanding students, they must meet high-level requirements. For those students with relatively limited abilities and learn at a slower pace, they need help to meet the basic requirements at this time because of their different learning styles.

	Basic requirements	Advanced requirements
Knowledge	• The basic idea of software engineering • Engineering methods and techniques for developing and maintaining software projects	• Be able to understand the cutting-edge theories of software engineering disciplines
Skills	• Software development ability • Software project management skills	• Literature search, analysis, and writing skills
Attitudes	• Abide by constitution, laws, and engineering ethics • Be kind to others, and have empathy and a team spirit	• Independent thinking and innovative spirit • Global perspectives

2.3.2 Learning Units

The learning unit of the course refers to a highly focused unit of instruction that contains a series of interrelated learning activities. Generally, a course contains multiple learning units, each of which is different from the learning content. Learning unit is grouped into different chapters, tasks, modules, projects, topics, or class schedule. The development of learning units needs to consider the logical relationship in the content first. Content in each learning unit needs to be independent, but also connected to each other. For cognition-focused content such as English, mathematics, physics, and pedagogy, by chapters/sections is the best way to organize the learning unit. For skills-focused content such as painting, carving, and equipment operation, projects, modules, or tasks is recommended for organizing the learning unit. For attitudes-focused content such as ideological, moral, and mental health, and other attributes, themes as a form of organization is suggested. Second, it needs follow students' cognitive development process. Third, it needs to consider feedback from previous teachers and students.

2.3.3 Unit Objectives

Same as learning objectives, unit objectives in blended learning is grouped into cognitive, skill, and attitude objectives. Table 2.5 provides an example of writing cognitive

Table 2.5 Reference table for writing cognitive objectives of learning units

Types of knowledge	Expected level of learning					
	Remembering	Understanding	Application	Analysis	Evaluation	Creation
Factual knowledge						
Conceptual knowledge						
Procedural knowledge						
Metacognitive knowledge						

Table 2.6 Reference table for writing skills objectives of learning units

Types of skills	Expected stage of skills development					
	Perception	Orientation	Guided response	Complex explicit behavior	Adaption	Innovation
Sensory and perceptual skills						
Physical or practical skills						
Expression skills						
Intellectual skills						

objectives. First, knowledge needs to be classified into four categories: factual knowledge, conceptual knowledge, procedural knowledge, and metacognitive knowledge (Anderson et al. 2001). Then, the expected learning level will be determined such as remembering, understanding, application, analysis, evaluation, and creation.

Table 2.6 provides an example of writing skills objectives. First, skills need to be classified into four categories: sensory and perceptual skills, physical or practical skills, expression skills, and intellectual skill. Then, the expected stage of skills development will be determined.

When writing the attitude objectives, three aspects should be considered: (1) students' cognition (e.g., group awareness, responsibility, endurance, self-management), (2) emotional state (e.g., self-confidence, enthusiasm, loyalty, honesty, integrity), and (3) behavioral tendency (e.g., initiative and enterprising spirit, cooperation with others, self-improvement of learning and performance).

The ABCD method can generate unit objectives. A (Audience) refers to the target audience. Because the audience are students, unit objectives will use "students" in the objectives' statement. B represents behavior and usually uses action verbs that explain what the work or task accomplished by the learners at the end of the unit. Students' behaviors can be directly observed by teachers and usually reflect whether the unit objectives have been achieved or not. Table 2.7 provides examples of writing behavior objective. C refers to conditions and describes the conditions or constraints that the learners expect to perform the learning tasks. It usually includes environmental factors (e.g., space, light, temperature, indoor and outdoor environment, noise), human factors (e.g., individual completion, collaborative group completion, teacher guided completion), equipment factors (e.g., tools and calculators), informational factors (e.g., data, textbooks, notes, pictures, dictionaries), time factors (e.g., speed and time constraints), and motivating factors (e.g., what stimulus is provided to induce behavior? How much stimulation is it?). D (Degree) refers to the degree of mastery and how well the learning activities are complete (e.g., speed, accuracy, quality).

Unit objectives are the refinement of the course learning objectives. It is necessary to check whether the course learning objectives are properly distributed across several levels rather than clumped together. Unit objectives provide a framework for devising ways to select instructional strategies and delivery media as well as evaluate student learning.

Table 2.7 Verbs to be used at different levels of learning objectives (Anderson et al. 2001; Mayer 2002)·

Levels	Description	Verbs to be used (and examples)
Remember	Retrieving knowledge from long term memory (Anderson et al. 2001, p. 67)	• Recognizing (identifying a piece of information that corresponds to knowledge in long-term memory) • Recalling (finding relevant knowledge in long-term memory)
Understand	Constructing meaning from instructional messages (Anderson et al. 2001, p. 67)	• Interpreting (expressing presented information in another form) • Exemplifying (giving an example of a concept or principle) • Classifying (determining that something belongs to a category) • Summarizing (determining a general theme or major point) • Inferring (drawing a logical conclusion from presented material) • Comparing (detecting similarities and differences between two or more things) • Explaining (describing a cause-and-effect relationship of a system)
Apply	Carrying out a procedure in a given situation (Anderson et al. 2001, p. 67)	• Executing (carrying out a procedure with a familiar task) • Implementing (carrying out a procedure with an unfamiliar task)

(continued)

Table 2.7 (continued)

Levels	Description	Verbs to be used (and examples)
Analyze	Breaking material into constituent parts and determining how the parts relate to one another and to an overall structure or purpose (Anderson et al. 2001, p. 68)	• Differentiating (distinguishing important from unimportant parts) • Organizing (determining how parts fit or function within a whole structure) • Attributing (determining the underlying point of view in presented material)
Evaluate	Making judgments based on criteria and standards (Anderson et al. 2001, p. 68)	• Checking (determining the consistency or effectiveness of a procedure or product) • Critiquing (judging the appropriateness of a procedure or product)
Create	Putting elements together to form a coherent or functional whole (Anderson et al. 2001, p. 68)	• Generating (generating alternative hypotheses) • Planning (devising a plan for accomplishing some task) • Producing (inventing a product)

 **Case 2.3**

"Application of Logistics Information Technology"

Unit 1: Task 1 Barcode Technology of Automatic Identification Technology.

• Objective 1: Students can explain the basic concepts and reading principles of barcode technology after reading the relevant materials of Project 2 and Task 1, with an accuracy rate of 90%.
• Objective 2: Complete the cognitive tasks of commodity barcodes and 2D barcodes by learning from the PPT courseware and teaching materials of project 2, task 1. Students can explain the types and structures of both commodity barcodes and 2D barcodes with an accuracy rate of 80%.
• Objective 3: By watching the video [Logistics Barcode Application], students can recite the types and structures of logistics barcodes, and students can explain the application process of barcode technology in storage and distribution management with an accuracy rate of 80%.

 **Case 2.4**

Example of writing learning unit's objectives "Basic Principles of Nucleic Acid Detection"

Learning unit	Learning objectives (ABCD method)	Learning content analysis
Learning unit 1–1: The Composition and Structure of DNA and The Basic Principles of DNA Replication	Students (A) can recall the composition of DNA strands, the structure of their connection, and the principles of replication (B) after watching the pre-class preview video and answering classroom questions (C), with an accuracy rate of more than 95% (D)	Knowledge points: Deoxyribonucleic acid and DNA double-stranded anti-parallel double helix structure, DNA base pairing, DNA replication
Learning units 1–2: Structure and Function of DNA Polymerases	Students (A) can match and describe the structure and corresponding functions of each part of DNA polymerase (B) after listening to the teacher's explanation (C), and the accuracy rate of answering relevant classroom questions is over 80% (D)	Knowledge point: How DNA polymerase works
Learning units 1–3: Principles and Processes of PCR Reaction	1: Students (A) can explain the role of primers, templates, DNA polymerase and DNTPs in PCR reaction (B) after watching an animated demonstration and listening to the teacher's lecture (C), with an accuracy rate of more than 80% (D)	Knowledge point: Principle and process of PCR reaction (key point) Skill point: Methods of applying PCR systems
	2: Students (A) can draw a schematic diagram of the principle of PCR utilizing group cooperation (B) after listening to the teacher's lecture (C) with an accuracy rate of more than 90% (D)	

(continued)

(continued)

Learning unit	Learning objectives (ABCD method)	Learning content analysis
	3: Students (A) can describe their own vocabulary and identify whether the vocabulary described by others is consistent with their own (B) after learning subunits 1–1, 1–2 and 1–3 and completing the group game (Similar to the rules of the game about who is an undercover agent, the description words need to conform to objective facts, undercover agents need to find commonalities, and civilians need to describe characteristics), without additional reading materials (C), and the success rate of the game is more than 50% (D)	
	4: Students (A) can distinguish the difference between PCR and DNA replication in vivo and consider the clinical application of the PCR system (B) after drawing a schematic diagram of PCR and listening to the contents of subunits 1–1 and 1–2 (C). The answer to each question considers at least two aspects, which are meaningful and consistent with the basic principle and logic (D)	
Learning unit 2–1: Principles of Fluorescence Resonance	Students (A) are able to describe the basic concepts of fluorescence resonance (B), after watching the animated demonstration and listening to the teacher's lecture (C), with an accuracy rate of over 80% (D)	Knowledge point: The principle of fluorescence resonance

(continued)

(continued)

Learning unit	Learning objectives (ABCD method)	Learning content analysis
Learning unit 2–2: Principle and Process of Fluorescence Resonance PCR	Students (A) can draw the diagram of fluorescence resonance PCR process and compare its similarities and differences with ordinary PCR (B), after listening to the teacher's instruction and reading the class notes and PPT (C), with an accuracy rate of more than 80% (D)	Knowledge points: principle of fluorescence resonance PCR (difficult point)
Learning unit 3–1: Basic Process of Nucleic Acid Detection	Students (A) can describe the basic process of nucleic acid detection (B), after watching the animated demonstration and listening to the teacher's lecture (C), with an accuracy rate of over 80% (D)	Knowledge point: the basic process of nucleic acid detection
Learning unit 4–1: PCR Operations in the Laboratory	Students (A) can prepare a PCR system, use PCR machines, and adjust parameters. At the same time, they can detect whether PCR products are obtained (B), after on-site viewing the experimental staff PCR operation under the guidance of teachers (C), and get target PCR products (D)	Skill point 1: Methods of using experimental instruments (such as pipettes, ice boxes, PCR machines) Skill point 2: Method of preparing PCR system Skill Point 3: Methods for detecting PCR Products

2.3.4 Learning Content and Media

The learning content is the sum of knowledge and experience and is purposefully selected and aligned with learning objectives and unit objectives. Learning content should be organized and arranged in a logical sequence. Learning resources represent learning content such as textbooks that are the most widely used learning resources. Textbook has two forms: print books and electronic books. In blended learning, most teachers use textbooks as the main resource as well as some supplemented materials from the Internet. Commonly used learning contents are cognitive (knowledge) and skill-based content (skills).

Selection of learning content. Learning content selection for learning units usually considers three aspects: scope, key points, and sequence. Scope refers to the breadth and depth of learning content. When determining the scope of the unit, we should start from the continuity of the course and the characteristics of society and students, and then determine the relative importance of various facts and concepts. Selecting the core content with an appropriate level of difficulty is next. Key points are the key to the learning content and usually grouped around specific themes. A theme may contain several sub themes that form the knowledge framework. Sequence is the progression of content expansion. Generally, when determining the sequence of materials, attention should be paid to the relationship between prior and new knowledge to ensure that new learning is connected to prior knowledge.

Selection of delivery media. After the content of the learning unit is determined, next step is to choose appropriate media to present the learning content and build the digital learning resources center in blended learning. Digital learning resources refer to network-based learning materials and multimedia materials digitally processed and run on computers or in a network environment. The selection of delivery media needs to match the content. For example, electronic lectures and electronic documents presents conceptual knowledge, while video presentations help with abstract knowledge. Animations demonstrate procedural knowledge.. Lecture-based teaching generally uses electronic lecture notes and electronic documents; inquiry-based teaching requires simulation programs and interactive animations; and collaborative teaching requires the support of collaborative electronic documents. When presenting learning resources, learners' characteristics, the learning environment, and technical equipment must be considered. For example, learning videos should be kept to 10 min to ensure the duration of the learners' highest level of attention. When students use mobile phones, designers need to consider whether the layout and style of learning materials are suitable for mobile screens. In blended learning, it is also necessary to consider the decomposition and logical arrangement of online and offline learning contents (as shown in Table 2.8).

Table 2.8 Suggestions for the arrangement of online and offline learning content for blended courses

Learning contents suitable for online arrangements
• Students prepare their own studies in advance and prepare knowledge before class
• What do students need to repeat?
• Factual knowledge and conceptual knowledge contents
• Content that takes too much time in the classroom, but is helpful to learning
• Consolidated and deepened content after class
• Extracurricular expansion readings to supplement textbooks contents

Learning contents suitable for offline arrangements
• Students have difficulties in autonomous learning
• What students need to answer
• What the teacher has mainly explained
• Content that requires face-to-face communication and communication between teachers and students
• Class discussions and presentations
• Complementary content with online learning

 **Case 2.5**

Learning unit objectives and learning content of "basic Principles of Nucleic Acid Detection"

Learning unit	Objectives (ABCD method)	Learning content
Unit 1–1: Composition and Structure of DNA and Basic Principles of DNA Replication	Students (A) can recall the composition of the DNA strand, the structure of its connection, and the principle of replication (B), after watching the pre-class preview video and answering the class question (C), with an accuracy of more than 95% (D)	Knowledge points: Deoxyribonucleic acid and DNA double-stranded anti-parallel double helix structure, DNA base pairing, DNA replication
Learning units 1–2: Structure and Function of DNA Polymerases	Students (A) can match and describe the structure and corresponding functions of each part of DNA polymerase (B), after listening to the teacher's explanation (C), and the accuracy rate of answering relevant classroom questions is over 80% (D)	Knowledge points: How DNA polymerase works
Learning units 1–3: Principles and Processes of PCR Reaction	Objective 1: Students (A) can explain the roles of primers, templates, DNA polymerases, DNTPs, etc. in the PCR reaction (C), after watching the animated demonstration and listening to the teacher's lecture (B), with an accuracy rate of more than 80% (D)	Knowledge points: Principle and process of PCR reaction **(emphasis)** Skilled: Methods of applying PCR systems
	Objective 2: Students (A) can draw a schematic diagram of the principle of PCR (B) after listening to the teacher's teaching and utilizing group cooperation (C), with an accuracy rate of more than 90% (D)	
	Objective 3: After the students (A) have studied sub-units 1–1, 1–2, and 1–3, without additionally reading the other materials (C), they can complete the group game (similar to the game rules of who is an undercover officer: describing words needed to conform to objective facts, undercover people need to find commonalities, civilians need to describe characteristics), when describing their own words and distinguishing whether the words described by others are consistent with their own (B), and the game success rate is more than 50% (D)	

(continued)

(continued)

Learning unit	Objectives (ABCD method)	Learning content
	Objective 4: After drawing the schematic diagram of PCR and listening to the contents of subunits 1–1 and 1–2 (C), students (A) can distinguish between the difference between PCR and DNA replication In Vivo and consider the application of the PCR system in clinical practice (B). The answer to each question considers at least two aspects, which are meaningful and consistent with the basic principle and logic (D)	
Learning unit 4–1: PCR Operations in the Laboratory	Students (A) can prepare the PCR system, use the PCR machine, and adjust parameters. At the same time, they can detect whether PCR products are obtained (B) and get the target PCR products (D) under the guidance of teachers (C)	Skill point 1: Methods of using experimental instruments (such as pipettes, ice boxes, PCR machines) Skill point 2: Method of preparing PCR system Skill Point 3: Methods for Detecting PCR Products

Selection of open educational resources. Digital learning resources can be open resources, imported resources, and self-developed resources. Open Educational Resources (OER) usually refer to digital resources based on non-commercial use, follow resource copyright requirements, and freely used and modified with the help of network information technology. Examples are open online courses (including MOOCs), open courseware (including micro-courses), open teaching materials, and open software (UNESCO 2002). Digital learning resources in blended learning should prioritize OER. The OER can be obtained through the Internet (as shown in Table 2.9). When the OER cannot meet teaching needs, schools can be advised to purchase or encourage donations externally. If the above two choices are not available, schools may choose to develop their own resources.

Development of digital learning resources. Six forms of media include text, graphics/image, audio, video, animation, and 3D model. The text-based materials should be as simple and clear as possible to avoid difficulty in reading. The text-based materials should not be too long or too short and avoid jargons. When presenting text-based materials, structures can be marked by numbering, and important words or sentences can be emphasized using bolding and highlighting to avoid a large amount of textual information on the screen.

Graphics/image materials are used for different purposes, and the presentations should also be designed accordingly. For example, embellished pictures used to

Table 2.9 List of some open educational resources

Types	Resource examples and their web addresses	Brief Introduction
Open courses	Khan Academy: https://zh.khanacademy.org/	Khan Academy, an online library of over 3,500 Khan teachers' instructional videos, provides free, high-quality education to people around the world
	Open Courses at MIT: https://ocw.mit.edu/	MIT put 240 courses on the Internet for free and offers a total of 2,000 courses in 33 disciplines in 2010, including course syllabus, lecture notes, homework and test papers
	Open Education Consortium: https://www.oeglobal.org/	The Open Education Consortium is a consortium of more than 200 higher education institutions and related educational organizations including Harvard, Yale, MIT, etc. Its mission is to promote the global sharing of educational resources for formal and informal learning, as well as the use of self-owned, open, and high-quality educational materials to form courses. Together, the consortium provides OCWC with 14,000 courses in more than 20 language environments
	Coursera: https://www.coursera.org/	Coursera is a large-scale public online course project founded by two computer science professors from Stanford University in the United States. It aims to cooperate with the world's top universities to provide online open courses. Coursera's first partner institutions include Stanford University, University of Michigan, Princeton University, University of Pennsylvania and other famous American universities
	TED-Ed: https://ed.ted.com/	TED convened many outstanding figures in the fields of science, design, literature, music, etc., and vowed to share their thinking and exploration about technology and society. Since 2006, videos of TED speeches have been uploaded to the Internet
	edX: https://www.edx.org/	edX is a massive open online classroom platform jointly created by MIT and Harvard in April 2012. It provides college-level online courses for free to the general public
	iTunes U: https://www.apple.com.cn/education/itunes-u/index.html	iTunes U is a free online open course. Many schools such as Harvard, MIT, Oxford, etc. have put their own classroom audio, video, and documents on the Internet, which can be downloaded through the iTunes U application
	Chinese University MOOC: https://www.icourse163.org/)	Chinese University MOOC is a high-quality Chinese learning platform, which was built by Icourse Network and Netease Cloud Classroom. The platform has more than 1000 courses provided by 985 universities

(continued)

Table 2.9 (continued)

Types	Resource examples and their web addresses	Brief Introduction
	Intelligent Vocational Education https://www.icve.com.cn/	Intelligent Vocational Education takes knowledge points/skill points as the basic granularity, takes the entire professional knowledge/skill tree as the overall structure, and systematically manages materials through a series of meta-data, so that each resource can be easily queried
	XuetangX: https://www.xuetangx.com/	XuetangX is a Chinese MOOC (Massive Open Online Course) developed by Tsinghua University. It was officially launched on October 10, 2013 and provides online courses to the world. Any student with Internet access can use this platform to learn course videos online
Open textbooks	American "Community College Open Educational Resources Alliance": https://www.cccoer.org/	The National Committee on Community College Reform launched the "Fulfilling Your Dreams" project to eliminate the economic burden of traditional educational resources on students. 38 community colleges in 13 states will launch degree programs based entirely on open education resources
	Flat World Knowledge: https://catalog.flatworldknowledge.com/	Online textbook and homework platform
	Gutenberg Course: http://www.gutenberg.org/	The Gutenberg Curriculum Project website is a library of over 60,000 free eBooks
Teaching materials	MERLOT: https://www.merlot.org/merlot/index.html	MERLOT is modeled after the NSF-funded project "Creating Tools and the Economy of Educational Objects (EOE)." It is a tool hosted, developed, and distributed by Apple and other industry, university, and government collaborators to form a community involved in building a shared knowledge base of learning materials
	Iconfont: https://www.iconfont.cn/home/index?spm=a313x.7781069.1998910419.2	A vector icon management and communication platform created by Alimama MUX. Designers upload icons to the iconfont platform, and users can customize and download icons in multiple formats. The platform can also convert icons into fonts, which is convenient for front-end engineers to freely adjust

attract learners' attention are usually placed at the beginning of paragraphs. Representational pictures present characteristics of the content and help learners quickly get to the key points. Procedural pictures can explain the context of information more concisely than text and used to show the steps of a series of operations. Explanatory pictures combined with text information help learners understand complex or abstract text information and used to support visual presentation of complex abstract information. When mixing pictures and texts, it is necessary to ensure that the content of picture information is accurate, and it relates to the text. Important is to avoid presenting irrelevant graphics and images to the transmitted information as it results in cognitive load (Jin 2017).

When designing video materials, the topic should be clear. Generally, one video reflects one topic. The video presentation should consider learners' characteristics and the attributes of the course content and determine whether to present portraits and subtitles. When combining video and audio, the content needs to follow the same topic. The sound should be as clear as possible and the speed should be moderate. The volume of the background music should not interfere with the voice of the explanation. The length of video materials should generally not exceed 10 min. If the video is too long, it can be appropriately divided into multiple pieces.

 **Extended Reading 2.3**

Several common video learning resources

- **Lecturer on camera**: The image of the lecturer appears in the video explanation. The lecturer can directly stand in front of the blackboard, electronic whiteboard, rear projection color TV, or the green curtain of the studio for later processing. Features: (a) it is easy to catch the students' attention, and (b) it is easy to form the feeling of one-on-one teaching.
- **Handwritten explanation**: You can save the handwritten explanation process in the form of camera shooting or screen recording on paper, blackboard, a tablet computer with an electronic pen, or a tablet with an LCD screen. Features: (a) absorbs all the advantages of blackboard writing in traditional courses, and (b) through post-editing, unnecessary procrastination can be cut, thus greatly improving the efficiency of derivation and explanation, and improving the learning efficiency of learners. This form is more suitable for courses that involve the explanation of the derivation process such as science and engineering, economics, and finance.
- **Real situation teaching**: Real-time recording of the traditional teaching process can give full maximization of the advantages of online teaching. Applicable to: (a) explaining relevant experiments while actually doing the experiments in the laboratory,; (b) explaining unearthed cultural relics and famous paintings such as going to the museum to give lectures; and (c) if visiting a factory workshop or financial trading market is necessary, going

directly go to the scene to feel the atmosphere and explain the relevant course content at the same time can be done.

- **Animation demonstration**: The animation demonstration is helpful for explaining abstract knowledge more vividly, thus making it easier to understand. Using it appropriately can arouse the learners' interest in learning and improve the efficiency of knowledge explanation.
- **Interview-style teaching video**: Shoot in the form of an interview or the process of discussion and dialogue between more than three teachers or students on specified topics. Features: (a) puts the knowledge in the dialogue step by step so that the learning content is full of stories and can attract the learners' attention, and (b) it is convenient for learners to be exposed to more people's views that broadens their ideas and horizons.

When developing multimedia materials, digitizing hard copy text, images, audio, video, and other materials occurs. For example, using Photoshop software to edit and make pictures, using audio and video recording software such as Premiere, Audition, and Camtasia Studio to create sound files or video files, and employing 3D Studio MAX, Animator Studio, Flash, and other software to make animations or 3D models can be accomplished. When uploading multimedia materials to the online learning platforms, teachers need to pay attention to the structure, file format, size (whether the image needs to be compressed), production difficulty and cost, and release time. Teachers are recommended to convert PowerPoint (PPT) formats into PDF formats, store image data in JPG or GIF formats, use MP3 formats much as possible for sound files, and convert video formats into streaming media video formats (e.g., WMV, ASF, MP4), to save space occupied by multimedia materials and facilitate transmission on the network.

Development of courseware, cases, and reference materials can use multimedia resources. Courseware is multimedia material or software that presents one or several knowledge pieces. Courseware can be divided into lecture-centered courseware (such as PPT lectures used by teachers) and learning-centered courseware (such as micro-videos for students' learning) according to different purposes. Learning-centered courseware can be categorized as presentation demonstrations, interactive learning, operation training, simulation experiments, and learning games. Learning-centered courseware provides learners with guidance, evaluation, and feedback, to promote autonomous learning while presenting learning content.

Cases are scenarios that resemble real-world examples that aim to achieve specific learning goals. Cases are important learning resources in learning as the problems presented in cases can stimulate students' critical thinking, debates, reasoning, and decision-making. Text or video has been used to present cases have been. The design and development of a case library is important in blended learning.

Reference materials refer to policies, regulations, rules, and educational regulations, records of major educational events, important articles, and books. Reference materials are important resources for inquiry-based learning such as researching a certain topic. Teachers can provide students with classic, important, and relevant reference materials to improve the efficiency in a certain field. When selecting and developing reference materials, necessary is to consider the file format and file size (whether it needs to be compressed).

2.4 Development, Implementation and Evaluation

Development and implementation phases build on both the analysis and design phases. The purpose of these phases is to generate learning activities and assessment instruments. Tasks completed include developing course activities, developing learning unit activities, and establishing assessment and feedback instruments. This section also provides implementation strategies of blended learning.

2.4.1 Course Activities

Design of course activities. Course activities are the sum of operations that learners need to complete to achieve the established learning objectives (He et al. 2006). Designing course activities includes the overall arrangement of course activities and the setting of learning activities for each unit. Special attention to the characteristics of online and offline learning activities and their internal connections is needed. Courses are usually scheduled by semesters. Course activities can be organized in three stages: initial stage, middle stage, and later stage. Emphasis of the learning activities varies in different stages (Feng et al. 2021).

The initial stage occurs generally during the first two weeks of the course when students review the course objectives, course content, and teaching methods and get familiar with teachers and other students. The design and implementation of course activities in this stage need to consider from the following aspects:

- Help students establish their identity and a sense of belonging and form a friendly and active learning environment. Typical activities include icebreakers, introducing the blended learning environment, facilitating group questions and answers, composing of groups for the following collaborative activities, encouraging students to express themselves freely, and more.
- Help students strengthen their understandings of the course and build a good teacher-student relationship. Typical activities include introducing the course contents and schedules, clarifying expectations and assessment methods, explaining the course's rationale to student development and talent training, and introducing teachers to students to get to know each other better.
- Promote students' interest and motivation in blended learning. Typical activities include clarifying rewards and punishments, notifying learning objectives, and explaining the significance of the course to stimulate the students' external

motivation. Other activities include fostering students' motivation by providing learning scenarios that adapt to students' a prior knowledge, group characteristics, and learning needs.

 **Case 2.6**

The organization of blended learning activities at the beginning of the course of "**Western Economics**" (Yuzhong Liang of Anshan Radio and Television University) is shown in the table below.

Activities	Learning method	Strategies
Activity 1: Welcome letter	Online	Create a sense of belonging and build a good atmosphere
Activity 2: Read course information	Online	Familiar with the learning environment
Activity 3: Teachers' self-introduction	Online and offline	Know the course and trust the teachers
Activity 4: Ice breaking	Online and offline	Create a sense of belonging and build a good atmosphere
Activity 5: Group building	Online and offline	Create a sense of belonging and build a good atmosphere
Activity 6: Objectives and standards informing	Online and offline	Stimulate learning motivation
Activity 7: Context importing	Offline	Stimulate learning motivation

Activities 3, 4, and 5 are carried out in online and offline environments. At the beginning of the course, teachers use WeChat, QQ and other instant messaging software to issue a "welcome letter" to inform students of the basic overview of the course including the schedule of specific instructional activities, details of the course objectives, and steps to use the platform. At the same time, teachers provide a "self-introduction" in the welcome letter allowing students to understand them and build a sense of trust, and helping students to quickly adapt to the new learning environment. Next, teachers design an "online icebreaking activity" and carry out "team building" activities. During the activity, group members introduce their age, occupation, etc., greet each other, and cooperate to conceive the group name and learning slogan. These activities further expand into face-to-face learning. According to online activities, teachers can design simple group tasks to shorten the distance between learners, help students establish identity and a sense of belonging, and initially form a learning community. On this basis, teachers encourage students to formulate basic rules for online discussions, to promote students' open communication, and create a relaxing and a freely communicative atmosphere. In the first face-to-face learning lesson, teachers should introduce themselves to students to strengthen students' academic trust in them. In addition, teachers design offline icebreaking activities to help students become more curious about scarcity, opportunity cost, and other related concepts and improve students' learning interest and motivation by connecting students' life experience and asking guidance questions. In addition, teachers introduce detailed evaluation criteria and rules to students, and emphasize the importance of online discussion to stimulate students' learning enthusiasm.

 **Case 2.7**

Example of the initial activity of the course: icebreaking activity—Eight Nouns (Bonk and Khoo 2014)

This example is derived from the undergraduate course "Blended Learning Design and Application" of Tsinghua University in China.

Activity content and purpose: Each student writes down eight nouns that best describe their own characteristics in the online discussion area and explain why they chose these attributes. The first few nouns are generally easy to think of, but when getting to the last three words, it often takes a while to think about. The words not easy to think of can later reveal characteristics that the students did not expect. This activity helps students become familiar with each other quickly. For example, a student from Turkey lists a dishwasher in the eight-noun activity because he likes washing dishes very much. Although the word is exaggerated and humorous, everyone will remember this classmate. The eight nouns are creating a social interactive learning atmosphere, which is often the starting point of curriculum learning. It enlivens the atmosphere of the whole team and establishes a social consensus among all participants (this activity applies not only to the network environment, but also to the real classroom environment).

Suggestions and tips: Teachers should make sure that all students have clarified the rules and requirements of the activities. Teachers themselves take the lead in posting their own eight nouns, or they can post several nouns of former classmates as examples. Each student should reply to at least one student's post.

The middle stage refers to the main part of course activities. The duration of middle stage in blended learning varies in different courses. The design and implementation of course activities at this stage need to consider from the following aspects:

- Guide students to learn effectively by organizing and implementing appropriate course activities. Typical activities include tutoring, listening to students, having conversations with students, and enhancing interactions between teachers and students through case analysis and discussions.

- Encourage individual students and groups to build knowledge and deepen cognition through continuous communication. Typical activities include brainstorming, focus group discussion, debate, role-playing, and problem analysis. Those activities can help students learn and grow collaboratively.
- Encourage students to actively participate in blended learning and avoid burnout in the middle stage. Typical activities include encouraging and praising in a timely manner, providing peers' role modeling, and evaluating peers. Those activities can improve students' self-efficacy and learning engagement.

 **Case 2.8**

"Paragraph Writing" course (an English education course offered by the University of Indonesia).

This course mainly adopts the flipped classroom model. Teachers provide students with the necessary learning materials in advance including writing cases and require students to read and study in advance. The organization of blended learning activities in the middle of the course is shown in the table below.

Activities	Learning method	Strategies
Activity 1: Face-to-face learning	Offline	Motivate students' continued engagement
Activity 2: Experience/case sharing	Online and offline	Guide effective learning
Activity 3: Brainstorming	Offline	Facilitate individual and group knowledge building
Activity 4: Case study	Offline	Facilitate individual and group knowledge building
Activity 5: Peer evaluation	Online	Motivate students' continued engagement

Teachers give face-to-face lectures once a week to create a high-intensity teaching presence. In class, teachers first chose a writing topic such as "definition" and "causality" to explain, and then provide students with difficult writing template cases corresponding to the topic through offline learning. Based on online case-sharing activities, teachers progress layer by layer to enrich blended learning resources. Students then brainstorm in groups during class, analyze the information, and discuss the central sentence, argument, and summary sentence of the case, and shared the discussion results with the whole class. After class, students write paragraphs according to the learning theme of the week and submit them to the homework area, where all students' work could be displayed. In addition to evaluating students, teachers also design online peer evaluation activities to stimulate students' continuous participation. In the next face-to-face class, teachers might provide face-to-face comments and guidance on students' homework from the previous week, which continues to stimulate students' enthusiasm for learning.

The final stage occurs in the last two weeks of the course. At this point, majority of the learning content has been completed. This stage focuses on summary, reflection, and presentation of students' course products. The design and implementation of course activities at this stage need to consider the following aspects:

- Promote presentation of students' course products. Typical activities include presenting learning products completed in the course and supporting the transfer of learned knowledge and skills to solve real world problems.
- Support students' self-reflection and evaluation. It refers to the execution of reflective evaluation activities to promote students' meaningful construction. Typical activities include teacher evaluation, peer evaluation, and self-reflection. Providing procedural scaffolds, presenting navigational maps or mind maps, and giving timely feedback and guidance can promote the smooth implementation of the above activities.

 **Case 2.9**

"Java Programming", undergraduate course at Peking University, China
The 15-week course is divided into three phases: Conceptualization, Construction and Dialogue. The latter stages of the course are the construction stage and dialogue stage, that is, students transfer the knowledge acquired in the early conceptualization stage. In the course, teachers provide expert code examples in the teaching materials for students to refer and help students solve similar programming problems. Students refer to the resources provided by the online platform, solve problems under the face-to-face guidance of teachers, design a variety of programming schemes, and then compare and self-evaluate to select the best scheme. After students submit their work to the platform, the teacher scores them, and other students can also communicate on the creation and transfer ability of the program. In addition to the evaluation and feedback of teachers and peers on students' work in the platform, teachers also design peer evaluation and independent evaluation activities in the offline classroom. Through face-to-face communication and discussion, students can more deeply reflect and summarize their own learning, thereby promoting development of their problem-solving ability and self-reflection ability.

Example of the organization of blended learning activities at the end of the course is shown in the table below:

Activities	Learning Methods	Strategies
Activity 1: Personal creation	Offline	Comprehensive display and self-development
Activity 2: Works demonstration	Online	Comprehensive display and self-development
Activity 3: Peer evaluation	Online and offline	Self-reflection and evaluation
Activity 4: Self-evaluation	Offline	Self-reflection and evaluation

Integration of online and offline learning activities. The schedule of school courses is different such as semester course, weekly course, and session course. Course schedule in universities and vocational colleges usually occur between 16–20 weeks in a semester. There are one to three face-to-face meetings each week, ranging from two to four hours. Instruction needs to match the course schedule. The characteristic of blended learning is that both offline learning activities and online learning activities are intertwined and run throughout the whole course (Neumeier 2005). Therefore, compared with face-to-face learning, the focus of designing course activities in blended learning is the connection between offline activities and online activities. For example, one of the two offline activities originally scheduled for face-to-face course each week can be scheduled as online activities in blended course.

To improve the connection between online and offline activities, teachers are suggested to utilize online tests and discussions to assess students' online learning performance, stimulate students to reflect online learning content, and timely adjust offline activities according to students' online learning performance. Teachers can also provide online feedback utilizing offline activities such as offline questions, quizzes, and discussions. The integration of online and offline activities is affected by same place/different place, online/offline, and synchronous/asynchronous.

Same Place/Different Place. It means whether teachers and students are in the same classroom and how long they can be in the same classroom. In most cases, teachers and students in universities can stay in the same classroom, which supports more offline activities. In some cases, for example, international students affected by the epidemic could not return to their campus. Therefore, course activities need to combine both offline and online activities so that teachers and local students can participate in the same classroom while international students can also participate remotely. In other cases, for example, learners in open universities work during the day and cannot go to school on weekdays. In those cases, more online activities will be more suitable.

Synchronous/Asynchronous. It means that teachers' instructional activities and students' learning activities could occur at the same or different time. Offline activities scheduled synchronously can create a collaborative learning environment where students can concentrate on completing learning tasks under the supervision and guidance of teachers directly. Students can also obtain real-time interactions and receive answers timely. Online activities can be delivered via learning management systems and scheduled asynchronously to allos students to study at their own pace and offer more flexibility of learning.

Online/Offline. Offline activities occur in physical spaces such as classrooms, training rooms, and more. Online activities require the support of technical systems (e.g., network teaching platforms, video conference systems). They all have different characteristics, so the arrangements are also different.

Items that are appropriate for online activities.

Learning Content. Learning content that requires repeated activities suitable for online activities such as watching the process of creating animation. Students can complete these activities independently.

Learning Process. The following activities are appropriate for online participation: (a) activities that require timely feedback such as online testing and online assignment submission, (b) activities that require advance communication and exchange with students such as submitting preview reports and learning the problems students encountered while working on the report, and (c) activities that must be carried out based on individual differences of students, for example, students can choose text or video to learn the content based on their proficiency level.

Study Time. Activities that permit flexibility are suitable for online learning. For example, students can participate in online discussions according to their timeframe.

Items that are appropriate for offline activities.

Learning Content. If the content contains many hands-on activities, those activities are more appropriate for offline. Other activities that need specific physical spaces, such as activities in specific training rooms, simulated factories, and real workplaces, are also suitable for offline activities.

Learning Process. Activities that require frequent interaction and cooperation between teachers and students, such as role-playing, cooperation to complete a task, and face-to-face discussion, are more appropriate for offline.

Learning Time: Any type of activities delivered offline using a face-to-face approach.

2.4.2   Unit Activities

Information technology expands the space and time of teaching activities for teachers and students, so the design of unit activities needs to consider not only the activities that take place in class, but also the activities before and after class.

Organizing Pre-class Blended Learning Activities. According to the unit objectives, teachers should construct and provide a learning unit guide, learning resources, learning tasks, and unit activities. Then, teachers should facilitate students with online learning and answering questions. Finally, teachers should evaluate students' pre-class learning results and adjust learning activities. Table 2.10 presents the objectives, instructions, tools, and implementation conditions of blended learning activities suitable for pre-class learning.

Organizing In-class Blended Learning Activities. Based on pre-class performance, teachers can conduct lectures and answer questions regarding students' challenges and difficulties. If learners have mastered the knowledge or skill during pre-class activities, teachers can reduce the lecturing time and increase time for facilitating collaboration with their peers. Teachers can also facilitate students with independent explorations, patrol inspection, and in-class tasks individually or collaboratively. Table 2.11 presents the objectives, instructions, tools, and implementation conditions of blended learning activities suitable for the in-class time.

Organizing After-class Blended Learning Activities. Teachers grade homework and provide feedback on students' learning performance. Teachers can also share some samples and guide learners to reflect the learning progress using prompting questions such as "what problems and difficulties have I encountered in blended learning?" and "What are the gaps between me and the samples, and how can I improve?" Table 2.12 presents the objectives, instructions, tools, and implementation conditions of blended learning activities suitable for after-class activities.

The connection of pre-class, in-class, and after-class blended learning activities. The load and time intervals of pre-class and after-class activities should be appropriate according to the course schedule. Classes with longer intervals are good for scheduling big projects such as homework and project-based tasks (i.e., one week). If a course's interval is short, review and preview tasks are good activities (i.e., one day).

At the beginning of offline activities, teachers need to provide feedback on students' pre-class activities whether it is homework and reviewing the previous stage or previewing the content of this lesson. This way, teachers can connect students' offline activities with online activities and thus, promote engagement in the pre-class and after-class activities. Figure 2.3 shows an example of the pre-class, in-class, and after-class blended learning activities, including students' learning activities, teachers' instructional activities, offline activities, and online activities.

Pre-class activities not only relate to in-class activities, but also after-class activities. For example, the preview report carried out during pre-class relates to after-class reflection activities. Then, students review the preview report after class in groups, conduct self-reflection, and reflect upon their experience, which is beneficial to optimize the effect of follow-up preview activities.

Table 2.10 Blended learning activities suitable for pre-class

Pre-class activities	Learning objectives	Instructions	Activity tools	Implementation conditions
Guide map	Students can clarify the knowledge structure of the learning content of this unit (chapter) and understand the logical clues of learning resources during preview		Chapter mind map, unit concept map, pre-class guide hand-out	The guide map can be released through the online learning platform, or printed on paper, depending on the specific situation
Self-test in pre-class	After completing the preview, students can use the pre-class test questions to self-check the preview effect, to clarify difficult problems, and identify key points of the class	Students should complete the self-test within the specified time, test their own learning effect, and supplement the preview, or discuss with their classmates	Pre-class self-test questions (subjective or objective)	This activity should be carried out after the students have finished the preview. Teachers need to set the pre-class self-test questions according to the preview contents
KWLQ (Know, Want-to-know, Learned, and Questioning) Preview Report	By associating the preview contents with previous knowledge to stimulate the curiosity of preview, sort out the preview content, put forward preview problems, and clarify the key and difficult points of lectures	K: Read the title, abstract and other summary information of the article, and write what you know about this article W: What do you want to know more about? L: After reading the article in detail, what have you gained? Q: What other questions need to be asked and discussed in class?	KWLQ list	The learning materials for the KWLQ list can be published through the online learning platform or printed on paper, depending on the situation

(continued)

Table 2.10 (continued)

Pre-class activities	Learning objectives	Instructions	Activity tools	Implementation conditions
Preview discussion area	Through preview discussion, students can find preview loopholes, strengthen the pertinence of the preview, and clarify the focus of classroom learning	Students post and reply in the preview discussion area, learn from each other's preview results, and help each other by answering questions	Preview materials or resources (audio, video, text, pictures, PowerPoint)	Teachers are required to clarify preview requirements, and preview discussion questions or topics before class

Table 2.11 Appropriate in-class blended learning activities

In-class activities	Learning objectives	Instructions	Activity tools	Implementation conditions
Review of previous knowledge	Learning new knowledge based on existing knowledge	At the beginning of class, students are organized to review the corresponding previous knowledge and establish the connection between the old and new knowledge by organizing students to review independently, answer questions, group discussion, etc	Discussion questions, problem designs, etc. for previous knowledge review	Teachers need to selectively design topics for previous knowledge review and strive to get to the point
Preview comments	Students clarify the problems existing in the preview process and clarify the focus of the lecture	Comments and explanations on students' preparations (such as preparation reports, pre-class self-evaluation)	Teacher's preview comments (tables, mind maps, etc. can be any form)	Teachers need to carefully analyze the feedback of the students' preview, extract the mistakes or problems that most students have in the preview, correct them in time at the beginning of the class, and guide students to focus on listening to the class
Focus on difficult points	Through the teacher's lectures or demonstrations, students master the key and difficult points of this lesson	Under the guidance of the teacher, the students listen carefully, take notes, and complete the exercises (practice or exercises) as required	N/A	It depends on the teachers' rigorous teaching design and sufficient lesson preparation to teach the important and difficult points in the classroom

(continued)

Table 2.11 (continued)

In-class activities	Learning objectives	Instructions	Activity tools	Implementation conditions
Ask questions	Students answer questions through the teacher's hints, and actively think during classroom learning	By asking questions from teachers and providing appropriate scaffolding for students, students can think actively in class and listen to the class while asking questions	Carefully designed questions and tools needed to create a real problem scene	The design of questions is very critical, and it is often based on the actual problems in workplaces. We should make full use of virtual simulation platforms or multimedia tools to create real problem situations or identify instances of problems for students as much as possible
In-class test	Check the classroom learning effect, and timely fill the knowledge gaps	Students should complete the in-class test published by the teacher within the specified time in class	In-class test questions (subjective or objective)	Pay attention to the time of the test and set the amount and difficulty of the questions reasonably. The test that takes place at the beginning of the class is used to detect the student's preparation is different from the test that takes place after the formal study in the class. The difficulty of the test questions should be changed
Operation/ pronunciation demonstration and correction	With the help of simulation training, enhance skill proficiency and achieve skill-based learning goals	Simulation is an effective way to enhance students' skill training when experimental practice is limited. Students' complete simulation training within the specified time in the classroom	Simulation software or platform	The smooth implementation of the activity depends on a relatively complete simulation software or platform

(continued)

Table 2.11 (continued)

In-class activities	Learning objectives	Instructions	Activity tools	Implementation conditions
Organizing role-plays	By acting in a professional capacity of the major they are studying, students perceive the connotation of the professional role in a real problem situation, experience the emotion of the professional position, and establish a correct understanding of the professional role and a certain sense of professional identity	Teachers act as the directors, and students act as the actors and observers in groups to participate in a real problem situation and experience the ways, methods, and results of dealing with practical problems through action learning. After the performance, the actors and observers comment on their roles and discuss their learning results of the activity	It depends on the specific performance needs	The smooth development of role-playing activities depends on the close cooperation and clear division of labor among students. Teachers should give full maximization to the functions of directors and help students create real professional situations
Organizing achievement display	Present and report the results of individual or group learning	Students, individually or in groups, complete the display of achievements and peer evaluation within the specified time through speeches, debates, exhibitions, etc., and optimize and improve themselves according to the suggestions of teachers and peers	Multimedia facilities or tools required for presentation	Suitable for the implementation in class as a summary of a unit

Table 2.12 Blended learning activities suitable for the after-class

After-class activities	Learning objectives	Instructions	Activity tools	Implementation conditions
After-class homework	Students use after-school homework to consolidate the knowledge and contents they have learned online, and fill in the gaps	Students complete and submit homework within the specified time	It depends on the specific homework	Teachers are required to clarify homework requirements, give timely feedback, and answer questions
Homework mutual evaluation	By giving reasonable evaluation and suggestions on the work of peers, students can learn from each other, and exercise their independent learning ability	Students submit their homework to the mutual evaluation area within the specified time and evaluate their peers' homework	Mutual evaluation standards	It is suitable for online learning after class, which is convenient for sharing opinions among students. The online learning platform needs to have a discussion area or a special homework mutual evaluation area
After-class discussion	Deepen the understanding of the knowledge learned in the classroom, and timely put forward or answer personal learning questions	Students are conducting discussions in the discussion area in the name of individuals or groups such as replying to the topic discussion posts set by the teacher, posting difficult questions and utilizing after-class reflection, and are asked to reply to as many posts other students as possible (optional)	Related tools for online platform discussion	This activity is suitable for online learning after class and is convenient for students to share their views. The online learning platform needs to have a discussion area, and teachers need to clarify the discussion topics and rules for topic discussions or Q&A

(continued)

Table 2.12 (continued)

After-class activities	Learning objectives	Instructions	Activity tools	Implementation conditions
After-class self-test	Timely test the classroom learning effect and carry out the targeted review	Students complete the after-class self-test and submit it within the specified time. The teacher stipulates the answering time, collects, and analyzes the students' self-test results, and answers the questions with a high error rate. The self-test can also be included in the final course evaluation system. According to the self-test results, students can carry out the targeted review for further discussion	Homework mutual evaluation standards, self-test questions can be published electronically or in paper through the platform	The number of self-test questions should not be too many, and it is appropriate to test the students' classroom learning effect
Practical exercises	Familiar with the key points of skills	Students in the form of individuals or groups, timely and repeatedly carry out practical exercises after the end of the class. If they encounter difficulties, they should seek help from their peers and teachers in time	Software or equipment required for practical exercises	It is suitable for independent learning after class, and its smooth implementation depends on the software, tools, and practical environment that support practical exercises
Provide expansion resources	Consolidate what you have learned and deepen your understanding of relevant content	After class, students can use the learning platform, or the supplemental resources issued by teachers to further their study	Various forms of expansion resources	It is suitable for the after-school online learning, and provides students with as many after-school development resources as possible
Classroom playback	Selectively review the classroom learning content, solve difficult problems, review, and consolidate what has been learned in the classroom	Watch the video of classroom teaching. Using various functions such as pausing, repetition and other ways (optional)	Learning platform/video conference system with playback function	Suitable for online learning after class

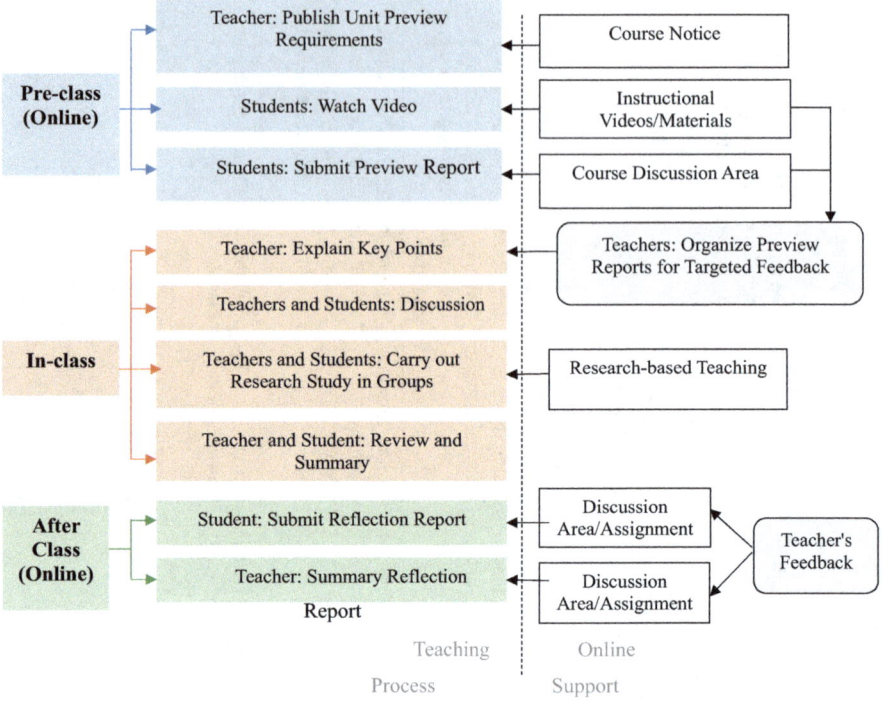

Fig. 2.3 Pre-class, in-class, and after-class blended learning activities for a learning unit

Extended Reading 2.4

The flipped classroom is a form of blended teaching. Researchers have sorted out the typical teaching modes of the flipped classroom (as shown in the table below). These flipped classrooms have organized different pre-class, in-class, and after-class activities.

Proposer	Pre-class	In-class	After-class	In the second class	Features
Sams and Bergmann (2013)	Video instruction	Problem solving			Through the video, superficial knowledge is moved into the pre-class and out-of-class learning, while the in-class teaching time is used for problem-solving and deep learning activities. The traditional teaching mode of "teaching first and then solving problems" is moved forward in both time and space
Talbert (2011)	Video instruction Self-test Exercise	Problem solving Sharing and communication Report display Answer questions Evaluation feedback Summary and reflection			Pre-class and in-class exercises can promote students' understanding of knowledge and help teachers know students' understanding on the content. Then, teachers provide feedback according to students' responses to the exercise
Lo et al. (2018)					Based on the First Principles of Instruction, blended teaching has been proved that the teaching effect in mathematics, Chinese, physics, and other subjects is significantly better than traditional teaching methods
Song and Kapur (2017)		Problem exploration	Video instruction		A flipped classroom model based on beneficial failure, which has proved to improve students' conceptual understanding of mathematics and problem-solving ability

(continued)

(continued)

Proposer	Pre-class	In-class	After-class	In the second class	Features
Musallam (2013)		Problem exploration	Video instruction	Test application Sharing and communication Report display Answer questions Evaluation feedback Summary and reflection	Explore-Flip-Apply: In the exploration stage, students carry out exploration activities in class to form necessary prior knowledge of the target content. In the flipping stage, students watch the teaching video outside class, systematically learn the teacher's explanation of knowledge, and submit video feedback to the teacher. In the application stage, the teacher explains the problems encountered in students' video learning in class, tests the students, designs application problems for the students to complete, and evaluates the students
Guo (2018)	Problem exploration Video instruction	Test application Sharing and communication Report display Answer questions Evaluation feedback Summary and reflection	Homework practice		The general mode includes seven links: objective, preparation, instructional video, review, test, activity, and summary

Selection of learning activities in blended courses. Teaching modes, knowledge types, and unit objectives determines specific unit learning activities.

Select learning activities according to teaching modes. There are two teaching modes: teaching-based and learning-based. The common teaching-based mode includes five-step teaching strategies (stimulating motivation, reviewing old courses, teaching new courses, applying consolidation, and checking the effect) and demonstration-imitation teaching strategies (demonstrating actions, students' practice under the guidance of teachers, independent practice, and skill transfer). Learning-based mode includes the discovery learning mode (problem situation, hypothesis-testing, and integrated application) and the anchored teaching strategy (creation of a situation, problem determination, independent learning, collaborative

Table 2.13 Learning activities according to the teaching mode

Teaching mode	Learning activities
Teaching-based mode	Listening, reading, watching videos, case studying
Learning-based mode	Discussion, collaboration, problem-solving, reflection, role-playing, online test, presentation, data searching

Table 2.14 FiveLearning activities according to the type of knowledge

Type of knowledge	Learning activities
Factual knowledge	Listening, reading, watching videos, data searching, discussion, collaboration
Conceptual knowledge	Listening, reading, material searching, watching videos, discussion, collaboration, problem solving, reflection
Procedural knowledge	Listening, reading, discussion, collaboration, problem solving, reflection, case studying, role playing
Meta-cognitive knowledge	Reading, discussion, collaboration, problem solving, reflection

learning, and effect evaluation). The learning activities selected according to different teaching modes are shown in Table 2.13.

Select learning activities according to knowledge types. According to Benjamin Bloom's taxonomy of educational objective, knowledge is classified into factual knowledge, conceptual knowledge, procedural knowledge, and meta-cognitive knowledge. The learning activities corresponding to different types of knowledge are shown in Table 2.14.

Selecting learning activities according to unit objectives. According to Benjamin Bloom's classification of educational objectives in the cognitive field, learning objectives are divided into six levels: memory, understanding, application, analysis, evaluation, and creation (Bloom 1956). There are also differences in instructional activities for different learning objectives, which can be seen in Table 2.15.

Table 2.15 Instructional activities according to teaching objectives

Learning objective level	Learning activities
Memory: Recognizing, listing, describing, distinguishing, retrieving, naming, locating	Simple mind maps, flash cards, online quizzes, basic web searching, social bookmarking, Q&A discussion areas, work presentations
Understanding: analysis, summary, rewriting, classification, interpretation, and comparison	Create mind maps, blog posts, categorize and tag advanced web searches, tag comments, and discussion areas

(continued)

Table 2.15 (continued)

Learning objective level	Learning activities
Apply: implementation, execution, usage, editing	Games or tasks, edit and develop shared documents (wikis, audio-visual tools), interviews (such as making podcasts), presenting work (using web conferencing or online tools), instructions (using online diagrams, creative tools)
Analyze: comparison, organization, structure, inquiry, construction	Survey/test, using database, mind map, report (online chart, online publishing)
Evaluation: confirmation, hypothesis, criticism, experiment, judgment, test	Debate or discussion (using online conference, online chat, or discussion), investigation (online tools), report (blog), persuasive speech (webcast, online document, mind map presentation mode), comment, coordination, reflection, and display (discussion area, blog), cooperation and communication
Creation: design, construction, planning, production, invention	Programming, movie production, animation, video, blogs, presentations, stories, projects, graphic art, advertisements, models

 **Extended Reading 2.5**

Strategies for implementing blended learning activities

- Provide a clear and complete unit guide (including learning objectives, learning activities, deadlines for task completion, and evaluation methods)
- Link classroom activities with extracurricular activities (Thai et al. 2017)
- Provide clear guidance and timely reminders, feedback, and incentives (Bernard et al. 2014)
- The difficulty of the learning task is appropriate, and sufficient time is given to complete the task (Kim et al. 2014)
- Give full maximization to the main role of students to be able to learn independently (Keller, 2008)
- Facilitate self-reflection and mutual evaluation of students (Shih, 2011)

Pay attention to the emotional interaction between teachers and students, and organize various forms of communication and interaction (Ma et al. 2015).

 **Case 2.10**

Blended Learning Design and Application, Tsinghua University 2021 Fall Undergraduate Course

Design of pre-class learning activities:	Learning objectives (ABCD method)	Learning content (knowledge points, skill points)	Resources/Tools	Online/offline	Time management
1. Preview learning resources: • Browse the learning video of the micro-course "Unit 1 Understanding and Designing a Blended Course - Teaching Activity Design" • Browse the learning video of the micro-course "Unit 2 Building a Blended Course-Unit Activity Building" • Watch the video above for ideas on the design of activities for the unit, as well as the construction of online activities After the preview, please think about the following questions and share them in the discussion area: • Among the courses you have taken before, what are the most impressive learning activities? What are the forms and processes of these activities? What resources you have used? • Why did the above learning activities impress you? If appropriate learning activities were selected and designed for your group's blended learning course, which activities would you choose? Give at least two reasons 3. Participate in the discussion of other students: browse the answers of other students before noon this Monday, select the answer with the clearest logic, praise the student's post, and reply with reasons 4. Submit questions: If you have any questions during the learning process, you can also submit them in the discussion area	1. Students can independently and accurately retell the types of instructional activities by browsing the micro-course videos 2. By browsing the micro-course videos, students can master the method of building instructional activities on the online course platform	1. Knowledge points: (1) The position and role of instructional activities in whole teaching design (2) The type of instructional activities 2. Skill Points: (1) Design of instructional activities (2) Construction of instructional activities in the online course platform	1. Micro-course video 2. Discussion area 3. Courseware	Online	Six days

(continued)

(continued)

Design of pre-class learning activities:	Learning objectives (ABCD method)	Learning content (knowledge points, skill points)	Resources/Tools	Online/offline	Time management
Design of in-class learning activities:	*Learning objectives (ABCD method)*	*Learning content (knowledge points, skill points)*	*Resources/Tools*	*Online/offline*	*Time management*
1. Listen to the teacher answer the questions raised by the students in the pre-class preview 2. Listen to the teacher explain the design of instructional activities	By listening to the teacher's explanation, students can remember the selection and design principles of instructional activities, and consciously apply relevant theories in the process of designing instructional activities, consider important matters, and design appropriate instructional activities in the group cooperation 2. Students can build instructional activities on the online learning platform through group cooperation by listening to the teacher's explanation and the learning video before class	Knowledge points: (1) Principles of selection and design of instructional activities (2) Relevant theories supporting the design of instructional activities (3) Precautions for the design of instructional activities	1. Courseware 2. Organizing students' homework 3. Online learning platform	Online & offline	2 classes
Design of after-class learning activities:	*Learning objectives (ABCD method)*	*Learning content (knowledge points, skill points)*	*Resources/Tools*	*Online/offline*	*Time management*
1. Complete the after-class reflection and post it in the discussion area: • What knowledge did you acquire in this class? What other questions are there? • A summary of the learning methods of this course. Deadline: x month x day 23:59 2. Complete the homework and submit it to the online learning platform: • Based on the course unit you selected, complete the design of instructional activities of the unit according to the teaching objectives and the matched teaching resources, and fill in the "Teaching Activity Design Form" • (2) Complete the addition of learning activities for this unit on the online learning platform, which may include micro-videos, tests, assignments, discussion areas, learning reflections, questionnaires, etc	1. Students can deepen their understanding and memory of the design of learning activities through reflection after class 2. By completing homework, students can apply the theoretical knowledge they have learned into practice, and design a learning activity that matches the teaching objectives and content of the selected courses	Skill points: Learning the application of activity design	Online learning platform	Online	Six days

 **Case 2.11**

Business Marketing and Negotiation

Stages	Activities	Objectives
Pre-class	Watch the micro-video of the quotation and complete the preparation for the simulated negotiation • Students who choose to act as job seekers comprehensively analyze their own abilities and job characteristics to reasonably formulate their own expected salary • Students who play the role of recruiters comprehensively analyze job requirements and reasonably formulate expected job salaries	Understand the factors, principles, and strategies to be considered in the quotation, as well as the way to deal with the other side's quotation, and be able to use it flexibly
	Watch a micro video of asking the price	Understand the way, frequency, and basic methods of bargaining, and analyze the opponent after bargaining
	Watch the micro-video of the counteroffer	Understand the preparations before counter-offering, the way of counter-offering, the determination of the counter-offer, and the skills of counter-offering
	Watch the micro video of bargaining	Learn basic strategies for bargaining
In-class	• Simulated negotiation 1: salary negotiation • Practitioners: flexibly apply the strategies and techniques they learned to negotiate and strive to achieve their goals • Observers to think: What are the steps in the bargaining process? What methods and techniques are there in each link? What price strategies can we use?	In the practical activities of simulated negotiation, let students use relevant strategies and skills flexibly, discover and solve problems
	Combine cases and learn new knowledge (negotiation deadlock and concession strategies)	Learn and understand the reasons for the negotiating deadlock and the methods and skills to deal with it in the case
	Teachers inspire students to think through cases by guiding and summarizing	Learn and understand the implementation steps, strategies, and skills of concessions in the case

(continued)

(continued)

Stages	Activities	Objectives
	Simulated negotiation task 2: purchase computer	Make corresponding preparations for the simulated negotiation practice in the next class
After-class	Prepare a plan before negotiation by forming a team, preparing negotiation information materials, formulating negotiation plans, etc	Circular review and application of knowledge, formulate a negotiation plan based on the content they learned in the previous units, and make corresponding preparations for the formal negotiation in the next class
In-class	• Purchase computer simulation negotiation 2 (1): group 1 and group 2 • Think: How do you feel about their negotiation? What aspects should we learn? What areas still need improvement? • Purchase computer simulation negotiation 2 (2): Group 3 and group 4 • Think: what do you think of their negotiation? What aspects are worth learning? What aspects need to be improved?	In the practical activities of simulated negotiation, let students use relevant strategies and skills flexibly
	Class discussion	Find and solve problems in practice

2.4.3   Evaluation

In blended learning, evaluation is to measure the degree to which learners have acquired the knowledge, can perform the skills, and exhibit changes in attitudes as required by the learning objectives of the blended courses (He et al. 2006). Evaluation in blended learning not only evaluates the final learning effect of students in the blended course, but also diagnoses the existing problems in the learning and provides feedback and guidance for further improvement.

2.4.3.1   Learning Unit Evaluation

In each learning unit, organization of learning activities takes place in the stages of pre-class, in-class, and after-class. Assessing the learning outcomes in these three stages helps determine the achievement of the learning objectives of each stage and provide feedback for revising the learning activities of the next stage. When conducting blended learning assessment, it is necessary to analyze students' performance at each learning stage in the learning unit and provide students with timely feedback and guidance accordingly. Table 2.16 presents the commonly used evaluation methods and feedback methods in the pre-class, in-class, and after-class stages of the blended course.

Assessment of pre-class learning. The main assessment items in this stage are students' participation in learning and the results of students' self-learning before class, including adaptability towards blended learning, acceptance, task completion, online learning behavior, learning effect, and more. Students' learning data,

Table 2.16 Learning assessment and feedback methods in blended course

	Pre-class assessment	In-class assessment	After-class assessment
Online data analysis	Participation/individual feedback/summary of the data and provide feedback in class		Participation/overall or individual feedback
Test	Online objective test/ instant score feedback		Online objective test/ instant score feedback
Discussion	The situation and content of posts and replies in the discussion area/reply/ summary discussion and provide feedback in class	Group discussion/observe the participation and guide at any time/show and comment according to the learning results	The situation and content of posts and replies in the discussion area/reply/ reply in the next class
Ask questions		Classroom questioning/ according to the situation, ask questions by name or randomly select students to ask questions	
Assignment			Online homework/ feedback scores and comments after reviewing
Experimental training	Virtual experiment training/individual guidance/summary of experience and provide comments in class	Operation of experimental training room/provide guidance to individuals/ groups at any time when needed/provide comments according to the results	Virtual experiment training/individual guidance/provide comments in the next class
Online teaching		Online test in class Instant grading in class Online opinion expression (e.g., voting, barrage) Discuss and comment in class	

completed tasks, questionnaires, and other methods used for assessment can be reviewed via the online teaching platform. The feedback and guidance given to students at this stage can be dynamic online Q&A and instance assessment message. Teachers can also provide thorough feedback and explanations in the next class. Teachers can timely adjust the learning activities in the classroom (in-class) according to the students' learning situation and difficulties. Table 2.17 presents the item, purpose, method, and evaluator of pre-class learning evaluation.

The ARCS model questionnaire is a tool to measure students' learning motivation in an information-based environment, which includes four parts: Attention, Relevance, Confidence, and Satisfaction perceptions. This tool assesses students' motivation in blended learning (Ma & Lee, 2021). Based on the assessment results of ARCS questionnaire, teachers can provide feedback and guidance to specific students such as presenting students' online learning time, the number of times they participated in discussions, and the number of comments received on their homework and thus, timely remind students of their progress. Students' interests can also be stimulated through various means such as video materials, group activities, and games.

Table 2.17 Items and methods of pre-class learning evaluation

Evaluation items	Evaluation purpose	Evaluation method	Evaluator
Adaptability of blended learning	Inspect whether students are comfortable with blended teaching methods, task difficulty, teamwork, etc	Student Self-Report Questionnaire	Teacher
Acceptance of blended learning	Investigate the students' acceptance of the blended learning objectives, the design of instructional activities, and the arrangement of blended learning methods	Student Self-Report Questionnaire	
Completion of learning tasks	Understand the achievement of students' preview behavior and their completion of tasks	The data recorded by the platform such as the number of times students log in to the platform, the amount of time used to watch videos, online test results, online speech frequency, etc	
Learning outcomes	Find out how well students are accomplishing their preparation goals	Test questions, discussion posts, etc. on the course website	

Extended Reading 2.6

Pay attention to the appropriate adjustment of teaching objectives and instructional activities based on the situation reflected by students' pre-class learning. The following figure presents an example of how to adjust subsequent learning activities based on the results of pre-class evaluation.

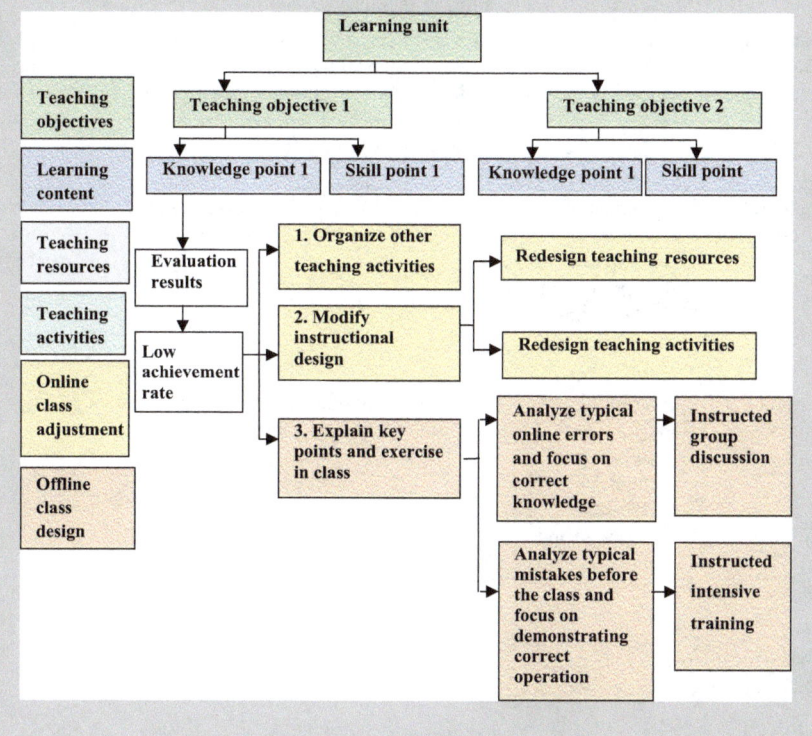

Assessment of in-class learning. The assessment items include students' online participation, classroom participation, completion of classroom tasks, and classroom learning results. In addition to using classroom observation, questioning, and tests to assess the learning effect in class, teachers can also use peer-evaluation and self-assessment for in-class assessment. Teachers then provide after-school learning resources and after-school learning tasks based on the in-class assessment results. Feedback and guidance at this stage completed in a timely manner in class can help. Table 2.18 presents the item, purpose, method, and evaluator of the in-class learning assessment.

Table 2.18 Items and methods of in-class learning assessment

Evaluation content	Evaluation purpose	Evaluation method	Evaluator
Online students' evaluation	Learn about students' participation in online learning activities	Evaluate through online learning behavior data such as the time of learners entering online courses, the total time spent on accessing learning resources, the completion of online tests, the number of completed online assignments, the number of posts and replies in the discussion area, etc	Teacher
In class students' evaluation	Understand students in class activities	Learn from classroom observation tools and teachers' personal teaching experience, fully mobilize students' mutual evaluation and learners' self-evaluation, and assess students' attendance, engagement, group interaction, etc	Teacher/ group peers/ student
Completion of classroom tasks	Investigate students' participation in the application of classroom knowledge and skills	Classroom questions, group discussions, experiments, results, presentations, etc	Teacher/ group peers
Classroom learning outcomes	Examining the mastery and application of students' classroom knowledge and skills	Exercises, assignments, extended discussions, reflection reports, etc. on the course website	Teacher

 **Extended Reading 2.7**

Action After Evaluation:

After obtaining the evaluation of students' classroom learning participation and task completion, teachers should timely adjust the content and focus of classroom teaching. They can appropriately change the classroom rhythm, and judge if necessary to interrupt the students' original activity process for unified guidance according to the actual teaching situation or provide targeted feedback and guidance for students. According to the evaluation of classroom learning results, it is important to formulate the contents and requirements of after-school activities and tasks.

Students' engagement is key to successful blended learning. Student learning engagement includes students' behavioral engagement, cognitive engagement, and emotional engagement. Behavioral engagement is explicit and observable such as attending classes on time, observing classroom rules, and completing work tasks. In addition, behavioral engagement reflects in the intensity of participation activities (e.g., attention, persistence, time investment, effort) and activity participation (e.g., participation in online and offline discussions). Cognitive engagement refers to the use of learning strategies. Different learning strategies lead to different levels of cognitive activities. Strategies such as exercising and summarizing to memorize, organize, and understand learning content, and using time management strategies to plan learning tasks (the OSLQ questionnaire, the Online Self-regulated Learning Questionnaires) can be used to assess students' ability to self-adjust in online learning (Barnard et al. 2009). Emotional engagement refers to students' emotional reactions including interest, boredom, happiness, sadness, and anxiety. It can also refer to feelings of belonging and upholding values.

Online learning behavior data can also assess students' engagement in blended learning. Table 2.19 presents the data in an online teaching platform in China including entering online courses, accessing learning resources, completing online tests, completing online homework, and posting replies in the discussion area.

Table 2.19 Learning behavior data in an online teaching platform in China

Role	Function name	Data items
Teacher	Resource function	1. The longest resource usage time
		2. The average resource usage time
		3. The shortest resource usage time
		4. The number of people who have participated by using the resource
		5. The number of people who did not participate by using the resource
		6. The total number of questions asked
		7. The number of questions answered by the teacher
		8. The texts and number of words
		9. The number of questions followed
	Voting function	1. The name of the voting item
		2.The number of participants who voted for each item
		3.The percentage of participation in voting for each item
	Communication function	1.The number of class members
		2.The number of speaking members
		3.The total number of times all ideas were approved
		4.The total number of people who approve of other people's ideas

(continued)

Table 2.19 (continued)

Role	Function name	Data items
	Test function	1. The number of people who should participate in the test
		2. The actual number of participants in the test
		3. Test time limit
		4. The longest test time
		5. The shortest test time
		6. The average test time
		7. The correct rate of each test question
		8. Number of people to choose each test item
Learner	Resource function	1. Study numbers
		2. Study time
		3. First visit time
		4. Last visit time
		5. The number of personal questions
		6. Personal attention to the number of questions
		7. The number of times the personal question is followed
	Salon function	1. The number of individual speeches
		2. The number of ideas approved by individuals
		3. The number of people who get approval for their personal ideas
	Test function	1. The number of tests submitted by individuals
		2. The number of correct questions on the personal test
		3. The number of wrong questions on the personal test

Assessment of after-class learning. The items of after-class assessment include the completion of homework and students' summary and reflection on the learned unit. Assessment of the achievements of students' unit learning objectives uses students' homework performance, reflection and summary reports, after-school extension tasks, and more. Comparing after-class learning assessment with pre-class learning assessment to check students' learning outcomes and progress is helpful in adjusting designated learning resources and learning activities in a timely manner. Feedback and guidance at this stage through individualized online tutoring lessons for students are useful. Comments and summaries provided in the next class based on the completion of homework in class and after class can reinforce learning.

Teachers are responsible for assessing the completion of the students' homework and the students conduct self-assessment through learning reflection. The reflection not only includes the reflection of the learning process, but also the overall reflection on learning outcomes via intrinsic psychological perception questionnaires. Through the analysis of learning satisfaction and self-efficacy, students could reflect on the learning process and teachers can adjust instructional strategies accordingly.

Table 2.20 The items and methods of after-school learning assessment

Items	Objectives	Methods	Responsible
Summary and reflection	To promote students to reflect on the learning process and adjust learning strategies in time	The feedback form of learning summary, intrinsic psychological perception questionnaires like learning satisfaction, self-efficacy	Students
The completion of homework	To check students' mastery of learning contents and knowledge	Homework, unit exercises, self-check	Teachers

Table 2.20 shows the items, objectives, methods, and responsibilities of after-school learning assessment.

 **Extended Reading 2.8**

Actions After Evaluation:

At the beginning of the next class, teachers will give feedback on the outcomes of students' after-class learning assessment, so students can obtain feedback and a sense of achievement. Targeted supplementary teaching for students who performed poorly after class can be offered.

 **Extended Reading 2.9**

Learning satisfaction refers to learners' pleasant feelings or attitudes towards the learning experience. Pleasant feelings or positive attitudes refer to "satisfaction," while "dissatisfaction" represents the opposite (Long 1989). In regard to assessing learning satisfaction, after-class questionnaires are usually adopted to get to know the students' subjective feelings. The questions often used include "Compared with other courses, I just feel that the quality of the course is good" "I would like to recommend this course to other students," "I am satisfied with XXX in this course," and so on in the context of self-reporting. The students choose from a scale that includes "strongly agree-agree-neutral-disagree-strongly disagree."

Bandura, an American psychologist, first proposed **self-efficacy**. Self-efficacy refers to people's beliefs in their capabilities to mobilize the motivation, cognitive resources, and courses of action needed to exercise control over environmental demands (Bandura 1977). It is an important reference for measuring and evaluating learners' inner psychological perception. The General Self-Efficacy Scale (GSES), developed by Schwarzer and his colleagues, is widely used and has been translated into many languages and marketed around the world. The general self-efficacy scale contains 10 questions, all of which are representative of 4-point Likert scale (strongly disagree- disagree-agree-strongly agree). Students are asked to choose from the scale according to different situations. The scale includes items such as "I can always solve problems if I try my best," "when faced with a difficult problem, I can usually find several solutions," and "it is easy for me to stick to my beliefs and achieve my goals."

2.4.3.2 Course Evaluation

In blended learning, summative evaluation measures the overall effectiveness of a blended course. Examples of summative evaluation include open/closed book examinations, project reports, course papers, academic defense, and so on. In social science, summative evaluation via research reports and papers can help judge the quality of learning. Science courses can use the final exam, and engineering and medical courses can use practical operation in simulated scenarios. Design-based courses can consider project design and presentation as summative evaluations.

 **Extended Reading 2.10**

There are three types of learning evaluation: summative evaluation, formative evaluation, and diagnostic evaluation, as shown in the following table.

Category	Summative evaluation	Formative evaluation	Diagnostic evaluation
Purpose	To improve the teaching effect	To identify problems in teaching and learning in time	To understand the knowledge students have mastered and their preparation
Time	Evaluating at the end of the course, at the end of the term, at the end of the school year, etc	The evaluation of the intermediate process, which is generally carried out during the course	The predictive evaluation at the beginning is generally conducted before class, before each semester, and the beginning of the academic year

(continued)

(continued)

Category	Summative evaluation	Formative evaluation	Diagnostic evaluation
Description	The overall evaluation of teaching means judging its effect after the completion of instructional activities The evaluation of the result at the end of the term is the summative evaluation	In the teaching process, it is used to understand student learning and discover problems in teaching and learning in time Tests, study reports, and other forms are often used. The test questions should be based on the predetermined objectives of unit teaching	Also known as preparatory evaluation. It generally refers to the investigation of students' knowledge, skills, and emotions before the teaching activity This kind of survey help teachers understand students' background knowledge and their preparation for learning so they know whether students are ready to learn

Combination of quantitative and qualitative evaluation. A complete learning evaluation system should combine quantitative and qualitative evaluations. Some learning activities, such as objective questions testing the memory and understanding of knowledge, are more appropriate for quantitative evaluation. Some learning activities such as students' participation in group cooperation and their passion for study, support, help given to peers, and other forms of cooperation are more appropriate for qualitative evaluation. Some learning activities need both qualitative and quantitative evaluations. For example, when two students have similar performance accuracy evaluated by a quantitative method, a qualitative method is needed to evaluate the quality of their performances. Results of qualitative and quantitative evaluations can show student differences in learning attitudes and cognitive levels.

Combination of formative and summative, online and offline evaluation. Formative combining summative evaluation and online combining offline data ensure a comprehensive learning evaluation (Choules 2007). Formative evaluation is the real-time monitoring of the whole learning process, and students' understanding of learning content. It includes students' independent learning on the online learning platform, performance in class, discussion of course topics, after-class homework quality, and reflection and summary of course learning. The summative evaluation is to evaluate students' learning effectiveness in the middle and at the end of semester. It includes the examination results in different stages, the proposal submitted at the end of term, and the final group project report. Online evaluation includes quizzes, online homework and work comments, a personal reflection of learning and feedback, as well as observation and measurement of a series of online learning behaviors such as discussion. The offline evaluation mainly includes tests in different stages, offline homework and work comments, observation, recording, and evaluation of classroom behaviors such as attendance, obedience to classroom rules, group discussion, Q & A, and group activities.

The combination of instructors' evaluation, peer-evaluation, and self-evaluation. There are two parts in blended learning: online and offline. Sometimes teachers are present, but sometimes they are not. Therefore, in addition to feedback provided by instructors, feedback provided by peers is also useful for evaluation (Vo et al. 2017). Self-evaluation can help students develop the habits of continuous reflection. Instructors' evaluation and peer-evaluation are helpful in receiving an objective and comprehensive evaluation of learning results from different perspectives. As collaborators in class, peers can directly observe each other's learning behaviors, attitudes, and outcomes. Diversified evaluation does not weaken the role of teachers but emphasizes the multi-perspectives in evaluation so that the evaluation results are objective and comprehensive. These three evaluation methods have different advantages. It is necessary to allocate the scores of different dimensions under the overall evaluation framework.

The explicit evaluation rubrics and the useful evaluation results. At the beginning of the course, students should be provided with evaluation rubrics such as the composition of process-oriented and result-oriented scores, the composition of online and offline evaluations, and the proportion of evaluation results from different sources, such as teachers and students. In the process of implementing blended learning, we should strictly follow the rubrics to ensure the transparency of the evaluation and the fairness of the evaluation results. Clear rubrics also can assist students' learning process. Analyzing the usability of the evaluation results is needed. Analysis not only includes the semantic meanings of the questions, but also whether they are universal and fair to all students to avoid Differential Item Functioning (Camilli and Shepard 1994). Besides, clearly distinguishing valid data from invalid data is important. For example, the time span of students' online learning, elapsed time of reading and watching materials, and activity levels (such as the number of "likes," the number of "being liked," the number of posts, the number of comments) are taken as the basis to measure students' enthusiasm. Restrictions should be set to avoid distortion of evaluation results. For example, if the student's online learning time is limited at the beginning, but increases rapidly in a short period of time, the data will be considered invalid or reduced. For the evaluation of student participation in the discussion forum, if the words of a post are too few (such as less than 10 words), it will be considered invalid.

Evaluation guiding students' learning. The function and purpose of evaluation is the assessment for or as learning rather than the assessment of learning. This requires teachers to provide students explicit evaluation goals in advance, help students recognize the expectations, motivate students to feel their "pulse," help students identify their current achievements and problems, and the gaps between goals and actual learning. Therefore, students can learn to narrow the gaps and achieve the goals. The goal of "promoting learning through assessment" through self-reflection can be truly achieved (as shown in Fig. 2.4).

The online learning data of each blended course allows each student to review their progress and results. Therefore, teachers should encourage students to share their learning experiences and shortcomings, actively engage in consistent self-reflection, rethink accurately, and adjust their learning (Davies et al. 2011). In terms of setting

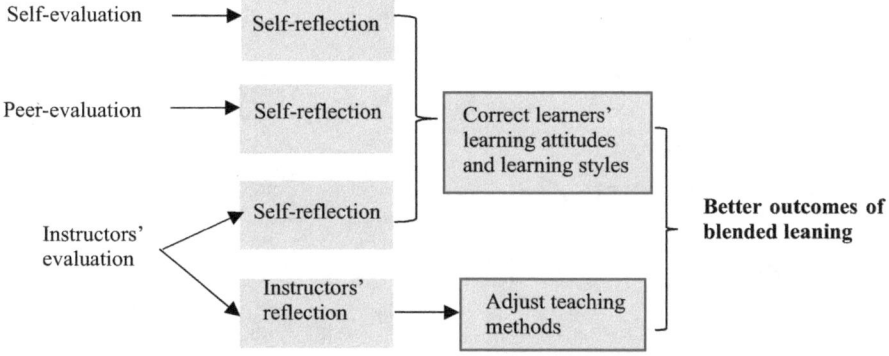

Fig. 2.4 The directive role of evaluation in learning and teaching

scoring goals, giving students extra incentive points and lessening punitive deduction points help directly engage students in evaluation.

 **Extended Reading 2.11**

Relevant Concept: The Purpose of Assessment

Assessment of learning: Exams taken as the major representation of summative assessment. As the absolute authority and evaluator, teachers assess students' learning results according to their test scores. As the main indicator to measure everything, standardized scores are used to assess the degree to which students achieve their goals at the end of the learning stage, with the aim of identifying, selecting, and classifying students.

Assessment for learning (Broadfoot et al. 1999): Assessment is no longer regarded as a standard to judge good or bad results, but as a tool to promote learning. The main purpose is to promote students' learning through assessment, make assessment a part of the teaching process to help students gradually achieve their learning objectives, pay attention to the formative assessment, and give a high degree of attention to the incentive and development function of assessment.

Assessment as learning (Dann 2014): Assessment is no longer a means or part embedded in the learning process, but a correction mechanism internalized in learning activities. Assessing others is a process of constantly deepening and reconstructing knowledge. In the process of constantly assessing others' answers and comparing them with their own knowledge, students can clarify the idea of the topic and gain a deeper understanding and mastery of knowledge. Therefore, they naturally enter into deep learning in the process of assessment.

 **Case 2.12**

Essential Biology: **An Undergraduate Course of Tsinghua University, China**

Design of	Learning Objectives	Resource/Tool	Distribution of Scores
pre-class learning assessment	Student (A) can recall the composition, structure, the basic principle of replication, and discovery history of double-stranded DNA (B) by watching the teaching video (C), and the accuracy of exercises for preview shall reach over 60% (D)	Learning management system (LMS)	• The total score of the pre-class part is 2 points • If student finished watching the preview video and homework for previewing before class, they would get 1.5 points • If the actual score is 5 points or more, students will get 2 points. But, if the actual score is lower than 5 points, one point lower will be deducted 0.1 points (for example, one would get 1.8 points, if the actual score is 3 points) • If the student only watched the video before class without finishing the exercises, or only finished the exercises without watching the required video, the student would get 1 point only • No score will be given if the preview is not completed before class
Design of in-class learning assessment	Learning Objectives	Resource/Tool	Distribution of Scores
	After listening to the lecture and completing the class games, students can: • Describe the process of PCR • Identify the similarities and differences between DNA replication and PCR (the above knowledge will be tested through in-class exercises and games, and the accuracy shall reach more than 60%) • Analyze the functions of various reagents in real PCR kits and the successful factors of the PCR experiment • Lay the necessary foundation for further learning using the nucleic acid detection method of novel Coronavirus which can be applied to clinical practice	Offline teaching and Rain Classroom	• The teacher assigns points according to the background data of Rain Classroom (a total of 1 point; 0.5 points for each question for example) • Answer the question within 1 min and students will get the score • No score is awarded without participating

(continued)

(continued)

Design of	Learning Objectives	Resource/Tool	Distribution of Scores
after-class learning assessment	Student (A) can use the basic principles of PCR (C) to analyze the effects of various reagents in real PCR kits (B) after completing the classroom learning, and the accuracy shall reach more than 60% (D)	Learning management system (LMS)	• 1 point for each correct answer to the question. Full marks given for two or more correct answers. For every 2 wrong answers, 0.5 points will be deducted (if one answer is wrong, no points will be deducted), until 0 points are left • 1 point for each correct answer. A score of 0.8 is given if the result of the formula is wrong or if the number of primers used in the last round is considered. Submitting the answer will earn 0.6 points • 1 point for each correct reason. Full marks given for three or more correct answers. For every wrong answer, 0.5 points will be deducted until 0 points are left

Describe the relationship between assessments:
The assessments before, after, and in class are gradual. The assessment before class can find out the basic level of students to guide teachers to change the key points and methods of teaching. The assessment in class can be compared with the assessment before class to understand the degree of students' mastery of new knowledge through courses. And, by contrasting the assessments in and after class, the teachers can know the students' final degree of mastery of the new knowledge and consolidate it
TIPS:
1. Consider the elements of learning assessment, comprehensively consider the assessment of the learning process and learning results (matching with learning activities and existing learning objectives)
2. Learning objectives: Elements and Design Methods of Learning assessment (Application)

 **Case 2.13**

Business Marketing and Negotiation, **a professional course of vocational college**

The course adopts a combination of unit assessment and final assessment of learning results

Unit assessment: This course consists of eight units, and each unit consists of a task, including fundamental learning, comprehensive practical training, and student tasks

Final assessment: Final assessment includes comprehensive simulated negotiation tasks and closed-book exams scheduled in the last two weeks of the semester. The topics and requirements of comprehensive simulated negotiation tasks are released in the second week of the semester. As the learning activity proceeds, students can complete the related preparation for the negotiation (e.g., building a negotiating team, collecting data, formulating negotiation plans, choosing negotiating strategies). The simulated negotiation is held in the penultimate week of the semester in class. Each student's score is based on their group performance and assessment of peers in groups. Closed-book exam: The final exam is held in the last week of the semester. The types of questions include multiple choice, true/false, short answer, and a case study. The criterion of assessment for the completion of comprehensive simulated negotiation tasks are shown in the following table:

Task	0 point	1 point	2 points	3 points	Score
Formulation of negotiation plan	Not submitted	The negotiating plan is incomplete and only a few of the stages have been considered	The negotiation plan is complete, but the application of strategies and skills is not strongly related to the goals	The negotiation plan is complete, including the basic principles, strategies, and skills of negotiation at each stage	
Simulated negotiation	Not participated	Vague roles without their own starting points and positions The pace of negotiations is disrupted by the other party	Having a clear position and starting point But, not being able to apply strategies and skills flexibly to achieve the goals. The negotiation is weak	Having a clear position and starting point And being able to flexibly use a variety of skills and strategies of negotiation	

2.4.4 Evaluation on Implementation of Blended Learning

At the end of a semester, teachers need to evaluate the effectiveness of implementing blended learning. Evaluation results are important for further improvement. Evaluation on the effectiveness of implementing blended learning includes two perspectives: (1) teachers' self-assessment on the implementation of blended learning and (2) students' learning experience of blended learning.

Teachers' self-assessment on the implementation of blended learning. Teachers can use the questionnaire as shown in Table 2.21 to conduct self-assessment.

Table 2.21 The questionnaire of self-assessment on the effectiveness of implementing blended learning

Criteria (Please rate the effectiveness of implementation of blended courses you want to self-evaluate.)	Yes	To a large extent	To some extent	No	Not Applicable
Course Objective					
The learning contents are consistent with the learning objectives	3	2	1	0	N/A
The learning activities are consistent with the learning objectives	3	2	1	0	N/A
The learning outcomes are consistent with learning objectives	3	2	1	0	N/A
Summary and improvement:					
Learning Assessment					
Learning assessment can reflect learning outcomes	3	2	1	0	N/A
Learning assessment is throughout the course	3	2	1	0	N/A
Being able to provide feedback to students throughout the course	3	2	1	0	N/A
Learning assessment makes full use of online behavioral data	3	2	1	0	N/A
Summary and improvement:					
Learning Resources					
Online learning resources can meet the demand of course learning	3	2	1	0	N/A
Pre-class, in-class, and after-class learning activities are supported by specific teaching materials and are associated with learning objectives	3	2	1	0	N/A
Course materials are presented in a consistent and logical structure and layout	3	2	1	0	N/A
Summary and improvement:					
Students' Involvement					
The aim of online discussions is to promote effective learning interactions (teacher-student, content-student, student–student)	3	2	1	0	N/A
The requirements for student's interaction and progress are clarified in the course	3	2	1	0	N/A
Summary and improvement:					
Support Service for Learning					

(continued)

Table 2.21 (continued)

Criteria (Please rate the effectiveness of implementation of blended courses you want to self-evaluate.)	Yes	To a large extent	To some extent	No	Not Applicable
The course makes it clear how students can get technical support	3	2	1	0	N/A
The course makes it clear how students can get access to support services (e.g., peer support services, counselling)	3	2	1	0	N/A
The course clearly provides guidelines for learning in the blended learning environment	3	2	1	0	N/A
Summary and improvement:					

Students' blended learning experience. Students' learning experience, especially student satisfaction, is important for further improvement in implementing blended learning. Satisfaction refers to students' pleasant feelings or attitudes towards learning activities, in this case, blended learning (Long 1989). There are many factors that influence students' learning satisfaction including class size, students' prior experience, age, the relationship between teachers and students, engagement, and technical skills. To measure students' learning satisfaction, questionnaires are used. A sample learning satisfaction questionnaire is shown in Table 2.22.

Additionally, teachers can self-assess their teaching by using students' learning performance in each learning unit and course data. Specifically, course tests and discussion posts on the course website help evaluate whether students have completed the pre-class activities. Student's in-class discussions, group activities, experimentations, and presentations evaluate students' in-class activities. Whether they reached their unit objectives through exercises, assignments, discussion forums, and reflection reports on the course website, students' achievement of pre-determined unit objectives is made. Behavioral data and statistical results on the course website assist in evaluating students' engagement and completion of after-class activities.

2.5 Suggestions for Implementing Blended Learning for Different Modes

The implementation of blended learning has different modes, which vary in learning objectives, time and space, and teaching environment. Thus, content and delivery methods should be adjusted when implementing blended learning.

Table 2.22   The learning satisfaction questionnaire on blended course

This questionnaire should be filled in anonymously. Based on statements from 1 to 9, choose the answer that best fits your situation by instinct. There is no right or wrong answer if it fits your situation. We will not count your answers in the grade of the course. For questions 10 and 11, just write down your thoughts briefly

1. The quality of this online course is better than other offline courses I have taken
□ strongly agree, □ agree, □ neutral, □ disagree, □ strongly disagree
2. I'm very satisfied with this course
□ strongly agree, □ agree, □ neutral, □ disagree, □ strongly disagree
3. I think this course meets my learning needs well
□ strongly agree, □ agree, □ neutral, □ disagree, □ strongly disagree
4. This course is well-discussed (both in class and online)
□ strongly agree, □ agree, □ neutral, □ disagree, □ strongly disagree
5. Part of this course is conducted online, which I think is very valuable
□ strongly agree, □ agree, □ neutral, □ disagree, □ strongly disagree
6. Compared with other offline courses I chose, the teaching of this course through the Internet has improved the quality of the course
□ strongly agree, □ agree, □ neutral, □ disagree, □ strongly disagree
7. I am very satisfied with the online learning style of this course (e.g.,demonstration video, online discussion)
□ strongly agree, □ agree, □ neutral, □ disagree, □ strongly disagree
8. For subsequent courses, I would like to choose similar online courses
□ strongly agree, □ agree, □ neutral, □ disagree, □ strongly disagree
9. Compared with other offline courses, it will be more difficult to learn content from this particular course through the Internet
□ strongly agree, □ agree, □ neutral, □ disagree, □ strongly disagree
10. What difficulties did you find in the previous stage of this course?
11. What are the differences between the previous stage of this course and other courses? Did you learn more from these differences?

2.5.1   Implementation of Blended Learning for Different Learning Objectives

When implementing blended learning for different learning objectives, blended learning is classified into two categories: (1) skill-driven blended courses and (2) competency-driven blended courses (Valiathan 2002).

Skill-driven blended courses. Skill-driven blended courses combine students' self-paced online learning and online learning support from tutors or teaching assistants. This type of blended courses works best for procedural knowledge and skills. In skill-driven blended courses, teachers need to provide students with a specific pre-class learning plan and requirements of the learning schedule. Teachers provide online assistance during students' self-paced learning. Offline in-class activities focus on practicing, forming group collaborations, and obtaining teachers' onsite guidance. When implementing skill-driven blended courses, teachers can consider the following steps:

- Before class: Teachers send out online learning tasks
- Before class: Teacher provide brief lectures of learning content

- Before class: Students complete self-paced online learning
- In class: Students practice and complete group tasks
- In class: Teachers offer onsite guidance and feedback
- In class: Teachers conclude the offline sessions
- After class: Teachers assess students' learning performance in an online learning environment

Competency-driven blended courses. Competency-driven blended courses utilize performance support tools and knowledge management tools. This type of blended courses works best for implicit knowledge and workplace competency development. In competency-driven blended courses, students are assigned workplace tutors and provided with learning tasks before class. Students can share their experience in the online learning communities. Students also need opportunities for observing and interacting with field experts in a real workplace. When implementing competency-driven blended courses, teachers can consider the following steps:

- Before class: Assign workplace tutors to students
- Before class: Build an online learning community
- In class: Students practice offline
- In class: Students discuss with the workplace tutors
- After class: The workplace tutors answer students' questions
- After class: Students complete homework and learning reflection in an online learning environment

2.5.2 Implementing Blended Learning for Different Time and Space

Blended courses include offline and online sessions. Teachers and students have different types of connections such as synchronous and asynchronous. Therefore, when implementing blended learning for different time and space, blended learning is lassified into three categories: (1) synchronous blended courses, (2) asynchronous blended courses, and (3) courses that combine synchronous and asynchronous courses (Li & Zhu, 2019).

Asynchronous blended courses. Asynchronous blended courses are the most widely used blended learning mode. Besides in-class lectures, after class online activities are added for independent learning and extended learning. When implementing asynchronous blended courses, teachers can consider the following steps:

- Before class: Teachers send online learning tasks
- Before class: Students complete self-paced online learning
- In-class: Teachers facilitate offline activities in class
- After class: Students complete homework and learning reflection in an online learning environment

Synchronous blended courses. Synchronous blended courses require both teachers and students have certain synchronous communication tools (e.g., video conferencing system, online real-time interaction tools). This type of blended course works best when teachers and students cannot come to the physical classroom. Teachers conduct lectures through video or audio-conferencing systems and interact with students in real-time. When implementing synchronous blended courses, teachers can consider the following steps:

- Before class: Teachers send online learning tasks
- Before class: Students prepare learning materials and synchronous communication tools
- In class: Teachers provide brief lectures of learning content via video conferencing system
- In class: Students interact with teachers online through video conferencing systems
- In class: Teachers conclude the session through video conferencing systems
- After class: Students complete homework and learning reflection in an online learning environment

The third category is a combination of the synchronous courses and asynchronous courses. This type of blended course works best when teachers are physically in-class while the students are either attending in person or online.

2.5.3 Implementing Blended Teaching for Different Learning Environments

The physical teaching environment can include many different spaces for learning. The space can include multimedia functionality, physical experimental training labs, virtual simulation training labs, virtual-real integration training labs, theory-integrated practical training labs, and actual workplace settings. The integration of online learning environment with these physical teaching environments generates different forms of blended learning. Details of these forms of blended learning are provided below.

Multimedia classroom + online learning environment. The multimedia classroom is the most widely used physical teaching environment. This model is suitable for courses with learning objectives focused on knowledge acquisition and developing intellectual and presentation skills. Students can acquire face-to-face assistance during self-paced online learning. When implementing this blended learning mode, teachers can consider the following steps:

- Before class: Teachers send online learning tasks
- Before class: Students complete self-paced online learning
- In class: Lecturing and tutoring are conducted in the multimedia classroom
- After class: Students complete homework and learning reflection in an online learning environment

Physical experimental training labs + online learning environment. The physical experimental training labs provide necessary physical equipment and devices for students to practice. This mode works best when learning content is primarily a motor, sensory, and perceptual skill. When implementing this blended learning mode, teachers can consider the following steps:

- Before class: Teachers send online learning tasks
- Before class: Students learn procedural skills in online learning environment
- In class: Teachers demonstrate procedural skills in the physical experimental training labs
- In class: Students practice procedural skills in a group or individually and teachers provide necessary assistance in the physical experimental training labs
- In class: Teachers conclude the learning sessions and provide feedback to students' performance
- After class: Students complete homework and learning reflection in an online learning environment

Virtual simulation training labs + online learning environment. Virtual simulation training labs provide students virtual simulation systems and software for practice. This mode works best when learning content is primarily operational skills and completed on computers or with other digital devices. When implementing this blended learning mode, teachers can consider the following steps:

- Before class: Teachers send online learning tasks
- Before class: Students learn operational skills in online learning environment
- In class: Teachers demonstrate operational skills in virtual simulation training labs
- In class: Students practice operational skills and teachers provide necessary assistance in the virtual simulation training labs
- In class: Teachers conclude the learning sessions and provide feedback to students' performance
- After class: Students complete homework and learning reflection in an online learning environment

Virtual-real integration training labs + online learning environment. Virtual-real integration training labs are equipped with virtual simulation software, virtual reality (VR/AR) software, Internet of Things, sensor networks, and more. The physical space and equipment integrate within an online learning environment in the virtual-real integration training labs to support students' physical operations as well as virtual simulation operations. This mode works best when learning content is primarily professional and requires complicated motor and high-risk motor skills. When implementing this blended learning mode, teachers can consider the following steps:

- Before class: Teachers send online learning tasks
- Before class: Students learn motor skills in online learning environment

- Before class: Students watch demonstration videos in an online learning environment and complete simulation operations in virtual simulation training lab
- In class: Teachers explain the key points of skill operation according to students' online learning
- In class: Teachers demonstrate the process of skill operation
- In class: Students practice operation in groups in the virtual-real integration training lab and teachers provide necessary assistance
- In class: Teachers conclude the learning sessions and provide feedback regarding students' performance
- After class: Students complete homework and learning reflection in an online learning environment

Theory-integrated practical training labs + online learning environment. Theory-integrated practical training labs integrate online learning environment with practicing labs (sometimes equip with virtual simulation systems) to meet students' different learning needs. This mode works best when requiring students to learn and apply the theories simultaneously. This mode also provides opportunities for deeper interactions between students and teachers, and fully develops students' abilities. When implementing this blended learning mode, teachers can consider the following steps:

- Before class: Teachers send online learning tasks
- Before class: Students learn declarative and procedural skills and complete pre-test in online learning environment
- Before class: Students watch demonstration videos in online learning environment and complete simulation operation using virtual simulation software
- In class: Teachers lecture on key points and procedures according to pre-test results
- In class: Teachers explain the key points and procedures according to simulation operation results
- In class: Students practice operations in groups in the virtual-real integration training lab and teachers provide necessary assistance
- In class: Teachers conclude the learning sessions and provide feedback to students' performance
- After class: Students complete homework and learning reflection in an online learning environment

Workplace + online learning environment. Workplace refers to the physical workplace with educational purposes, including on-campus and off-campus workplaces. Students are employees in the workplace and participate in related activities to obtain professional skills. They will conduct real tasks under the direct or indirect guidance of skilled employees. When implementing this blended learning mode, teachers can consider the following steps:

- Before class: Assign workplace tutors to students
- Before class: Create an online learning community

- In class: Students complete offline practice and conduct workplace tasks
- In class: Students discuss with workplace tutors
- After class: Workplace tutors conclude the learning sessions and provide feedback regarding students' performance
- After class: Students complete homework and learning reflection in online learning environment.

In summary, this chapter has demonstrated how to implement blended learning in three phases as well as provided implementation strategies when teaching in different modes, such as different learning objectives and learning environments. Information presented in this chapter could serve as references for researchers and practitioners to implement blended learning in their own contexts.

References

Akkoyunlu, B., & Soylu, M. Y. (2008). A study of student's perceptions in a blended learning environment based on different learning styles. Educational Technology & Society, 11(1), 183-193.

Anderson, L. W., Krathwohl, D., Airasian P, Cruikshank, K. A., Mayer, R. E., Pintrich, P., Raths, J. & Wittrock, M. C. (2001). A taxonomy for learning, teaching, and assessing: A revision of bloom's taxonomy of educational objectives. New York: Longman.

Ausburn, L. J. (2004). Course design elements most valued by adult learners in blended online education environments: An American perspective. Educational Media International, 41(4), 327-337.

Bandura, A. (1977). Self efficacy: Toward a unifying theory of behavioral change. Psychological Review, 84, 191-215.

Barnard, L., Lan, W. Y., To, Y. M., Paton, V. O., & Lai, S. L.. (2009). Measuring self-regulation in online and blended learning environments. Internet and Higher Education, 12(1), 1-6.

Battelle for Kids (2019). Framework for 21st Century Learning. Retrieved from: https://static.bat telleforkids.org/documents/p21/P21_Framework_Brief.pdf.

Bernard, R. M., Borokhovski, E., Schmid, R. F., Tamim, R. M., & Abrami, P. C. (2014). A meta-analysis of blended learning and technology use in higher education: From the general to the applied. Journal of Computing in Higher Education, 26, 87e122.

Binkley, M., Erstad, O., Herman, J., Raizen, S., Ripley, M., Miller-Ricci, M., & Rumble, M. (2012). Defining twenty-first century skills. In Griffin, P., McGaw, B., & Care, E. (Eds), Assessment and teaching of 21st century skills (pp. 17–66). Springer, Dordrecht. Retrieved from: https://doi.org/10.1007/978-94-007-2324-5_2

Bloom, B., Englehart, M. Furst, E., Hill, W., & Krathwohl, D. (1956). Taxonomy of educational objectives: The classification of educational goals. Handbook I: Cognitive domain. New York and Toronto: Longmans, Green.

Bonk, C. & Khoo, E. (2014). Adding some TEC-VARIETY: 100+ activities for motivating and retaining learners online. United States: Open World Books, 181-208.

Broadfoot, P., Daugherty, R., Gardner, J., Gipps, C., & Stobart, G. (1999). Assessment for Learning: beyond the black box, 1–12. Retrieved from: https://www.researchgate.net/publication/271 848977.

Camilli, G., & Shepard, L. A. (1994). Methods for identifying biased test items. Thousand Oaks: Sage Publications, 174.

Chen, M. L. (2009). Influence of grade level on perceptual learning style preferences and language learning strategies of Taiwanese English as a foreign language learners. Learning and Individual Differences, 19, 304-308.

Choules, A. P. (2007). The use of eLearning in medical education: A review of the current situation. Postgraduate Medical Journal, 83(978), 212-216.

Clark, R. E., Yates, K., Early, S., & Moulton, K. (2010). An analysis of the failure of electronic media and discovery-based learning: Evidence for the performance benefits of guided training methods. In K. H. Silber & W. R. Foshay (Eds.), Handbook of training and improving workplace performance (pp. 263-297). John Wiley & Sons, Ltd.

Conroy, D. E. (2001). Fear of failure: An exemplar for social development research in sport. Quest, (53), 165-183.

Cui, Y. (2004). Course objectives: The starting point of teaching should not be forgotten. People's Education (in Chinese), 16–18.

Dann, R. (2014). Assessment as learning: Blurring the boundaries of assessment and learning for theory, policy and practice. Assessment in Education: Principles, Policy & Practice, 31, 149-166.

Davies, A., Pantzopoulos, K., & Gray, K. (2011). Emphasizing assessment 'as' learning by assessing wiki writing assignments collaboratively and publicly online. Australasian Journal of Educational Technology, 27(5), 798-812.

Feng, X., Wu, Y., Cao, J., & Guo, L. (2021). Designing blended learning activities for the Internet Plus age. Distance Education in China (in Chinese), (06), 60-67.

Ferreira-Meyers, K. A. F. (2019). Book review: Guide to blended learning by Martha Cleveland-Innes with Dan Wilton. Journal of Learning for Development , 6(2), 187-190.

Gardner, H. (1999). Intelligence reframed: Multiple intelligences for the 21st century. New York: Basic Books, (Kindle), 41–66.

Grover, S., Pea, R., & Cooper, S. (2015). Designing for deeper learning in a blended computer science course for middle school students. Computer Science Education, 25(2), 199-237.

Guo, J. (2018). Flipped classroom and teaching innovation in higher education (in Chinese). China: Xiamen University Press, 190.

Han, X., Wang Y., Zhang, T., & Cheng, J. (2016). Translation, interpretation and research of "Preparing for the Digital University: A Review of the History and Current State of Distance, Blended, and Online Learning" (in Chinese). China: Tsinghua University Press, 325.

He, K., Lin, J., & Zhang, W. (2006). Instructional system design (in Chinese). China: Higher Education Press.

He, K., Zheng, Y., & Xie, Y. (2002). Instructional system design (in Chinese). China: Beijing Normal University Publishing Group.

Jin H. (2017). Theory and practice of online learning: A curriculum design perspective (in Chinese). China: Tsinghua University Press, 134.

Keller, J. M. (2008). First principles of motivation to learn and e3-learning. Distance education, 29(2), 175-185.

Kim, M. K., Kim, S. M., Khera, O., & Getman, J. (2014). The experience of three flipped classrooms in an urban university: An exploration of design principles. The Internet and Higher Education, 22, 37-50.

Li, B. D. (1991). Theory of instruction (in Chinese). China: People's Education Press.

Li, X., & Zhu, Q. (2019). A study of live broadcasting in blended teaching and learning in higher education--An action research in the University of Hong Kong. Modern Educational Technology (in Chinese), 2, 80-86.

Lim, D. H., & Morris, M. L. (2009). Learner and instructional factors influencing learning outcomes within a blended learning environment. Educational Technology & Society, 12(4), 282–293.

Lo, C. K., Lie, C. W., & Hew, K. F. (2018). Applying "First Principles of Instruction" as a design theory of the flipped classroom: Findings from a collective study of four secondary school subjects. Computers & Education, 118, 150-165.

Long, H. B. (1989). Contradictory expectations? Achievement and satisfaction in adult learning. Journal of Continuing Higher Education, 33(3), 10-12.

Ma, J., Han, X., Yang, J., & Cheng, J. (2015). Examining the necessary condition for engagement in an online learning environment based on learning analytics approach: The role of the instructor. The Internet and Higher Education, 24, 26-34.

Ma, L., & Lee, C. S. (2021). Evaluating the effectiveness of blended learning using the arcs model. Journal of Computer Assisted Learning, 37, 1397-1408.

Maccoby, E., & Jacklin, C.(1974). The psychology of sex differences. Redwood: Stanford University Press.

Mayer, R. E. (2002). A taxonomy for computer-based assessment of problem solving. Computers in Human Behavior, 18(6), 623-632.

Ministry of Education of the People's Republic of China. (2020, June 24). The Ministry of Education issued the Norms for Digital Campus for Vocational Colleges (in Chinese). Retrieved from: http://www.moe.gov.cn/srcsite/A07/zcs_zhgg/202007/t20200702_469886.html.

Musallam, R. (2013). Cycles of Learning. Explore-flip-apply: Introduction and example. Retrieved from: https://www.cyclesoflearning.com/home/apedagogy-first-approach-to-the-flipped-classroom.

Neumeier, P. (2005). A closer look at blended learning--parameters for designing a blended learning environment for language teaching and learning. Recall, 17(02), 163-178.

Oxford, R. L. (2003). Language learning styles and strategies: An overview. In Proceedings of the GALA (Generative Approaches to Language Acquisition) Conference, 1–25.

Padilla- Meléndez, A., Del Aguila-Obra, A. R., & Garrido-Moreno, A. (2013). Perceived playfulness, gender differences and technology acceptance model in a blended learning scenario. Computers & Education, 63, 306-317.

Reid, J. (1984). Perceptual learning style preference questionnaire. In J. Reid (Ed.), Learning styles in the ESL/EFL classroom. Boston, pp. 202–204, MA: Heinle & Heinle Publishers.

Rodríguez-Ariza, P. L. (2011). Blended learning in higher education: Students' perceptions and their relation to outcomes. Computers & Education, 56, 818-826.

Sams, A., & Bergman, J. (2013). Flip your students learning. Educational Leadership, 6, 16-20.

Shi, Q. (2015). What is the learning situation of college students? China Higher Education (in Chinese), 68–70.

Shih, R. C. (2011). Can Web 2.0 technology assist college students in learning English writing? Integrating Facebook and peer assessment with blended learning. Australasian Journal of Educational Technology, 27(5), 829–845.

Smaldino, S. E., Lowther, D. L., & Mims, C. (2005) Instructional technology and media for learning (12th edition). United States: Pearson Education, Inc.

Song, Y., & Kapur, M. (2017). How to flip the classroom-productive failure or traditional flipped classroom pedagogical design? Educational Technology & Society, 1, 292-305.

Stein, J. & Graham, C. R. (2014). Essentials for blended learning: A standards-based guide. New York: Taylor & Francis, 13.

Talbert, R. (2011). Inverting the linear algebra classroom. Retrieved from: http://prezi.com/dz0rbkpy6tam/inverting-the-linear-algebra-classroom.

Thai, N., Wever, B. D., & Valcke, M.. (2017). The impact of a flipped classroom design on learning performance in higher education : Looking for the best 'blend' of lectures and guiding questions with feedback. Computers & Education, 107, 113-126.

UNESCO. (2002). Forum on the impact of open courseware for higher education in developing countries. Retrieved from: http://unesdoc.unesco.org/images/0012/001285/128515e.pdf.

Valiathan, P. (2002). Blended learning models. Retrieved from: https://www.purnima-valiathan.com/wp-content/uploads/2015/09/Blended-Learning-Models-2002-ASTD.pdf.

Vo, H. M., Zhu, C., & Diep, N. A. (2017). The effect of blended learning on student performance at course-level in higher education: A meta-analysis. Studies In Educational Evaluation, 53, 17-28.

Woltering, V., Herrler, A., Spitzer, K., & Spreckelsen, C. (2009). Blended learning positively affects students' satisfaction and the role of the tutor in the problem-based learning process: Results of a mixed-method evaluation. Advances in Health Sciences Education, 14, 725-738.

Wu, B. L. (2010). Impact of self-regulated learning on acquisition efficiency in collegiate physical culture: An experimental study (in Chinese). Doctoral dissertation, East China Normal University.

Xu, Y., & Xu, D. (2012). Research on the situation and countermeasures of higher vocational students' learning involvement. Journal of Vocational Education (in Chinese), 30, 77-81.

Zhang, L. & Jiao, J. (2015). Research on student perception and attitude of e-schoolbag. Open Education Research (in Chinese), 21(02), 98-105.

Chapter 3
Development of Academic Programs in the Digital Age: Practice from China

Shusheng Shen, Hao Yang, and Qian Zhou

Abstract One of the main purposes of higher education is to prepare students to adapt to the needs of a changing society. On the basis of discussing the function of academic programs and the interdisciplinary revolution in the digital age, this chapter summarizes the Chinese higher education system from three main dimensions: the catalog of disciplines, the framework of "four new" disciplines and the action plan of vocational education. In response to the new requirements of academic curriculum reform in the digital age, this paper describes the concrete measures taken by China's academic program reform to cultivate compound talents and strengthen the collaboration of universities. This paper expounds the future trends in the development of higher education programs, such as blended teaching, interdisciplinary talent training, diversification, information literacy training, university cooperation, new systems and new methods of project evaluation, and puts forward operational strategies for reconstructing academic programs.

One of the primary purposes of higher education is to prepare students to meet the demands of an ever-changing society. This means not only equipping them with tangible skills that are in high demand in today's industries, but also immersing them in a learning culture that reflects the values and processes of the day—ways of thinking and seeing the world that, when placed in a societal context, lead to great personal and professional enrichment. As society changes, university academic programs must be continually revised to reflect current learning needs. The Internet has had a profound impact on social and economic patterns, creating new demands that must be considered in the development of academic programs. As demand shifts away from well-defined specialties and toward skills that cannot be easily replaced

S. Shen (✉)
School of Education Science, Nanjing Normal University, Nanjing, China
e-mail: ssshen_nj@163.com

H. Yang
School of Education at the State University of New York at Oswego, New York, USA

Q. Zhou
Institute of Education, Tsinghua University, Beijing, China

© The Author(s) 2024   125
M. Li et al. (eds.), *Handbook of Educational Reform Through Blended Learning*,
https://doi.org/10.1007/978-981-99-6269-3_3

by automation, these programs could use a thoughtful refresh. Other chapters in this handbook describe how the mediums through which education is delivered are becoming a mix of physical and digital; this chapter seeks to illustrate how the content of academic programs themselves should change in a similar way.

While the impact of the Internet is undoubtedly global, higher education is generally administered independently by each nation-state in accordance with its own history, culture, and resources. This has led to different approaches to developing academic programs suitable for the digital age. This chapter will highlight China's recent approaches to developing academic programs in the digital age. We chose China because the country has clearly articulated its plans for academic program reform, because it is relatively far along in the reform process, and because of the authors' area of expertise. While there is no one-size-fits-all strategy for higher education, we hope that this deep dive into China's program development will prove useful to the global community.

The first section of this chapter provides an overview of the Chinese higher education system and defines key terms. The second section will describe the new requirements for academic program reform in the digital age and how China has chosen to implement such reform. The third section will provide further reflections on China's implementation and explore generalizable strategies for systematically rebuilding academic programs. We hope that this chapter will serve as a reference for university leaders, organizers, and researchers as they develop their academic programs in the digital age.

3.1 Key Definitions and Overview of the Chinese Higher Education System

In this section, we will provide a brief overview of the Chinese higher education system, including recent policy initiatives like the "Four New" construct for universities and the "Vocational Education Action Plan" for vocational institutions. While the granular details of Chinese national education policy may not be directly applicable to the development of other academic programs worldwide, we hope the content here conveys some focus areas to consider prioritizing and provides the necessary context for understanding the academic program reforms described in the next section.

3.1.1 The Role of the Academic Program

While the general concept of an academic program has been alluded to above, we take some space here to elaborate on what such programs consist of. An academic program is the combination of courses and related requirements that a student must complete in order to receive the higher education degree they are pursuing. This can include not only curriculum systems, but also evaluation standards, capstone projects, work experiences, regulations, and the management personnel and faculty members involved with the student's path through higher education. From a societal standpoint, academic programs exist to cultivate qualified graduates that can adapt to social needs and are equipped to engage in a specific profession after graduation. Historically, such programs have cultivated specialized talents that address our modern society's wide spectrum of needs—they help cultivate the next generation of electricians, filmmakers, chemists, politicians, etc. Increasingly, such programs emphasize interdisciplinary and innovative thinking over pure specialization, as those are traits expected of the next generation of professionals.

The "development of academic programs" is an umbrella term we use to describe the reforming and rebuilding of academic programs in response to societal changes brought on by factors like scientific discoveries, the adoption of new technologies, and evolving cultural norms. Developing academic programs is both a science and an art—a good program should incorporate insights from empirical research, like that described in this chapter, while still being tailored to the unique needs of the community of learners that it serves. Much of the design and implementation of academic programs need to actively adapt to changes in national strategy, target the frontiers of professional development, and align with the general trend of global higher education development.

3.1.2 Interdisciplinary Revolution in the Digital Age

In most current societies, digital technologies have become a ubiquitous factor in almost everyone's lives. The combination of modern science and technology with evolving professional fields has brought significant changes to traditional concepts of academic programs and disciplines, strengthening the interaction between disciplines. Reconstructing new disciplinary relationships from our old ways has become an important proposition in current education reform at universities. Historically, academic programs have been divided by discipline, with a heavy emphasis on the student developing specialized skills for a particular industry. We argue that the efficiency brought on by automation-related technologies has shifted the set of skills in high demand from more specialized industry expertise to more cross-disciplinary expertise. This may not apply in every case, but the advantages of emphasizing more "blended" disciplines in academic programs appear compelling.

In other chapters, we discussed the term "blended learning" in reference to the mediums of education—combining physical and virtual learning experiences into a distinctly hybrid one. Here, we introduce the idea of blending academic programs. This blending refers not to the medium, but to the subject matter being taught and learned. For example, instead of separate course paths for architecture and urban planning, a blending academic program might include more pathways that incorporate both fields or individual courses that address the intersection between the two. Academic programs can include both blended learning and blended subjects; in fact, we argue that both approaches should be employed when designing the higher education model of the future.

3.1.3 Overview of the Chinese Higher Education System

To provide some context, we will provide a brief overview of the Chinese higher education system here—including some recent national objectives—before discussing the implementations of academic program reform the country in the digital age has tried in the next section.

The current higher education model in China is composed of institutions of various types and levels, including universities and vocational colleges. These universities and colleges undertake the mission of cultivating professional talents—students attend these institutions to complete their studies in a specific academic program. These academic programs were constructed with several considerations in mind, including the requirements of division of labor in society, changing employment trends, and achieving some level of well-roundedness within each degree. After participating in their academic program, individuals are ideally able to competently enter a relevant profession and continue to meet the requirements of that profession well into the future.

At the turn of the century, China began exploring its approach to higher education in earnest. "The construction of a powerful country in higher education" has been the theme of the International Forum on Higher Education hosted by the China Higher Education Association for four consecutive years since 2009. In 2015, the "*Overall Scheme to Promote the Construction of World-class Universities and Disciplines*" issued by the State Council of China proposed that by the middle of the twenty-first century, the number and strength of China's world-class universities and disciplines should be at the forefront of the world. This scheme provides a clear timetable for the Chinese strategy of "constructing a powerful country in higher education" and illustrates the high priority the nation is placing on higher education reform.

The Ministry of Education of the People's Republic of China issued "Opinions of the Ministry of Education on Accelerating the Construction of High-level Undergraduate Education and Comprehensively Improving the Ability to Cultivate Talents" on September 17, 2018. The opinions proposed that to implement the "*Double Ten-Thousand Plan*" for the construction of world-class disciplines, academic programs are the basis of talent cultivation as well as the pillars of the construction of world-class undergraduate education and top talent cultivation. To build these world-class disciplines that meet society's emerging needs, the Ministry of Education will construct 10,000 national world-class academic programs and 10,000 provincial ones to lead and support high-level undergraduate education".

Academic Program Specialty Catalogs

In the talent cultivation system of its higher education model, China has established a series of catalogs for academic programs according to the country's social needs and continuously revises these catalogs as needed. The catalogs serve to guide different colleges and universities in designing programs that suit both their institution and the broader educational development goals of the nation. For example, undergraduate universities set up their academic programs based on the Undergraduate Specialty Catalogue of Higher Education issued by the national government, which includes fields of academic study, academic programs, and specialties. The 2020 edition of this catalog has a total of 12 disciplines: philosophy, economics, law, education, literature, history, science, engineering, agriculture, medicine, management, and art. Under each disciplinary category, there are special categories, and under those are academic programs. Overall, the edition listed 93 specialty categories and 703 academic programs. Vocational colleges set up their academic programs based on the Specialties Catalogue of Vocational Education, which divides academic programs into three levels: program, major, and specialized direction. The institutions for cultivating postgraduates (including graduate and doctoral students) set up their academic programs according to the Training and Degree-Granting Academic Catalog, which contains disciplinary categories, first-tier disciplines, and second-tier disciplines. Together, these catalogs guide Chinese institutions of higher education, leading to a national system with a fairly high level of standardization. Within each university, the more granular facets of academic program development are delegated to sub-organizations like colleges, departments, or research institutions.

Disciplines of Focus—the "Four New" Framework

On top of understanding the catalog system of academic programs in China, it's helpful to be familiar with the "Four New" framework that describes the nation's disciplines of focus in the current era. On October 17, 2018, the Ministry of Education of China decided to implement the "Six Excellence and One Top-notch" 2.0 Plan, which aims to improve the ability of universities to serve economic and social development by targeting seven specific fields. The plan includes "2.0 plans" for excellent education and training in the fields of engineering, medicine, agriculture and forestry, teaching, law, journalism, and fundamental disciplines—the last four are sometimes grouped together and referred to as the "new liberal arts". Thus, this series of 2.0 plans can be broken down using the "Four New" construct, with the four fields being engineering, medicine, agriculture, and liberal arts. The relevant administrators of the Ministry of Education view engineering as the country's critical power, medicine as the country's health, agricultural science as the country's growth force, and liberal arts as the country's soft power (Wu 2020). Thus, the goal of building "a powerful country in higher education" will be realized through these Four New constructs. Next, we will briefly introduce each of the Four New.

The construct of "new engineering" is in a "pioneer" position in the Four New strategy. Relevant universities in China jointly issued Beijing guidelines for new engineering principles, emphasizing the need to explore "new opportunities brought by the new industrial revolution, the new needs of the country, and the new development of engineering education". Additionally, the guidelines also proposed constructing a new engineering education system, attaching importance to craftsmanship, and implementing the international concept of certification for engineering education.

In addition, the guidelines urged upgrading and reforming existing engineering academic programs and the deployment of emerging engineering programs—paying attention to both cutting-edge and less popular specialties. Universities are encouraged to explore new practice patterns for university-enterprise alliances and interdisciplinary platforms and promote the internationalization of engineering education. In alignment with the Belt and Road Initiative, China looks to build a strategic partnership of national engineering universities along the route and jointly build an engineering education community that will usher in a new round of scientific, technological, and industrial transformation.

The second of the Four New is medicine. China's new medical education aims to serve the modern health care and improve the quality of health care. Medical education is an important foundation for health care and essential to a powerful and healthy country. The construction of new medical education needs to emphasize the integration of science and industry. The outbreak of COVID-19 can be regarded as the "trigger" that is driving structural changes in the healthcare industry, and it is also a "challenge" to the current "habituation" of the healthcare industry. Medical education plays two important roles in the national strategy and structural system. The first is that it serves the construction of a "Healthy China" and the second is that it drives the innovation of medical science and technology. New medical education has to adapt to the multidisciplinary trend of medicine and set up emerging specialties like intelligent medicine, translational medicine, and precision medicine that are conducive to the cultivation of interdisciplinary talents. It also needs to strengthen the cultivation of medical professionals that have expertise in the whole life cycle and the holistic process of health. Lastly, it is also necessary to coordinate between the decisive forces of the market and government regulation to build dynamic and scientific control mechanisms for the professional coordination of medical talent.

As for the construction of "emerging agricultural education", Chinese agriculture-related universities and agricultural experts put forth in the "Anji Consensus" that China's emerging agricultural education has four development tasks: winning the battle against poverty, implementing a rural revitalization strategy, promoting the construction of ecological civilization, and building a beautiful and happy China". To strengthen the construction of new agriculture, new countryside, new farmers, and new ecology, the country must develop emerging agricultural education. The missions of emerging agricultural education can be encompassed by the following four aspects. First, it aims to transform and upgrade the agricultural, industrial, production, and management systems and improve education on these systems. Second, it focuses on product development and innovation management as it relates to the new countryside. Third, it attaches importance to cultivating qualified new farmers who have mastered modern technology and knowledge to become the creators and defenders of the new countryside. Fourth, emerging agricultural education contributes to constructing the governance system of water, forest, field, lake, and grass with a notion of "lucid waters and lush mountains being invaluable assets". Beijing guidelines further clarified the main areas of emerging agricultural education construction, emphasizing the innovation of concepts and the optimization and reform of academic programs. These guidelines are promoting significant changes in the structure of higher agricultural and forestry education in China, including the establishment of a three-level accreditation system, and clarified standards for related academic programs.

The construct of "new liberal arts" is necessary for informing China's disciplinary system, academic system, and discourse system. The new liberal arts pay attention not only to excellent traditional culture, but also to the integration and development of both Chinese and foreign cultures, thus contributing to China's wisdom, solutions, and strength as it helps build humanity's collective global future. It is also necessary to promote the integration of philosophy and social sciences with new scientific, technological, and industrial transformations. The nation's leaders hope that this holistic approach to philosophy and social science in the new digital will foster a new and exciting Chinese liberal arts culture that becomes highly respected in the world.

In the construction of this "Four New", Chinese universities advocate exploring information technology tools in the development of teaching methods. With the help of "Internet + " (Internet integration into traditional industries), big data, and artificial intelligence, universities incorporate new technologies into the development of not only engineering education, but medical, agricultural, and liberal arts education as well. As we have seen in other chapters of this handbook, universities have been initiating a student-centered teaching reconstruction by deeply integrating online and offline teaching into a blended hybrid experience. In the following section, we will highlight some ways that Chinese institutions of higher education have also been developing academic programs within the Four New framework.

Vocational Education Action Plan

Running parallel to the Four New framework is China's efforts to reform its vocational higher education offerings. In 2020, China's Ministry of Education and other departments jointly promulgated the "Vocational Education Action Plan for Enhancing Quality and Cultivating Excellence (2020—2023)", which designed 10 tasks and 27 measures for the development of vocational education. These objectives include fostering virtue through education, promoting and coordinating the development of vocational education, improving the institutional system that serves lifelong learning for all, deepening industry-education integration and university-enterprise cooperation in vocational education, and improving the examination and enrollment systems in vocational education. The action plan also proposed some specific actions. For example, it suggested that the governance of vocational education should be improved, and the reform of "three educational aspects" (i.e., the quality of teachers, learning materials, and pedagogy) must be implemented. Additionally, it also incorporated points about international cooperation and the improvement of innovative abilities.

Notably, the Vocational Education Action Plan said that institutions should "actively adapt to the requirements of the scientific and technological revolution and industrial revolution, upgrade traditional academic programs with 'information technology+ ', and develop merged academic programs derived from the digital economy promptly. Vocational schools are encouraged to reform the model of talent cultivation through modern information technology to meet the diverse learning needs of students. It also urges to build a new form of education that is based on 'Internet +' and 'Intelligence +' and promote the reform and innovation of education and teaching".

In addition to the Vocational Education Action Plan, recent revisions to the vocational education specialties catalog also reflect trends in the nation's approach to vocational education. In 2021, the Ministry of Education of China conducted a comprehensive revision of the specialties catalog and issued the "Specialties Catalogue of Vocational Education (2021)" which mirrors the specialties catalog for undergraduate programs at universities in structure. The catalog is broken down into disciplines, specialty categories within disciplines, and academic programs within specialty categories. It constructed academic programs at different levels, including secondary vocational education, higher vocational education, and undergraduate higher vocational education, with a total of 19 disciplinary categories, 97 specialty categories, and 1349 academic programs. Among the academic programs, there are 358 specialties for secondary vocational education, 744 for higher vocational education, and 247 for undergraduate higher vocational education. The construction and adjustment of these vocational academic programs focused on connecting industries and occupations, prioritizing innovation to keep pace with the times, and promoting industry-education integration. It also sought to incorporate principles of the new economy, new technology, new business models, and new occupations.

Examining the adjustments to the specialties catalog of vocational education generally reveals the following focus areas:

(1) Modern service industry: supply chain operations, intelligent logistics, digital design, intelligent manufacturing, infant care, smart health care, modern housekeeping, winter sports, cave maintenance, temple protection, mitigation of occupational hazards, etc.

(2) Construction infrastructure: 5G mobile communication, industrial internet, intelligent transportation, intelligent water conservancy, hydropower engineering, distributed generation and intelligent microgrid technology, high-speed railway trains, new energy vehicles, etc.

(3) Industrial digitization and information security: big data, cloud computing, artificial intelligence, embedded technology, integrated circuits, information security technology, cryptography, bio-information, etc.

(4) Rural revitalization and food security: modern agricultural economics, new rural economic organization, leisure agricultural business, forage production, intelligent livestock breeding, grain storage, transportation, and quality safety,

(5) Sustainability and environmental protection: green and low-carbon technology, new energy material application, ecological preservation, intelligent monitoring and protection of water environments, ecological environment restoration, marine engineering, etc.

(6) National governance emergency management: emergency rescue technology, intelligent security monitoring, digital security technology, smart community management, etc.

(7) Emerging businesses: cultural tourism, prefabricated buildings, blockchain engineering, customized travel management and services, guesthouse operations, e-commerce, all-media advertising and marketing, webcasting, etc.

 **A Case Study 3.1**

Certificate Program of Worldwide Blended Classroom for Logic

In January 2021, the Logic Center of the School of Humanities of Tsinghua University in China released the "English-only Certificate Program of Worldwide Blended Classroom for Logic", which consists of four logic courses jointly taught by a group of four professors from the School of Humanities of Tsinghua University, including "Logic, Language and Philosophy", "Modal Logic and Its Application", "Basic Theory of Logic" and "Logic, Computation, and Games". This program is the first global blended classroom certificate program launched by Tsinghua University, whose goal is to target high-quality international students and attract more students to pay attention to Tsinghua Logic and Tsinghua Humanities, starting from East Asia and Southeast Asia. All courses are taught in English, with Logic as the core, including such basic disciplines as Philosophy, Mathematics, Linguistics, Computer Science, and Cognitive Science. It not only cultivates students' basic thinking abilities but also fosters their broad interdisciplinary horizons and innovative spirits. This certificate program is not only open to students at Tsinghua University but also to students from universities in the Global MOOC Alliance, such as St. Petersburg University in Russia, Nanyang Technological University in Singapore, and other world-class universities. Each course in the program will employ a blended teaching method to introduce high-quality college students at home and abroad into Tsinghua University classrooms through online teaching, which builds a global classroom and enhances students' international communication and understanding. Students can participate in courses through synchronized or asynchronized online learning. After completing all four courses and passing the examination, they can obtain the project certificate. Tsinghua University is expecting to launch a number of certificate programs for the global blended classroom and MOOC certificate programs. By sharing high-quality educational resources and strengthening international exchanges and cooperation, Tsinghua University will respond to global challenges with an open mind and promote higher education innovation.

3.2   China's Academic Program Reform in the Digital Age

The development of high-quality academic programs is not only the foundation of survival for higher education institutions but also part of their responsibility and mission in the digital age. After entering the information age, nuanced academic programs have become increasingly abundant, and more importance is attached to academic program construction, with specialties becoming more open and blended than before. This section aims to explore these changes to academic program reform in the context of the Chinese higher education system and national objectives described in the previous section, with particular attention paid to how programs are shifting from rigid specialties to inter-disciplines.

3.2.1   From Specialist to Interdisciplinary Talents

In the information age, the attributes of academic programs are changing. In the past, programs aimed to cultivate specialist talents, focusing on developing the unique abilities and skills associated with specific professional fields. But now, they attach more importance to the comprehensive abilities that will be increasingly prevalent in future society. Professional and cultural trends suggest that more and more attention should be paid to the complementarity between different professionals and the position of professional talents in the entire talent system. In the digital age, there is far more cross-pollination and communication between specialties and the boundaries of specialties are being expanded and continuously enriched. Cooperation between industrial sectors, enterprises, and foreign institutions is also far more common than before and often requires different skill sets than what previous generations are familiar with. To feed this shift, Chinese higher education institutions have taken a number of measures. They are taking full advantage of the Internet in breaking the boundaries between different disciplines and academic programs, in conjunction with the implementation of blended learning mediums that seek to combine the best of in-person and digital platforms and pedagogies. Students are also being encouraged to choose cross-major courses and work on cross-major and cross-school learning and research teams to improve their overall professional competence.

In addition to meeting society's demand for more cross-disciplinary talent, these new cross-discipline approach also alleviates some of the growing pains associated with rapid and radical academic program reform. A problem faced by many universities in practice is that they are often confronted with the inadequacy of teaching resources, teachers, and experimental facilities when constructing new academic programs. Another prominent problem is that many newly constructed programs have no special features. The development of academic programs will be subject to many constraints if it relies solely on the strengths of different specialties and pure addition rather than a combination. Therefore, it is necessary for talent cultivation and disciplinary development to establish an open, collaborative, and shared training path for modern professional talents. The practice of incorporating cross-disciplines into academic paths ought to help not only students but program architects and administrators as they adapt their university's resources to meet this new challenge in a timely manner.

Adjusting Academic Program Structure

The combination of modern and traditional technologies in our current moment has given birth to many emerging industries and sectors. The Ministry of Education of China pays much attention to these shifting winds and seeks to adjust program categories and academic programs options accordingly, removing outdated programs and adding new programs. In 2017, the Chinese government issued the "Opinions on Deepening the Reform of the Education System and Mechanism" (No. 46 [2017] of the General Office of the State Council), proposing to "establish and improve a dynamic adjustment mechanism for disciplines and academic programs". Since then, the Chinese system has been looking to dynamically adjust its overall academic program offerings accordingly. For example, the Ministry of Education of China listed 37 new, emerging academic programs in the "Undergraduate Specialty Catalogue of Higher Institutions" in 2021. That year, universities added 2,046 recorded academic programs that had already existed in the original specialty catalog and 177 newly approved programs that had not been recorded in the original specialty catalog. Ninety-three academic programs were adjusted for degree-granting categories or years of study, and 518 majors were canceled.

When we look at what programs are being added, we see that the country is paying more and more attention to the cultivation of specialized talents in the field of modern science and technology and the integration of science and technology with new academic programs is a top priority. Among the 37 emerging programs, 14 have been added to the engineering category. The top five programs are artificial intelligence, intelligent manufacturing engineering, data science and big data technology, big data management and application, and robotics engineering. Furthermore, more than 130 higher education institutions have set up artificial intelligence programs as well as other emerging interdisciplinary programs that incorporate novel science and technology. On the other hand, some universities have gradually reduced or canceled academic programs such as public affairs management, information management, and information systems. However, we also see from 2020 additions to the catalog that new programs from other disciplines are also being included. That year, the specialty category with the largest number of newly-added academic programs was foreign language and literature, with a total of 40 new programs, accounting for 21.2% of the total number of academic programs. New programs were also added in public security, automation, traditional Chinese medicine, management science and engineering, public management, music, and dance. This suggests a desire to expand the breadth of offerings available to students while retaining a focus on the "Four New" core disciplines of engineering, medicine, agriculture, and liberal arts.

Structural adjustments to academic program offerings should follow a common understanding of exactly what the word "new" means. First, it is necessary to establish a new type of thinking pattern for academic program construction that avoids falling into our previous understanding of existing programs and focuses on the transformation and upgrading of traditional specialties. Second, "new" means breaking old thinking patterns to understand the technological revolution and its impact on the industry. Third, "new" means emphasizing the connection between different programs, starting with the relationship between specialty categories and between different programs—looking at these intersections optimizes the specialty setting, reduces narrowness, and enhances integration.

As mentioned in previous chapters, the blended teaching model—that is, the practice of combining physical and digital teaching mediums—has become an important form of education and teaching in the digital age. A similar "blended" thinking pattern can and should be adopted in the restructuring of specialties. While the general trend is towards cross-disciplines, the need for specialized talents in niche industries must be considered and preserved during program restructuring. The goal is not to erase narrow expertise entirely, but to infuse interdisciplinary education into every student's academic programming so that they have a broader set of skills to apply to their future profession(s) of choice, however, niche those careers may be.

Other considerations when adjusting the overall systematic structure of academic programs are the demands of the times, the demands of current industries, feasibility, specialty coverage and continuity, school conditions, faculty member input, recent innovations, and the country's development strategies. Incorporating all these variables into broad academic program structure changes can help reduce short-sightedness and arbitrary decisions throughout the reform process.

Establishing Quality Standards of Academic Programs

In addition to having the right composition of academic program offerings, it is crucial to create systems that promote and evaluate the quality standards of such programs. Different countries have varying degrees of centralization and standardization when it comes to this objective. For example, in the United States, private institutions of higher education have much autonomy over dictating how these quality standards are drawn and assessed; their model is on the decentralized end of the spectrum. In China, the system is more centralized, with more guidelines and requirements provided by national government agencies. Here, we continue our focus on the Chinese system and the quality standards for academic programs established there.

China's reasoning behind having uniform quality standards has much to do with trying to even out extreme disparities in the quality of education at different individual institutions. Suppose the development goals of academic programs and disciplines are designed and implemented solely by each university's own program development management groups. It is argued that such a system could be too susceptible to restrictions stemming from each institution's operational conditions. Therefore, to mitigate this factor, it is common practice in modern Chinese academic program development for the Ministry of Education to establish guidelines for program construction and conduct regular assessments and evaluations of adherence to these guidelines through specialized audit groups.

In 2013, the Ministry of Education of China launched the development of "National Standards for the Teaching Quality of Undergraduate Specialties in Higher

Education Institutions", which covers 92 undergraduate specialty categories and 587 undergraduate academic programs in the catalog of undergraduate specialties in higher education institutions. In the development of academic program standards, it adhered to the values of unity and change, foundation and excellence, and qualitative and quantitative research. The document highlights the bottom line of running sustainable academic programs and encouraging innovation in program construction. In 2018, China officially released quality standards of specialties, which stipulate basic principles for the running of specific academic programs. These standards include specialty scope, training objectives, talent specifications, faculty members, teaching conditions, quality assurance, and assessment. The Ministry of Education hoped that these standards would establish uniform "rules" for universities, while still providing some "room" for them to engage in free development.

Accreditations and certifications are a large part of how the quality standards of academic programs are assessed and described. As part of establishing standardized accreditations, the Ministry of Education has launched various professional certifications in industries like engineering, medicine, and teaching. For example, China's engineering education certification began in 2006. By the end of 2019, 1,353 academic programs in 241 colleges and universities in China had obtained the engineering education certification, which includes 21 engineering disciplines. In 2008, the Ministry of Education and the former Ministry of Health jointly promulgated the "Standards of Undergraduate Medical Education—Clinical Medicine (Trial)" and established the Working Committee for the Accreditation of Medical Education or MOE. By the end of 2019, the Working Committee had completed on-site inspections of the accreditation of 106 medical education institutions, accounting for 76.3% of all accredited institutions. In October 2017, the Ministry of Education officially issued the "Implementation Measures of Teachers' Professional Accreditation in Colleges and Universities (Interim)", which included implementation methods and a three-level tier of certification standards for preschool education, primary education, and secondary education. Professional accreditation standards for vocational and technical normal education and special education were issued in October 2019. By the end of 2019, more than 4,000 academic programs for higher normal education in China have undergone first-level monitoring, and there are 188 programs with second-level accreditation. Moreover, 26 pre-pilot specialties have been re-evaluated according to second-level accreditation standards, and 6 normal programs have received third-level certification.

Since 2015, the Ministry of Education of China has also advocated exploring how to establish a novel credit recognition mechanism—one that emphasizes the capacity of using online curriculum resources to achieve credit recognition while still adhering to robust quality standards. Researchers have also begun to investigate how to optimize intercollegiate credit recognition while following quality standards. Some universities have established credit recognition mechanisms for courses from national, high-quality resource platforms. For example, the China University of Geosciences encourages students to take elective courses through course platforms like Gaoxiaobang, Zhihuishu, CNMOOC, and Chaoxing Erya Platform. The credits in these online platforms can be recognized after the university provides confirmation. Tianjin Medical University recognizes the credits of the courses offered by the Coursera online courses and by 985 colleges in the Ai Course Network.

In a related example, China Pharmaceutical University proposed strengthening its resource construction through the establishment of university-level alliances, online platforms, and university-enterprise cooperation. To do this, the university has been relying on support from government policy, industry institutions, and news media. Critically, the success of the initiative and others like it depends on improvements to the mechanisms of credit and certificate attainment for MOOC-based academic programs. As academic programs become increasingly blended in both teaching medium and discipline, we expect that credit recognition mechanisms will become increasingly standardized, more collaborative across institutions, and reflect students' interdisciplinary expertise rather than the narrow expertise of traditional accreditations.

At present, the Ministry of Education of China maintains an Education Steering Committee for Academic Program to carry out theoretical and practical research on best practices in undergraduate professional education. The committee provides specific guidance on academic program construction, teaching material construction, curriculum construction, teaching laboratory construction, and teaching reform. It also formulates specialty norms and education quality standards and guides undergraduate education evaluation. Moreover, it strengthens and guides teachers' training and organizes professional academic seminars for teachers to learn from information exchanges and international communications. The guidance provided by the committee has become more flexible, adapting along with the rest of the industry. Annual face-to-face meetings gradually became a combination of online and offline meetings that take place more regularly. In this way, the scope and benefits of this guidance have become wider, as there is more participation from all players involved in the development of academic programs. Additionally, students themselves have had more opportunities to provide their input and actively participate in the discussions surrounding academic program reform.

Composition of Course Credits Within Academic Programs

So far, we have discussed the macro-level structure and quality standards China is trying to achieve with its modern academic program development. Here, we describe trends in how course credits are distributed within an academic program. To meet the graduation requirements for a certain academic program, the enrolled student needs to obtain certain credits. Recently, higher education institutions have been rethinking this credit composition to allow for more cross-discipline study in students' course selection. Previously, credit requirements at Chinese institutions included three main buckets: "public courses", "professional basic courses", and "professional essential courses". This has gradually shifted to a composition of "public platform courses", "quality development courses", "basic and core courses", and "independent development courses". The net effect of this shift is that the proportion of credits allocated for independent development courses has increased.

This trend has been aided by the construction and development of online teaching resources, which has allowed the conditions for cross-discipline and cross-university courses to become more mature. Research shows that since 2012, the forms of credit recognition have become more diversified after China carried out the construction of MOOC resources. Some universities have tried recognizing credits of MOOC platform courses that are no longer limited to the courses offered at their own institution. Some universities have also begun to recognize credits from their ally universities or other universities in the area. As a result of this maturation of technology-enabled cross-university and cross-discipline diffusion, credit recognition from some universities has become more flexible. Credit composition now reflects the trend of "quality over quantity", emphasizing the formation of students' core competence and intellectual exploration over pure technical skill.

This trend in credit composition has extended to more profession-based institutions of higher learning as well. In the past decade, Chinese universities have paid attention to their professional education programs and adjusted the proportion of professional credits in their programs. For example, Tsinghua University and the China University of Mining and Technology historically have very different credit compositions in their respective academic programs. As a top comprehensive university, Tsinghua University has a higher proportion of credits in cultural courses and basic knowledge courses while China University of Mining and Technology's namesake disciplines have aligned with a higher proportion of credits in engineering technology courses, professional knowledge courses, and independent development courses. However, with the development of online and blended educational resources like MOOCs, some scholars suggest that universities are now able to diversify and enrich course composition in profession-based academic programs too. Instead of being limited by faculty members, universities can jump out of their habitual and stereotyped ways of thinking to design profession-based academic programs that meet the holistic needs of their high-quality talents. For example, it may be possible for the China University of Mining and Technology to start offering its students more cultural and social science courses by leveraging new technologies and collaborative practices with other institutions. Diversifying credit composition at these professional education institutions is a key aspect of integrated cross-disciplines into the lifeblood of higher education.

Adjusting Teaching and Learning Methods

As already mentioned, new pedagogies that leverage modern technology have contributed greatly to the proliferation of academic program reform that promotes cross-disciplines. These new platforms, tools, and models come with new learning methods that fundamentally change the way education is conducted. Course models like MOOC require a radical departure from traditional in-person, lecture, and assessment-based college courses. The impacts of these new learning methods are discussed throughout this handbook, but here we hone in on how they have affected the development of China's academic programs.

At the beginning of the century, the Massachusetts Institute of Technology (MIT) initiated the trend toward more collaborative and online education through its Open Course Ware Movement (MIT OCW-Open Course Ware), which opened its curriculum resources to countries around the world. Since then, countries around the world latched onto this principle of constructing open educational resources. The first attempt at online course development in China was organized by Nanjing Normal University in 2001. However, due to the limitations of technology and management platforms of the time, those courses mainly presented teaching and learning materials in the form of static pages. In 2003, the Ministry of Education of China launched the construction of high-quality courses for teaching quality and reform projects in colleges and universities. In 2011, it also initiated the construction of national high-quality open courses, this time including video open courses and resource-sharing courses. In 2015, it once again renewed its efforts to construct and identify national high-quality online open courses. By 2019, having learned from all these previous iterations, the Ministry issued its opinions regarding the implementation of national world-class undergraduate courses. They outlined a plan to start building out national world-class courses that are online (MOOCs), offline, and blended in nature; they also expressed interest in more experimental options, like courses that incorporate virtual simulation and social practice courses. As we have seen, the medium of education is highly tied to the content of education, so these new formats will play an influential role in how students experience their academic programs moving forward.

Research on the Quality of Blended Teaching and Learning Methods

As part of the switch towards more blended teaching and learning methods, research is being done globally and within China to investigate the quality of such forms of education. Since 2013, Central China Normal University has been supporting research that explores blended learning practices. In the early stages of blended learning uptake, universities found that the overall situation of curriculum education remained relatively the same, but the new style affected different groups differently. Plenty of learning resources were provided, but there was much room for quality improvement. Students in those early programs often completed their tasks but lacked a certain proactiveness and excitement about their education. The operation inside the physical classroom was functional, but the network platform's supportive role was insufficient. To some degree, these problems still persist in more current blended learning practices. Therefore, universities are trying to strengthen course resource construction, implementation conditions, the nature of some curricula, learning adaptability, etc.

Since then, as the methods and technologies matured, studies have identified some favorable impacts of blended teaching and learning and some inconsistencies that remain. Jinzhou Medical University found that students' language competence and communication abilities were improved after the blended teaching method was employed in the teaching of sectional anatomy—communication between teachers and students was also enhanced. However, students' autonomous learning and management abilities were inconsistent. By comparing studies on blended teaching in both China and abroad, the research team of Beijing Normal University found that it is necessary to strengthen research and practice on the blended teaching model, teaching ability and training, teachers' professional development, evaluation, and learning analysis.

Other areas of research have included: the relationship between teacher-student and student–student communication, learners' use of online resources, and the impact of interface design and content design on the learner. Furthermore, many teaching support platforms employed in the blended teaching model have been joint projects between universities and enterprises that also utilize research studies to examine the efficacy of their platforms and approaches. The Jilin Institute of Chemical Technology has found that different teaching models can be constructed to improve the teaching effect after the use of learning support platforms. Shangqiu Vocational and Technical College has explored how vocational colleges adapt to blended learning needs and build blended learning spaces. Jiangsu Vocational and Technical College of Architecture has explored how to use the "superstar" mobile learning platform for blended teaching. The upshot is that the move towards blended learning and teaching methods is being supported and informed by rigorous research efforts, rather than arbitrary hunches about what constitutes the best learning environment or an overreliance on traditional methods.

Innovation and Entrepreneurship Education

Another aspect of modern academic program development is the emphasis on innovation and entrepreneurship education, which is by definition a cross-discipline pursuit. Innovation and entrepreneurship go hand in hand, with innovation providing the creative fuel and entrepreneurship providing the confidence and practical knowledge to develop a great idea into fruition. Thus, innovation education in colleges and universities cannot be separated from professional education. Instead, universities should integrate innovation education with professional education and promote a combination of creativity, critical thinking, and entrepreneurial spirit in their academic programs.

Many leading educational institutions around the globe have established entrepreneurship centers in hopes of cultivating the conditions for innovative ideas and bringing them to life. Since 2014, China has participated in this trend by trying to strengthen college students' innovation and entrepreneurial abilities. China has specially designed training courses for teachers on the topic and has also released corresponding online courses. Additionally, universities have built up a number of innovation and entrepreneurship courses for satisfying the needs of different college students and established ways of sharing these courses with other institutions. Similar to its other initiatives, China has advocated for a coordinated implementation of standardized training objectives for innovation and entrepreneurship at colleges and universities.

One example of the cultivation of innovative and entrepreneurial students can be found at Sichuan University, where special attention is paid to the interdisciplinary nature of arts, science, engineering, and medicine. The university has not only designed some interdisciplinary courses that reflect innovation at the intersections of content areas but has set up interdisciplinary research teams that focus on complex societal problems that are not confined to a single discipline. The university has also established an international course week, where experts and scholars from high-level universities around the world provide students mentorship and exposure to the global context of innovation and entrepreneurship. Another example is found at Nanjing Normal University, where students are encouraged to obtain innovation credits by designing a credit plan for comprehensive practical courses. In addition to dedicated programs for innovation and entrepreneurship, much can be gained from infusing these principles into courses from all fields—this will help blend innovative spirit into whatever subject matter students have chosen to study based on their interests and talents.

Educational researchers and practitioners have also found that in order to accelerate innovation and entrepreneurship education in higher education institutions, the medium of information transfer should gradually transition from paper materials to the internet. The reason for this is that the internet helps build university-enterprise cooperation and diffusion of creative practices that foster innovation and excitement.

"1 + X" Certificate System—Pilot Program in Vocational Education

Reforms that emphasize interdisciplinary talents over specialist ones are also being tested in vocational education institutions. Recently, a pilot program called the "1 + X" was launched in vocational colleges and application-oriented undergraduate colleges. The "1" refers to the student's main academic certificate; the "X" refers to several vocational skill-level certificates. The academic programs involved in the pilot program need to implement teaching and training models such as the flipped classroom, blended teaching, and integration of theory and practice. The goals of this pilot program include promoting the diversification of academic program offerings, encouraging graduates of vocational colleges to adapt to the changing needs of their jobs, making their professional certificates more powerful and multifaceted, enhancing their professional adaptability, enhancing their innovation and entrepreneurship abilities, and promoting high-quality employment of vocational college graduates.

3.2.2 From Independent to Collaborative Higher Education

In this part, we elaborate on the impact of collaboration between education institutions on academic program development. In traditional models of professional education, more rigid distinctions are drawn between colleges and universities; such distinctions often reflect different levels and types of education. Under that model, universities would often improve their educational quality through their internal administration, changes to faculty structure, and in-house adjustments to academic programs. However, in the digital age, higher education institutions have initiated collaborative initiatives that connect academic programs from different universities. This is especially true in China, given the public and nationalized nature of its higher education system.

Establishment of Curriculum Sharing Alliances

If universities rely solely on resources and courses of their own, they tend to limit the scope of their talent cultivation. When they participate extensively in the building of high-quality online open course resources and other collaborative initiatives with other institutions, learners obtain access to more high-quality resources and opportunities for growth. These connections strengthen the co-construction and sharing of resources among different universities and academic programs, leading to sustained alliances in the long term. In April of 2013, higher education institutions in the East and West of China established the "Course Sharing Alliance" to realize the sharing of high-quality curriculum resources through online courses. The impact has been profound—in 2019, 27.6 million people from 2,200 colleges and universities earned credits by taking courses from the Alliance. Such prolific sharing enables students to access courses in fields from subject matter experts they wouldn't otherwise be able to, contributing greatly to the blended nature of their course composition.

The "2011 Plan" and Collaborative Innovation Centers

In addition to curriculum-sharing alliances, Chinese universities have participated in the building of shared, collaborative innovation centers. In 2011, the Chinese Ministry of Education and the Ministry of Finance jointly launched a plan to improve the innovation capacity of colleges and universities—the "2011 Plan". Led by higher education institutions and with the help of scientific research institutes, industrial enterprises, local governments, and other advantageous resources, this plan aims to promote innovation and research through "collaborative innovation centers". It serves the country's domestic innovation needs and its desire to participate in international competition on research frontiers in major fields. By 2020, 38 new national collaborative innovation centers and 125 new provincial collaborative innovation centers were built; in total, over 1000 provincial collaborative innovation centers have been established nationwide.

Establishing Regional Academic Communities for Professional Development

In addition to the collaborative innovation centers from the 2011 Plan, another type of academic collective being formed in China are regional academic communities. One example of this can be seen in the Jiangsu Province of China. Under the direct guidance of the province's Education Department, Jiangsu established its Education Technology Research Association for Higher Education Institutions—an academic community for developing informative teaching research, practice, and talent cultivation in the province. The association has wide participation from universities in the province. It organizes relevant academic exchange activities every year to study the reform of modern education and teaching practices in higher education. Additionally, it has built a secondary community for professional construction, teaching reform, resource construction, network application, vocational education, and social services. This type of hub enables collaborative professional development from neighboring institutions that will ultimately benefit administrators, faculty, staff, and students.

Collaboration During Times of Crisis

The benefits of collaborative higher education become highly evident when the system is tested by unforeseen and unprecedented challenges. The global outbreak of COVID-19 in the spring of 2020 presented perhaps the largest test that higher education systems have faced in recent history. It triggered massive switches to online teaching throughout the globe and many universities took the opportunity to explore online teaching models in earnest. China and many other countries that were forced to test out new online and hybrid models out of necessity experienced a renaissance of education reform. In China, this renaissance was aided by coordinated efforts between institutions to tackle the problem together. The Ministry of Education's Teaching Guidance Subcommittee of Educational Technology Specialty in Colleges and Universities, together with relevant experts and scholars in China's colleges and universities, worked together to disseminate relevant wisdom about new ways of conducting education. They have given nearly 50 non-profit lectures for teachers in colleges and universities. The contents are quite diverse, covering topics like blended teaching, teaching design, organization and implementation of teaching activities, and teaching evaluation.

Individual universities have also taken initiative to organize collaborative efforts during this challenging time. For example, the Institute of Educational Technology of Tsinghua University organized experts from different disciplines across the country to conduct a large-scale survey on the current situation of blended teaching in vocational education and carried out several large-scale online lectures and forums on the topic that were attended by over one million audience members. Beijing Normal University, Jiangnan University, East China Normal University, Central China Normal University, South China Normal University, and Nanjing Normal University have also designed various activities for groups inside and outside of their respective schools to help teachers and students adapt to the sudden change of teaching environment and conditions.

3.3 General Strategies for Systemic Reconstruction of Academic Programs

In the previous section, we dove into specific approaches and initiatives China has implemented in its recent academic program development. In this section, we will provide general strategies for systematically reconstructing academic programs that are inspired by and expand upon the Chinese strategies previously discussed.

3.3.1 Trends in Higher Education Program Development

Professional talent training aims to meet social development needs and provide high-quality professional talents for society. Under the background of globalization, social development has crossed national borders, reflecting the coexistence and inclusiveness of cultures and the realistic demands of increasing common ground while reserving differences. According to the overall development and future trend of the world, professional settings and talent training should be in line with the trend of the times and promote the common progress of human society. A professional setting and talent cultivation program needs to break the inherent barriers, emphasize students' professional capabilities in modern society, and be able to adjust themselves in time to adapt to dynamic social development. For example, specialties in vocational education are constructed mainly based on the requirements of industries and the future development of society. The new technologies in the digital age and their combination with industries make the demand for different jobs in different industries much clearer, which requires students to have professional skills in specific occupations and the ability to transfer their knowledge positively.

The design of the professional talent training program needs to reflect the appropriate orientation of academic program development, which is, in turn, reflected in the process of talent cultivation.

Blended Teaching and Learning Methods

Given the heavy exploration of this topic elsewhere in the chapter and handbook, we include this trend here mainly to serve as a reminder rather than a place for elaboration. Blended teaching methods have been proven effective, and ought to be incorporated into academic programs of the future when feasible and appropriate.

Cross-Disciplines and Interdisciplinary Talent Cultivation

Like the previous trend, we include this here to serve as a reminder of a major shift we have covered extensively throughout the chapter.

Internationalization and Globalization

Alongside many other fields, higher education has become increasingly globalized. In large part due to the application of modern information technology, the interdependence of global higher education has become stronger and stronger. The international flow of talents and resources in the field of higher education has generally accelerated, promoting changes in the fundamental structure of higher education in various countries. This increased contact has led to symbiotic cooperation and relationships, as well as healthy competition among global higher education institutions.

To understand the advantages and disadvantages of certain academic programs in the global landscape, it is necessary to design such programs with the context of globalization in mind. Gaining this understanding of how a nation's academic programs are positioned in a global context is beneficial for not only learning from the approaches of other nations but for contributing the nation's unique culture to international higher education development. Achieving this awareness of the global context can take many forms, including the establishment of programs that allow international scholars and professionals to interface with students through presentations, workshops, research projects, field trips, and more.

Emphasis on Science and Technology Innovation

As evidenced by the government guidelines of the previous section, this trend is especially prevalent in China, where fields like artificial intelligence and engineering are given elevated priority status. However, the trend has also taken root to varying degrees in most nations, as new scientific discoveries and technological inventions dramatically transform how societies function and are governed.

This trend toward an emphasis on science and technology innovation attaches great importance to the integration of STEM principles in academic programs and the development of skills that are not discipline-specific like creative problem-solving. Higher education institutions should help students understand modern trends in scientific research and industrial development through teaching methods that include experiential learning. Through participating in scientific research, students can begin to understand the knowledge landscape and gaps in current industries, the evolution of industries over time, integration between theory and application, and pioneering frontiers of cutting-edge experimentation. In this way, they can not only optimize their professional learning about science and technology but also practice transferrable skills that are conducive to innovative thinking. In our modern world, this level of science and technology innovation literacy is beneficial to students of all disciplines, not just those in academic programs related to hard science or engineering.

It is worth noting that this trend can also be seen as a call to action to ensure that the value of non-STEM fields is preserved in the next generation of academic programs and not overshadowed by the massive excitement surrounding new science and technology innovations. In the same way, that science and technology literacy can benefit students focused on liberal arts disciplines, liberal arts literacy also benefits students in STEM-oriented academic programs. Both scenarios enable a valuable blending of disciplines that will cultivate more well-rounded and profession-ready graduates.

Diversification Within Uniformity

This is another trend that is perhaps more prevalent in China's strategy than in other nations but provides a useful perspective for the global community to consider when developing their own higher education academic program standards. In the national standards for the teaching quality that the Chinese Ministry of Education released in 2018, there was a stated desire to strike a balance between "rules" and "room"—that is, enough standardization enforced by the Ministry's rules while saving some room for individual institutions to creatively structure their programs to their unique needs. Striking an appropriate balance between national—or even international—uniformity and cultivating diversity of academic programs and institutions is a difficult conundrum that all higher education systems must grapple with. Providing individual institutions, the autonomy to experiment with their academic programs often results in innovative teaching and learning models, like MIT's Open Course Ware Movement. On the other hand, establishing uniform standards for academic programs across institutions levels the playing field provides a common language for program development and lends itself to intercollegiate collaboration due to the presence of shared constraints.

Cultivating Information Technology Literacy

In the digital age, being able to understand and use information technology is a crucial skill set for students to develop. Students' competence in information technology is reflected in the following aspects:

(1) Foundational information technology competence: Students should internalize basic knowledge about information technology, master common information terminals, be able to use professional software relevant to their field(s), and learn to employ information technology to acquire professional skills.

(2) Information proficiency: Students should be able to apply information tools to collect, evaluate, and use effective and accurate information; they should also be able to put forth their own thoughts and suggestions upon digesting information about a certain topic.

(3) Critical thinking, problem-solving, and decision-making: Students should be able to use appropriate digital resources and information tools to aid in conducting research, managing projects, solving problems, and making effective decisions founded on critical thinking.

(4) Cooperation and communication: Students should be able to use digital media environments to communicate respectfully and effectively with peers and mentors across different learning settings. Such communication can be for an individual or collaborative learning moments.

(5) Innovation and reform: With the help of information technology, students should be capable of carrying out creative professional activities according to the characteristics of their academic programs, including the generation of new ideas and potential solutions to existing problems in the world.

(6) Social responsibility: Students should be able to better understand human, cultural, and social issues through their use of information technology. Furthermore, they should conduct themselves responsibly, and online in ways that comply with legal and ethical standards.

Open Education and Collaboration Between Universities

After the open education movements of courses in the United States and other countries, the research and construction of online courses in colleges and universities have gradually been upgraded from university-level research projects to national research projects. Online courses in universities are becoming the main channel for sharing global educational resources. Educators in many countries have participated in researching and constructing online courses, making it an international collaboration. This collective effort promotes the reproduction and development of knowledge, the reuse of resources between modern universities, as well as the coordination between different academic programs. The openness of modern professional education resources and curriculum sharing among higher education institutions is a top priority. There are various ways to enhance the coordination between different academic programs, including building a suitable learning support system or platform, establishing a curriculum management system that combines private and open courses, and designing a management process to govern private and open courses.

Collaboration Between Education Institutions and Industries

Nowadays, academia is greatly linked to the market and industries. It is of great necessity to strengthen students' connections with industries and employers. To achieve this, education institutions should consider creating spaces and tools like professional virtual-real integration laboratories, virtual factories, virtual teaching, and research rooms, and virtual simulations of inter-school collaboration for students to gain exposure to the nature of different industries of interest. This can be combined with traditional methods of industry exposure like internships or day trips to shadow professionals in their jobs. Adding blended medium options for this exploration offers more flexibility for off-campus teachers and enterprise personnel to instruct students, makes such experiences more accessible to schools geographically isolated from some industries and promotes more convenient school-enterprise cooperation. Moreover, industry-university-research collaborative innovation centers can be constructed through cooperation among universities and between universities and enterprises to expand professional teaching outside of the walls of individual universities. The alignment and collaboration of these major institutions allow a more seamless transition for students upon graduation and assist with matching the reforms of academic programming to the current demands of industry and society.

New Systems and Methods for Academic Program Evaluation in the Digital Age

The new academic program reforms triggered by all these prevalent trends will reshape higher education significantly. The systems and methods for tracking the efficacy of these changes and evaluating the success of academic programs must modernize alongside the programs themselves. Research must be done on how to construct "institutional guarantee systems" that provide mechanisms for evaluating the development of an academic program itself and the cultivation of high-quality talents through the program.

The following aspects should be represented in the institutional guarantee systems:

(1) It must check that the development mission of academic programs and talent training objectives are aligned with the overall development orientation of the university, the nation, and/or the international community.

(2) It must formulate and monitor the enforcement of policies related to blended teaching and establish leadership and implementation groups for ensuring such blended practices are incorporated into program construction.

(3) It should promote cross-department and other cross-cutting discussions across academic institutions to ensure that disciplines are being blended in logical ways for students to develop interdisciplinary, high-demand skills.
(4) It should establish a monitoring and management mechanism for the quality of professional talent training that considers student learning achievement, employment after graduation, and student health and satisfaction, among other metrics.
(5) It should iterate courses and other pieces of academic programming based on previous feedback on the quality and usefulness of such programming.

In regards to the last point, feedback on the quality of student learning and ultimate employment can be obtained immediately and regularly with the help of the internet and big data technology. Based on the statistics and analysis of big data and information, industry development trends and demands can be analyzed and predicted along with other channels of feedback, allowing for timely adjustments that optimize the benefits and relevance of the academic program.

 **A Case Study**

Reconstruction of Academic Programs in the Digital Age

In order to adapt to the development requirements of the digital age, a university in Shandong, China, has reconstructed the undergraduate training program in mining engineering.

Part 1: In School Training Phase

〔Talent Training Objectives〕
1. Knowledge Objectives (it is better to increase professional knowledge of informatization)

   • Master the basic knowledge of information technology.
   • Master the basic knowledge of information technology application in mining engineering.

2. Ability Objectives (it is better to increase the information ability)
2.1. Information literacy and autonomic learning

   • Master the ability to judge when and through what network channels to discover, collect and optimize the information and understand the latest developments in mining engineering.
   • Have strong abilities in information analysis and processing as well as analogy learning and can quickly master new mining engineering technology. (Note: Information analysis: information classification, synthesis, error checking, and evaluation; information processing:

information sorting and retrieval, organization and expression, storage and transformation, control and transmission, etc.)

- Have the ability to effectively use information technology to carry out a variety of blended learning methods such as "network-based collaborative learning" and "research-based learning".

2.2. Effective Communication

- Have the ability to transfer information through information multimedia and use technical language to communicate in a cross-cultural environment.
- Have the capability to discover and flexibly apply a variety of communication media to improve communication efficiency in cross-campus, cross-city, and cross-country environments.

2.3 Possess good informatization professional ethics, reflecting responsibilities for occupational, societal, and environmental aspects.

- Comply with information technology standards, information security standards, and occupational safety standards, and assume relevant security responsibilities.

【Curriculum System】

1. Curriculum setting
1.1. Course teaching content:

In order to adapt to the digital transformation of the mining industry, it is necessary to sort out all professional courses and analyze whether to increase the teaching contents of cultivating informatization ability.

1.2 Course teaching method:

The characteristics of all professional courses are analyzed, and the blended teaching method is determined for different types of courses.

Part 2: In Enterprise Training Phase

(1) Arrangements for project training and learning

The network-based research teaching will be carried out by project teams. It is suggested to modify the assessment method of this teaching period as follows: periodic work report (online submission) + online discussion participation + real scenario examination.

(2) Arrangements for practical training of enterprise projects

It is suggested to modify the assessment method of this teaching period as follows: project design of mining engineering practice (which can be completed through network collaboration) + project implementation effect.

(3) Arrangements for Graduation Thesis

At this stage, it is recommended to modify the instruction process to online guidance of dissertation + traditional face-to-face defense.

3.3.2 Summary of Actionable Strategy Suggestions

(1) Implement blended teaching and learning mediums
(2) Prioritize blending disciplines in academic programs
(3) Learn from the international higher education context
(4) Be competitive in emerging fields of science and technology innovation while preserving the advantages of developing non-STEM disciplines
(5) Enforce standardization while allowing room for diversification to breed creative education innovations
(6) Cultivate students' information technology literacy and digital citizenship
(7) Participate in open education and collaboration between universities; promote curriculum sharing and collaborative innovation and research centers
(8) Create channels between education institutions and industries to give students exposure and improve education and market alignment
(9) Implement modern methods of evaluating academic programs and providing an "institutional guarantee" of high quality

 **A Case Study 3.2**

Grass-Root Teaching Organizations for Promoting Teaching Ability

In 2021, the Jiangsu Education Department in China issued the "Guiding Opinions of the Jiangsu Education Department on Strengthening the Construction of Grass-root Teaching Organizations in Universities to Promote Teaching Ability", requiring universities to make "a long-term plan and a top-level design" for teachers' teaching ability improvement. A "Grassroots teaching organization" is regarded as a third-level organization together with universities and departments. It reflects the specific requirements and process of professional talent training and serves the real needs of modern professional talent cultivation. Grass-root teaching organizations in universities with no specified forms are constructed on the basis of the requirements of the Ministry of Education of China on the quality of undergraduate talent training and the construction of virtual teaching and research rooms. It is necessary to "explore the new path and mechanism for the construction of grass-root teaching organizations in universities, promote the construction of relevant functional departments for teachers' teaching ability improvement, improve teaching standards and teaching skills, reform teaching evaluations, enhance teaching motivation, and further improve teaching quality evaluation as well as guarantee and provide incentive mechanisms, and continuous improvement mechanism". Additionally, "open and diverse new grass-root teaching organizations should be established, including "teaching workshops, lectures by famous teachers, teaching diagnosis" and so on. A number of training rooms for improving the teaching ability of college teachers are constructed, such as "microteaching classrooms, teaching study rooms, teaching consulting rooms", etc., to support teachers' growth in professional abilities. Finally, with the help of the practical exploration of grass-root teaching organizations, teachers are able to "carry out various forms of online and offline blended teaching, virtual simulation experimental teaching, and promote the deep integration of modern information technology and education and teaching" in the process of professional talent cultivation.

 **A Case Study 3.3**

Systemic Reconstruction of Academic Programs with Information Technology in Central China Normal University

Central China Normal University has regarded "education informatization" as its development strategy. Based on demonstration projects of the Ministry of Education in China in terms of information-based pilot universities, it, with a five-year exploration and practice, has built an appropriate new talent training system in the digital age, which is student-centered and emphasizes connection, sharing, independence, and openness. The new system pays much attention to the reconstruction of teaching concepts, the reorganization of teaching resources, the innovation of teaching methods, the reform of teaching evaluations, and the construction of teaching culture. To be specific, this university has conducted the reform in the following eight aspects. It revised the talent training programs to build a student-centered talent training model; it reconstructed the teaching environment to realize the deep integration of virtual and real spaces; it carried out advanced training programs to improve teachers' information-based teaching ability; it enriched digital teaching resources to provide a more open education service; it reformed teaching methods and promoted blended classroom teaching; it reformed evaluation methods and carried out a comprehensive evaluation on the basis of data; it optimized management services and built a new ecology of education; it set up teaching festivals to construct teaching cultures. Central China Normal University has fully and deeply integrated information technology into the whole process of talent cultivation, which has effectively solved three problems. First, with the help of information technology, a student-centered talent cultivation system of higher education has been established in the digital by systematically reshaping the teaching environment, contents, methods, evaluation, etc. Second, big data and other technologies have been employed to share high-quality resources and innovate teaching methods, which ensures the implementation of large-scale teaching and provides personalized resources for students according to their differences. Thus, the contradiction between massiveness and individualization in teaching activities has been solved. Third, the teaching culture in which colleges and universities attach great importance to teaching and advocate innovation in the digital age has formed, and a good atmosphere in which teachers are both interested and talented at teaching and education has been created. (see Chap. 6 "Exemplars of Typical Practices in Blended Learning" for details).

Foreign studies:

Boyer Commission on Educating Undergraduates in the Research University released "*Reinventing Undergraduate Education: A Blueprint for America' Research Universities*" in 1998, followed by a group of researchers published "*Reinventing Undergraduate Education: Three Years After the Boyer Report*" in 2001(Kenny et al. 2001). Both of them analyzed how research universities view undergraduate education. Harvard University, Stanford University, The Massachusetts Institute of Technology (MIT), and other universities have focused their attention on undergraduate education and launched undergraduate teaching reform. In 2006, Harry Lewis, Dean of Harvard University's undergraduate school, proposed that a "world-class university" without a world-class undergraduate education is soulless. In the UK, Department for Business, Innovation and Skills released a white paper called *Success as a Knowledge Economy: Teaching Excellence, Social Mobility and Student Choice* in 2016, which pointed out that the success of the knowledge economy is reflected in teaching excellence, social mobility, and student choice.

Stanford University proposes that the goals of undergraduate education in the twenty-first century should include four aspects. The first is to own knowledge, which emphasizes the integration of professional education and general education as well as the integration of the depth and breadth of knowledge; the second is to hone skills and capacities, such as expression and writing skills, critical reading ability, aesthetic ability, reasoning, and analytical skills; the third is to cultivate personal and social responsibility, including personal and social responsibility, ethics and morality, cross-cultural and cross-racial identity, tolerance and compassion, etc.; the fourth is to adaptive learning, also including how to respond to challenges and opportunities and enhance innovation. MIT also emphasizes the urgency to strengthen curricular and pedagogical changes and advocate active learning, inquiry learning, project-based learning, etc.

Every country in the world pays attention to interdisciplinary construction, especially the construction of modern engineering, and actively promotes the reform of engineering education. For example, from 2011 to 2013, the United States successively launched the "American Advanced Manufacturing Partnership Program", "American Advanced Manufacturing National Strategic Plan" and "American Manufacturing Innovation Network Program". In addition, Germany issued the "German Industry 4.0 Strategy Implementation" in 2013. In 2014, many countries issued a series of national strategies for engineering education reform. For example, Japan released the "Manufacturing White Paper"; the United Kingdom promulgated the "Made in Britain 2025" strategy, and France proclaimed the "New Industrial France" strategy.

Promotion of Opening and Sharing Course Resources in the Rise of MOOC

Canadian professors Stephen Dow Enns and George Simmons proposed MOOC (Massive Open Online Courses) in 2008. In 2011, the "Introduction to Artificial Intelligence" opened by Sebastian Sirui and Pete Norwich of Stanford University in the United States attracted 160,000 people from more than 190 countries to register online for learning. In 2012, Sebastian founded Udacity, an online education business company that provides free, non-credit college courses to the public. In the same year, Andrew Ng and Daphne Kohler of Stanford University co-founded the education technology company Coursera. Additionally, Harvard University partnered with MIT to establish edX, an online education platform. Since the emergence of MOOCs, there have been a series of changes in higher education around the world. The educational methods in universities have changed, which has promoted the openness and virtuality of universities and the expandability and economic values of curriculum resources.

TAFE (Technical and Further Education) College in New South Wales, Australia, is a government-funded vocational training institution whose main goal is to provide flexible and timely solutions to meet the needs of students, industries, communities, and the ever-changing economy. Courses in TAFE include online, distance, and face-to-face courses as well as a combination of these courses in an attempt to provide a flexible and high-quality education for all (Bliuc et al. 2012).

Promotion of the Opening and Mutual Recognition of Course Credits Through Resource Sharing

Learners have the chance to learn when course resources are open to all learners, but it does not mean that students can obtain corresponding professional academic certificates. For example, Stephen Jackson, director of accreditation at the Quality Assurance Agency for higher education in the UK, believes credibility is the most important thing. In other words, "credits should be awarded only if it is demonstrated that learners did finish the corresponding learning tasks". However, it has become a natural trend to achieve credit certification between academic programs after some time. The Universal College of Colorado State University in the United States became the first university in the United States that recognized credits in MOOCs in 2012. In 2014, Tsinghua University in China announced the recognition of some of the classroom credits in "XuetangX". The "CNMOOC" independently developed by

Shanghai Jiao Tong University has started the mutual recognition of MOOC credits among 19 universities in Southwest China for the first time.

American research universities are still exploring the value-added services of MOOCs. Traditional American higher education often charges based on credits. Through the credit certification of The American Council on Education, MOOCs truly enter the traditional American higher education market. Universities are actively exploring new ways of learning certifications, such as Udacity's "Nano Degree Certificate", Coursera's "Professional Course Package Certificate", edX's "Vocational Qualification Certificate", etc. Columbia University has also cooperated with the edX platform to develop MicroMasters courses. Students who complete the course can receive an electronic course certificate that is accredited and can be used as a credential for degree-awarding. Based on the needs of in-service professionals for further education or professional qualification certification, MOOC platform operators also conduct systematic evaluations of the learning process in MOOC. For example, edX has designed a signature tracking project to evaluate the learning process of learners(Wu and Qian 2021).

Promotion of Blend and Creation of Academic Program Construction Through Mutual Recognition of Credits

In 2013, Udacity announced a partnership with Georgia Tech and AT & T to develop an online master's degree program in computing. edX is also actively exploring a blended method that integrates MOOCs and traditional campus learning. In August 2015, Udacity launched an innovative project named "Global Freshman Academy" with Arizona State University, allowing students to apply to different universities, including Arizona State University, and different academic programs after completing all credit courses in the first year of college and passing the exam. They are also endowed with on-campus learning opportunities from the second year of college. Arnett Angerwal, the founder and CEO of edX, called this new model for college application and admission "flipped admission". In 2016, edX launched a MOOC program for a "Micro Master's Degree". Students who have obtained the certificate can apply for the on-campus courses of the master's degree programs in many universities that can accept the certificate. Therefore, students can spend less time and money acquiring a formal master's degree. In 2016, Coursera and the University of Illinois at Urbana-Champaign launched the "Master of Data Science (MCS-DS)" program and the "Online Master of Business Administration (iMBA)" programs, respectively.

The medical students of Imperial College London in the UK need to specialize in one of their selected disciplines in the fourth academic year. Pharmacology is one of the optional courses. About twenty medical students and five biomedical students choose to complete this course every year. The course construction team carried out the modular design of the course and organized the teaching material of neuropharmacology in a blended teaching model. This course was originally only open to graduate students, and then the blended teaching model was also applied to undergraduate education. It was proven that students become very interested in studying this subject with the blended teaching model, but the premise is that the curriculum should be highly structured, high-quality, and supported by tutorials.

Students believe that "blended" learning is more beneficial than purely learning online (Morton et al. 2016).

Universities in many countries not only attach importance to the practice of blended teaching but also strengthen the research on the quality of online teaching. For example, Massey University in New Zealand established the Distance Education and Learning Future Alliance in 2012. It also brought together scholars and practitioners in distance education, online education, and blended education to explore how to form a new model and method of modern higher education in the digital network environment, global link, and rapid change of higher education (Brown and Xiao 2013).

References

Bliuc, A. M., Casey, G., Bachfischer, A., Goodyear, P., & Ellis, R. A. (2012). Blended learning in vocational education: teachers' conceptions of blended learning and their approaches to teaching and design. The Australian Educational Researcher, 39, 237-257.

Boyer Commission on Educating Undergraduates in the Research University. (1998). Reinventing undergraduate education: a blueprint for American's research universities. State University of New York at Stony Brook for the Carnegie Foundation for the Advancement of Teaching.

Brown, M., & Xiao J.(2013). The new normal of online, blended and distance learning: the Massey University experience (in Chinese). Distance Education In China, 452(11): 27–35, 95.

Department for Business, Innovation and Skills. (2016). Success as a knowledge economy: teaching excellence, social mobility and student choice. Gov. uk.

Kenny, S. S., Thomas, E., Katkin, W., Lemming, M., Smith, P., Glaser, M., & Gross, W. (2001). Reinventing undergraduate education: three years after the boyer report.

Morton, C. E., Saleh, S. N., Smith, S. F., Hemani, A., Ameen, A., Bennie, T. D., & Toro-Troconis, M. (2016). Blended learning: how can we optimise undergraduate student engagement. BMC Medical Education, 16(1), 1-8.

Wu, Y. (2020) Brave the tide and empower the future—the reform of higher education led by emerging engineering education (in Chinese). Research in Higher Education of Engineering, (2): 1-5.

Wu, D., & Qian, X. (2021). An analysis of the transformation of the MOOC business model of Chinese universities: based on the practice of American research universities (in Chinese).Research in Education Development, 41(1): 79–84.

Chapter 4
Implementation of Blended Learning at the Institutional Level

Qian Zhou, Yue Huang, Yangyang Luo, Xiaojing Bai, Yiran Cui, Yuping Wang, and Nan Chen

Blended learning has become the new normal in higher education. Research and practice have demonstrated its learning effectiveness (Siemens et al. 2015). At the institutional level, however, there is a lack of systematic planning strategies and implementation guidelines for promoting blended learning, as well as methods for evaluating the effectiveness of blended learning. How to implement blended learning more effectively and sustainably in institutions has become a key issue in the digital transformation of higher education.

Section 4.1 of this chapter explains two frameworks for the implementation of blended learning from the perspective of institutions and stakeholders; Sect. 4.2 discusses the main components for the implementation of blended learning in institutions; Sect. 4.3 proposes strategies for institutions to implement blended learning; Sect. 4.4 describes the qualitative and quantitative evaluation methods for the institutional implementation of blended learning. This chapter provides strategies and

Q. Zhou (✉)
Institute of Education, Tsinghua University, Beijing, China
e-mail: zhouqian@tsinghua.edu.cn

Y. Huang
School of Online Education, Beijing University of Posts and Telecommunications, Beijing, China

Y. Luo
Institute of Higher Education, Lanzhou University, Lanzhou, China

X. Bai
Beijing Open University, Beijing, China

Y. Cui
School of International Education, Shandong University, Jinan, China

Y. Wang
School of Humanities, Languages and Social Science, Griffith University, Brisbane, Australia

N. Chen
Beijing Academy of Educational Sciences, Beijing, China

© The Author(s) 2024
M. Li et al. (eds.), *Handbook of Educational Reform Through Blended Learning*,
https://doi.org/10.1007/978-981-99-6269-3_4

approaches for implementing blended learning for higher education administrators, support and service staff and other stakeholders. At the same time, this chapter can be used as a reference by government departments when formulating policies to promote blended learning in institutions.

4.1 Frameworks for Implementing Blended Learning in Institutions

4.1.1 A Framework for Institutions to Implement Blended Learning

According to a series of studies on blended learning in institutions in the USA, three aspects of approaches have been identified, namely strategies (purpose, advocacy, implementation, definition, policy), organization (management, infrastructure, teacher professional development, course arrangement, evaluation), and support (technical, pedagogical, incentives). With the support of UNESCO, Lim and Wang (2016) proposed an implementation framework including eight aspects, namely vision and planning, curriculum, professional development, learning support, infrastructure, facilities, resources and support, policy and institution structure, partnership, research, and evaluation.

Based on the research results and implementation cases of various countries, this section proposes a framework for institutions to implement blended learning (Boelens et al. 2017). The framework consists of nine components (as shown in Fig. (4.1). Setting goals and developing action plans are a start for an institution to implement blended learning and are the basis for evaluating the implementation's effectiveness (Graham 2006). According to the developed goals and action plans, the institution sets up an organizational structure, issues corresponding policies and norms, and establishes a technical-support environment and staff-supporting system (Machado 2007). The institution then implements blended learning through redesigning programs and curriculum and enhancing the staff's capabilities with information technology. The cultural atmosphere of implementing blended learning in institution will gradually be created through this process. Finally, the use of effectiveness evaluation allows the institution to assess progress against the set goals, which can provide the basis for adjusting goals and action plans in the next round.

Set goals and develop action plans: An institution determines the positioning of blended learning in student cultivation according to the requirements of the institution's vision and characteristics. Based on the current situation of blended learning, the institution sets the goals (including the overall objectives of implementing blended learning and operable objectives), and major tasks and safeguard measures in action plans.

Set up an organizational structure: The institution should build and enhance the corresponding organizational structure for implementing blended learning in

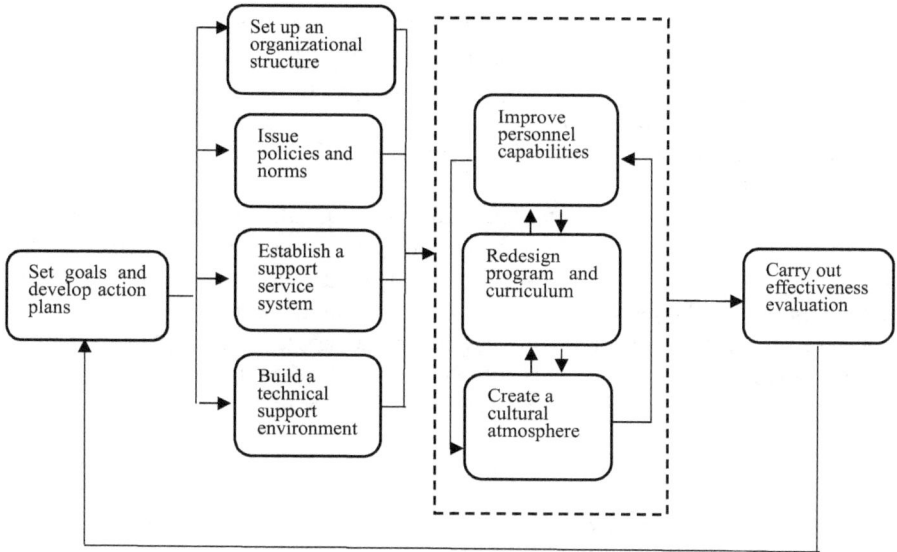

Fig. 4.1 A framework for institutions to implement blended learning

order to accommodate innovations in teaching and learning, refine procedures in the information age, as well as ensure the smooth implementation of blended learning.

Issue policies and norms: To promote the implementation of blended learning, the institution should formulate and issue relevant policies and norms including the design and development, application, management, and evaluation of implementing blended learning.

Enhance capabilities with information technology among staff: To successfully implement blended learning, an institution is necessary to continuously enhance teachers', students', and management staff's capabilities with information technology. Teachers' capacity is key for the implementation of blended learning. The institution should develop a capacity developing system, including training content, implementation plans, safeguard measures, and evaluation. In addition, the institution should also improve leaders' information leadership, staff's capacity of information management and service.

Redesign programs and curriculum: To meet the needs of talent cultivation in the information age, the institution should reposition the goals of program development and redesign the content of courses and programs.

Establish a support service system: To ensure the implementation of blended learning among teachers and students, the institution should establish a support service system, including services to support teachers' teaching and students' learning. The primary role of teaching support services is to provide teachers with relevant information technology support services, as well as to offer students with learning guidance, technical guidance, and humanistic care related to blended learning at the curriculum and institution levels.

Build a technical support environment: The development of the technical support environment required for blended learning is crucial to its effective implementation. The information technology environment and digital resources necessary to support the institution's implementation of blended learning include information infrastructure, the physical teaching and learning environment, and online learning spaces and resources.

Create a cultural atmosphere: The institution gradually creates a corresponding meaningful perspective and team atmosphere in the process. A good cultural atmosphere can promote teachers' recognition of the value of blended learning implementation and their willingness to participate in the process.

Carry out evaluation: In the process, it is necessary to develop evaluation plans and systems in line with the goals set. Regular evaluation throughout the process should be adopted to improve the process of implementing blended learning.

4.1.2 A Framework for Stakeholders to Implement Blended Learning in Institutions

The abovementioned framework presents the elements and interrelationships involved in implement blended learning in institutions. It is also crucial to consider the responsibilities and interrelationships between different stakeholders, such as teachers, students, institution leaders, managerial staff in internal supporting units, and external support units.

Based on relevant research, this section proposes a framework for stakeholders to implement blended learning in institutions (as shown in Fig. 4.2). Teachers play a central role in the implementation of blended learning, designing, developing and delivering blended courses to help students achieve learning outcomes. Institutional leadership, staff in internal support units, and people outside the institution have different roles to play in supporting teachers (Bai and Han 2020).

Teacher

When teachers design, implement and evaluate blended courses, they are influenced by various factors, including personal factors, institutional factors, course factors, technological factors, students, etc. Personal factors include teachers' awareness, attitudes, skills and teaching experience. Institutional factors include the institution's requirements, investment and evaluation for teachers to implement blended learning. The course factor is relatively complex and varied. The ability to develop digital learning resources, design online and offline learning activities, and carry out data-based learning evaluation for blended courses will affect teachers' adoption of blended learning. Technological factors include technical support, technical training and technical infrastructure. Student factors include student characteristics, learning needs and online learning experience.

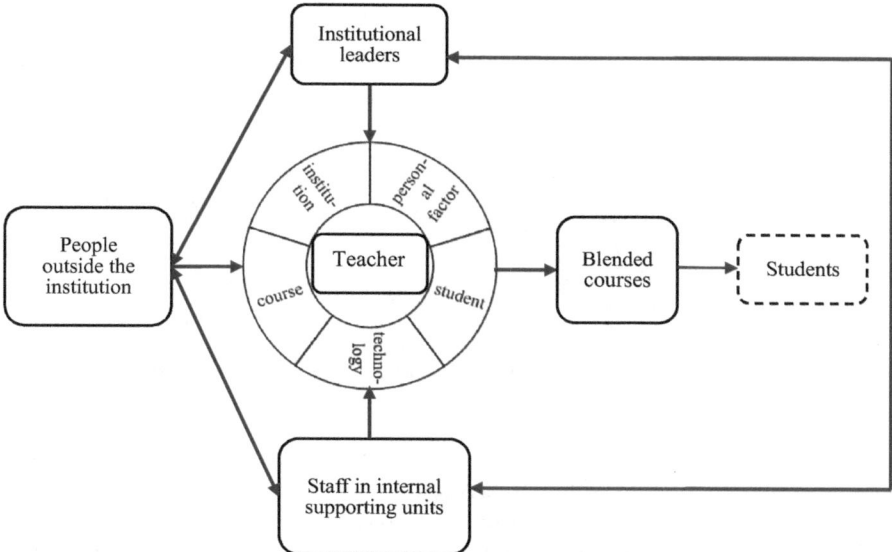

Fig. 4.2 A framework for stakeholders to implement blended learning in institutions

Institutional leaders

Institutional leaders always set the direction and focus of blended learning implementation, making strategic decisions and leading the way in terms of what goals the school wants to achieve, what subjects are involved, and how blended learning implementation will be supported. Teachers, staff in internal support units and people outside the institution all implement the leadership's thinking. It can be said that the effectiveness of leaders' decisions and leadership directly determines how far and how steadily the institution can go with blended learning. Leaders should consider the following key points when promoting blended learning (As shown in Fig. 4.3) (Boelens et al. 2017).

Based on the current status. Institutional leaders should confront the actual conditions of institutional development, especially the current situation of teachers, which will be considered as the starting point for blended learning.

Clarify the desired goals. Institutional leaders need to be clear about what needs to be achieved in the institution's digital transformation (e.g. to achieve the transformation goals, to build faculty capacity, etc.), but the goals are not clear and unambiguous at the outset and require a gradual process of exploration.

Focus on teacher capacity development. Institutional leaders should plan the institution with teacher guidance at its core. They are generally not directly involved in specific teacher training, but rather exercise their responsibilities by introducing policies and norms, formulating development strategies, setting up special programs and conducting effectiveness evaluation to guide teachers to clarify their direction, improve their skills, motivate them and broaden their horizons.

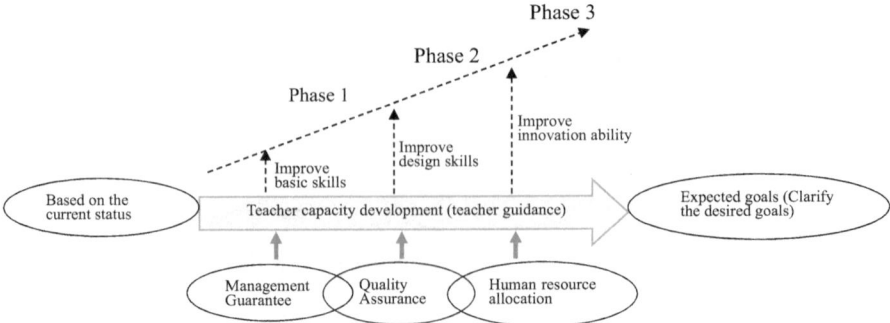

Fig. 4.3 The focus of institutional leaders in implementing blended learning

Implement blended learning in a phased and focused manner. Institutional leaders should adopt a phased approach to promoting the construction of blended courses by focusing on different capacities, such as improving teachers' basic skills, design skills and innovation abilities, to achieve the milestones of blended learning implementation and showcase the results.

Provide support services. Institutional leaders can support blended learning through management guarantee, quality assurance and human resource allocation. Specifically, the management and service support provided by staff in internal support units facilitates a suitable environment for the implementation of blended learning. The development of curriculum standards and requirements enhances the quality of blended learning. People outside the institution, such as experts, peers and technical staff from companies, can help provide practical support for the implementation of blended learning.

Staff in internal supporting units

Staff in internal support units are responsible for promoting and supporting teachers' blended teaching. Whether blended learning can actually be implemented, whether the implementation plan can be carried out, and whether teachers can be effectively supported is often closely related to the effectiveness of the work of these staff. They play a central role in communication between institutional leaders and teachers, and between people outside the institution and internal stakeholders. Staff should be aware of the following points when supporting the implementation of blended learning (Fig. 4.4).

Implementation and feedback. The institution's vision is implemented in the day-to-day management and support of blended learning so that teachers are guided by the vision. Feedback on teachers' blended learning needs and opinions should also be provided to leaders in a timely manner. This requires staff to have a comprehensive understanding of teachers' blended learning situation and to reach out to teachers to actively identify and solve problems.

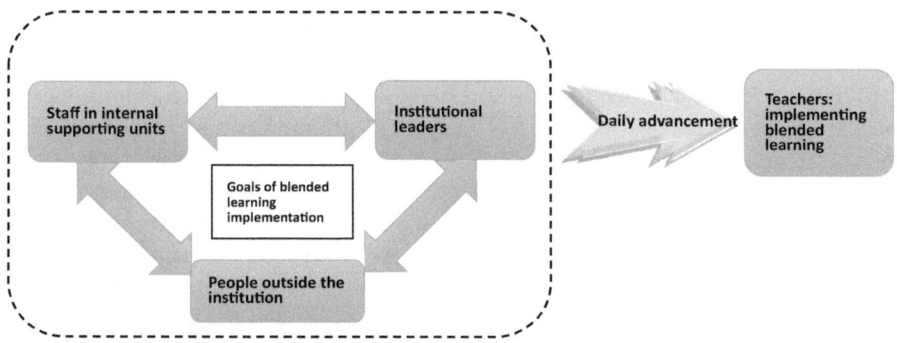

Fig. 4.4 Roles of staff played in implementing blended learning

Act as a bridge between internal and external cooperation. Staff should play an active role in communication and collaboration between the university and its external partners in order to facilitate cooperation.

Smooth and effective communication. Staff should use school leadership, external support and themselves as the three fulcrums to form a synergy that creates smooth and good communication. Practice shows that the smoother the communication function, the more support it will receive and the smoother the multi-party cooperation will be (Baier-D'Orazio and Mukuza Muhini 2016).

Forming management leadership. Around the goal of implementing blended learning, staff should gather institutional leaders and people outside the institution to form "management leadership", and closely link inside and outside the institution to form the willpower and action force to grasp the implementation, and continue to promote the progress of work and consolidate its effectiveness.

People outside the institution

People outside the institution refers to people from external institutions, companies and individuals who work in partnership and cooperation with the institution to better implement blended learning. Practice shows that relying on the institution's own capacity to promote blended learning is not only too slow, but also easily misleading. It is therefore necessary to build a collaborative and cooperative blended learning community with the help of external forces. Institutions should consider the following points when implementing blended learning with external support (Johnson and Graham 2015).

People outside the institution include experts from other similar institutions, companies, research institutions, etc. The types of experts include teaching experts, technical experts, research experts, etc. Expert support is introduced at the appropriate time according to the stage and needs of blended learning implementation.

The focus and content of the support provided by the external experts differ from stage to stage: the initial stage is to map the overall situation of the institution and provide planning support for the institution to implement blended learning; in the construction stage, the focus is on supporting the construction of the pilot course; in the application stage, the pilot course should be provided with tailor-made teaching support to form institution-based examples and lead the whole institution's curriculum reform. The content of the support includes updating the teaching concept, teaching design guidance, educational technology training and services, and data-based teaching effectiveness evaluation.

The institution should establish a trusting, close and harmonious relationship with the external experts. The institution should ask these experts to land the ideas of the management, to establish a co-planning relationship with staff, to help teachers with guidance and to be deeply involved in the whole process of implementing blended learning.

4.2 Main Components for Implementing Blended Learning in Institutions

The framework for institutions to implement blended learning consists of nine main components (Fig. 4.1). The following five components are discussed in more detail in this section: setting goals and developing action plans, setting up an organizational structure, issuing policies and standards, creating a cultural atmosphere, and building a technical support environment. Evaluation of the effectiveness of implementation is discussed in Sect. 4.4. For the programs and curriculum redesign, please refer to Chap. 3 Development of Academic Programs in the Digital Age and Chap. 2 Implementation of Blended Learning at the Course Level. For establishing a support service system, please refer to Chap. 5 Supporting Students and Instructors in Blended Learning in this book.

4.2.1 Setting Goals and Developing Action Plans

An institution should set clear goals and action plans to support the implementation of blended learning. The process of the setting goals and plans is illustrated in Fig. 4.5. Based on the overall vision, the institution sets the direction for blended learning. At the same time, by analyzing the status quo of blended learning, the institution clarifies the existing basis and the key problems of the blended learning. The institution then sets development goals for blended learning, including long-term objectives and milestones, taking into account national policies and standards about blended learning. Based on the objectives and milestones, the institution plans the main tasks and support measures for the implementation of blended learning.

Setting the direction for blended learning

The implementation of blended learning must be subordinated to the overall vision of an institution. When formulating objectives and action plans for blended learning

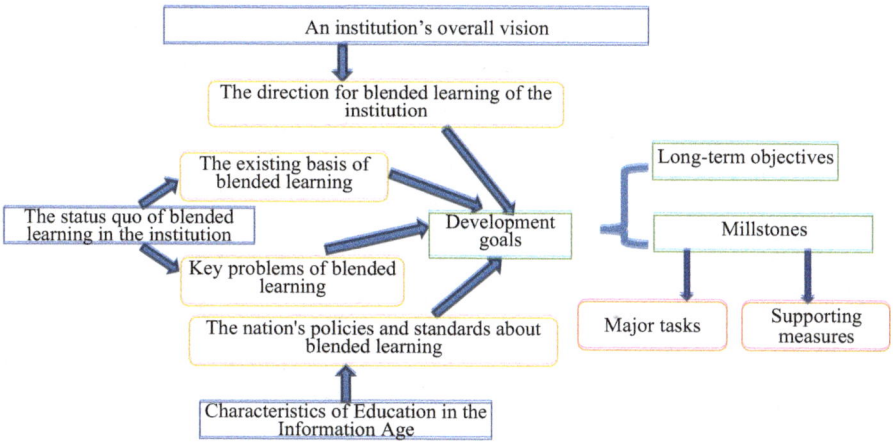

Fig. 4.5 Set goals and action plans for implementing blended learning

implementation, the institution needs to clarify the positioning and the role that blended learning can play in talent development. The digital age has put new demands on human resources, which requires the institution to reconstruct its teaching philosophy, methods and tools to meet the needs of the digital age for talent development. Based on the student-centered approach, blended learning cannot simply copy traditional teaching onto the Internet or combine online and offline teaching. It requires the institution to reintegrate and redesign curricular elements such as learning outcomes, content, activities and assessment in a learning environment that integrates virtual and real life. In this way, students are more likely to be engaged and have a personalized learning experience according to their own learning characteristics and abilities.

Analyzing the status quo of blended learning in the institution

In order to set goals and action plans for implementing blended learning, the institution should analyze the existing basis of blended learning. In order to facilitate the institution's examination of the achievements and key problems of blended learning, this book provides the following diagnostic framework as shown in Table 4.1. The framework consists of a total of 41 specific diagnostic indicators in 8 sub-dimensions under 3 dimensions, namely basic information about the institution, the current situation of blended learning, and the supportive environment for blended learning. Depending on the situation in the institution, managers can use this framework as a tool to select the relevant diagnostic indicators or add additional indicators and develop a customized diagnostic tool for the current situation of blended learning in the institution.

The implementation of blended learning should address the real problems of talent development, especially those that arise in the teaching and learning process. The problems to be solved in institutions vary. For example, research-oriented universities need to solve the problem of students' basic knowledge learning and research innovation. Application-oriented universities need to solve the problem of students'

Table 4.1 The diagnostic framework for the implementation of blended learning in an institution

Diagnostic dimensions	Diagnostic sub-dimensions	Diagnostic indicators
1. Basic information about the institutions	1.1. Profiles of the institution	Institutional features and advantages
		Academic colleges and departments
		Faculty and staff
		Teaching
		Research
		Transfer of scientific and technological achievements
		Admissions and employment
		Others
2. The current situation of blended learning	2.1. Designing and delivering blended courses	Blended course classification
		Blended course development
		Blended instructional design
		Blended course delivery
		Blended learning resource creation
	2.2. Evaluating blended course teaching	Teaching evaluation mechanism
		Assessment of achievement of learning objectives
		Quality assurance and monitoring of blended learning in the institution
		Feedback on teaching assessment
	2.3. Development of academic programs	Academic program planning
		Academic program diagnosis and improvement
		Dynamic optimization mechanism for academic programs
3. The supportive environment for blended learning	3.1. The institutional systems for blended learning	Organizational development
		Institutional standard building
		Construction of management mechanisms
	3.2. Information technology environment construction	Building IT-based teaching environments
		Creation and use of digital learning resources

(continued)

Table 4.1 (continued)

Diagnostic dimensions	Diagnostic sub-dimensions	Diagnostic indicators
		Creation and use of learning resources in cooperation between institutions and enterprises
		Use of open educational resources
		Establishing standards for database construction
		Integration of IT applications
		Building a campus network
		Building information systems and services
		Building logistics service systems
		Building network security management systems
		Building network public opinion management and disposal systems
		Situation of network security management
	3.3. Human resources capabilities of the IT applications	Staff skills in IT applications
		Teachers' IT-based teaching skills
		Students' IT-based learning skills
	3.4. Services provided by external forces	Technology support systems for blended learning
		Blended learning support services
		Blended learning evaluation

knowledge application ability, and vocational colleges need to solve the problems of students' basic work ability and vocational skill development.

Setting development goals for blended learning

The institution sets long-term goals and milestones based on the direction of blended learning, taking into account the status quo of blended learning and relevant national policies and standards. Long-term goals should be sustainable and consistent with the institution's long-term development strategy, including values, beliefs and visions. The implementation of blended learning in an institution involves a variety of roles, including institutional leaders, departmental support staff, teachers and students. It has been found that when teachers and students are aware that the institution's goals are aligned with their own, it has a significant impact on the implementation of blended learning. The institution must first build consensus among senior management and determine the long-term goals for blended learning. Once management has chosen the long-term goals, the various supporting staff in departments, teachers and students can have a common and consistent direction to achieve these goals). To gain the support of teachers and students for the long-term goals of blended learning, the institution can organize an institution-wide pep rally for blended learning to motivate teachers. On the other hand, a symposium of student representatives can be held to mobilize the power of student organizations and spread the ideas of blended learning (Halverson et al. 2014). In addition, the use of a variety of institutional promotional channels can bring the ideas of blended learning to every teacher and student and gain their understanding, recognition and support.

Milestones are specific, measurable outcomes that the institution will achieve in implementing blended learning. Milestones usually describe what the implementation is trying to achieve, with a focus on short-term results. Milestones can also be seen as short-term goals that need to be reflected in the institution's annual action plans. Setting specific targets for activities in the implementation process can provide direction for action across departments and units. In setting milestones, an institution may wish to refer to the elements in the Framework for Institutions to Implement Blended Learning, mentioned earlier in this section (Fig. 4.1).

Planning the main tasks and supporting measures for the implementation of blended learning

Implementing blended learning in an institution is a long-term, systematic undertaking. Once the goals have been set, the institution should formulate the action plans and clarify the means and strategies for achieving these goals, including the tasks, time, methods, persons responsible and supporting measures required. In formulating the plans, it is necessary to carry out a comprehensive analysis in terms of feasibility, expected results, costs and timing. According to implementation experience and relevant studies, the strategy of "pilot before promotion" is more appropriate for the institution to implement blended learning in a systematic way. Therefore, when formulating plans, the institutions can plan the implementation in phases in terms of program and curriculum, technical support environment, support service systems, and staff capacity. Evaluation will take place at the end of the pilot phase and the ultimate goal of implementation will be achieved through adaptation and improvement during the promotion phase.

4.2.2 Setting up an Organizational Structure

In order to ensure a smooth and stable implementation of blended learning, an institution needs to establish a customized organizational structure that addresses the management, processes and staff involved in the implementation. Such an organizational structure aims to clarify the roles and responsibilities of relevant departments and to establish a management process for blended learning. In this way, problems are more likely to be resolved efficiently and risks avoided during the process, contributing to the effectiveness of blended learning.

In terms of the organizational structure for the implementation of blended learning, special committees and working teams should be added to the existing administrative and service departments in the institution (Moskal et al. 2013). According to organizational design theory (Daft et al. 2010), three aspects of work activity design, reporting relationships and departmental combination should be considered in the organizational setting. Work activities refer to the specific tasks assigned to each responsible department. Reporting relationships refer to the chain of command or line of authority to which members of the institution should report their work. The departmental combination includes functional grouping, divisional grouping, multi-focus grouping, horizontal grouping and virtual network grouping. Multi-focus grouping is often referred to as matrix grouping. It includes both horizontal and vertical grouping alternatives suitable for organizations with significantly changing environments and objectives that reflect dual requirements. Such a structure can facilitate the communication and coordination needed to respond to rapidly changing environments. As the implementation of blended learning involves many departments and staff in an institution, it lends itself to the departmental grouping of a matrix structure.

To facilitate the implementation of blended learning in a systematic way, the institution should establish a leadership group, an expert advisory committee, and dedicated offices and working teams to guide the relevant functional departments in coordinating design, implementation and evaluation. The organizational structure for the implementation of blended learning is shown in Fig. 4.6.

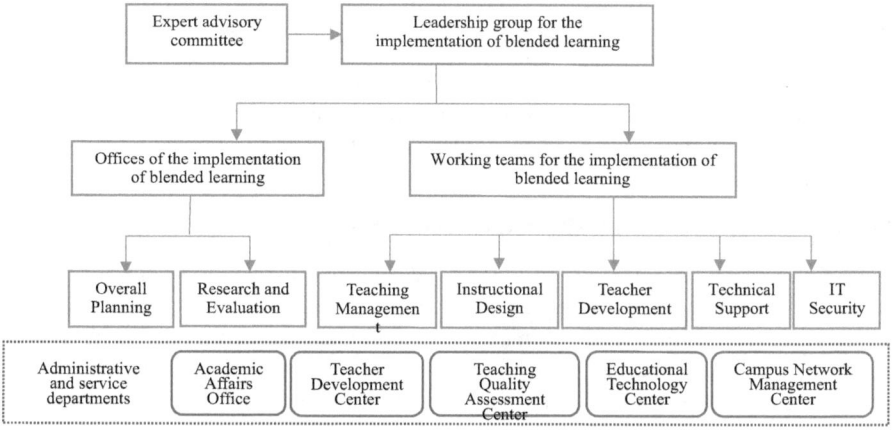

Fig. 4.6 Organizational structure for implementing blended learning

The leadership group for the implementation of blended learning

The implementation of blended learning involves several aspects, including program and curriculum development, teaching and learning support services, staff capacity, technical support environment, cultural atmosphere, etc. It is therefore necessary to develop a leadership group, centered on institutional leaders, to coordinate the overall implementation. The group will be chaired by the president or vice-president responsible for teaching. The group will be chaired by the President or Vice-President for Teaching and Learning and will include as members the Deans of Faculties and the Heads of relevant Administrative and Service Departments. Its main functions are to formulate long-term goals and milestones for implementation, to formulate and issue relevant policies and standards, to co-ordinate implementation tasks as a whole, and to conduct research and evaluation to meet the needs of blended learning implementation.

The expert advisory committee

The expert advisory committee for the implementation of blended learning is made up of experts and academics in education management, instructional design, blended learning, information technology and experienced frontline teachers. The main role of such a committee is to provide guidance and think-tank support for the implementation of blended learning.

The offices of the implementation of blended learning

The office of implementation of blended learning works under the guidance of the leadership group. With the help of staff members from administrative and service departments, such as Academic Affairs Office, Teacher Development Center, Teaching Quality Assessment, Educational Technology Center etc., the office carries out planning, research, and evaluation.

The working teams for the implementation of blended learning

Different working teams can be set up according to different functions, including the teaching management team, the instructional design team, the teacher development team, the technology support team and the IT security team. The composition and responsibilities of each group are shown in Table 4.2.

Administrative and service departments in the institution

The Academic Affairs Office is the operational administrative department responsible for managing the institution's blended learning. It directs and coordinates the institution's teaching, builds the teaching system and improves the management system. It also conducts the management of blended learning projects and the day-to-day management of independent research projects on blended learning to improve the quality of teaching.

The Teacher Development Centre is committed to promoting blended learning by providing professional development for teachers, research on teaching and learning, and consultancy services. In addition, it strives to build a communication platform

Table 4.2 The working teams for implementing blended learning

Name of team	Composition	Responsibilities
Teaching management team	• Administrators from the registrar, the education administrators of faculties and departments • Staff from education technology center and teaching and learning quality assessment center • The registrar should be the leading unit for the reform	The team promotes teachers' participation in the reform of blended learning, supervises and evaluates the effectiveness of the blended learning, and manages the implementation process of the reform
Instructional design team	• Staff of educational technology center • Faculty and departmental support staff • Staff from teaching and learning quality assessment center	The team is responsible for providing teachers with educational technology services, such as instructional design and resource development
Teacher development team	• Staff of teacher development center • Registrar managerial staff • Faculty and departmental support staff • Staff of educational technology center • Staff of teaching and learning quality assessment center	The team is responsible for teacher capability development, such as professional development for blended learning and teaching and learning quality monitoring and evaluation
Technology support team	• Staff from campus network center, or educational technology center	The team is responsible for implementing the technical system plan for the reform, including the technical environment construction, operation and maintenance, user services and information technology training
IT security team	• Staff of information center or network center	The team is responsible for preventing network security incidents such as security, public opinions, and copyright infringement in the process of reform

within and outside the institution, to address teachers' challenges in blended learning, and to improve teachers' skills in blended learning.

The Teaching Quality Assessment Centre formulates various evaluation rubrics and plans, implementation methods and related documents required for monitoring blended learning. It also organizes the implementation of blended learning supervision and teaching and learning evaluation. It is responsible for collecting and processing information on teaching and learning quality, such as supervision and evaluation, and publishing evaluation results.

The Educational Technology Centre is mainly responsible for developing, managing and maintaining the blended learning environments, including physical multimedia classrooms and online learning management platforms. It is also responsible for training in educational technology skills, developing multimedia resources for blended learning, monitoring online usage and analyzing resources.

The Campus Network Centre (or IT Centre) is responsible for building and maintaining the campus network and other information infrastructure, including the management of the backbone network, egress bandwidth, virtual desktops, hardware, software and the data center. At the same time, it must work with the operators of the online learning management platforms to provide technical support for blended learning.

 **Case 4.1**

The organizational structure for blended learning in Central China Normal University (CCNU) includes the Academic Affairs Office, the IT Office, and the Teacher Development Center. A leading group for educational informatization is established, led by the president of the university. The responsibilities of the leading group include:

- reviewing the medium and long-term development plans, annual work plan, and important work systems of informatization;
- listening to the feedback from the experts of the evaluation committee;
- guiding, monitoring, and evaluating the IT Office of the university.

By cancelling some traditional departments such as the Audio-visual Center, and the Information Center, etc., and integrating the original departments, CCNU established the Center for Digital Teaching and Learning Resource Development and the Informatization Office as the functional office dedicated to informatization. Moreover, The Teaching and Learning Quality Assessment Center and the Teacher Development Center cooperate with departments such as the Registry, the Student Labor Office, and the National Engineering Technology Research Center for Digital Learning. They perform their duties; collaborate; rectify the management system; clarify the boundaries of power and responsibilities; eliminate information isolation islands; and develop a new system that can provide teaching and learning, research, technology, management, and support led by department leaders, which is conducive to information technology

4.2.3 Issuing Policies and Standards

The systematic promotion of blended learning requires the guidance of policies and standards. Policies and standards serve as a foundation to support managers, staff and teachers in the implementation of blended learning and to set goals for them to achieve. At the same time, policies and standards can be used as a reference for administrative and service departments to manage, support and evaluate the implementation of blended learning.

The policy framework for implementing blended learning

To implement blended learning at an institutional level, it is necessary to formulate policies that reflect the values, vision and goals of the institution. Policies also determine the strategic direction and focus of blended learning and optimize the allocation of resources. The policy framework for implementing blended learning includes specific actions, role allocation, staff development, resources and evaluation. To be clear, specific actions refer to the actions an institution needs to take to achieve the milestones of blended learning implementation. Role allocation refers to policies that clarify the specific responsibilities of teachers, students, staff and other stakeholders in the process. Staff development refers to the skill requirements of staff and their development pathways, of which teacher competence for blended learning is considered the most important. Resources refer to the teaching and learning resources and financial investment involved in implementing blended learning. Evaluation refers to the monitoring and quality assessment of the effectiveness of the implementation of blended learning.

Classification of policies and standards

Policies and standards formulated in the process of implementing blended learning can be grouped into four categories, namely those related to design and development, application and management, evaluation, and incentives and assurance, as shown in Fig. 4.7.

Guidelines and standards for design and development mainly include those for blended course design and development, resource development and technical support environment development. Guidelines and standards for blended course design specify the process, rationality and legality of curriculum design by teachers and support staff, such as emphasis on student-centered design, allocation of online and

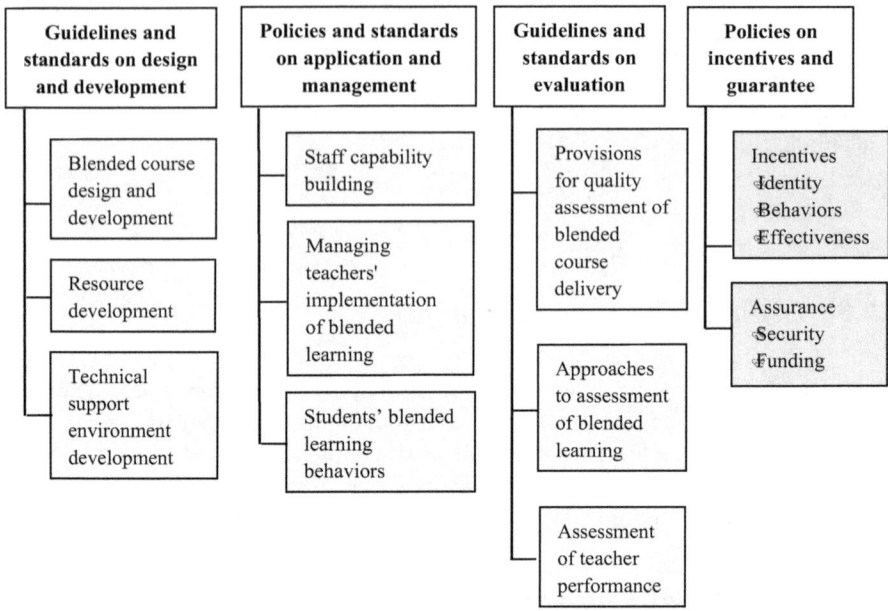

Fig. 4.7 Classification of policies and standards for implementing blended learning

offline learning hours, and other requirements based on the institution's professional certification. Guidelines and standards for blended course development specify the content, presentation formats and technical requirements for teachers and support staff to develop blended courses. Guidelines and standards for resource development mainly clarify the requirements for the digital learning resources that teachers and support staff develop when implementing blended learning. These include the classification, presentation and technical requirements of such digital resources, as well as the access conditions, terms of use and evaluation methods for integrating such resources into blended courses. Guidelines and standards for the development of technical support environments mainly include uniform requirements for IT hardware facilities, equipment and software for blended learning, with the aim of ensuring that the above aspects meet the relevant standards and the needs of teachers and learners in blended learning environments.

Policies and standards for application and management include policies for staff capacity building and specifications for managing teachers' implementation of blended learning and students' blended learning behavior. Staff capacity building policies refer to a set of hierarchical and classified policies formulated to build the capacity of leaders, teachers, departmental administrators and support staff in the process of implementing blended learning. Such policies aim to change staff perceptions of teaching and learning, to make them understand the value of blended learning, and to enhance their skills in instructional design, teaching and learning management, and the use of information technology required for the implementation of blended learning. Standards for the management of teachers' implementation of blended learning specify requirements for teachers, including teaching concepts, teaching behaviors (such as online teaching process, online homework assessment, online discussion and feedback, and online testing and grading), and ethics and other related behaviors in the online learning space. Standards for students' blended learning include requirements such as learning time and attendance, code of conduct, and ethical requirements in the online learning space.

Guidelines and standards for evaluation include provisions for quality assessment of blended course delivery, approaches to assessment of blended learning, and assessment of teacher performance. Standards for quality assessment specify content and methods for assessing the effectiveness of blended course delivery (see Chap. 2 Implementation of Blended Learning at the Course Level in this book). Assessment guidelines for blended learning include requirements for assessing students in the process of blended learning. When planning assessment approaches for blended learning, the focus should be on student learning and academic achievement based on formative assessment. By using information technology to record students' learning processes, taking into account students' online learning behaviors, classroom learning performance and academic performance, a formative assessment system can be established for course assessment (Welker et al. 2017). Based on some basic standards at the institutional level, teacher autonomy should be fully realized so that teachers are encouraged to optimize assessment approaches for their students based on the actual situation of the courses. The guidelines for the evaluation of teachers' performance include participation in blended learning as one of the criteria for promotion in the context of the annual evaluation at institutional and departmental level.

Incentive and assurance policies include incentive policies and assurance policies. Incentive policies include identity incentives, behavioral incentives and effectiveness incentives. Identity incentives motivate teachers through identity propaganda. For example, special identities are given to teachers who have made great contributions to the promotion of blended learning. These teachers are invited to attend relevant exchanges or academic conferences to encourage them and publicize their important contribution to blended learning. Behavioral incentives refer to the validation of specific behaviors that can motivate teachers to continue with the stated behaviors. For example, research and implementation projects related to blended learning can be awarded to pioneers of blended learning to support them in continuing to implement blended learning through research projects. Another way of incentivizing behavior is to recognize the workload of teachers in promoting blended learning by multiplying their original teaching hours by a certain coefficient, or by increasing the corresponding teaching salary to financially reward excellent courses. Teachers can be subsidized with information-based facilities and equipment for blended learning. Preferential policies can also be formulated for teacher tenure and promotion. The above list is just a few of the possible measures that can be adopted. Effective incentives recognize achievement, which in turn gives teachers a sense of identity. For example, teachers who are successful in blended learning can be awarded 'Outstanding Teacher', 'Outstanding Contribution to Blended Learning' and other similar awards. Support and security policies include security policies and funding assurance policies. The purpose of security policies is to ensure the security of technical systems and various types of data in the process of blended learning. The content of security policies includes objectives, targets, content, organization and staffing requirements. The purpose of a financial security policy is to ensure a long-term and sustainable financial investment during an institution's implementation of blended learning. When formulating a financial security policy, the following aspects should be considered:

- The formulating a sustainable institutional funding mechanism,
- Establishing a normalized reserve fund for the implementation of blended learning,
- Considering an appropriate allocation of funds for the development of hardware, software, teaching and learning resources, maintenance of technical systems and staff development,
- Improving the cost–benefit analysis of funding investments,
- Developing a long-term method of monitoring project effectiveness, and
- Establishing a tailor-made project evaluation and audit mechanism.

4.2.4 Creating a Cultural Atmosphere

Organizational culture is the sum of a set of values, beliefs, perceptions and attitudes shared by all members of an organization and passed on to new members. Organizational culture plays the role of guiding, regulating, unifying and motivating organizational behavior. Organizational culture expresses the sense of identity of its members and encourages them to recognize and strive for a higher level of things than their own self-interest. It sets appropriate standards of behavior for members of the organization and binds the organization together. As an ideology and control mechanism, it guides and shapes the attitudes and behavior of its members. Cultural change is a deep embodiment of organizational change (Daft 2015). Therefore, the development of a cultural atmosphere enables the institutional implementation of blended learning in a more systematic, deeper and sustainable way (Basir et al. 2010). In general, the creation of a cultural atmosphere of institutional implementation of blended learning can be divided into three layers, namely the first layer, which reflects the material layer related to blended learning of an institution; the second layer, which refers to the regulations and codes of conduct to maintain the implementation of blended learning in an institution; and the third layer, which refers to the goals, values, basic beliefs and principles that the institution prevails in the implementation of blended learning.

In the process of blended learning implementation, it is necessary to start from the first layer culture, the second layer culture to the third layer culture, thus gradually creating a cultural atmosphere for blended learning implementation. The first layer culture is a carrier for the development of institutional culture. In this process, an institution can demonstrate its philosophy and determination to implement blended learning by developing and optimizing the physical learning environment and the online learning space, and by promoting it through appropriate channels. The second layer culture is gradually developed through the implementation of routine management requirements of an institution. It is an intellectual norm that is recognized and followed by all members of an institution. It reflects the unique values and behaviors of the institution. In the process of implementing blended learning, an institution should try its best to listen to the opinions of teachers and students in the formulation, introduction and implementation of its policies and standards in order to build consensus, incorporate cultural construction into the implementation and develop a cultural atmosphere in line with the institution. The third layer culture teaches teachers and students how to put the values into practice from a practical perspective and how to internalize the values, beliefs, opinions and attitudes of blended learning in their hearts and externalize them in practice. In order to actively create a cultural atmosphere for the implementation of blended learning, institutions can start from the following aspects.

- Focusing on the role of leaders. Cultural development requires values-based leadership. The awareness, enthusiasm and initiative of institutional leaders for cultural development will determine the breadth and depth of institutional cultural development. Institutional leaders should integrate the long-term goals and milestones of blended learning implementation to develop the values of blended learning. In addition, institutional leaders should disseminate and implement these values throughout the institution;
- Emphasizing the role of public relations. Public relations are an important force in guiding the psychology and behavior of teachers and students. The institution can increase the scope and intensity of publicity about blended learning through the intranet, newspaper, bulletin board and various new media channels, and guide teachers and students to understand the benefits and necessity of blended learning through mobilization meetings, expert lectures, teacher-student representative symposiums, etc.;
- Using role models as examples. It is necessary to bring into play the role of teachers as pioneers. The institution can introduce incentive mechanisms to recognize and reward those senior teachers who actively implement blended learning, thus encouraging them to take a leading role; and
- Promoting Blended learning. It is necessary for the institution to implement blended learning through some routine actions, special ceremonies and symbols.

 **Case 4.2**

Create of cultural atmosphere for blended learning by Central China Normal University

Through a series of measures such as establishing teaching and learning festivals, setting up the Teaching Innovation Award, and promoting cooperative education on the basis of the integration of science and education, CCNU has created a cultural atmosphere of emphasizing on teaching, advocating innovation, excellence in teaching, and eagerness to teach. During the Teaching and learning Festival, open classes, teaching and learning workshops, teaching and learning reform forums were held. The Teaching Innovation Award has been set up since 2014, focusing on the teaching effectiveness of teachers in the information environment, with the aim to mobilize teachers' enthusiasm in implementing blended learning. In addition, under the guidance of the National Center for Engineering and Technology Education and the National Engineering Laboratory for Educational Big Data, the institution has facilitated teachers who need to implement innovative research on teaching and learning in the context of information-based learning, realized cooperative education based on the integration of science and education, and promoted the interaction between research and teaching and learning, as well as the integration of research and talent training

4.2.5 Building a Technical Support Environment

An environment that supports blended learning is one that combines face-to-face and computer-mediated instruction. The goals of creating such an environment include making learning accessible, facilitating small-group instruction, meeting diverse needs, increasing productivity, providing a variety of instructional methods and techniques, increasing student and teacher engagement, and providing additional support for complicated and abstract content (Neumeier 2005). The technical support environment generally consists of three parts: the physical teaching environment, the cyber learning space and the IT-based teaching tools (as shown in Fig. 4.8).

The technical support environment described above is used to support the needs of blended learning participants (teachers and students), such as fair, fast and convenient visit and access, motivation and perception, management and control, interaction and collaboration, communication and reflection, content and resources, evaluation and feedback, activity and method, and agent and support (Weller 2007).

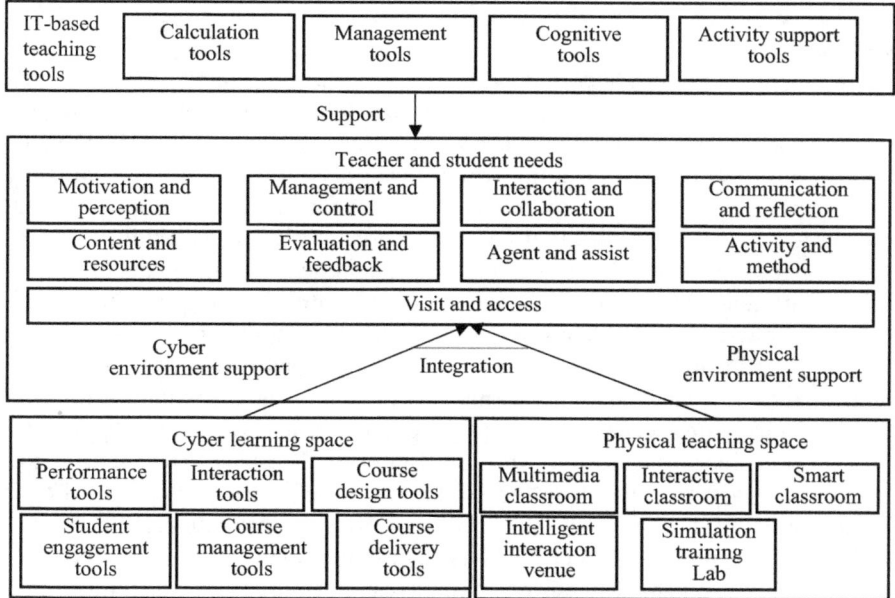

Fig. 4.8 Components of a technical support environment for blended learning

Visit and access needs. Blended learning requires that the technical system provides teachers and students with fair, fast, and convenient visit and access, and supports teachers and students to participate in teaching and learning without barriers in various natural environments (Moskal et al. 2013). It is vital to ensure that teachers and students can have access to the virtual environment through mobile devices, PCs, electronic whiteboards, augmented reality, and other devices in the physical environment. It's also crucial for teachers and students to be able to access the cyber environment through learning management systems, simulation, virtual reality, and other technologies.

Motivation and perception needs. Blended learning requires the technical system to enhance the motivation of teachers and students to participate in blended learning, or to sustain their motivation using various strategies (Geng et al. 2019). In addition, the system needs to be easily perceived by teachers and students to enhance their presence in teaching and learning. It is reported that enhancing the user friendliness of technical systems can help teachers and students build and maintain motivation for effective learning (Rafiola et al. 2020).

Management and control needs. Blended learning requires teachers and students to manage and control the teaching and learning process (Bärenfänger 2005). They can adjust the teaching and learning process individually, categorize different learning objectives according to the characteristics of students, and customize their learning progress. At the same time, the technical system needs to automatically record various data generated in teaching and learning management and control process.

Interaction and collaboration needs. Blended learning requires the technical system to assist teachers and students to interact and collaborate with each other (Sun et al. 2017). The system should be able to encourage teachers and students to have different types of interactive learning activities, such as asynchronous, synchronous, one-to-many, and many-to-many modes of communication, as well as encourage students to form collaborative groups of various organizations to help build a learning community. At the same time, the technical system needs to automatically record various data generated in the interactive and collaborative learning activities.

Communication and reflection needs. Blended learning requires the technical system to provide teachers and students with asynchronous, active, one-to-one, one-to-many, many-to-many and other forms of communication in formal and informal teaching and learning scenarios, including text, picture, audio and video, application software, and other formats of information (Bidarra and Rusman 2017). The system should allow teachers and students to record and insert reflective content into different teaching and learning stages, such as instructional design, instructional intervention, and learning progress adjustment. At the same time, the system needs to automatically record various data generated during communication and reflection activities.

Content and resource needs. Blended learning requires the technical system to provide blended learning with various forms of teaching and learning content and resources and provide teachers and students with content and resources design, construction, subscription, and iterative optimization services (Tucker et al. 2016). The system offers teachers and students fast and convenient access to external teaching content and resources. The system supports collaborative editing and refinement of content and resources and provides real-time customization of content and resources during the implementation of blended learning. At the same time, the technical system needs to automatically record various data generated in the design and optimization of content and resources.

Activity and method needs. Blended learning requires that technical system to provide support for teaching and learning activities and methods in conventional teaching and learning scenarios, as well as unconventional teaching and learning scenarios flexibly, such as classroom observation, fieldwork, and tours in science museums (Watson 2008). The system can provide cases, procedures, and other information for reference to enhance the effectiveness of teacher-student activities and the feasibility of teaching and learning methods.

Agent and auxiliary needs. Blended learning requires students to be more autonomous in the learning process. Therefore, the technical system needs to provide teaching agents to help teachers respond to students promptly and provide auxiliary analysis to help teachers and students understand the current learning situation in a timely manner (Montgomery et al. 2015). The system can effectively reduce the difficulties for teachers and students to participate in blended learning, improve the outcomes of teachers and students in blended learning, and reduce the rate of students' incomplete and withdrawal from courses.

Evaluation and feedback needs. Blended learning requires the technical systems to provide learning evaluation in multiple formats, multi-individual participation, and implementation methods for blended learning. It can provide a variety of feedback methods to help teachers and students to optimize blended learning and adjust teaching methods timely at each stage according to the evaluation results (Shih 2011). At the same time, the system needs to automatically record various data generated by evaluation and feedback.

According to the above requirements, the technical support environment is generally co-constructed by various information systems and tools, including the physical teaching environment, the cyber learning space and the IT-based teaching tools, which should enable intelligent teaching and learning activities, differentiated teaching process and personalized student support.

The physical teaching environment. When building a such environment, the IT department should work with faculty to analyze blended learning needs in different scenarios, including classrooms, labs, internships and practical. The physical environments that support blended learning in the above scenarios are mainly multimedia classrooms, smart classrooms, and internship and training environments.

Multimedia classrooms. They can support various teaching and learning activities in the classroom, enhance students' observation and listening skills, and increase opportunities to choose teaching and learning strategies through all ICT-based media in blended learning. At the same time, multimedia classrooms can provide teachers and students with support in terms of connecting electronic equipment, accessing network, displaying multimedia content and interacting with information (a power supply, a laptop/computer, an Internet connection, a projector, a screen/white walls and a sound system, etc.).

Smart classrooms. They can provide intelligent services for various forms of blended learning (course teaching, experimental teaching, etc.). They include perception and intelligent adaptation of the teaching and learning environment, intelligent control of the teaching and learning process, intelligent push of teaching and learning content, various intelligent evaluation of teaching and learning quality, intelligent analysis and optimization of the teaching and learning process, and intelligent suggestions for teaching decisions, and so on. Smart classrooms add a variety of sensors, data collection and analysis systems, and various forms of feedback and intervention devices based on multimedia classrooms (Chong et al. 2010).

Internship and training environment. It can provide information-based support for work experience and training. Specifically, it provides access to the most authentic information-based training scenarios for the target learners, support for information-based needs analysis for work experience and training products, different work experience and training options, control methods of different durations and many simulation formats of work experience and training. Such environments can fully integrate the information technology needed to train professional competences and related skills, provide flexible, adaptive and innovative training formats, and offer psychological follow-up support as well as information-based physical health testing and support for students.

The Cyber learning space. A cyber learning space is an Internet-based virtual learning environment that reflects the key attributes of online learning spaces, mainly including learning and society. Learning refers to the basic attribute of an online learning space, which is to facilitate learning for students and teaching for teachers. Society refers to the attribute of the online learning space that supports interaction between teachers and students, parents, etc. The cyber learning space consists of unique characteristics, including individualization, openness, connectivity, interactivity and flexibility. The individualization of the cyber learning space is mainly reflected in the provision of different resources, tools, activities, services and designs for users with different roles. Openness is mainly reflected in the openness of resources and spaces. In other words, it is open to all users, other systems and other resources and tools within it. Connectivity refers to the communication between users-users, users-objects (space, resources, tools, technologies, services, etc.) and objects-objects. Interactivity emphasizes that it can provide a platform for interaction between users with different roles, between learners and resources, and between resources and resources. Flexibility refers to its scalability in both time and space dimensions. In the time dimension, the learning space can store learners' lifelong learning records or query the learning records of a particular time node. In the spatial dimension, the cyber learning space can be large or small, depending on the needs of the users. The more nodes the cyber learning space is equipped with, the larger the learning space will be. The cyber learning space has to be built systematically by the institution. According to their different functions, cyber learning spaces can be divided into four categories: course services, live teaching, learning resources and role-playing.

Course service space. It is based on learning management systems and helps teachers to build a website for blended courses with functions such as course design, course management, course delivery, communication and learning assessment. This type of system is usually used by institutions, e.g., Moodle, Canvas, Tsinghua Education online, etc.

Live teaching space. It can provide real-time online video or live audio instruction. In this type of space, teachers teach in real-time video or audio, and students can interact through speeches, messages, bullet screens and comments during the learning process. This type is usually built by the institution or provided by social institutions as a cloud service, such as ZOOM, Skype, Tencent Meeting, etc.

Learning resources space. It is characterized by the provision of teaching and learning resources such as video, audio, lesson plans, lecture notes, courseware, exercises and multimedia materials. In this type of space, students can download or browse independently according to their learning needs. Such spaces are cloud services provided by social institutions such as TED (www.ted.com), Baidu Wenku (wenku.baidu.com), etc.

Role-playing space. It is characterized by role substitution to carry out inquiry-based learning. In this type of space, the individual student enters a virtual learning situation with a particular role to discover and explore. Knowledge construction takes place in groups. This type of space needs to be developed, such as Second

Life (www.secondlife.com). The metaverse, based on VR technology, can provide unprecedented immersive experiences for students in the future.

IT-based teaching tools. In addition to the powerful and highly integrated network learning space, there are also special IT-based teaching tools that can assist teachers and students, such as MATLAB (for scientific data visualization calculation, nonlinear dynamic system modeling and simulation, etc.) and Mindmap tools (for visualization of ideas and presentation of knowledge framework), and language translators (or apps), etc.

4.3   Strategies for Institutions to Implement Blended Learning

4.3.1   The Focal Point for Institutional Efforts in the Implementation of Blended Learning

Graham et al. (2013) proposed three stages for the adoption and implementation of blended learning at the institutional level that starts with "institutional awareness". However, in practice, as a large number of institutions have little knowledge of and no foundation for reform through blended learning, there is a need to add one more stage to indicate the reform process from the scratch. Therefore, there are four stages for systematical institutional implementation of blended learning, namely, the unawareness stage, the awareness/exploration stage, the adoption/early implementation stage, and the mature implementation/growth stage. Several key dimensions are involved in the systematical institutional implementation of blended learning, which demonstrates different characteristics at different stages of the reform (Porter et al. 2014). The key dimensions and their characteristics at the aforementioned four stages are shown in Table 4.3.

For an institution passing from the stage of unawareness to the stage of mature implementation/growth, it has to go through three transitional processes. The focus is different in each process, namely the leaders, teachers and students of the institution (as shown in Fig. 4.9).

Transition I: In the transitional process from the unawareness stage to the awareness/exploration stage, the focus is to enhance the institutional leaders' understanding of blended learning, to formulate goals and plans for the reform and to put them into action;

Transition II: In the transitional process from the awareness/exploration stage to the adoption/early implementation stage, the focus shifts from leaders to teachers, that is the implementation of training programs to enhance teachers' awareness, attitude, and ability to adopt blend learning. The key point is that the management of the institution needs to have a clear awareness of blended learning and to formulate plans to implement blended learning;

Table 4.3 The key dimensions and their characteristics in each stage of a blended learning implementation

Key dimensions	The unawareness stage (0)	The awareness/exploration stage (1)	The adoption/early implementation stage (2)	The mature implementation/growth stage (3)
(1) Vision plan	Lacking general planning and design for blended learning implementation	Having the awareness to begin considering carrying out blended learning from several specific aspects, and initially formulated planning documents	Having started to formulate and issue relevant planning documents, and made unified arrangements for institutional learning reform	With clear overall and operational goals of the implementation of blended learning, which are unanimously recognized and accepted by teachers and students, with a reasonable time schedule
	Lacking a proper understanding of the basic philosophy of blended learning	With basic recognition of the role of blended learning and its related concepts, but without integrating it with the institutional context	Recognizing the role and philosophy of blended learning, and contemplating on its positioning in view of the actual situation of the institution	Having clarified the role and positioning of the blended learning in talent training of the institution, and adhered to the correct and distinctive blended learning philosophy and ideas
(2) Organization	Lacking a specialized organization to lead and support blended learning	With a dedicated organization to lead and support the implementation of blended learning	With a dedicated organization to lead and support the implementation of blended learning, with the institutional leader as the main person in charge	With a customized matrix (body) for blended learning with a reasonable hierarchy, clear responsibilities, appropriate staff, and division of labor, which runs well and continues to promote implementation of blended learning

(continued)

Table 4.3 (continued)

Key dimensions	The unawareness stage (0)	The awareness/exploration stage (1)	The adoption/early implementation stage (2)	The mature implementation/growth stage (3)
(3) Policies and regulations	Lacking policies to support blended learning	Having implemented some policies to support blended learning	With well-established policies to support the implementation of blended learning, and such policies are implemented at all different levels of the institution	The overall planning, corresponding policies, and functional mechanisms of the institution to promote blended learning are well-aligned
(4) Personnel capability	The leaders lack awareness of blended learning	The leaders have an awareness of blended learning and have started training teachers for a pilot reform	The leaders, teachers and students, and staff in functional departments have begun to develop the ability to implement blended learning	The leaders, teachers, students, staff in functional departments, and external forces are all qualified to continue to promote blended learning
(5) Curriculum structure	Not any pilot reform conducted to any course yet	Blended learning is adopted in a few courses	Blended learning is adopted in a number of courses with good results	Blended learning has been established as a regular teaching form in most courses, with the overall teaching and learning quality enhancement
(6) Supporting service system	Lacking favorable conditions to support the implementation of blended learning	Provides some support services to facilitate the implementation of blended learning limited to technical services	Having started offering support services for blended learning, including teaching support and technical services	With a complete blended learning support service system, including facilitation of students' learning and teachers' teaching

(continued)

Table 4.3 (continued)

Key dimensions	The unawareness stage (0)	The awareness/ exploration stage (1)	The adoption/early implementation stage (2)	The mature implementation/growth stage (3)
	Lacking support for students' learning	Provides support for students' technical issues only	In addition to an ICT technology service platform, online Q&A services to support students' blended learning are also provided	The students are not only provided with blended learning support, but also guided to become active, self-directed learners
(7) Technical environment	Lacking physical environments, online learning spaces, and digital resources for teachers to implement blended learning	Having started building physical environments, online learning spaces, and digital resources that support blended learning	Teachers and students can easily have the physical environment, online learning space and digital resources for blended learning	Teachers and students have easy access to physical environments, online learning spaces, and digital resources for blended learning and teachers develop and share their digital resources online

(continued)

Table 4.3 (continued)

Key dimensions	The unawareness stage (0)	The awareness/exploration stage (1)	The adoption/early implementation stage (2)	The mature implementation/growth stage (3)
(8) Cultural atmosphere	Lacking a cultural atmosphere that supports blended learning	Having begun to create a cultural atmosphere that is conducive to promoting blended learning	Having gradually built a culture conductive to blended learning, which is recognized and accepted by teachers and students	A common belief and cultural identity about blended learning have been established among the teachers and students of the whole institution, which has become the internal driving force of blended learning in the institution
(9) Effectiveness evaluation	Lacking an evaluation scheme for the effectiveness of blended learning	Having begun to formulate an index system for evaluating the effectiveness of blended learning, and attempted the evaluation	Having formulated an evaluation scheme with multi-subject participation and a multi-dimensional indicator system, which is applied to diagnose the effectiveness of the institution's blended learning	Having formed an evaluation scheme and system for the effectiveness of blended learning, which is in line with the institution's characteristics, and provided assessment reports on a regular basis to improve the reform process

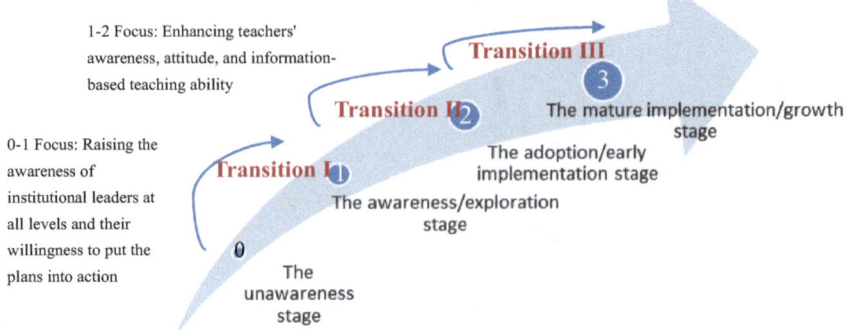

Fig. 4.9 The different stages of institutional implementation of blended learning and their focus

Transition III (The adoption/early implementation stage): In the transitional process from the adoption/early implementation stage to the mature implementation/ growth stage, the focus shifts from teachers to students, that is, that teachers implement blended learning with the ultimate goal of improving learning effectiveness and information-based learning ability.

4.3.2   Strategies Adopted by Institutions to Implement Blended Learning

For an institution to systematically implement blended learning, it needs to formulate specific strategies based on its predetermined goals, status quo, and its own characteristics. Given that the reform can be initiated by different subjects, the reform promotion strategies can be divided into two types, namely top-down and bottom-up strategies.

The top-down strategy

The implementation of the top-down strategy refers to the case when the institution's top management initiates blended learning, conducts overall planning starting from top-level design, and gradually promotes the reform to the bottom level, i.e., teachers and students. The specific sequence for an institution to implement blended learning by adopting the "top-down" strategy is shown in Fig. 4.10. Starting from (1) formulating goals and plans, the institution (2) sets up organizations, (3) issues policies and regulations, (4) establishes a support and service system, (5) builds a technical support environment, (6) enhances staff capabilities and reforms the curriculum system, (7) reforms the program and curriculum system, in order to obtain staged evaluation results, and continuously adjusts all aspects, during which (8) a corresponding cultural atmosphere is gradually developed. Then (9) an overall

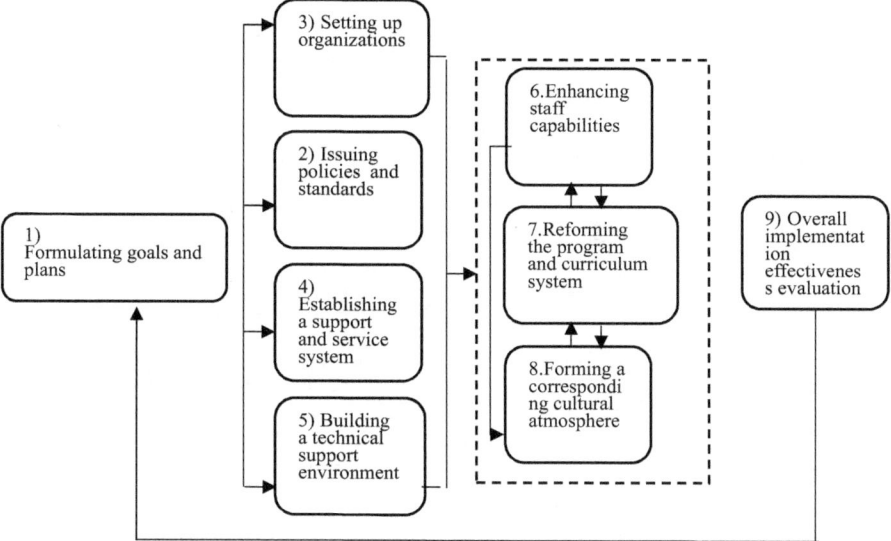

Fig. 4.10 A reference sequence for institutions to implement blended learning by adopting the "top-down" strategy

evaluation result of implementation effectiveness is generated for this stage. Based on the evaluation result at this stage, the institution revises (1) its goals and plans. Some of the abovementioned steps are iterative throughout the entire reform process (such as iterative revision of policies and regulations, improvement of information capabilities of staff in cohorts, iterative adjustment of the evaluation system, etc.).

The main advantage of the "top-down" strategy is that it allows the institutions to formulate their overall goals and plans, making it possible for them to concentrate their strength and resources on designing and supporting implementation of blended learning in a holistic fashion. Also, the promotion of blended learning can be conducted with clear time nodes and can achieve expected milestones. Such a strategy sets high requirements on the information leadership of institutional administrators and the management ability of its organizations, as well as requires close cooperation of various departments to ensure the effective planning and implementation of all kinds of policies and measures (Porter and Graham 2016). In addition, since a top-down reform is mandatory, if a consensus cannot be reached during the process, it is likely to encounter resistance from teachers.

The "bottom-up" strategy

The implementation of the "bottom-up" strategy refers to the case that teachers voluntarily explore blended learning first and expand the scope after receiving support from the institution. The sequence of implementing blended learning by adopt the "bottom-up" strategy is shown in Fig. 4.11. The premise of adopting this strategy

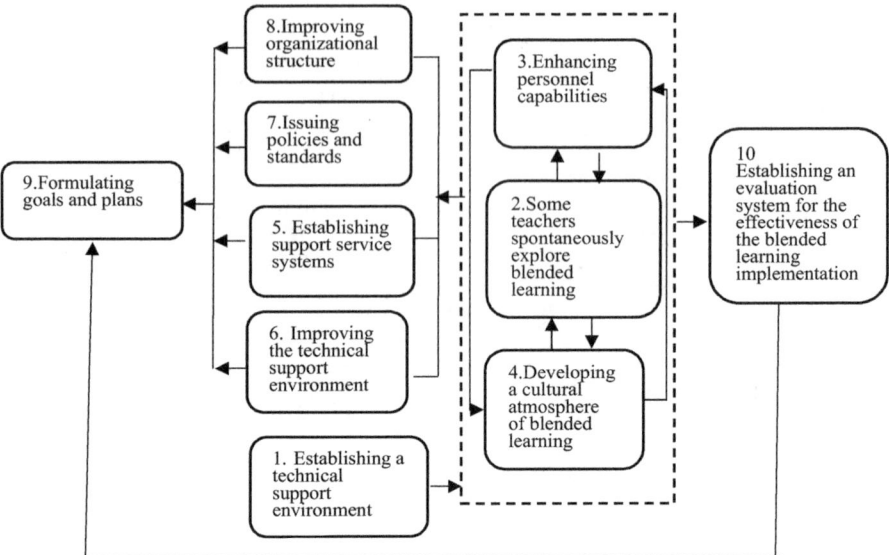

Fig. 4.11 A reference sequence for institutions to implement blended learning by adopting the "bottom-up" strategy

is that (1) a technical support environment is established, (2) some teachers spontaneously explore blended learning, and in this process (3) personnel capabilities are enhanced. When such teachers make up an increasingly large share of the entire faculty, (4) a cultural atmosphere of blended learning is developed in the institution. In this way, the institution is urged to (5) establish support service systems, (6) improve the technical support environment, (7) issue policies and regulations, (8) improve the organizational structure, and finally (9) formulate goals and plans at the institutional level and establish (10) establish an evaluation system for the effectiveness of implementation of blended learning. And then, based on the evaluation result, the (9) goals and plans are revised.

The main advantage of the bottom-up strategy lies in that since teachers are the initiators of the reform, they share a common internal motivation to drive the reform. Following the trend brought about by the teachers, the institution then promotes the implementation of blended learning gradually, which is not likely to cause great turmoil in the institution. However, due to the lack of preliminary overall planning and strong organizational management, the nodes of the entire implementation of blended learning are clear, and the implementation process can be protracted. It can be difficult to achieve clear milestones in the short term. At the same time, because the demand for teachers is scattered and short-term, the institutional support services for teachers' blended learning implementation will not be sustainable and sufficient, and therefore it will be difficult to ensure sustainable advancement of the reform with high quality.

Each of the abovementioned two strategies have their own advantages and disadvantages. The institution can choose either one strategy based on its own needs and conditions. In the process of promoting blended learning, the institution can also integrate the abovementioned two strategies. In this way, the institution still leads the progress of the implementation of blended learning and conducts overall planning and implementation. At the same time, the institution encourages teachers to adopt blenden learning, allows a longer transition period, and provides different training mechanisms and multi-level incentive mechanisms to guide teachers to sustainably implement blended learning.

4.4   Evaluation of Institutional Blended Learning Implementation

In the process of institutional promotion of blended learning, it is necessary to evaluate the effectiveness of the reform, identify the problems, and adjust the measures in the implementation process accordingly.

4.4.1   A Self-evaluation Framework for Implementation of Blended Learning in Higher Education Institutions

Based on Rogers' Diffusion of Innovations Theory, Graham and Robison (2007) examined the situation of implementation of blended learning in universities in the U.S.A., and proposed three categories with 12 dimensions of measures, namely: Strategy (Purpose, Advocacy, Implementation, Definition, Policy), Structure (Governance, Models, Scheduling, Evaluation) and Support (Technical, Teaching Pedagogical, Incentives). In his subsequent research, he revised the "model" under "structure" into "infrastructure" and "professional development". In order to facilitate higher education institutions to evaluate the effect of their implementation of the blended learning, he developed an institutional self-evaluation checklist based on the blended learning adoption framework. The checklist contains relevant questions around 12 indicators under the three categories: strategy, structure, and support, which can be used by higher education institutions to qualitatively judge which of the above three stages their implementation of blended learning is in just by answering these questions, and to find out areas for improvement.

4.4.2 UNESCO Self-assessment Tool for Implementation of Blended Learning in Higher Education Institutions

In a book titled *Blended learning for quality higher education: Selected case studies on implementation from Asia–Pacific* published by UNESCO, based on the implementation of information-based learning reform or reform through blended learning by organizations and higher education institutions in the Asia–Pacific region, Lim and Wang (2016) developed a framework that illustrates the four stages of blended learning practices, i.e., under consideration, applying/emerging, infusing, and transforming., and eight key dimensions of strategic planning for driving blended learning practices, namely vision and philosophy; curriculum; professional development; learning support; infrastructure, facilities, resources and support; policy and institutional structure; partnership; and research and evaluation. Based on this framework, a framework and self-assessment tool for building the capacity of higher education institutions for blended learning was developed, which can be adopted by institutions to analyze the progress and stages of their blended learning reform from the above eight dimensions. An online system based on this tool was also developed for self-assessment by institutions.

4.4.3 A Quantitative Assessment Framework for Implementation of Blended Learning Based on Online Behaviors of Teachers

Blended learning reform involves a complex and continuous process. We need to understand not only the stages of the reform at an institutional level, but also the dynamic progress of the reform in a timely manner (Taylor an Newton 2013). Teachers, as the practitioners of the reform, constitute as one of the key factors that determine the success of the reform. No reform will succeed without complying to the will of teachers and the involvement of active participation of teachers. Therefore, by evaluating teachers' involvement, we can understand the dynamic progress of the blended learning reform of the institution. At the same time, the continuous emergence of big data technology related to education and the data analysis methods make it possible to conduct quantitative assessment of blended learning reform based on the online teaching behavior of teachers.'

Based on the data of teachers' involvement in online teaching, Han et al. (2019) from the Institution of Education at Tsinghua University proposed a quantitative assessment framework for the implementation effectiveness of blended learning in higher education institutions. The proposed framework was proved to be technically adequate in assessing teachers' online presence in blended learning at an institutional level. Using this framework, institutions can gain a comprehensive understanding of their blended learning implementation so as to refine their strategies and advance their blended learning agenda.

The Quantitative Assessment of Online Teaching Presence (QAOTP) in institution-wide BL implementation consists of three key constructs–the intensity, the regularity, and the interactivity. The degrees of each construct can be quantitatively assessed.

The intensity of online teaching presence can be assessed by the frequency of the teachers' overall course site visits in any given period of time (e.g., an academic year, or a semester). In other words, the more visits to the course sites, the stronger the online teaching presence would be during this period. Thus, the frequency that teachers visit their course sites is a primary indicator of the developmental stages of BL at an institution. A more detailed picture can be depicted by grouping teachers according to the number of course visits and calculating the percentage of each group to see the frequency of course visits by a group.

The regularity of online teaching presence can be assessed by dividing the period under investigation into smaller time units and then calculating the frequency of teachers' course visits in each unit. The unit can be a month, a week, or any meaningful division of a time period. This is the second primary indicator indicating the level of BL normalization by checking the regularity or irregularity of the teachers' course site visits incrementally throughout the whole period under investigation. This will further explain the first construct by showing a more detailed course site visit status phase by phase. Hypothetically and ideally, along with the normalization of BL, in regular teaching weeks (excluding exam and self-study weeks) in a semester, the total number of teachers' visits to their course sites as a whole should be more or less evenly distributed throughout the teaching weeks. The rationale is that after teaching begins, teachers should moderate and/or teach the course online on a regular basis to maintain student engagement during this period of time. Thus, if the total number of teachers' course visits for the whole institution is 100% for the teaching weeks in a semester, the average percentage of visit per teaching week should be 100% divided by the number of teaching weeks in the semester. This average can be used as a baseline to judge institution-wide teachers' online participation phase by phase.

The third construct seeks data on the level of interactivity that a teacher engages students online. As the QAOTP framework uses the log data from an LMS, it is not easy to determine the depth of the interactivity of an action generated by a teacher. Thus, the interactivity construct is only qualified as being non-interactive or interactive. The teaching presence in this research only concerns the design and facilitation of online learning in a BL course. Teaching activities in the design category are usually non-interactive, while in the facilitation category, teachers engage learners in either interactive or non-interactive fashion. The interactivity construct should cover all the activities generated by the teacher in the course design and facilitation, both interactive and non-interactive.

The three constructs in the QAOTP framework should be equally important and indispensable. They complement one another in generating a more accurate and comprehensive picture of the degrees and features of online teaching presence than a single construct is able to achieve. That said, this is only an overarching framework that is designed with special attention to its applicability and replicability in that all three dimensions are only broadly defined with no specific requirements for how data should be categorized and treated. This leaves room for individual universities to integrate their specific data within the broad boundaries of this framework.

References

Bai, X., & Han, X. (2020). Introducing blended learning in a community college: how teachers can be prepared. In 2020 Ninth International Conference of Educational Innovation through Technology (EITT) (pp. 64–69). IEEE.

Baier-D'Orazio, M.G. and Mukuza Muhini, V.B. (2016). Guide for practitioners of vocational training. CAPA-Centre d'Apprentissage Professionnel et Artisanal Bukavu, Dem. Rep. of the Congo. https://unevoc.unesco.org/up/CAPA_practitioners.pdf.

Basir, H. M., Ahmad, A., & Noor, N. L. M. (2010). Institutional strategy for effective blended e-learning: HCI perspective of sustainable embedding. In 2010 International Conference on User Science and Engineering (pp. 71–76). IEEE.

Bärenfänger, O. (2005). Learning management: a new approach to structuring hybrid learning arrangements. Electronic Journal of Foreign Language Teaching, 2(2), 14-35.

Bidarra, J., & Rusman, E. (2017). Towards a pedagogical model for science education: bridging educational contexts through a blended learning approach. Open Learning: the Journal of Open, Distance and E-learning, 32(1), 6-20.

Boelens, R., De Wever, B., & Voet, M. (2017). Four key challenges to the design of blended learning: a systematic literature review. Educational Research Review, 22, 1-18.

Chong, S., Cheah, H. M., & Low, E. L. (2010). Perceptions of student teachers in a blended learning environment. International Journal of Innovation and Learning, 8(4), 345-359.

Daft, R. L., Murphy, J., & Willmott, H. (2010) .Organization theory and design. Mason, OH: South-Western Cengage Learning, 101–104.

Geng, S., Law, K. M., & Niu, B. (2019). Investigating self-directed learning and technology readiness in blending learning environment. International Journal of Educational Technology in Higher Education, 16(1), 1-22.

Graham,C.R. (2006). Blended learning systems. The handbook of blended learning: global perspectives, local designs.Pfeiffer, 1, 3–21.

Graham, C. R. , Woodfield, W. , & Harrison, J. B. (2013). A framework for institutional adoption and implementation of blended learning in higher education. The Internet and Higher Education, 18, 4-14.

Graham, C. R., & Robison, R. (2007). Realizing the transformational potential of blended learning: comparing cases of transforming blends and enhancing blends in higher education. Blended Learning: Research Perspectives, 83–110.

Halverson, L. R., Graham, C. R., Spring, K. J., Drysdale, J. S., & Henrie, C. R. (2014). A thematic analysis of the most highly cited scholarship in the first decade of blended learning research. The Internet and Higher Education, 20:20-34.

Han, X., Wang, Y., & Jiang, L. (2019). Towards a framework for an institution-wide quantitative assessment of teachers' online participation in blended learning implementation. The Internet and Higher Education, 42, 1-12.

Johnson, M. C., & Graham, C. R. (2015). Current status and future directions of blended learning models. Encyclopedia of Information Science and Technology, Third Edition, 2470–2480.

Lim, C. P., & Wang, T. (2016). A framework and self-assessment tool for building the capacity of higher education institutions for blended learning. In C. P. Lim & L. Wang (Eds.), Blended learning for quality higher education: Selected case studies on implementation from Asia-Pacific (pp. 1-38). Paris, France: UNESCO.

Machado, C. (2007). Developing an e-readiness model for higher education institutions: Results of a focus group study. British Journal of Educational Technology, 38(1), 72-82.

Moskal, P., Dziuban, C., & Hartman, J. (2013). Blended learning: a dangerous idea? The Internet and Higher Education, 18, 15-23.

Montgomery, A. P., Hayward, D. V., Dunn, W., Carbonaro, M., & Amrhein, C. G. (2015). Blending for student engagement: lessons learned for MOOCs and beyond. Australasian Journal of Educational Technology, 31(6).

Neumeier, P. (2005). A closer look at blended learning—parameters for designing a blended learning environment for language teaching and learning. ReCALL, 17(2), 163-178.

Porter, W. W., Graham, C. R., Spring, K. A., & Welch, K. R.. (2014). Blended learning in higher education: institutional adoption and implementation. Computers & Education, 75, 185-195.

Porter, W. W., & Graham, C. R. (2016). Institutional drivers and barriers to faculty adoption of blended learning in higher education. British Journal of Educational Technology, 47(4): 748-762.

Rafiola, R., Setyosari, P., Radjah, C., & Ramli, M. (2020). The effect of learning motivation, self-efficacy, and blended learning on students' achievement in the industrial revolution 4.0. International Journal of Emerging Technologies in Learning (iJET), 15(8), 71–82.

Richard L. Daft.(2015). Organization theory and design, tenth edition. South-Western Cengage Learning, 60–64,101–104.

Shih, R. C. (2011). Can web 2.0 technology assist college students in learning English writing? Integrating facebook and peer assessment with blended learning. Australasian Journal of Educational Technology, 27(5).

Siemens, G., Gasevic, D. and Dawson, S. (2015). Preparing for the digital university: a review of the history and current state of distance, blended, and online Learning. https://researchmgt.mon ash.edu/ws/portalfiles/portal/256525723/256524746_oa.pdf.

Sun, Z., Liu, R., Luo, L., Wu, M., & Shi, C. (2017). Exploring collaborative learning effect in blended learning environments. Journal of Computer Assisted Learning, 33(6), 575-587.

Taylor, J. A., & Newton, D. (2013). Beyond blended learning: a case study of institutional change at an Australian regional university. Internet and Higher Education, 18:54-60.

Tucker, C. R., Wycoff, T., & Green, J. T. (2016). Blended learning in action: a practical guide toward sustainable change. Corwin Press.

Welker, E.W., Kelter, P. and Motschenbacher, J.M.D. (2017). Classroom design manual. North Dakota State University. Available at: https://www.ndsu.edu/fileadmin/provost/LSEC/NDSU_ Classroom_Design_Manual.pdf.

Watson, J. (2008). Blended Learning: The convergence of online and face-to-face education. North American Council for Online Learning. Available at: https://files.eric.ed.gov/fulltext/ ED509636.pdf.

Weller M. (2007). Virtual learning environments: using, choosing and developing your VLE. Routledge.

Chapter 5
Supporting Students and Instructors in Blended Learning

Qingtang Liu, Li Chen, Xiaoying Feng, Xiaojing Bai, and Zhiqiang Ma

Blended learning is the integration of online learning and face-to-face instruction. This type of learning integrates innovative technology and multimedia with the best aspects of the traditional pedagogical approach in a way that creates a richer learning experience for students. With the potential to enhance the student experience, the key to success is how to effectively support students and instructors. In this chapter, Sect. 5.1 provides an overview of the fundamental principles for building a blended learning support system; Sect. 5.2 covers the approaches to supporting students in blended learning, including planning and guidance, diagnosis and monitoring, and intervention and evaluation; and Sect. 5.3 discusses a variety of strategies that have been used to support instructors, such as training, pedagogy, policy, and evaluation. This handbook serves as a guide for instructors, support staff, and administrators who want to offer blended courses to their students, with relevant cases and approaches.

5.1 Overview

Four fundamental principles of support for blended learning are proposed in light of what has been done to support students and instructors n distance education and what has made blended learning unique.

Q. Liu (✉)
Faculty of Artificial Intelligence in Education, Central China Normal University, Wuhan, China
e-mail: liuqtang@mail.ccnu.edu.cn

L. Chen · X. Feng
School of Educational Technology, Beijing Normal University, Beijing, China

X. Bai
Beijing Open University, Beijing, China

Z. Ma
School of Humanities, Jiangnan University, Wuxi, China

© The Author(s) 2024
M. Li et al. (eds.), *Handbook of Educational Reform Through Blended Learning*,
https://doi.org/10.1007/978-981-99-6269-3_5

5.1.1 Fundamental Principles of Building Support System for Blended Learning

Systematization: Single-Service to System-Wide Service Transition

Systematization is critical for the success of the blended learning support system. Instructors and students must be at the center of the support system so that diverse parts may work together to strengthen relationships. Changes are expected to be made, from the content-fragmented and department-isolated series to the one that is intersectional, integrated and cohesive (Wu et al. 2021).

Integration: Transforming from Actual Classroom into Virtual Space

For blended learning to work, it must be built on the concept of "integration," which means that to meet certain learning goals, both physical classrooms and online virtual learning environments must be carefully planned and connected. It is therefore vital to create conditions and support for learning that may occur at any time and in any location (Yang et al 2020).

Process-Oriented: Transition from Single Point of Support to a Support System Throughout the Teaching and Learning Process

Instructor preparation and learner support teams should work together to develop a comprehensive approach to blended learning that covers all aspects of the process before, during, and after sessions.

Personalization: Transition from Group to Individual Support

Students' educational level and capabilities for self-regulated learning should be taken into consideration while providing support services for blended learning. Traditional learner support services are frequently fixed and rigid in their approach. However, by means of learning analytics and adaptive technology, blended learning support services may accomplish tailored instructional design, curriculum management and learning assessment, satisfy students' individualized learning requirements, and assist students in overcoming specific learning difficulties (Li 2018).

5.1.2 The Core Elements of the Blended Learning Support System

Globally, different approaches to classifying the elements of learner support have been employed. Simpson classified learner support into teaching and nonteaching support (Simpson 2002), whereas Tait argued that three components need to be taken into consideration in learner support: systematic, emotional, and cognitive support (Wang and Ding 2004). Brindley further characterized learner support as tutoring and teaching (support in connection to the content of the course), advising and consulting (support not connected to the content of the course), and administrative and technical support (Chen 2011).

With respect to early studies conducted in other parts of the world, Ding (2002) first introduced learner support to China and provided detailed taxonomies of learner support: manpower, facilities, instruction, information desk, supply service, and assessment and evaluation. As the practice of blended learning is quickly developing in China, scholars have continued to synthesize the many elements of learner support. For example, Huang (2004) broke down learner support into the following five categories: resource support, advisory support, technical support, instructor support, and managerial support. Although pedagogical instructional support dominated discussions in the early days, Chen (2011) subsequently advocated cognitive support and peer support in addition to management support, instructional support and technical support. Huang further added emotional support to technical support, course logistical support, and teaching support, etc. (Huang and Zhou 2006).

The primary goal of the learner support system is to meet the needs of both instructors and their students. Instructors and students must be at the center of a blended learning support system that allows students to actively participate in the instructional activities initiated by the instructors. This handbook incorporates the most recent research findings in distance education and best practices to help educators and students alike get the most out of a blended learning support system. To effectively provide learner support, a blended learning environment, digital learning materials, and organizational and operational management are all essential prerequisites (see Chap. 4 of this handbook).

5.2 Supporting Students in Blended Learning

Blended learning is characterized by more substantive learning material, flexible and diversified learning activities, and greater student autonomy, but it also demonstrates that students are increasingly dependent on digital platforms; therefore, instructors and schools must give more systematic support to students.

There are several types of learning support services targeted specifically toward students, all of which focus on the needs of the students themselves.

5.2.1 Guidance and Preparation

Introducing the Course

In the beginning, we should make the most of the course platform to offer an overview of the courses in the blended learning program. In addition to providing students with a better understanding of their learning objectives and plans, it may also help them to become more motivated and engaged in their studies.

The Association for Educational Communications and Technology (AECT) produced the AECT Instructional Design Standards for Distance Learning, which states that clearly defined goals and objectives (both those of the institution/instructor and those of the students) are a necessary precondition for productive collaboration between educators and students (Piña and Harris 2019).

In practice, a well-designed course overview may help students better understand the course's objectives, structure, materials, codes of conduct, required prior knowledge and skills, information about professors, and class members. The QM (Quality Matters 2020) organization of the United States has developed a national standard framework for online courses (Lowenthal and Hodges 2015), which includes the course overview and introduction. It is necessary to take into consideration the following nine factors:

- Instructions make clear how to get started and where to find various course components.
- Learners are introduced to the purpose and structure of the course.
- Communication expectations for online discussions, email, and other forms of interaction are clearly stated.
- Course and institutional policies with which the learner is expected to comply are clearly stated within the course, or a link to the current policies is provided.
- Minimum technology requirements for the course are clearly stated, and information on how to obtain the technologies is provided.
- Computer skills and digital information literacy skills expected of the learner are clearly stated.
- Expectations for prerequisite knowledge in the discipline and/or any required competencies are clearly stated.
- The self-introduction by the instructor is professional and available online.
- Learners are asked to introduce themselves to the class.

The course overview should address all or part of the abovementioned nine factors in an effective blended teaching design, and it is recommended that each school consider and create additional factors according to their actual circumstances.

Making a Learning Plan

The blended course platform must provide guidance to students so that they may create learning plans and become accustomed to online learning. Guidance in making learning plans prior to the official start of learning helps students manage their time and complete assignments more efficiently and thus meet their learning goals. Learning plans often include information such as the days and times of classes, the modules or subjects covered, the number of hours of instruction, the assignments to be completed, and so on. In a nutshell, making a learning plan refers to the process of breaking down the material covered in the class into individual learning units and carrying out the activities associated with each learning unit according to predesigned instructions.

- Teaching Weeks: In a learning program, the dates of study are commonly stated in the form of weeks;
- Learning Modules or Themes: A module or theme in a class often consists of multiple chapters, and students are expected to devote a significant amount of time to studying for it;

- Learning hour: Also known as class hours, they are 50 min in length.
- Assignments: Quizzes, formative assessments, and summative evaluations (examinations) are included.

 Exemplar 5.1

The Open University in the UK offers a course package for learners, which includes learning materials, the course schedule and assessments, allowing students to acquire all the information and advice they need prior to beginning their studies (Sun et al. 2015).

 Exemplar 5.2

Table 5.1 is the schedule for a university's *Child Psychology* course of the Open University of China. For students who are new to the course, the table provides an overview of the study dates, units, chapters, class hours, and formative assessments.

Table 5.1 Schedule for *Child Psychology*

Weeks	Theme	Chapter	Class hours	Formative assessment (The full score is 100 points, equivalent to the final assessment score of 50 points)		
				Discussions (40 points for 5 topics)	Tests (60 points in 5 tests)	Case sharing (1~5 bonus points)
1~2	Basic theory of psychological development in preschool children	I Introduction	7	Topic 1 (8 points)	Test 1 (12 points)	Provide relevant cases (1–5 bonus points)
2~3		II Theoretical schools of preschool child psychology	5			
4~5		III Biological factors affecting the development of preschool children	6	Topic 2 (8 points)	Test 2 (12 points)	

6~7	Age characteristics and development principles of preschool children's psychological and behavioral development	IV Physical development of preschool children	8		
8~9		V Cognitive development of preschool children	8	Topic 3 (8 points)	Test 3 (12 points)
10~11		VI Language development of preschool children	6		
12~13		VII Emotional development of preschool children	10	Topic 4 (8 points)	Test 4 (12 points)
13~14		VIII Development of personality and sociality	8		
14~15	Impact of environmental factors on child development	IX Family and child development	7	Topic 5 (8 points)	Test 5 (12 points)
15~16		X Child development outside the family	7		

Learning Requirements

Having explicit learning requirements at both the course and individual levels helps to establish a positive learning environment and ensures that the course progresses in a timely manner.

According to Adams et al. (2020), blended learning calls for multidimensional engagement on the side of students, including their cognition (the needed knowledge and skills), behaviors (students actively participating in course activities), and emotions (emotions expressed to the instructor and peers). On the basis of the aforementioned three dimensions, the learning needs of blended courses should also consider the features of face-to-face courses and those of online courses (Visiting group of Jiangsu RTVU and Zhou 2006).

Learning requirements for blended learning, which are similar to those for face-to-face courses, need to further address the following points:

- The amount of time students must devote to the course;
- The minimum number of credit hours they must earn;

- The essential knowledge and abilities students should acquire as a result of taking the course; and
- The standards students must adhere to prior to, during, and following class (such as the class code of conduct, completing coursework on time, etc.).

Blended learning, however, presents a new set of challenges:

- Usage of the course website and any appropriate application software;
- Adherence to the rules for managing online courses;
- Compliance with the criteria for online class attendance;
- Adherence to the norms for participation and discussion in online class groups.

 Exemplar 5.3

Before the beginning of the *General Psychology* course, a university disseminated the learning requirements using a WeChat group. These requirements included specifics on the amount of time that must be spent on the course, the live broadcast platform, the management of learning groups, attendance, and prerequisite reading. Moreover, instructors are advised to notify students in a timely manner to ensure that the course progresses as expected.

 Exemplar 5.4

During the course of a Business English class, a professor at the university released the particular learning requirements for students to the original WeChat group. These requirements included:

(1) a questionnaire that students needed to complete before the class;
(2) learning groups that needed to be added, personal information that needed to be amended, and learning materials that needed to be downloaded;
(3) an application that needed to be downloaded for the course and explanations regarding check-in and attendance concerns;
(4) a requirement that students check in and be present during class.

Learning Strategies

A learning strategy is an approach for a student to accomplish a certain learning objective and master subject knowledge. Because of the unique nature of blended learning, students must not only have the skills they need to master specific subject content but also have the information technology skills they need to make effective use of relevant online learning resources. It is vital to have knowledge of learning strategies to increase learning efficiency and effectiveness.

In contrast to traditional teaching, blended learning places greater emphasis on student autonomy and self-regulated capacities. The utilization of software, communication, material, and after-class time are all important considerations for instructors in blended learning (Ushatikova et al. 2019). Learner support includes not only the assistance students receive from their lecturers (Dwiyogo and Radjah 2020) but also the help offered by other students in online communities of practice and learner–content interaction.

- Providing cognitive support in connection with the learning material
- Students should be given cognitive support such as mnemonics if the course requires them to remember knowledge. This will help them create their own cognition map.
- Asking to take notes in class
- The purpose of having students take notes in class is so they may organize their information and revisit it as needed.
- Supporting the learning of new tools
- Students would benefit from our support in becoming proficient in the use of various learning tools, such as computers, the software that goes with them, and the apps that they run.
- Motivating students to learn. For blended learning to be successful, we need to give students more control over their own learning, allow them to understand the notion of self-directed learning, and help them create their own learning trajectories.
- Learning how to engage with and be supported by others in the community. We might assist students in establishing online learning communities, creating online classes, fostering a positive community environment, and obtaining peer support inside the communities.

 Exemplar 5.5

The learning strategies contribute to the overall success of the course. A university's *government economics* course primarily focuses on the following aspects of teaching and learning:

(1) understanding what the course is about;
(2) putting theory and practice together;
(3) making mastering basic principles and knowledge your top priority;
(4) paying attention to the summary of each chapter; and
(5) doing exercises in different ways on the computer.

5.2.2 Diagnosis and Guidance

Diagnosis of Learning Status

Blended learning integrates traditional teaching with online instruction, and its primary goal is to improve students' overall academic performance. Nevertheless, when blended learning is put into practice, can students actually experience better learning outcomes? If not, how can we make it better? Because of this, it is crucial to understand how students learn and be able to see difficulties with their progress in real time. This handbook can help educators better understand the challenges that can occur when putting blended learning into practice and enable them to make timely adjustments to the instructional design to obtain the best possible learning experience.

Learners have to contend with twice as many learning challenges while using blended learning. Therefore, both their own personal challenges, such as learning fatigue, and the challenges posed by the nature of blended learning, such as the mismatch between face-to-face instruction and online learning, obsolete learning materials, lack of resources, and inappropriate activity designs, must be addressed.

Challenges Using Learning Resources

There are various concerns with online learning resources, including a lack of overall design, poor quality, and disconnection from face-to-face instruction (Li and Ma 2014). In terms of how resources are organized, they are almost always a copy of offline materials, and the creation of online content is not guided by any pedagogical theory. The quality of the available technological resources is also poor, and they are not kept up to date. Some examples of this include obsolete courseware, blurry images, and video that has been segmented. Learners are unable to select learning resources according to their individual needs, as there is a dearth of learning resources that are specifically geared toward their needs. In addition, the learning resources that are now available are inadequate, uninteresting, and lacking in integration (Xiao and Jiang 2009). Online courses are sometimes limited to course materials and online assignment submissions because they do not include other learning tools, such as references and resource links. It is also difficult for students to utilize library resources, with just 47.1% of institutions providing e-library services for distance learners (Cai and Zhuang 2006).

Challenges Arising from Interaction

There is a lack of online interaction currently available for blended learning. The community of inquiry theory developed by Garrison and Kanuka (2004) brought attention to the vital role that interaction plays in blended learning. In their article "Designing Mixed Environments," Osguthorpe and Graham (2003, page 231) also include "social interaction" as one of the six aims that instructors should strive toward while creating blended environments. However, instructors seldom respond to student queries online, so student questions cannot be answered quickly; in addition, the online learning community lacks behavioral rules, so student interaction cannot be assured. Moreover, there are few interactive activities for students to participate in, resulting in challenges in mobilizing their excitement.

Problems Caused by Technology

On the one hand, technological issues prevent students from accessing materials. Because of this, some students are unable to participate in online learning because they do not have access to computers, the internet, or even online resources (Lu and Sun 2015). Existing learning platform resources are also inadequately accessible, with just a small subset of materials readily available to students whose network is not part of a campus network. On the other hand, the current technological level of the platform is not sufficient to facilitate the fulfillment of the requirements of the learners. First, the network environments (platform security and stability) are poor, the network speed is slow, and the courseware cannot be opened during peak hours; this causes a great deal of inconvenience for students in regard to logging in, studying, submitting homework and even taking exams. Adaptive mobile terminal support is also missing from the network learning platform, as are intelligent interactive features (Jin et al. 2018).

Inappropriate Learning Strategies

Blended learning relies heavily on effective and efficient blended learning strategies, which may be classified into two categories: content and technology. Many blended learning courses do not include instructions on how to employ techniques and tools in the design of the course, despite the presence of advice in teaching practice. Learning tactics and approaches, such as helping learners define objectives, making acceptable plans, monitoring their progress, strengthening community ties, and so on, are often overlooked in instructional design. As a direct result of this, it is difficult for students to master knowledge and become proficient with it. It is difficult for certain learners to understand how to use computers and related software on the learning platform since there is no matching operating guide or demonstration. This has a negative impact on the learning process and the learning outcomes of these learners.

Personal Emotional Factors

Learners who are less likely to participate in learning tend to feel depressed and exhausted (Li and Lei 2012). Learners' attendance rates are poor owing to conflicting work and study schedules, and as a result they are more likely to have a negative view of blended learning. Furthermore, some students continue to favor and become accustomed to the conventional face-to-face classroom because they find it difficult to adjust to the new notion, find it difficult to grasp the new technology, and believe that the new blended learning pattern is ineffective. In addition, some students lack the capacity to study on their own and the ability to manage their time and plan ahead. One final aspect to consider is that students who participate in online education report feeling a great deal of isolation, and it can be challenging to genuinely become a part of online learning communities and to realize the potential for communication and engagement with professors and other students.

Provision of Guidance and Support

A complete approach is needed to address the challenges that students face in blended learning, which includes providing them with relevant information and tools and strategies to help them learn.

Resource Allocation

Face-to-face and online instruction should be designed in a way that takes full advantage of the strengths of each medium in a blended learning environment (Lu and Sun 2015). It is important that the way educational materials are presented is tailored to their content's distinctive features. Face-to-face instruction may be used, for instance, to teach students key and difficult concepts, and then those concepts can be videotaped and made available for students to examine after the session has ended.

At the same time, learners should have access to courses that are more individualized and tailored to their specific needs. In face-to-face classes, it is difficult to give one-on-one instruction for each student because of the limited time and faculty resources. Students' log data may be used to create individualized resource suggestions for online learners with the use of learning analytics (Liu and Sun 2021). Accrington & Rossendale College in the UK emphasizes tailored courses, such as preschool counseling, development evaluation, teaching group support, and IT help (Wu 2009).

Courses should be integrated, but so should the design of relevant resources to ensure that students are connected to one other in an effective manner. There are advantages to using printed materials and electronic materials. One plus one is more than two; therefore, the presentation of learning resources may be tailored to suit varied learning content and objectives. In the absence of students attending in-person classes, we should make clear which online resources they may use instead. Attention should be given to new knowledge points developed during face-to-face sessions, such as common issues of learners in the learning process, new challenges originating from debate and interaction, and a summary of blended learning activities, to design more focused and practical learning materials.

As a last step, the richness and variety of learning materials should be enhanced. First and foremost, network information technology may deliver multimedia courseware, audio and video, and the video recording and streaming of courses, successfully supplementing face-to-face course materials mostly focused on textbooks. After attending face-to-face sessions, students can continue their education at a distance using a digital library. For example, libraries in American universities provide students with one-on-one consultations. Students can contact library staff by phone, email, or online chat with questions regarding using the library's resources, borrowing items, or other academic concerns (Bai et al. 2008). Additionally, to build a "strong alliance" and prevent wasting resources and repeating efforts, high-quality digital learning resources have to be made available to everyone.

Interactive Activities and Environmental Design

One of the most important goals of blended learning activity design is encouraging learners to take the initiative to participate in the course and actively engage, communicate and share. Interactivity is increasingly important in the design of blended learning activities because of the nature of online learning. Bates(1991) identifies two types of learning interactions: individual interaction and social interaction. Individual interaction happens when students connect directly with the learning material (such as a book, television show, or computer program), while social interaction occurs when students interact with one other. One of the purposes of creating blended learning programs, according to Osguthorpe and Graham, is to promote social interaction (Osguthorpe and Graham 2003).

Instructor–student interaction and student–student interaction are the two main types of social interaction. Micro and macro strategies for designing learner–instructor interactions before, during, and after lessons are shown in Tables 5.2 and 5.3, respectively (Chen and Tong 2006).

Typical instructor–student interactions include explanation, questioning and feedback, exercises and discussion, whereas student interaction usually consists of competition, collaboration and communication. There are a number of strategies that can be used to deal with the issues that arise in the blended learning environment, including first, making learning content more engaging by including a variety of hands-on activities such as group discussions, role plays, and brainstorming sessions; second, keeping the online learning community engaged by publishing the rules and norms of communication, evaluation, and standards; third, creating a conducive environment for students to interact with each other; and fourth, responding to online inquiries from students promptly and gathering their questions in a variety of formats, such as real-time queries, forum messages, surveys, and so on.

Learning Strategies Support

Effective learning strategies are the key for learners to better understand what they are learning. One of the most fundamental aspects of education is mastering the art of effective reading from textbooks and other educational resources. For instance, schools are able to coordinate with qualified instructors to routinely organize seminars and lectures on how to read instructional materials and take notes in a manner that is most beneficial to their students. Additionally, students should learn how to "self-regulate" their learning, which means they should be able to plan their own activities and keep tabs on their progress. The majority of students who struggle to learn do a poor job of planning their education and making necessary adjustments to their learning practices. It is possible to increase learning outcomes by providing students with effective support, such as directing them to finish course objectives in stages, customizing learning assignments according to the student's progress, and increasing the student's sense of accomplishment upon completion of the course. This improves the students' motivation and helps them develop into more self-regulated learners.

Table 5.2 Learner–Instructor Interaction Strategies

Learner	Instructor	Timeline	Strategies		
			Macro Level	Micro Level	Object
		Before session	Building communities	Account registration	The forming of the online community will help instructors and learners get to know each other and be ready for study
				Self-introduction	
				Exchanging information	
				Creation of course folders	
				Answering questions	
		During session	Organization and management	Clarification of the purpose of communication	It helps to guide the interaction and arouse motivation
				Communication rules	
				Clarification of evaluation methods and criteria	
				Presentation and evaluation	
				Praise and reward	
			Evaluation and feedback	Homework and feedback	It is to help learners solve problems and enhance their understanding
				Notification of exam results	
			Development of learing skills	Cognitive skills development	It is to develop learner's skills
				Organizational management skills development	
				Emotional skills development	
			Conversation and communication	Questions and answers	It is to provide opportunities and encourage learners to participate in interactions
				Topic-based discussion	
				General social interaction	

(continued)

Table 5.2 (continued)

Learner	Instructor	Timeline	Strategies		
			Macro Level	Micro Level	Object
			Summarization and generalization	Systematical explanation	It helps learners understand the key points and systematically master what they have learned
				Highlights and difficulties	
			Problem solution	Advice on methods	It helps to achieve knowledge transfer and develop learner's innovative ability
				Q&A in time	
				Innovative thinking encouragement	
		After session	Evaluation and feedback	Organizing final exams	It is to make a comprehensive assessment and give feedback
				Marking exam papers	
				Collecting other evaluation information	
				Completing evaluation reports	
				Evaluation report feedback	

In addition, it is vital to provide students advice on how to use the many learning resources available to them. Learners can benefit from tools such as mind mapping and tomato clocks, which help them organize and integrate the information they have acquired.

Emotional Support

Emotional support is meant to help students communicate with each other through technical means and then strengthen two-way emotional interaction to improve learners' positive emotional experiences (Li and Lei 2012). There are many ways that network and multimedia technologies may be used to enhance student engagement and participation and minimize students' feelings of isolation. As a first step, there are a range of educational circumstances and activities that may be used to help students better express their emotions, such as teaching games and role plays. Second, a CSCW (computer-supported collaborative work) should be implemented to facilitate communication and collaboration among students in an online learning environment (Liu and Zhong 2011).

Table 5.3 Student–student interaction strategies

Learner	Learner	Timeline	Strategies		
			Macro level	Micro level	Function
		Before session	Building communities	Logging in	It is to help learners get to know each other and the learning community
				Self-introduction	
				Classmate communication	
		During session	Individualized communication	Questions and answers	One-to-one communication can make communication more direct and attract learners to participate
				General social interaction	
			Observation	Reading forum messages	It is to facilitate effective learning through alternative interaction
				Observing the discussion among other learners	
				Observing other learners' records and achievements	
			Competition and cooperation	Online games	It is to stimulate and engage learners for learning and develop problem-solving and cooperation skills
				Role play	
				Brainstorming	
				Group discussion	
			Presentation and communication	Group presentation	It is to facilitate mutual learning
			Discussion	Questions and answers	It helps to solve problems, make social connections and take others' perspectives
				Topic discussion	
			Mutual evaluation	Mutual evaluation among groups	It is to stimulate and engage learners for learning and understand the criteria for effective learning
				Peer evaluation within groups	

(continued)

Table 5.3 (continued)

Learner	Learner	Timeline	Strategies		
			Macro level	Micro level	Function
		After session	Individual communication	Exchanging learning experiences	It can help learners improve their skills and stay focused on learning

It is imperative that we further diagnose and analyze students' emotional status to provide emotional support at the appropriate moments. First, questionnaires, barrage exchanges, and forum postings can be utilized to learn about students' learning styles, difficulties, and expectations and to offer emotional encouragement while giving knowledge and then to find solutions to problems in a timely fashion. Second, the affective computing model-based expression recognition system can identify learners' emotional states and provide relevant emotional support in real time during the learning process. Third, a real-time support platform might be built to provide personalized emotional support services for learners.

To help students develop a feeling of belonging, blended learning should make full use of the ease of online instruction and the sense of presence provided by face-to-face learning.

5.2.3 Monitoring and Intervention

The quality of blended learning is dependent not only on a well-designed learning plan and appropriate instructional support but also on timely intervention in the learning process.

Academic Early Warning

Academic early warning is a strategy for evaluating, warning, and assisting students in their academic development. Academic early warning is mostly based on data created in the online education environment, which has grown in popularity since the introduction of online education. Early warning models can be built using relevant methodologies and theories, and we can evaluate the data, send feedback to students and instructors based on the analytical results, and quickly provide targeted interventions. For instructors, educators and administrators, early warning is a "prevention in advance and in process" advisory service that enables students and instructors to learn and teach more effectively (Zhu et al. 2020).

Early Warning Indicators and Their Levels

There are a number of indicators of academic early warning that may be used. According to the findings of one study, college students' daily behavior, attendance in class, and academic performance are all crucial indicators for determining whether they are experiencing learning difficulties (Liu 2017). Academic early warning indications should, of course, be comprehensive rather than focused only on academic achievement (Lin 2021). According to provincial criteria for comprehensive quality evaluation, a higher vocational college uses ideological and moral character as the major indication of early warning for full-time junior college students' academic achievement, creativity and entrepreneurship, and social practice. Academia's early warning level is strongly influenced by students' grades, but comprehensive quality evaluation data also have a significant impact. Students' daily attendance, internships, and certifications obtained via practical training may also be considered by some vocational institutions. At the same time, the design of early warning should be improved in accordance with the features of various disciplines and courses (Yang et al. 2021).

As the semester progresses (such as at the beginning, in the middle, and at the end of the semester), risk levels (e.g., low, medium, and high) are utilized to determine the extent to which academic early warning is given to students and instructors. For instance, the academic early warning of a higher vocational school is organized in a hierarchical structure that ranges from a Level 1 warning (very light) to a Level 2 warning (there are many failing courses or truancy hours) to a Level 3 warning (it is possible to fail to earn the graduation certificate) to a dropout early warning (there will be an inability to continue studying in school) and so on (Chen 2021).

Early Warning System

In blended learning, the learning platform serves as both a means of disseminating knowledge and a means of monitoring student progress. The accuracy and effectiveness of academic early warning may be greatly improved by collecting and evaluating data on learning behavior according to theoretical models.

Students at Purdue University, for example, are assessed for their academic risk based on a variety of factors, including their demographics, academic achievement, amount of effort, and prior academic history. Using a color-coded system, the system offers "course signals" with rising danger levels for each course. Using this information, instructors can send students text messages or set up face-to-face meetings with them. One tool that certain platforms offer is referred to as "Student Explorer," and it is designed to analyze data on students' participation and performance. For example, it analyzes the relationship between students' utilization of online courses, the number of activities they complete, and their final grades to determine the likelihood of students' academic failure. This information can be used by student advisors to take the necessary actions based on a rising risk level for a student. Some early warning systems include "learning analytic dashboards," which compare a student's risk level to that of other students with comparable features in the system. For example, students at University College Dublin (UCD) can be warned about their progress in class via an early warning system.

 **Exemplar 5.6**

Academic early warning systems that are powered by big data have the potential to successfully identify students' actual learning difficulties and provide them with accurate and consistent support. Many aspects of data collection and analysis must be considered while developing an effective early warning system. One of the key considerations is the availability of data (such as student engagement and performance statistics). There are a variety of additional factors to consider, such as instructional approaches (such as the flipped classroom), assessment techniques (such as formative evaluation), geographic location, and the demographics of the students. Concerning the method, there is not yet a widely accepted optimal algorithm for academic early warning, thus the one that is used must be chosen based on the specific circumstances (Liz-Domínguez et al. 2019).

Support Systems

To improve students' learning outcomes, a warning system in blended learning is simply the beginning; what students truly need is a support system that comes after the warning system.

There are a number of laws and regulations that need to be established to assist students in improving their present level of learning and to find solutions to difficulties that arise throughout the learning process. There must be a defined division of work, detailed evaluations, and incentives in place in the regulations of the support system.

Establishing a Support Team and Working Mechanism

Creating a committed support team comprised of representatives from each party is essential to the successful implementation of the support system.

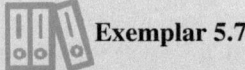 **Exemplar 5.7**

There are many factors to consider when providing support, including the nature of disciplines and courses, students' difficulties, and their own characteristics. However, effective implementation of support work must also consider the diversity and division of responsibilities of the staff involved while integrating and connecting the functions of various departments so that all parties can work together to achieve the goal. Regarding student academic challenges, instructors play a critical role; regarding issues with student students' motivation, instructors, counselors, and tutors must work together; and regarding learning challenges, instructors and the school's special student service management department may work together.

Universities and colleges have created an accountability framework that puts an individual in charge of each intervention to guarantee the timely and efficient implementation of support programs. For example, in a vocational college, the counselor, class advisor, and subject instructor are in charge of the primary warning; the deputy dean, deputy secretary of student management, and director of the teaching and research office are in charge of the intermediate warning; and the party secretary and dean of the college are in charge of the senior warning (Lin et al. 2021). It is not just students who are informed by the academic early warning system; the warning information and studying advice are also sent to the person in charge of helping them out. Working together as a team, they divide their tasks and responsibilities according to established protocols.

When determining whether or not a support system is effective, an evaluation must consider both the rate at which the number of students who require assistance has decreased and the success of the interventions given to students who struggle with learning.

Creating Repositories of Supporting Records

When students receive an academic early warning, the institution should keep a complete record of all interactions between counselors and students, the academic guidance given by instructors to students, the effect of this support on their subsequent performance in school and other information. The documentation of support files may be used by students to monitor their progress and by management to supervise and examine the work of support staff and to assist with the regulations that govern it. The institute can hold the individual in charge accountable if inadequate files were documented and insufficient support was found and order him or her to reform within a time limit. Building a repository of case studies and best practices for student assistance is a long-term investment that helps build a stronger system of support and early warning for students.

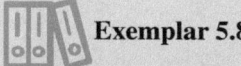 **Exemplar 5.8**

Sichuan University issued the "Sichuan University Undergraduate Early Warning Notice" to students who were not doing well in their studies and urged their counselors to inform their families. At the same time, the university forwarded the list of warned students, transcripts and the "Warning Notice" to the dean and class advisers, seeking their assistance for the students, including interviewing the students and their parents to understand their difficulties and providing them with necessary support services (Yin et al. 2020).

Incentive System for Support

The course instructor is frequently the best resource for support since he or she is the one who is most familiar with the curriculum and the students' current level of understanding. There must be an incentive system for instructors to participate in support work because it is an extra obligation that is separate from their regular teaching duties.

Instructors should be rewarded for the time and effort they invest in supporting students, and their efforts could be linked to their professional advancement (Yuan et al. 2014). Instructors' morals and manners, along with the criteria for applying for research projects at universities, should include consideration of instructors' involvement in the support work as a means to acknowledge the time and effort they put in and encourage them to engage in the support work.

5.2.4   Evaluation and Feedback

 Exemplar 5.9

After determining the dimensions of evaluation model, it is necessary to confirm which indicators can be obtained and how to obtain them. Generally, the evaluation of student's participation in blended learning should combine the characteristics of traditional classroom and online learning organically. For example, the classroom data is generated by students in the traditional classroom, and the online data mainly comes from platform records. Of course, a variety of data collection methods could be explored, such as questionnaire survey.

 Exemplar 5.10

The blended learning course "College Computer Foundation" at Jianghan University was evaluated, with a focus on both face-to-face and online education. Attendance, experiments, computer time, classroom quizzes, assignments, and exercises are just a few examples of the types of information collected in the classroom. Online learning data comprises online learning length, online test results, online learning video watching time, online roll call, online check-in, online discussion, and other data (Zhu et al. 2021).

Evaluation of effectiveness of blended learning

Students' face-to-face learning and online engagement should be considered when evaluating blended learning, and both formative and summative assessments should be used. Both formative and summative assessments are used to gauge the effectiveness of blended learning. Formative assessment primarily examines the performance of students in the learning process, helping students to identify their learning status, change learning strategies, and improve learning results. Summative assessment measures how well students have learned after completing a course. The process of developing a scientific and appropriate course evaluation system necessitates constant experimentation and optimization. The dimensions of the evaluation model are the ways in which the student's learning effect is measured.

Blended learning may make use of a wide range of evaluation methods. To assess students' understanding of certain topics, questions in the classroom or on bullet screens, voting, and surveys might have a significant impact. An online self-assessment, peer review, or online demonstration can be used to evaluate a chapter or module as a whole. Summative evaluation analyzes whether students accomplish the learning objectives, course knowledge, and competence, and it may be done in various ways, such as an open/closed paper test or a paperless test, oral questions, classroom observation, self-evaluation and peer review, online live broadcast interaction, etc. (Gao et al. 2021).

Feedback to students

Feedback creates a connection between assessment and student growth. For students to learn more effectively, it is important to provide clear and concise feedback. The three pillars of feedback are timely feedback, real-time feedback, and feedback that is specifically tailored to the individual. It is important to provide students with timely and real-time feedback to address any difficulties they may be having with their learning. Providing students with feedback that is specifically tailored to their individual needs and circumstances is known as personalized feedback. Student gains may be boosted by providing them with frequent and detailed feedback on their progress in their studies. Feedback that focuses on how students solve problems rather than their final grades is extremely beneficial to students. To encourage students to reflect on their current learning situation, change their learning strategies, and gain an in-depth understanding of the material, it is important to provide students with timely and constant feedback on their progress. In addition, it can help instructors adjust their teaching methods and improve the quality of classroom instruction (An 2014). We have seen a shift in learning feedback due to educational big data: from delayed to instantaneous, subjectivity to objectivity, contextualizing to standardization, and from text to visualization as the feedback's format changes (Chen and Wang 2018).

There are three possible components to feedback: the current state of learning, learning objectives, and strategies for achieving those objectives. ① Students' grades, knowledge, information, progress, and reasons for studying are some of the most important aspects of a student's learning status. ② Students' learning objectives may include mastery of current knowledge and mastery of related information.

③ Strategies to motivate students to achieve their goals are presented through instructor suggestions and recommendations. Instructors' suggestions are largely to help students recognize problematical behaviors in learning and provide learners with feasible learning approaches. The recommendation for instructors is to recommend learning materials, peer resources and activity alternatives for students (Chen and Wang 2018).

By analyzing learning data, student portfolios will be more accurate, and the academic early warning and support system will be more intelligent. As a result, students are able to complete their studies and achieve their personal growth via effective and timely interventions. Using "virtual teaching assistants" allows students to obtain answers to simple queries about the course and enables online supervision and other consulting. Distance education's low student-to-instructor interaction and professors' incapacity to respond to every student in a timely manner can be alleviated, and students can be encouraged to study to improve their self-discipline in learning (Zhang 2018).

The support system will become more tailored and accurate. Students' tailored learning paths have become more precise thanks to the use of technology, and each learner's unique learning priorities and obstacles have become more clearly defined. More importantly, these support systems may meet students' learning demands, give them tailored assistance and exact answers, and improve their learning efficacy. The FutureLearn platform, for example, has taught over one million students from all over the world, amassed countless amounts of data about the usefulness of the content, and then used patented algorithms to determine exactly what the learners themselves need to learn.

An individual's emotional well-being is critical to his or her success. Students' emotional and psychological difficulties, such as anxiety, loneliness, and a sense of powerlessness, are increasingly being addressed through support systems in blended learning to improve learner support and enable students to finish their studies in a healthy manner. Over time, the number of people on the learner support team has increased.

The establishment of a working group (including the heads of the institutions) and a framework for cooperation is necessary to help students overcome their real-life issues. There should be some sort of organization set up to help troubled students, and the person in charge of support should be identified and the support policy publicized in a timely and effective manner.

Learner support is expected to increase in scope as intelligent technology develops, and learner support is expected to be improved to better satisfy students' different learning needs in the future.

5.3 Supporting Instructors in Blended Learning

Instructors face additional challenges when they transition from conventional to blended courses, which have more fragmented resources and more flexible instructional approaches. To enable instructors to more effectively implement blended courses, timely and constant support should be provided, including training, pedagogy, policy, assessment, and so forth.

5.3.1 Training Support

Training for instructors is unquestionably required at every step along the way, from the early examination of blended courses through the design and delivery of instruction and the ultimate evaluation of its success. Instructors must also keep up with the quick changes in instructional technology and tool systems, which necessitate a constant learning and adapting process. As a result, it is more important than ever to institutionalize instructor training to foster the development of blended learning.

The institute's teaching faculty is led by the institute's most experienced professors. Their attempts to incorporate information technology into teaching are beneficial for strengthening their teaching skills and favorably directing new instructors. Blended teaching, or online learning, in which instructors and students are separated during the whole process, is a new concept for most lead instructors. Training for blended teaching that specifically targets lead instructors is critical. It is critical to give lead instructors training tailored to their own teaching requirements and background and to the unique challenges of online instruction. Educators should be taught in the design, implementation, and assessment of online classes in blended learning so they can change quickly.

Instructors who have a solid foundation are known as "backbone instructors." Aside from helping them improve as instructors, their attempts to use information technology in course instruction serve as a positive example for future generations of instructors. It is vital to carry out tailored training since the great majority of backbone instructors are experienced with face-to-face technology-enhanced teaching. However, they are less comfortable with online teaching in which instructors and students are totally separated. On the basis of their extensive teaching experience, this group of instructors should be trained in the theory and practice of designing, implementing, and evaluating online learning.

Young educators are the new driving force behind the faculty team, and as such they are deserving of attention and specific training to achieve quick development. It is advised that role play can be used in the training approach when schools conduct training on blended learning for new instructors, as it is necessary to evaluate their initial teaching competence before the training.

Training takes many formats; in addition to the more conventional expert lectures and workshops, educational institutions can also increase training by creating

communities of practice. The development of the community highlights the importance of teaching and research that is done together. Along with instruction in the use
of blended tools and technologies, instructors must also receive instruction in instructional design, classroom management, student–instructor interaction, feedback and
assessment. In addition, internet research, training, and case sharing among institutions and regions are also possible methods of communication. The community
must be given constant support, such as planning long-term teaching and research
initiatives to address the genuine issues in teaching practice and foster the long-term
development of blended learning.

5.3.2 Support for Pedagogy

Blended course syllabuses, instructional activities, and websites should all be clearly
defined by institutes to ensure that instructors are on the same page while building
these courses. The syllabus should have a clear allocation of time for online and
offline instruction, an evaluation methodology that includes both online and offline
grades, and so on. Delivering online course materials on time, and reminding and
motivating students to complete their online learning are just a few of the requirements. Instructors should explain the learning requirements and schedule to students
during the first week of the course and provide online technology training to students.
In addition, students' questions should be answered promptly through online contact.

 **Exemplar 5.11**

The following are the writing requirements for the Central China Normal
University Undergraduate Blended Course Syllabus:
   Introduction: Information such as course category, major application,
number of hours and credits, course content and subjects, faculty members
who will teach the course, and a brief description of the course are all included.
   Methods and requirements for online learning: There are suggested strategies and resources for differentiating the learning experience and step-by-step
directions on how to get started with the online learning system.
   Course content: The main modules of the course and a resource in text or
multimedia are included in the course. As such, it should include the course
syllabus in chapters. There should be a variety of media and cases available
in each chapter to help students learn the fundamentals and expand on their
knowledge.
   Course video: Classes conducted in small groups should be videotaped and
divided into smaller units called "micro videos," which may be viewed on a
computer's hard drive. There is a 15-min limit on the length of each video.

To ensure that the whole course's instructional material is covered, all video materials must be seamlessly integrated.

Design and arrangement of activities: Assignments, exercises, and examinations, as well as grade books, Q&A sessions, group discussions, and other forms of group learning, can all be utilized to help students learn more effectively.

Assessment design and scheduling: Learning activity data, course information management, etc., are all part of assessment design and scheduling.

Blended courses need a website where digital teaching resources are given to interconnect online and offline teaching activities. In addition, the institute should offer timely technical assistance to instructors and students, including the creation of a teaching environment, technical help in the teaching process, technical system monitoring, data management and utilization, etc. It is imperative that educational institutions provide online learning spaces, digital materials, and classrooms in a consistent manner to make it easier for instructors to use blended learning.

Technical Support in Teaching

Technical issues may arise during the implementation of blended learning, including issues with uploading teaching materials; information cannot be viewed, replied to or published; the system cannot calculate how much time students spend on online learning; and logging in difficulties. To ensure the smooth progress of classroom instruction, institutions should work more closely with communication operators, increase the platform's stability, and reinforce the system's maintenance. The use of online manuals, operation demonstration videos, and 7*24-h Q&A services might be made available to assist instructors and students with software operation issues that may arise during blended teaching (such as mailboxes, WeChat, and Whatsapp). Students who are unable to attend class for a variety of reasons, such as an epidemic, disease, or being overworked, might have the school set up appropriate online learning materials and create a learning environment on how to utilize them through the internet, phone, or other means.

Monitoring and Troubleshooting of Technical Systems

Real-time monitoring of a technical system's condition is essential for catching any instances of anomalous service functioning or resource usage at any time. The state of learning support services and general operational conditions should be evaluated in time to identify potential dangers in important daily service reports. An irregularity in the technical system must be dealt with as quickly as possible in the process of blended teaching to prevent the problem from spreading or possibly resulting in the end of the service. Exceptions such as network outages, software flaws, and other issues must be anticipated and addressed in advance so that the plan may be implemented either automatically or manually in the event of a problem. Consider the recovery of the product under various degrees of damage, such as the circumstance when the data of online teaching are deleted, causing the platform to be rendered unusable.

Management and Utilization of Data in Technical Systems

Data generated by the technological system must be sorted out in a timely manner and sent back to teaching support to increase the data's usefulness. Online teaching platforms such as Blackboard and Google Classroom can provide a window into the challenges and opportunities faced by instructors in their day-to-day work.

5.3.3 Incentive Policy Support

The implementation of blended learning requires the long-term development and timely maintenance of courses by instructors. It is therefore critical to have an incentive system. Blended teaching should be regulated in a way that ensures that the rights and interests of instructors who use it are protected, that instructors are encouraged to experiment with it, and that its instructional value is realized.

It is the responsibility of educational institutions to encourage the systematic and efficient implementation of blended learning based on the premise of combining economic and intellectual gain.

First, create a separate fund to support the creation of blended learning and provide financial support to instructors who choose to do so on an annual basis in accordance with the development plan. Second, encourage instructors who have completed the blended teaching course evaluation to be rewarded and subsidized. Last, faculty members with a more diverse range of teaching styles are encouraged to apply for relevant projects and further their education. High-quality study findings might be used as a basis for the future design and implementation of blended learning. An increase in instructor involvement and a clearer understanding of incentives are necessary for the long-term sustainability of blended learning. Details on the creation of incentive policies may be found in Chap. 4 of this handbook.

5.3.4 Course Evaluation Support

Because of the increasing reliance on technology, the conventional methods of course assessment are no longer adequate for assessing blended learning. Blended course evaluations are critical to ensuring their long-term sustainability and effectiveness.

It is inevitable that the evaluation viewpoint will shift as a result of putting students first in a blended learning context. It is important to consider both the involvement of instructors and students in a blended evaluation system. In terms of the techniques of assessment, several methods should be adopted, such as process evaluation, summary evaluation, qualitative evaluation, and quantitative evaluation, to achieve generalizability; in terms of the format of evaluation, the combination of online and offline evaluation should be used to avoid becoming one-sided. Instructors' and students' performance should be evaluated based on both online and offline teaching procedures, whereby data should be immediately and properly reflected in the quality of teaching.

 Exemplar 5.12

To standardize blended teaching, Central China Normal University has successively issued the documents "Administrative Measures for Blended Classroom Teaching", "Specifications for the Construction of Blended Course Resources", "Administrative Measures for the Construction of Blended Teaching Curriculum", etc., which clarified the norms of course construction, course management, platform operation and other aspects of blended teaching, along with the evaluation standards of online and offline content and activities of mixed courses. The requirements and evaluation contents of blended courses include:

(1) Instructors build resources according to the curriculum construction specifications, upload the resources to the cloud-based integrated learning platform, implement open online classrooms or blended classrooms for undergraduate students through the space, and are responsible for updating and improving the resources.

(2) The lecturer determines the type of class according to the needs of the course, and after the approval of the college, a unified arrangement of classes is adopted according to the institute's plan each semester. The online class and the blended class information is required to be reported to the Academic Affairs Office.

(3) Courses offered for freshmen in the first semester do not offer online classes or blended classes.

(4) The first lecture of the online class and the blended class is arranged in the classroom, and the lecturer introduces the learning method, requirements, and assessment to the students. Except for the first time, the online class generally no longer arranges fixed classrooms. If needed, students or instructors can temporarily apply for a classroom at the Academic Affairs Office. The instructor determines the proportion of class time allocation between online and face-to-face teaching in the blended class according to actual needs.

(5) Instructors are responsible for the instruction and management of the online or blended class. Instructors should strengthen contact with students, for example, guide them to study independently, regulate their online behavior, engage them to participate in learning, and timely answer students' questions and correct their assignments online, etc.

(6) The overall evaluation of the course is composed of the formative evaluation and the final exam. Instructors should formulate detailed quantitative

evaluation standards for their performances and inform the students. The formative evaluation includes but is not limited to the following aspects: students' autonomous learning status (online learning time and the number of speeches recorded by the platform), assignment grades (depending on electronic assignments, essays, online communication, and discussion, etc.), participation in online discussions (number of speeches, effectiveness, enthusiasm for discussion, etc.), and participation in face-to-face seminars (attendance, preclass preparation, classroom performance, etc.).

(7) The university inspects and evaluates the teaching of online classes and blended classes by organizing supervisors and experts to attend lectures from time to time. Other inspections include checking the creation of digital curriculum resources, holding student symposiums, and communicating with lecturers.

This handbook includes the following form to make it easier for the institute to assess its own support services for instructors and to offer specific actions for improvement.

Exemplar 5.13

Self-Examination of Support Services for Instructors

No	Contents	Current State	Improvement
1	Are department managers encouraging?		
2	Are institutional leaders encouraging?		
3	Has the institute formulated related policies and rules? (such as specific implementation norms, evaluation mechanisms, etc.)		
4	Are the institution and individual instructors aligned in their need to improve technological (and teaching) integration?		
5	Does institutional policy require instructors to implement blended instruction?		
6	Can students successfully find internet devices and environments on campus for online learning?		

7	Can students view online teaching resources smoothly on campus?		
8	Does the institute provide the professional resources required for the construction of course content on the internet?		
9	Is there access to other instructors' successful experiences?		
10	Is there access to the pedagogical support needed to implement blended instruction? (e.g., ongoing communication with course designers and developers)		
11	Do you have access to the one-to-one professional mentoring/training needed to implement blended teaching?		
12	Do you have access to the professional face-to-face instruction/training in small groups needed to implement blended teaching?		
13	Do you have access to the online professional guidance/training needed to implement blended teaching?		
14	Do you have access to the technical support you need to implement blended teaching?		
15	Is the evaluation data needed to judge whether the implementation of blended teaching is effective available?		
16	Will the implementation of blended teaching receive financial subsidies?		
17	Will the implementation of blended teaching affect the evaluation of professional titles and promotions?		

Summary and improvement measures:

References

Adams D., Mabel H. J. T., Sumintono, B., & Oh S. P. (2020). Blended Learning Engagement in Higher Education Institutions: A Differential Item Functioning Analysis of Students' Backgrounds. *Malaysian Journal of Learning and Instruction*,17(1),133-158.

An F. (2014). Research on Classroom Teaching Strategies of Promoting Deep Learning(in Chinese). *Curriculum,Teaching Material and Method,34(11)*,57-62.

Bai B., Gao Y., & Chen L. (2008). Learning Support Services of Onlinge Higher Education in the United States (in Chinese). *International and Comparative Education, (11)*,81-85.

Bates, A. W. (1991). Interactivity as a Criterion for Media Selection in Distance Education, *Never Too Far, (16)*,5-9.

Cai J., & Zhuang X. (2006).Study on Some Systems of Learning Support Service in China(in Chinese). *Open Education Research, (01)*,74-79.

Chen L. (2011). *Fundamentals of Distance Education (in Chinese)*. Beijing: Higher Education Press,2011.

Chen J. (2021). Research on the Reform of Academic Early Warning of Higher Vocational Colleges under policies of stringent admission and elastic graduation(in Chinese). *PR World,(16)*,92-93.

Chen L., & Tong Y. (2006).Social Interaction Strategies and Methods in Distance Learning (in Chinese). *Distance Education in China, (08)*, 14–17+ 78.

Chen M., & Wang S. (2018). Research on Design of Learning Feedback Supported by Big Data on Exercise (in Chinese). *e-Education Research, 39(03)*, 35–42+61.

Dai B. (1999).Psychological obstacles and education of students with learning difficulties (in Chinese). *Theory and Practice of Education, (06)*:46-49.

Ding X. (2002).*Distance Education Research (in Chinese)*. Beijing: Capital Normal University Press.

Dwiyogo W. D., & Radjah C. L. (2020).Effectiveness, Efficiency, and Instruction Appeal of Blended Learning Model. *International Journal of Recent Technology and Engineering,16(04)*,91-108.

Feng X., Guo W., & Song J. (2021). Teachers' Blended Teaching Competency Development Model: Principles, Preparations and Strategies(in Chinese). *Open Education Research,27(05)*,53-62.

Gao Y., Zhang X., & Han J. (2021).Design and Thinking of Teaching Evaluation Based on Blended Courses(in Chinese).*Education and Teaching Forum,(36)*,161-164.

Garrison, D. R., & Kanuka, H. (2004). Blended learning: Uncovering its transformative potential in higher education. *The Internet and Higher Education, 7(2)*, 95-105.

Huang Z. (2004). *Distance education course(in Chinese)*. Beijing:Science Press.

Huang R., & Zhou Y. (2006). *Theory and practice of blended learning(in Chinese)*. Beijing: Higher Education Press.

Jin Y., Huang J., & Yin B. (2018). Analysis of the Current Situation of the Research on the Blended Curriculum in China Universities(in Chinese).*Education Teaching Forum,(03)*,70-72.

Li X., & Lei J. (2012). The composition of teachers' emotional support to students in Distance Learning—theoretical and empirical research (in Chinese). *E-Education Research*, 33(05), 57–62+84.

Li Q., & Ma D. (2014).Research on the current situation, problems and countermeasures of network resource construction in Blended Learning(in Chinese). *Software Guide,13(05)*,48-49.

Li X. (2018).*Research on the Personalized Learning Support Service of Distance Education based on Education Data Mining(in Chinese)*.JiangNan University.

Lin X, Huang X., & Chen C.(2021).Difficulties and Improvement Strategies of Academic Early Warning Mechanism of Higher Vocational Colleges(in Chinese).*Education and Vocation,(18)*,44-48.

Lin X. (2021).Analysis of academic early warning based on the comprehensive quality assessment of students in higher vocational colleges. *Hunan Education(C version), (08)*,34–36.

Liu M. (2017).*Study on academic early warning System of Undergraduate students(in Chinese)*.Shanxi:Shanxi Normal University.

Liu X., & Sun M. (2021).Overview and Characteristics of Student Support Services at the UK Open University(in Chinese).*Adult Education,(04)*,83-87.

Liu J., & Zhong Z. (2011).Lack of Sensation in On-Line Teaching and Countermeasure(in Chinese). *Distance Education in China, (06)*,15–17+79.

Liz-Domínguez, M., Rodríguez, M. C., Nistal, M. L., & Mikic-Fonte, F. A. (2019). Predictors and early warning systems in higher education—A systematic literature review. In LASI-SPAIN, 84–99.

Lowenthal, P. R., & Hodges, C. B. (2015). In search of quality: Using quality matters to analyze the quality of massive, open, online courses (MOOCs). International Review of Research in Open and Distributed Learning, 16(5), 83-101.

Lu D., & Sun H.(2015).The study of the current situation and measures of the Open University learning support services based on blended Learning model(in Chinese). *Adult Education, 35(05)*, 36–39.

Osguthorpe, B. R., & Graham, C. R. (2003). Blended Learning Environments: Definitions and Directions. *The Quarterly Review of Distance Education, 4(3)*, 227-233.

Piña, A. A., & Harris, P. (2019). Utilizing the AECT Instructional Design Standards for Distance Learning. *Online Journal of Distance Learning Administration, 22(2)*, n2.

Simpson O. (2002).Supporting Students in Online, Open and Distance Learning. Taylor & Francis Group.

Sun W., Du R., & Liu Y. (2015). *A Study on Open University of United Kingdom (in Chinese)*. Central Radio & TV University Press.

Ushatikova I, Konovalova E, & Ling V, et al. (2019). The Study of Blended Learning Methods In Higher Eeducation Institutions. Astra Salvensis, (13),367-387.

Visiting group of Jiangsu RTVU, & Zhou W. (2006). Supported open learning——successful practice and its inspiration of Open University (in Chinese).*Journal of Jiangsu radio and television university*,(2),25-30.

Wang X., & Ding X. (2004).The research of Allan Tait(J) (in Chinese).*China Educational Technology*,(11),39-43.

Wang W., & Gu Z. (2020).Construction and application practice of learning effectiveness evaluation index system of online open courses in higher education under hybrid teaching mode (in Chinese). *Education and Vocation,(21)*,85-91.

Wang J., Ma X., & He J. (2007). Investigation and Countermeasures of Emotional Deficit in Modern Distance Education(in Chinese).*Modern Distance Education, (04)*,29-31.

Wu R. (2009).Comparative View of Learning Support Services' Theory and Practice in Distance Education (in Chinese). *Open Education Research, 15(2)*,97-101.

Wu B., Zuo M., & Song Y. (2021). The Mechanism and Strategy of Blended Learning Support Service: Under the Theory of Holistic Learning. Journal of Distance Education,39(04),83-93.

Xiao A., & Jiang C. (2009).Investigation and research on web-based learners. *Open Education,15(01)*,75-80.

Xiao X., & Xiao Y. (2020). Building a teaching evaluation system based on hybrid courses (in Chinese). *China CIO News,(10)*,173-174.

Yang X., Li Y., Wang D., & Xing B. (2020). Integration of learning spaces in the intelligent age: pattern and path (in Chinese). *Distance Education in China, (1)*,46-53.

Yang Q., Deng Y., Wu Li. Nie B., & Huang L. (2021). Discussion on the Optimization Measures of Medical Academic Early Warning System: Taking University of South China as an Example(in Chinese). *The Science Education Article Collects,(09)*,135-137.

Yin J., Li W., Feng Juan, & Xie H. (2020).Study on Academic Early Warning Support Measures and Their Effectiveness(in Chinese). Education and Teaching Forum, (49),87-89.

Yuan A., Zhang N., & Shen H. (2014).The construction and application of the evaluation index system of college students' academic early warning. *Heilongjiang Researches on Higher Education,(03)*,79-83.

Zhang X. (2018). Research on the Construction of Adult Learning Support Service Model Under the Background of Intellectualization—Illustrated by the Case of Open University (in Chinese). *Adult Education, 38(12)*,26-30.

Zhu Z., Li Z., Liu Y., & Zou Y. (2020).Research Process Review on Learning Early Warning(in Chinese).*Modern Educational Technology,30(06)*,39-46.

Zhu J., Chen G., & Xiang H. (2021). Hierarchical evaluation model of students' learning ability based on mixed teaching big data(in Chinese). *Information Technology and Informatization,(10)*,203-205.

Chapter 6
Typical Practical Cases in Blended Learning

Mingxuan Chen, Zhuli Wang, Linmei Liang, Zhiqiang Ma, and Yingqun Liu

This chapter presents 16 practical cases from 11 countries, including China, Australia, Egypt, Morocco, Peru, Serbia, Indonesia, Malaysia, the Philippines, and Vietnam. These cases aim to present the implementation background, core problems, solutions, effects and impacts of the cases, to help teachers and administrators understand the educational and teaching concepts reflected in the cases, to learn the teaching design and practice methods and teaching management strategies in the cases, to reflect on the experiences and lessons learned from the implementation of the cases, and also to provide researchers with research materials with their own characteristics.

6.1 Introduction to Blended Learning Exemplars

6.1.1 Function and Value of Exemplars in Blended Learning

The three exemplary cases presented in this chapter have been summarized and refined based on real world application practice, especially the core characteristics of blended learning. These cases serve as practical guidance to assist teachers better

M. Chen (✉) · Z. Ma
School of Humanities, Jiangnan University, Wuxi, China
e-mail: chenmx@jiangnan.edu.cn

Z. Wang
Center for Faculty Development, Sun Yat-sen University, Guangzhou, China

L. Liang
Faculty of Education, Henan University, Kaifeng, China

Y. Liu
Institute of Education, Tsinghua University, Beijing, China

© The Author(s) 2024
M. Li et al. (eds.), *Handbook of Educational Reform Through Blended Learning*,
https://doi.org/10.1007/978-981-99-6269-3_6

understand and implement blended learning by comparing and contrasting similarities and differences of the cases. It is our hope that by examining the cases, teachers can apply the theories and model presented in this *Handbook* to their own contexts and practice related professional knowledge, theory, and skills in blended learning, and ultimately, carry out blended learning independently.

6.1.2 How to Use the Blended Learning Exemplars

Blended learning exemplars aim to guide teachers to analyze blended learning in specific situations, reflect blended learning practice (e.g., knowledge management, instructional design, and implementation), and generate practical knowledge. Blended learning exemplars can be used in three ways as following[1]:

Internalize the practical knowledge of blended learning

Blended learning exemplars contain internalized practical knowledge that can help teachers to integrate uncertain knowledge into practice to a large extent. Practical knowledge is obtained from "learning by doing". In other words, practical knowledge is acquired from experience and activities and then integrated it into teachers' own cognitive structure. In this way, teachers can, on the one hand, "re-construct" educational problems. On the other hand, teachers can transform their teaching practice as a special type of research activities. Additionally, teachers can obtain deep understanding of blending learning by discussing these exemplars with others.

Understand blended learning theory

Blended learning theory contains concepts, propositions, and principles, which are interrelated. Blended learning practice not only represents the application of blended learning theory but also reflects educational practice in specific contexts. Exemplars presented in this chapter demonstrate teachers the real-world educational problems and show them how to respond to those problems as the role models included in the exemplars. These exemplars can help teachers fully understand blended learning theory.

Analyze and reflect on practical problems of blended learning

Explicating practical problems could promote wider adoption of blended learning. Blended learning exemplars not only can help teachers understand how to implement blended learning but also assist teachers reflect blended learning practice as these exemplars demonstrated the "dilemma" situations in blended learning practice. Teachers will gradually learn how to analyze and reflect on practical problems of blended learning by analyzing the issues involved in the exemplars.

---

[1] Zheng, J. (2002). Case teaching: A new approach to teacher professional development. *Educational Theory and Practice, 07*, 36–41.

Table 6.1 Blended learning cases at the institutional level

General requirements	The data of selected cases is authentic and closes to the theme of blended learning reform in colleges and universities. The cases have an extensive and important social impact
Specific requirements	• Contain advanced conceptualization, clear objectives, essential questions, and empirically supported ideas • Clarify the background, significance, solutions, processes, effects, and implications • Highlight the key points, catch the gist, and clearly clarify the solutions
Structural requirements	• Background and problem statement • Environment and resources • Design and implementation • Features and innovation • Effectiveness and impacts • Reflection and learned lessons

6.1.3 Content Structure of the Exemplars

There are two types of exemplars collected in this chapter: institutional cases and class cases. Institutional cases are educational reforms of blended learning in higher education institutions. Class cases are the blended learning practice in courses. Content of the cases is structured as background and problem statement, design and implementation, effectiveness and reflection, and features and innovation according to the standards of exemplars as shown in Tables 6.1 and 6.2.

6.2 Case 1: Blended Learning in a Public Elective Course: *Innovative Thinking Training*[2]

Background and problem statement

The Innovative Thinking Training course was an elective course and first offered in 2010 for students in educational technology masters' program at Sun Yat-sen University. Starting in 2013, partial content of this course was included in undergraduate curriculum. In 2015, the instructor re-designed this course as a Massive Open Online Courses (MOOCs) and related course materials were published as a textbook. In 2016, this course was offered in blended learning mode that combines online and offline teaching. This course lasted for 18 weeks, a total of 36 h. Each week there was one offline session, lasting about two hours. The course was limited to 120 students. All students on campus can take this course. Most of students were freshmen and sophomores, with the former being represented more. Two problems revealed in the teaching process:

---

[2] Edited by Zhuli Wang, Sun Yat-sen University, China.

Table 6.2 Blended learning cases at the class level

General requirements	The data of selected cases is authentic and highlights teachers' innovation in blended learning. The cases provide guidance and references to solve practical teaching problems
Specific requirements	• Contain real-world activities that could inspired and be referred by practitioners • Clarify the background, conceptualization process, implementation methods, and effectiveness • Clarify specific case situation, learning objectives, evidences that support the practice • Highlight the key points, catch the gist, and clearly clarify the solutions • Reflect on advantages and disadvantages in the implementation, significance and implications, and reasons for success • Contain necessary resources, such as data and tools
Structural requirements	• **Background and problem statement** include course category, student analysis, instructional objective, and problem statement • **Design and implementation** explain course design, pedagogical ideas, instructional methods, learning activities, implementation, and evaluation • **Effectiveness and reflection** include evaluating and reflecting the learning outcomes, successes, and shortcomings • **Features and innovation** summarize the features, innovation, and implications of the case
Additional requirements	Additional essential resources, such as data and tools can be provided as attachments

- Students reluctant to spend too much time in this course since it's a public elective course. It's difficult to ensure the quality of online learning in this course?
- It's difficult to conduct specific in-class exercises and interactions in offline session because of the large class size.

Design and implementation

(1) Design

Five learning objective were designed for this course: raising the consciousness of innovative thinking, developing the habit of innovative thinking, understanding the principles of innovative thinking, mastering the method of innovative thinking, and practicing innovative thinking. Five objectives should be progressively achieved from low to high.

The classroom was a multimedia classroom that was equipped with basic equipment such as computers and projection screens. The teacher sometimes may switch to classrooms where desks and chairs can be moved to assist group activities. Most students have laptops and all students have smartphones.

Since this course was already available in MOOCs, blended learning was adopted in this course. Flipped classroom was also used in this course since it focused on thinking training rather than information delivery. In this class, students familiarized themselves with factual knowledge online via MOOCs and participated in learning activities related to thinking training during offline session. Online session in MOOCs was 12 h, accounting for 1/3 of the total hours. Offline session was 24 h, accounting for 2/3 of the total hours. Online session and offline session were often completed alternately to coordinate the course content. In the last few weeks of the course, students would work on final project independently and present and evaluate the project publicly such as class presentation.

The learning assessment consisted of three parts: class participation, final exam, and final project. Class participation accounted for 60% of the total score, which was mainly composed of online learning performance and offline learning performance. Final exam accounted for 20% of the total score, including subjective and objective questions that tested whether students mastered and used course knowledge. Final project accounted for 20% of the total score.

Calculation of class participation score relied on an application, *Superstar Chinese Study*, which is an instructional software that can be accessed via cloud, computer, and mobile devices. The teacher can upload MOOCs, E-textbooks, and other digital resources to the cloud where students can access through computers and mobile phones and complete related learning activities. This application can also assist online teaching and offline teaching, such as sign in, conduct class discussion, assign homework, conduct peer evaluation, choose students to answer questions, initiate quick answers, project mobile interfaces onto a screen, live streaming, PowerPoint slides page turns, group students, and collect and analyze learning statistics. Students' learning activities can be recorded through the *Superstar Chinese Study* and converted into numbers that be used to calculate students' class participation score.

(2) Implementation process

This course was divided into 15 sections altogether. Each semester started from the first week of the semester and proceeded week by week according to the schedule. The schedule did not follow the sequence of textbooks and made appropriate adjustments according to actual teaching needs. The offline classroom exercises were adjusted to match the online learning progress. Generally, students would complete three online sessions before one offline classroom session.

The online session was scheduled as follows. Study guide was provided one week in advance to assist students get familiar with the course content. When meeting online, students would first sign in via *Superstar Chinese Study,* then complete assigned learning activities and assignments independently in MOOCs for about one hour. After that, the instructor would initiate discussion and assign in-class exercises via *Superstar Chinese Study* by using the functions of selecting students for quick answers. When the class was over, students would sign out and the teacher would summarize the online session and answer questions through live streaming, which is a function of *Superstar Chinese Study*.

The offline session was scheduled as follows. Students would sign in 5 min before class, and the teacher asked the students to some warm-up activities. Then the teacher would assign the thinking training activities. Students could complete these activities in groups or individually. After that, the teacher would post questions and evaluate students' activities in *Superstar Chinese Study*. Finally, the teacher would assign the learning tasks for next week. At the end of the class, students would sign out the offline session.

Effectiveness and reflection

(1) Effectiveness

At the end of each semester, the teacher gave out questionnaires to students and conducted anonymous surveys. The scores were above 90, with an average of 95. For the open-ended questions at the end of the questionnaire, most students evaluated the course highly and were impressed by some games and training activities. Some of our teachers and those from other universities also spoke highly of the course after listening to it. When applying for the national quality course, an expert committee headed by the former vice president of teaching highly rated this course. In 2017 and 2020, the course was recognized as national high-quality MOOC, the national first-class undergraduate online course, and first-class blended learning course.

(2) Reflection

① How to ensure the quality of online learning?

This course used to provide 1/3 of the total class hours for students to study online. However, it was found that students did not actively participate in online learning activities as expected although they were given enough time. There were two reasons. One was the passive learning habit formed under the influence of long-term exam-oriented education. Second, online learning lacked a collective learning environment and required high independence from the students. Therefore, the teacher made some adjustments, such as releasing study guide in advance, creating online virtual classrooms, asking students questions in class, and increasing the grade proportion of class participation. The online virtual classroom, delivered via *Superstar Chinese Study*, assisted with online course sign-in and online discussion and created a collective online learning environment. All online and offline learning activities were included in class participation, and the grade proportion increased from 20 to 60%. This adjustment has effectively promoted class participation that students who completed online learning tasks increased from 40–50% to 90–100%.

② How to conduct specific in-class exercises and interactions in offline session due to the large class size?

In the case of large class size (more than 50 students), the teacher used to divide students into several groups, assign a teaching assistant to each group, and provide them with necessary guidance and help. The questions discussed in the group were varied according to the specific situation, and the teacher gave his/her guidance on these questions. The problem, however, was that the learning requirement could not be too high and the teacher could not expect too much from the students because students could drop the course or even not to select this course after two weeks according to the university policy. If teachers expect too much of students and the learning pressure is too high, students may not choose this course or give up and change to other courses after choosing them. Therefore, teachers need to balance the teaching quality and students' needs.

Features and Innovation

(1) This course provided practical experience in carrying out blended learning in the elective course, in particular several effective practices in ensuring the quality of students' online learning.

(2) This course made full use of smartphones and educational applications, such as *Superstar Chinese Study*, which features learning management and mobile learning. This course also played an important role in connecting online and offline learning, motivating students to participate in learning and interaction and recording students' daily learning activities. It provided a successful experience for using smartphones in the classroom.

(3) This course explored several innovative ways of training innovative thinking at university. In addition, a number of teaching cases were accumulated. Three textbooks and reference books, and many research papers were published.

6.3 Case 2: Promote the Reconstruction and Practice of an Undergraduate Training System with the Help of Information Technology[3]

Background and problem statement

Located in Wuhan, China, the Central China Normal University has over 31,000 full-time students, including over 18,500 undergraduates, 12,000 graduate students, and 1,100 international students. Based on the national education informatization desig-nated by the Ministry of Education, the university has newly built an appropriate student-centered talent training system that features connection, sharing, indepen-dence, and transparency under the extensive integration of information technology after five years of continuous exploration and practice.

Central China Normal University fully integrated information technology into talent training, effectively solving three problems. Firstly, how to develop a student-centered talent training system in the era of information by making full use of information technology to re-design learning environment, contents, methods, and evaluation? Secondly, how to share high-quality educational resources and improve teaching methods by using big data and other technologies to ensure quality of teaching activities in large class size and individual learning needs? Thirdly, how to create the university's culture that not only emphasizes educational quality but also encourages innovative?

---

[3] Edited by Qingtang Liu, Central China Normal University.

Design and implementation

The university has reshaped teaching philosophy by establishing the student-centered talent training system that pays attention to quality, knowledge, and competencies and building an open educational support system that prioritizes learning and competencies. The *"four changes"* has been used as the guiding principle of the talent training program. That is, the teaching method has changed from the teaching-oriented to the learning-oriented, learning content has changed from professional content to the combination of general and professional content, learning environment has changed from the offline classroom to the combination of online and offline classrooms, and learning assessment has changed from summative assessments to the combination of formative and summative assessments. The extensive integration of information technology and teaching not only effectively improved students' participation in learning and their abilities of critical thinking, cooperation, communication, and creativity (4C), but also promoted students' self-management, self-learning, and self-service (3S) qualities in digital age.

The university also formulated standards for digital course resources so that all required courses could be offered online. Besides, the university further expanded the educational resources supply by encouraging developing and introducing high-quality digital course resources independently. The university optimized the course structure, including general courses, professional courses, and personalized courses to provide diversified learning content. Teachers and students were provided with cyberspace on a self-developed cloud teaching platform so that they can share high-quality educational resources. Students' socialist core values were cultivated through the innovation of online ideological and political courses.

Additionally, the university proposed and implemented a three-dimensional integration teaching theory, namely "physical space, resource, and social interaction", to develop and deploy the cloud teaching platform and smart classroom. The university implemented blended learning that combined online and offline learning, cut down in-class hours, and strengthened guidance and in-class discussion to achieve the goal of *returning time to students and teaching students the methods*. By using big data, the university tracked and analyzed students' learning process to timely find weaknesses in the teaching process, accurately find students with learning difficulties, provide appropriate guidance, and promote individualized teaching according to the students' learning situation.

The university has established a comprehensive evaluation system based on data to form diversified, procedural, and developmental evaluations for teachers, students, courses, and classes. Lastly, the university organized activities, such as *Teaching Festivals*, to create a culture of *valuing teaching and advocating innovation*. The university made full use of the advantages of the two national educational informatization research labs—the National Engineering Research Center for E-Learning and the National Engineering Laboratory for Education Big Data, to promote the combination of science and education and collaborative education.

Effectiveness and reflection

In 2017, the number of students choosing blended learning classes reached 30,000, and students who took online courses reached 100,000. Students' learning motivation and satisfaction have been increasingly improved for five years. 85% of students often studied online, and 75% of students perceived that blended learning is beneficial for them to analyze and solve problems. In the past five years, students have won a total of 1,026 prizes in discipline competitions at all levels, including 349 prizes in national competitions.

More than 1,500 teachers have been trained and 80 seeded teachers were selected to study in the United States. Teachers have produced a total of 6.58TB of digital teaching resources and have developed 746 blended classes in 2017. 88% of the teachers were able to conduct self-evaluation and reflection on teaching activities by analyzing the students' online learning, activities, and learning achievements.

Central China Normal University has invested more than 200 million yuan in information construction and teaching and learning reform since the university carried out a unified and centralized use of its funds in information technologies since 2012. Through the establishment of the hall of students' affairs, a one-stop service, one-table monitoring, one-network management, the allocation of various resources such as teaching resources and office space in the university has been significantly optimized. Besides, the utilization rate of public spaces, like classrooms, dramatically increased. In addition, teachers have gradually gotten rid of tedious form-filling work, and their workload has been significantly reduced.

Features and Innovation

Features and innovations of this case are presented in eight aspects.

(1) Revised the current training curriculum and built a student-centered talent training model. The student-centered education concept was implemented, which pays attention to quality, knowledge, and ability. A three dimensions of theoretical research, an interdisciplinary approach, and innovation and entrepreneurship were designed, and the talent training program was revised systematically. The course structure and proportion of general courses, major courses, and personalized courses was adjusted. In terms of the distribution of class hours, 20–30% of in-class hours were reduced, and the remaining time was returned to students. In terms of teaching methods, research-based teaching that combines online and offline learning was fully executed. The organization form of teaching and discussion "2:1" was advocated. In terms of evaluation, data-driven formative assessment was implemented.

(2) Reconstructed instructional environment to realize the integration of the three dimensions. The university emphasized the three-dimensional integration theory, *physical space, resource, and social interaction*, and transformed the education and instructional environment. In terms of physical space, unified standards and norms were set up. More than 60 smart classrooms with high-quality display equipment, various interaction equipment, and intelligence analysis equipment were built. In terms of resource space, the university developed

and introduced high-quality digital to share on campus. In terms of cyberspace, teachers and students can occupy the same cyberspace using the self-developed cloud platform. Teaching was carried out in cyberspace and a ubiquitous intelligent instructional environment that integrates online and offline learning, curricular and extra-curricular activities, and physical and virtual spaces was constructed.

(3) Carried out advanced training to improve teachers' digital teaching competencies. The university has established a training program for the development of teachers' digital teaching competencies to facilitate the change of teachers' role (Fig. 6.1). The university customized training for different types of teachers. Firstly, for new teachers, well-known national and international scholars were invited to conduct training for digital teaching competencies and application of media technology and cloud integration platforms. Secondly, for lead teachers, a training for in-depth integration of information technology and teaching and learning was carried out, in order to address the difficulties and problems in improving learning effectiveness, and design and development of resources. Thirdly, overseas training in digital teaching competencies for seeded teachers was carried out. 20 seeded teachers were sent to study TPACK (Technological Pedagogical Content Knowledge) at the State University of New York every year to cultivate a group of excellent teachers for digital teaching and educational reform.

(4) Enriched teaching resources and provided open education
The university has set up standards of digital course resources, gathered high-quality resources through self-construction, sharing, and purchase, completed the digital construction of more than 800 required courses, and introduced more than 220 major courses and online courses of general education from colleges and universities at home and abroad. All courses were open and shared by

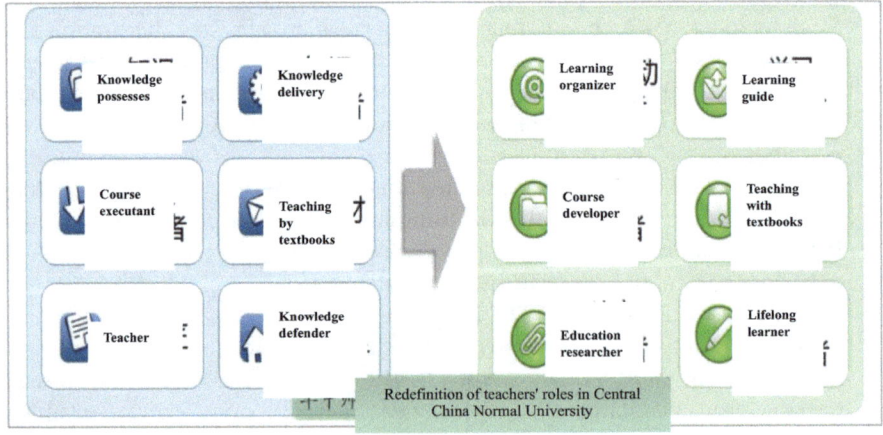

Fig. 6.1 Redefinition of teachers' roles

the university on a unified cloud platform, which broke the physical barriers between colleges. The main position of ideological and political education was consolidated, and the visualization of online ideological and political education was realized by using new media technology. The "1 + X" mode of ideological and political courses hosted by university leaders was carried out through the cloud platform in 2017 and generated good results. The university took the lead in establishing the Hubei Teacher Education Network Alliance and provided high-quality courses that contributed to the development of local colleges and universities. The channel for normal university students to study online for their master's degree of Education two years after graduation was opened to provide a more continuous and open education.

(5) Reformed teaching methods and promoted blended classroom learning
Blended classrooms were implemented into daily teaching, accounting for 20% of all courses. Over 30,000 students chose blended courses, and a large number of information-based teaching innovation cases emerged. Besides, high-quality teacher resources were shared. The new flipping teaching mode that combined the traditional teaching method and blended learning was implemented. An effective way to solve personalized teaching problems for large class size was formulated. For example, Dai Jinjun from the School of Mathematics and Statistics, who taught *Linear Algebra,* won the first prize in the Teaching Competition in Hubei Province. Mr. Dai used to teach only one session of this course and other sessions were taught by junior teachers, which affected the teaching quality. After adopting the "1 + N" blended learning, Mr. Dai could teach eight sessions simultaneously with junior teachers as teaching assistants and utilized the cloud platform to conduct learning analysis and provide guidance for each student in a timely manner. In this way, the high-quality teacher resource was shared and the average scores of eight sessions were improved. The personalized teaching and learning for a large number of students was realized.

(6) Reformed the evaluation method and executed a comprehensive data-based evaluation. A basic teaching and learning database were established to collect data from students' learning behavior in the smart classrooms, online homework, discussions on the cloud teaching and learning platform, exams, and daily life, which supported student analysis, comprehensive evaluation, and academic planning. With the support of the cloud platform with big data, formative assessment was adopted. The proportion of class participation was increased from 20–40% to 50–80%.

(7) Optimized management services and constructed a new education ecosystem
Through the one-stop service based on the information portal, a network management mode based on campus grids and students' track records, the whole learning process from students' enrollment to their graduation was tracked, reflecting the 3S educational concept (self-management, self-learning, and self-service). A "five-in-one" education ecosystem that integrates ideological and political, general, major, practical education and management services based on information technology was created (Fig. 6.2).

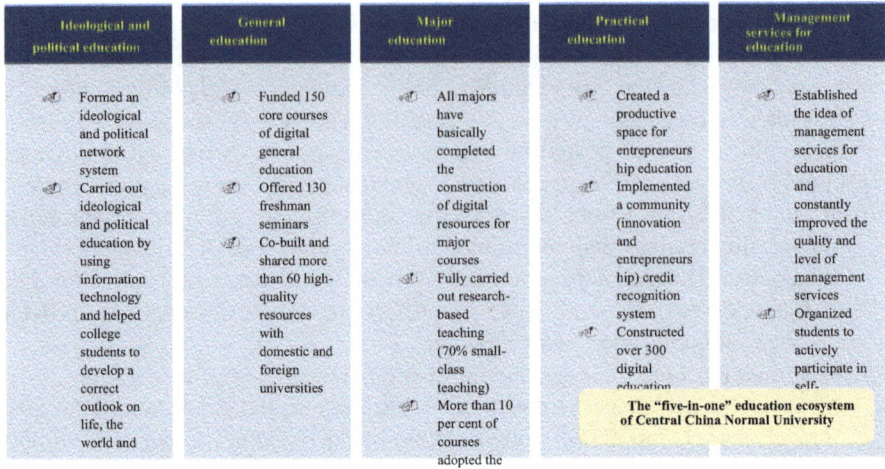

Fig. 6.2 The education ecosystem based on information technology in Central China Normal University

(8) Created *Teaching and Learning Festivals* and blended learning culture. Since 2015, the *Teaching and Learning Festival* was first created and held every year for one month. Each festival consists of a variety of activities, such as demonstration lessons, teaching and learning workshops, forums of teaching and learning reform, the International Symposium on Teacher Education in East Asia, Competition of students' information technology competencies, and "excellent digital teacher" –a teaching skill competition for pre-service teachers. A cultural atmosphere of teaching and learning was created, and innovation was advocated in university. Since 2013, the university has awarded teaching innovation prizes to teachers every year that focus on innovative teaching strategies and students' learning effectiveness. Award-winning teachers were provided with customized reward policies and gives preferential treatment to them in their appraisal and promotion.

6.4 Case 3: Systematically Promote Educational Reform via Blended Learning in Vocational Education Institutions[4]

Background and problem statement

Located in Weifang, Shandong Province, China, Shandong Vocational College of Science and Technology is a full-time public vocational college. With 20,490 students, the college offers 51 majors, including textile and garment, mechanical and

---

[4] Edited by Zongbao Zhang, Shandong Vocational College of Science and Technology, China.

electrical engineering, machinery manufacturing, and information engineering. The college began to build an information-based campus in 1997. In 2008, the Tsinghua Education Online (THEOL) platform was used to implement education and teaching management reform. In 2013, the project of students' learning behavior analysis was launched. In 2014, under the principle of "integrated design, structured organization, and granular construction", the college updated the evaluation model of blended learning and created "modern vocational education courses" which feature "online and offline learning and workplace training", and comprehensively implemented blended learning. In 2015, virtual simulation platforms were built to support the reforms of classroom teaching, such as flipped classrooms and collaborative learning.

Design and implementation

(1) Established an online teaching platform that served the talent training process. THEOL is a comprehensive teaching platform that integrates teaching, learning, management, evaluation, and testing. "Teaching" and "learning" support the development, implementation, and online learning management of blended courses. "Testing" optimizes real-time analysis and feedback on learning progress and results. "Evaluation" executes a systematic evaluation and guarantees teaching quality. "Management" represents teaching management and provides data sources for data empowerment.

(2) Built a smart instructional environment to help achieve the *Four Changes*. The college has built 49 professional-smart classrooms, like smart classrooms for Fashion Design major and the Internet of Things according to the needs of different majors. There were also 168 classrooms for theory learning and skill practice and 32 BYOD (Bring Your Own Device) classrooms built for students to complete work in the workplace. Specifically, according to the needs of different majors, the college built several smart classrooms with their major characteristics, such as Fashion Design and Production, Internet of Things Technology, and Business Management, to assist with teaching demonstration, group discussion, group teaching and difficulties in collaboration. Focusing on the concept of integrating "teaching, learning and doing" and major needs, the college created an information-based environment for teaching, discussion, guidance, and training in the training room to solve the problems of being "watched by a large number of students", and of guiding offline training and testing. The college improved the information-based and "workplace" environment and achieved the change from the traditional classroom teaching mode to the "student-centered" classroom teaching mode.

(3) Created a large number of teaching resources and promoted individualized training for students. The college has offered more than 1,000 online courses and 813 courses based on the excellent MOOC teaching platform and more than 200 courses on other platforms. The college has constructed 81 sets of virtual simulation teaching systems partnered with Siemens, East Simulation Software Technology, and Shanghai JingGe, which has solved the problem of high investments, high challenges, high risks, and difficulties in implementing, empathic learning

and re-demonstrating, in practical teaching. The college also built two national resource libraries for Fashion Design and Automotive Electronics majors and took charge of 19 sub-projects related to resource library.

(4) Constructed a big data center that empowered teaching and learning. The college constructed a teaching database using data from the big data center and the teaching platforms. This teaching database supported an intelligent instructional environment that empowered teachers to understand the students' learning needs before class more accurately, better engage students using the "data thermometer" in the database, and provide more accurate guidance that supported personalized teaching after class. At present, the big data center updates more than 5 million pieces of data every day.

(5) Improved information literacy and enhanced the vitality of teaching and learning reform. The college focused on improving teachers' teaching competencies, scientific research, and social-service ability and thus, established training program that improved teachers' information literacy. Teachers' information literacy has been developed in two formats in the training system (online and offline) and at three levels (off-campus, on-campus, and departmental). A development center was also developed to integrate resources inside and outside the campus. The college also established a training program for improving students' information literacy. The students' training program focused on reforming basic information technology curriculum and created a students' information technology support team to develop information literacy. In addition, various forms of information technology competitions were held to promote information literacy development.

(6) Carried out formative assessment to improve the quality of education. The college has established standards for formative assessment, made full use of the big data in the course platform and the system for diagnosis and improvement, tracked students' development process, visualized students learning trajectories, monitored the instructional process, and conducted self-diagnosis. A formative assessment mechanism of "early-warning, improvement, and development" has been gradually developed.

Effectiveness and reflection

Effectiveness and reflection are represented by the following two aspects.

(1) *Four Changes* have been achieved in classroom teaching. The classroom teaching mode has changed from the traditional classroom featuring theory teaching to the task-oriented, student-centered, and flipped classroom. Evaluation for students' learning in classrooms has changed from traditional questioning to an online testing system. Classroom management has changed from traditional experience-oriented management to scientific data-driven management. Learning assessment has changed from summative only assessment to the combination of multiple assessments.

(2) The quality of education has improved significantly. The learning habits of more than 35,000 students in the college have been changed after six years of exploration and practice in blended learning. The overall graduates' job placement rate has been over 97% for consecutive years, and the promotion rate of positions in three years after graduation has reached 69.27%. In addition, the satisfaction with their Alma mater is 99.43%, and the employers' satisfaction with graduates is relatively high and stable, approaching 100%.

Features and innovation

Features and innovation are represented by the following four aspects.

(1) Constructed a "two-line and three-level" teacher development system to improve teachers' digital teaching competencies. The college systematically promoted teaching overall ability to develop and implement information-based courses through the blended training that combined "online learning" and "face-to-face hands-on training", such as teacher workshops and teaching salons. The college also invited experts in education informatization from the Ministry of Education, Shandong Province, Tsinghua University, and other universities to train their teachers, such as innovating the blended learning mode, developing informatization courses, and reviewing course design. The college trained full-time teachers and lead teachers to learn online training courses such as the Flipped Classroom Teaching Method and take a MOOC course as students. The college also created some online video portfolios for teachers to document and analyze their learning process. Last, the college created an online communication platform for interaction and communications among teachers. The college innovated the working mechanism of teachers' professional development by using information technology.

(2) Innovated informatization environment. The college has built a THEOL platform that comprehensively covered teaching, learning, management, and evaluation. The college implemented reform through blended learning, featuring "online learning, offline learning, and workplace training". Regarding online learning, more than 1000 courses were offered online and the implementation of blended learning was supported by virtual simulation teaching software, curriculum resource databases, and other online resources. Regarding offline learning, a professional workplace environment was created so that information technology support is everywhere, every time, for everyone. According to "one plan for one major", the college designed professional-smart classrooms for Fashion Design, Internet of things, and Business Management majors that solved the problems of group teaching, collaborative learning, collaborative development, and other teaching activities that reflected a more dominant role for students.

(3) Innovated data application. The online classroom and smart classroom systems were used to accurately track the data of students' blended learning process and form data portraits to describe students' learning status and behavior in a timely manner. The data empowered teachers to design courses more accurately before

class that meet different learning needs. The "thermometer" data promoted students to participate in classes actively. Teachers provided accurate guidance and implemented personalized teaching after class.

(4) Innovated **quality** assurance mechanism. The college formulated a set of quality assurance systems and mechanisms, such as the *Diagnosis and Improvement Implementation Plan for Internal Quality Assurance System of Shandong Vocational College of Science and Technology, Implementation Plan for Modern Vocational Education Curriculum Improvement, Management and Evaluation Measures for Modern Vocational Education Curriculum.* It also connected the learning objectives and teaching standards and created a closed-loop mechanism to ensure teaching quality. Besides, the college rewarded teachers who were excellent in curriculum construction or achieved remarkable results in course implementation. In this way, teachers and students could be fully motivated to actively participate in the reform through blended learning.

In summary, three exemplary cases that reflect typical practices of blended learning at class and institutional levels were presented in this chapter. Case one presented how to implement blended learning at class level and case two and three showed the implementation of blended learning at institutional level. Findings of case one demonstrated that implement blended learning in class needs the support of other technological tools, such as smartphone applications and teachers need to actively participate in the teaching activities to facilitate and engage students. Case two and three demonstrated the effectiveness of blended learning in supporting educational reforms in higher education institutions. Case two showed that blended learning is an efficient tool to develop teachers' digital teaching competencies, which are the core component of educational reform in four-year university. Case three revealed that blended **learning** also can benefits students in vocational colleges, such as combining virtual simulation training and workplace hands-on training to develop professional skills. Although challenges still exit to implement blended learning, researchers and practitioners will continue exploring and advancing the field of blended learning as we understand its challenges but nevertheless promising future.

6.5 Case 4: Fiji: A University's Immediate Response Strategies for Learning and Teaching Amidst COVID-19 Crisis[5]

Executive Summary

Indisputably, the COVID-19 pandemic has had an unprecedented global impact on the higher education system. After a horrendous second wave of COVID-19 in Fiji,

---

[5] Authored by Dr. Wahab Ali, Associate Professor and Head of the Education Department, School of Humanities & Arts, The University of Fiji.

all education institutes immediately closed their doors on 19th April, 2021. Subsequently, the majority of the higher institution swiftly adopted online modalities using platforms such as Zoom and Google Meet, later switching to the Top Hat learning platform as a more practical and measurable tool.

Interview findings reveal that, besides resources, staff readiness, confidence, student accessibility, and motivation play essential roles in building equitable and quality online and blended teaching and learning (OBTL). This paper proposes that staff members use technology and digital gadgets to enhance learning, especially during these exceptional times. Findings also suggest online and remote learning as necessary in times of lockdowns and social distancing due to the COVID-19 pandemic. The University employs Top Hat as the learning platform assisted in addressing the quality assurance aspect of OBTL because the staff performance could be well-monitored in terms of their preparation, content knowledge, delivery style and attendance. Similarly, students' progress could be monitored through assessment, participation and attendance. Appropriate feedback could be provided to the students, and a positive learning experience could be observed as students could learn at their own pace and time.

The lockdown situation also led to the strengthening of internal and external partnerships. Online student support services were created within the Student Affairs Section to provide online mentoring and counselling services to the students. Likewise, the IT Department revamped its online service delivery, and the University launched its first-ever radio station known as VOX to keep the University community socially connected. The finance team advised students to use their scholarship money to buy technological gadgets and data. Partnership with external stakeholders like Vodafone led to students getting smartphones at reduced prices with special data packages. It was not all plain sailing for the tertiary education provider, but a concerted effort from all departments and sections paved the way forward for uninterpreted learning to take place.

Introduction and Context

Against the backdrop of this pandemic, various policy initiatives have been launched by governments and educational institutions worldwide to cater to students' learning. There has been a widespread and rapid move to online learning and the reorganization of the learning process (UNESCO 2020). The COVID-19 pandemic has revealed emerging vulnerabilities in education systems around the world. It is now apparent that society needs more flexible and resilient education systems as we face unpredictable futures (Zhang et al. 2020). After a horrendous second wave of COVID-19 in Fiji, all education institutes immediately closed their doors on 19th April, 2021. The university is physically closed to students, but the learning and teaching have been least affected through the concerted effort of the staff through OBTL. Staff have been diligently working online and attending to all university academic and administrative matters from the safe vicinity of their homes.

This case study was based at a University located on the main island known as Viti Levu in The Republic of Fiji. Fiji's two large major islands are Viti Levu and Vanua Levu, and the archipelago consists of some 300 smaller islands scattered over 3,000,000 square kilometers. Out of Fiji's population of 884,887 people, 54% are I-Taukei, and 38% are Fijians of Indian descent (Indo-Fijians)–descendants of Indian labourers (girmityas) brought to the region by the British in the 1800s. The remaining 8% are the people of other races who have made Fiji their home (Fiji Bureau of Statistics 2017) (Fig. 6.3).

The University was established in December 2004 by a religious organization and opened its doors to students in March 2005. The University is on a journey to provide the university community with its dream of providing excellence in learning and teaching; excellence in research; student experience; partnerships; environment; leadership, and governance. The journey is an exciting one. It provides a defined route for far-reaching progress, expansion, and most importantly, the envisioned future of the University as a leading tertiary institution in Fiji and the region and beyond.

The study is significant in the sense that it aims not only to ascertain the challenges and opportunities brought about by the COVID-19 pandemic and swift transition to OBTL but also discusses a few projects, programmes and policies instituted by the University to aid the rapid shift to online learning and minimize the disruptions to learning. In essence, this study addresses the following research questions:

1. What are some of the challenges and opportunities brought about by the swift transition to OBTL?
2. How did university-initiated projects, programmes and policies combat the challenges caused by the pandemic and reinforce the influences towards quality OBTL?
3. To what extent have the projects, programmes and policies concerning OBTL achieved the goals and expective outcomes?

Fig. 6.3 Fiji's location. *Source* https://www.mapsnworld.com/fiji/fiji-map.html

The findings of this paper aim to provide tangible results, solutions and amicable way forward during a crisis of such magnitude delivering quality OBTL. This paper is crucial to higher education providers in consolidating learning and teaching, considering that their decisions are sustainable and that learning is ongoing, and parity is maintained across all education providers.

Design and Implementation

This study examines the university's coping mechanisms in response to 'the new normal' state. This research was conducted within the interpretivist paradigm as the key concern was understanding the phenomenon under study from the participants' perspectives. The interpretivist paradigm is characterized by a concern for the individual and focuses on the importance of understanding, interpretation and meaning (Lincoln and Guba 1985).

Hence, a case study research design was implemented to probe the measures undertaken by the University to ensure their core business of serving the learners was least uninterrupted. A research design is an overall structure that enables researchers to map out strategies to collect relevant data. Subsequently, qualitative research methodology was adopted using telephone interviews with certain university community members due to the lockdown situation. It was not easy to have unfettered access to all the target population as mobile contacts were unavailable or their calls diverted. Ultimately, only purposive sampling could be implemented in such a situation. A few of the staff willingly agreed to participate and share their candid views, including Senior Managers, Heads of Departments, and Teaching Staff. Purposive sampling is widely used in qualitative research to identify and select information-rich cases related to the phenomenon of interest (Boddy 2016).

Prior approvals were sought, appointments were made with the respondents and interviews were held using mobile phones. A few respondents preferred to send in written comments to elaborate their views further. Bazeley's (2009) work informed this analysis–a thematic approach was executed for analytical purposes. This study reveals the challenges and opportunities created by the rapid switch to OBTL and presents some of the achievements and expected outcomes of the reforms and initiatives undertaken by the University.

Impact on Equity, Quality and Efficiency

The most promising education systems combine equity with quality and efficiency in service delivery. They provide all learners opportunities for good quality education. This report presents policy recommendations for education systems to help learners succeed in online and blended education. It discusses some university-level initiatives, policies and programmes that were implemented with the aim of promoting equity and quality in OBTL. The University was fully aware of the challenges and opportunities associated with OBTL. Table 6.3 shows some of the challenges and opportunities mentioned by the institution's staff.

Undoubtedly, the emergency transition to OBTL in light of COVID-19 brought along with its share of challenges and complications. The University tried to address

Table 6.3 Challenges and opportunities of OBTL

Challenges	Opportunities
Staff working in isolation	Going fully online
Creating of conducive workspace	Ability to expand the program abroad
Students not reachable	Implement alternative assessment strategies
Online teaching	Working safely at home
Adequacy of digital gadgets	Awareness created in public about OBTL
Internet accessibility	Increased parental participation in student learning
Infrastructure support	Webinars as an aspect of professional development

the challenges by making policies and plans to minimize the disturbances and make the most of the opportunities.

Reforms in ways of new Projects, Programmes and Policies

Work from Home

The first policy change was the work-from-home arrangement for staff due to the physical closure of the University since the lockdown. Though forced by the abrupt COVID-19 outbreak, this arrangement protects staff from contracting the coronavirus to a certain extent (Susilo 2020) while facilitating them to adapt to remote working mode using the video conference platforms.

Pedagogy and Practice

As the COVID-19 has abated, the institution intends to keep the OBTL mode running parallel to face-to-face ones, with an intention to create a robust educational ecosystem to provide perpetual access to OBTL by crafting strategies through the lens of a quality assurance framework (Cheng 2003; Pond 2002). Quality assurance strategies, including internal and external review, collecting students' feedback, and evaluation of recorded lectures, will potentially contribute to reviewing and upgrading pedagogy and practice; and it will further motivate and incentivize the inputs of relevant stakeholders for continuous improvement.

Setting up of IT Labs

To ensure equitable access to IT gadgets, IT labs were set up throughout Viti-Levu and Vanua-Levu for students. Concerning the digital divide among students, these IT labs promote greater equity in education and allow students to have hands-on experience of using high-tech equipment and gaining a necessary edge to survive in this competitive world (Ali 2020).

Digital Learning Platforms

With virtual training and the help from online mentors, students can conduct experiments, record observations, collect data and submit results virtually. These functions enable students to conduct lab experiments even while studying from home, and teachers can follow students' progress constantly. This modus operandi ensures access to resources from anywhere in the world as well. Thus, resource sharing, information dissemination, and connection became the focal point of the University's overall operation.

Webinars and Symposiums

Various webinars and educational symposiums, thus, were held as the University catered to the dire needs of keeping the staff and the students connected. This increased connectivity reduced isolation and increased collaboration and provided a strong platform for bonding and socialization among students and academic staffs.

Enhanced Student Support

University-sponsored financial and mental support from counselling services or internet providers has facilitated students to complete their studies. As revealed by the data recorded in the Top Hat, improvements have been made in both attendance and participation rate in lectures and tutorials. This progress has translated into students' better pass rates across the University.

Vox Populi-Online Radio

Communication efficiency has been improved with the launch of the project Vox. The Vox Populi is seen as the bridge between the University and the community and has gained a steady growth in listenership from Fiji and abroad.

Flexibility in Assessment

Taking account of the equity issue, the University allowed for flexibility in the assessment system as all students may not have access to computers and laptops with high-speed internet service. As such, the majority of the schools opted for 100% course work, while some chose online examination and take-home examination or "open-book examinations" systems. An adapted approach to assessment also allows students to use higher-order thinking rather than regurgitation.

Effectiveness of the Reforms in the way of new projects, programmes and policies

In essence, the programmes and policies have been beneficial in maintaining a conducive learning environment despite the lockdown and staff working from their homes. While it is too early to discuss the achievements in detail but holistically, they all have contributed towards creating a great online teaching environment. It is too early to evaluate each of the initiatives either. Still, the Quality Assurance team at the University has already analyzed Top Hat and has found that most staff members can deliver online lectures and provide a collaborative learning experience to all students. Since the semester is still in progress, the actual effects can be established at a later time.

The figure below captures the essence of the study in the way of a stairway pyramid for inclusive and quality education, ensuring building institutional capacity to manage equity, quality, and efficiency in OBTL (See Fig. 6.4).

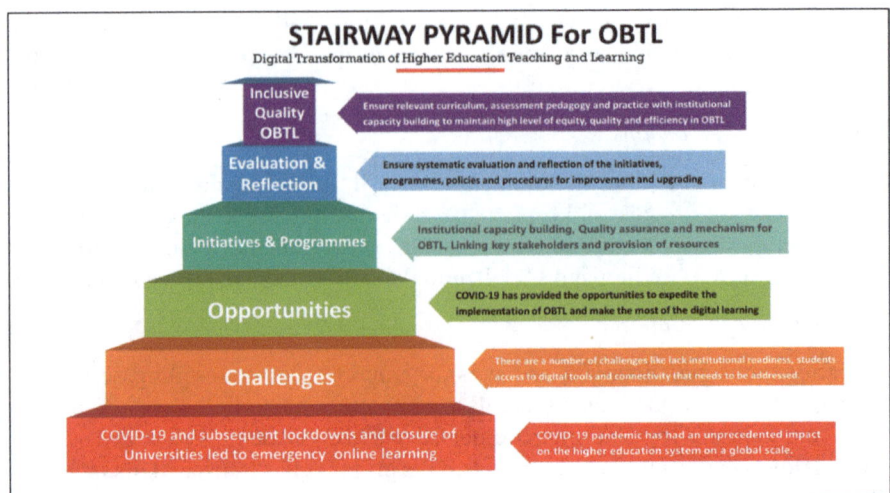

Fig. 6.4 Stairway pyramid for OBTL

Conclusion and Implications

The COVID-19 pandemic is creating fear and pandemonium worldwide. This unprecedented situation has revealed emerging vulnerabilities in education systems around the world. It is now clear that society needs flexible and resilient education systems as we face unpredictable futures. The global higher education landscape is shifting rapidly towards the digital transformation of learning and teaching. However, providing inclusive and quality OBTL, ensuring the relevance of existing curriculum and assessment, and building institutional capacity to manage equity, quality, and efficiency are brimming with challenges and opportunities.

Summary of key findings

Findings reveal several challenges associated with inclusive and quality OBTL. Some of the challenges as mentioned in the study were as follows:

- The absence of high-quality, consistent and fast internet service due to the demographical location of the staff and students has been a fundamental challenge of OBTL implementations;
- There is a need for more institutional capacity building to build staff readiness through professional development to craft and implement effective OBTL strategies;
- Administrators have not yet provided staff with sufficient access to equivalent hardware and software to what they use in their on-campus office to ease the transition and support all aspects of academic productivity;
- Higher education institutions (HEIs) lack a holistic approach to craft strategies through the lens of a quality assurance framework ensuring the relevance of

existing curriculum and assessment to manage the challenges of equity, quality, and efficiency;

- There is a need to leverage key stakeholders and partners to work towards the shared vision of equitable and quality OBTL to build future-ready HEIs; and
- Resistance to reforms of new projects, programmes and policies could hinder universities in maintaining the rigor and quality of their programs and at the same time assist in managing the challenges of equity, quality, and efficiency.

Implications for practice and scholarship

From the study, it is evident the following measures need to be implemented in order to create a robust online university in the new norm:

a. **Multilateral collaborative partnerships will facilitate OBTL**—There is a need to cultivate concerted partnerships across all sections/faculties when approaching and addressing educational needs for effective OBTL;
b. **Institutionalized dialogues should be implemented**—Ensuring learner and facilitator voices feature as a major aspect of the solution will be helpful for the OBTL implementation;
c. **Flexibility is key when planning for OBTL**—the learner is as important as the facilitator and both their needs in terms of resources, skills, support and conditions to learn and teach, infrastructure and support to learn should be given due consideration;
d. **A detailed review of the Top Hat learning and teaching platform will be helpful for OBTL evaluation**—It is suggested to gauge its acceptance, user demand, and the need to enhance online learning should there be apposite gaps;
e. **Quality Assurance mechanisms** are feasible and rewarding at all times—A quality assurance view will closely monitor curriculum and analyze staff recordings in order to ensure the learning experiences for students are differentiated and pedagogically focused.

The way forward for future practices and research

While this study has focused on the key insight of "Lead, innovate, and support online and blended teaching and learning" mentioned in the introduction chapter, it has also touched on Building capacity of the higher education workforce: Competency framework and professional learning pathways. This is because a future-oriented competency framework can specify the knowledge and skills that the higher education workforce needs to possess, so that equitable and quality OBTL is implemented effectively. This study lays down a solid platform for further research for HEI leaders and policymakers in regards to strengthening the institutional capacity to provide a system-level guideline on implementing equitable and quality OBTL

The COVID-19 pandemic and the sudden move to online modality has presented undue challenges for all stakeholders in higher education to work in a time-constraint and resource-restraint situation. It must be established that adopting an online learning environment isn't just a technical issue but is also a pedagogical and instructional challenge. Closing universities and taking students and lecturers out of the classroom is a pedagogical transformation that requires rapid mobilization across university staff and resources. The University in Fiji is of the view that it will continue with the online option by strengthening the reforms and policies even after the lockdowns are removed. The pandemic has provided an opportunity for virtual learning; as such, the online and face-to-face modalities will continue simultaneously in the post-COVID-19 era. In essence, COVID-19 has provided us with the opportunity to adopt online learning as education systems need to be abreast with the rapid emergence of new technologies, thus making online, blended and remote learning a necessity in universities not only in Fiji but the world over.

6.6 Case 5: Indonesia: Online Learning Development in Higher Education[6]

Executive Summary

While online learning has been embraced by Indonesian higher education since the 2010s, its development has been strongly pushed forward by the COVID-19 Pandemic. Within a month of the Pandemic, higher education institutions transformed into online learning without proper preparation. Indonesia Cyber Education Institute (ICE-I) is a government initiative launched in 2021 as Indonesia's digital marketplace for online learning courses. It aims to assist the higher education community in Indonesia in implementing online learning, especially during the Pandemic, and increasing the higher education participation rate through access, equity, and quality of online courses from leading universities in Indonesia and abroad.

Designed to be a marketplace of quality online courses, ICE-I's main functions are to curate, verify, and register online courses; to manage online courses gallery; to conduct research and innovation in online learning; to manage partnership and certification of online courses, and to use blockchain technology to link the relevance of online courses and participants' competencies to the job market. With 275 courses from the ICE-I Consortium and 1420 EdX courses and subsidies from the Government, ICE-I serves 3800 students from 69 higher education institutions in Indonesia involved in the MBKM (Merdeka Belajar Kampus Merdeka, Freedom Learning Freedom Campus) activities, i.e., independent education institutions study, students exchange, or micro-credential. In the future, ICE-I will need to strengthen its network, collaboration, coverage, and services.

---

[6] Authored by Dr. Habibah Ab Jalil, Associate Professor, Faculty of Educational Studies, Universiti Putra Malaysia (UPM).

Introduction and Context

Realizing the role of higher education in nation-building, Indonesia's higher education is expected to be transformative and agile to adapt to global changes. In July 2021, the Indonesian Government through Universitas Terbuka launched the Indonesia Cyber Education Institute (https://icei.ac.id/) as a strategy to improve access, quality, and relevance of tertiary education.

ICE-I has been initiated to answer the emerging challenges as follow:

a.   4th Industrial Revolution

The 4th Industrial Revolution (IR) has imposed a new mindset, new way of thinking, and new way of doing things. 4th IR introduces the digital revolution in which a fusion of technologies blurs the lines between the physical, digital, and biological spheres. The high-speed transformation that 4th IR brings has been a global disruption in every aspect of human life. In such a situation, Indonesia puts higher education at the forefront to prepare the country for the transformation caused by the 4th IR. The Government is determined to improve Indonesian competitiveness in the world market, prioritizing the development of science, technology, and innovation while infusing humanist and inclusive goals into its higher education program. Furthermore, the Government is endorsing the emergence of online learning in higher education to provide accessible quality education for all.

b.   Goals of Indonesia's higher education program

Indonesia's higher education program aims to increase the gross tertiary enrolment from 31,34% (9,034,972) to around 38% by 2024, according to a policy document. Currently, the country has 4,516 higher education institutions (HEIs) with over 37,553 study programs and 298,347 lecturers. The Government expects higher education to play a significant role in developing competent, skilled, and professional higher education resources to meet the needs of industry and the community in the twenty-first century. These goals will be measured by (a) the proportion of graduates who are immediately employable and or able to create employment through entrepreneurship, (b) an increase in the number of graduates able to compete in both regional and international markets with skills and professional certificates; (c) the increase in human resource productivity contributing to the competitiveness of the nation, and (d) innovations produced by HEIs and streamlined to industry needs. The country needs to overcome the current challenges to achieve these goals: only around 62% of HEIs and 68% of the study programs are accredited. There is a shortage of quality lecturers to teach specialized subjects, particularly those needed for the 4th industrial revolution.

In early 2020, the Ministry of Education, Culture, Research, and Technology (MOECRT) has launched the Merdeka Belajar Kampus Merdeka (MBKM, Freedom Learning Freedom Campus) Policy that offers flexibility for the undergraduate students to study outside of their study programs for three semesters starting the 5th semester. This policy is supported by eight categories of activities: students exchange, independent study, field service, teaching in rural schools, developing a village, entrepreneurship project, internship, and research. This MBKM policy is expected to answer the challenge of graduates' quality and productivity of the HEIs in Indonesia.

c. COVID-19 Pandemic

COVID-19 Pandemic has brought immense ramifications to global human life, including the education sector in Indonesia. Suddenly, 90% of higher education institutions in Indonesia turned into implementing "online learning" (Belawati and Nizam 2020) with minimal preparation. At that time, Universitas Terbuka has been the only distance learning university serving more than 500 thousand Indonesian students. In 2020, the MOECRT established three other distance learning universities: Universitas Siber Asia, Universitas Insan Cita Indonesia, and Muhammadiyah Online University. On top of that, the MOECRT also launched Indonesia Cyber Education Institute (ICE-I) as the marketplace for online courses in Indonesia to make online education in Indonesia a vehicle for quality learning that is widely accessible in Indonesia.

ICE-I is expected to significantly increase participation in higher education, improve the quality and productivity of higher education institutions and their graduates, and facilitate the implementation of MBKM policy.

Design and Implementation

The ICE-I was designed to be a marketplace of online courses in Indonesia. It collects and provides a collection of quality online courses both from top national universities and international higher education institutes to the higher education community in Indonesia. It was officially launched by the Director General of Higher Education, Research, and Technology on July 28, 2021.

The establishment of ICE-I became increasingly strategic in higher education practice in Indonesia. It was reinforced by the fewer contact principles of the COVID-19 Pandemic that calls for "online emergency remote learning" that was supported by an inadequate ecosystem. The World Bank (2021) found that the extent of learning and learning loss is determined more by the effectiveness of online learning than by the duration of school closure or any other factors. Quality online learning is predicted to result in good learning.

Based on such consideration, ICE-I has been designed as follows (Picture 6.1): The functions of ICE-I are as follows:

1. To curate, verify, and register online courses or online study programs in Indonesia, specifically the e-learning courses from Indonesian universities and online courses from international universities and global MOOC platforms. ICE-I carries out the curation process and supervises compliance based on ICE-I standards. In this process, curation is not merely verifying the validity of the content and reviewing the design of the online learning experience, but also verifying the interoperability of each course within the ICE-I marketplace system. Afterwards, a registration number will be assigned as the unique identifier for the course in the ICE-I marketplace.

Picture 6.1 Design of ICE institute

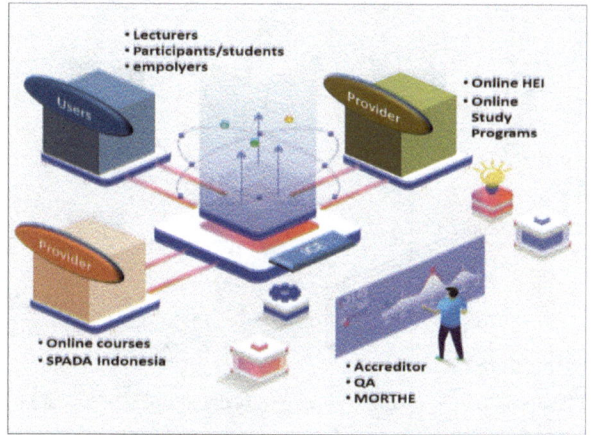

2. To manage the marketplace of online courses in the ICE-I gallery. Online courses in the gallery have been well-curated and are accessible by the users. Expectedly, the quality assurance of online courses in the ICE-I marketplace will facilitate transfers and recognition of courses across institutions or countries.
3. To improve its system and services continuously through collaborative research. The research is intended to extend collaboration to partner universities, improve the ICE-I system, and disseminate research results applicable to the online learning context in Indonesia or elsewhere.
4. To network and partner with various institutions to ensure the availability of online courses. Thus far, ICE-I has partnered and networked with 14 institutions in Indonesia and EdX as online courses providers.
5. The completion of courses, certification, and other student transactions through ICE-I will be recorded using blockchain technology as digital credentials which will later be linked to the job market.

Meanwhile, the operation of the ICE-I is evolving as illustrated in the following business (Picture 6.2).

There are 275 courses available from the ICE-I Consortium members and 1420 EdX courses. Some other partner institutions are also coming in to provide services through ICE-I. For the first three years of its establishment, ICE-I service offers free unbundled courses that can be recognized toward independent study, students exchange, or micro-credential under the Policy of MBKM.

ICE-I services have been free for all parties involved based on the Government's and partner universities' subsidies until 2023. Afterwards, it is expected that a new business model will be implemented to cater to the contribution of the Consortium, pricing for the users, listing all possible fee-paying services from ICE-I, while still carrying out the Government's mandate for ICE-I to assist the unreachable and those needing to upgrade its quality.

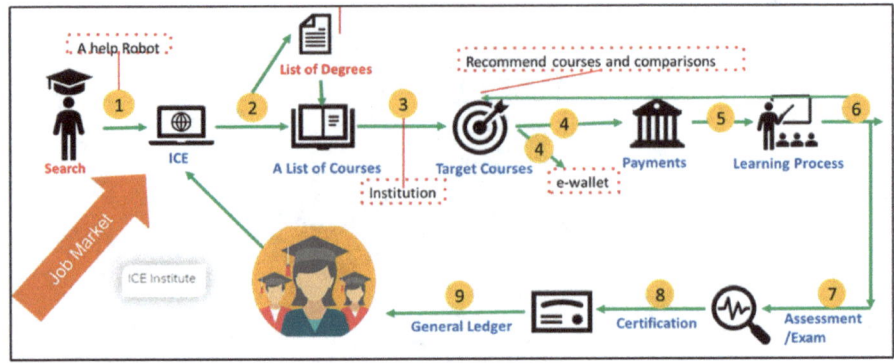

Picture 6.2 ICE institute and digital education in Indonesia (Gullapalli and Ren 2019)

Impact on Equity, Quality, and Efficiency

Equity

ICE-I has been perceived as a strategic means for access to quality knowledge to Indonesians and beyond. Employing cloud-based technology, ICE-I becomes a platform to disseminate quality online courses to all Indonesians across countries, and even across the globe. The platform features online courses from leading universities in Indonesia. This has increased students' access to quality education and transformed the learning process of Indonesian higher education institutions.

ICE-I operates based on the contribution and collaboration of the partner universities. It promotes the strengthening of working relationships among Indonesian HEIs involved, both public and private institutions. The 14 partner universities are the top leading universities in Indonesia, with a history of offering the highest quality education in the country. This collaboration has also provided strong support for implementing the MBKM Policy. Through ICE-I, a university is expected to sign an only one-time agreement with ICE-I to access the online courses market from various institutions, including EdX collection. Taking online courses through ICE-I has been recognized for independent study and students exchange or micro-credentials activity.

Thus far, 3800 students are enrolling through ICE-I. Each student can take up to 20 credit hours or more than one course. As such, 8857 students enrolled in various courses from ICE-I Consortium and EdX. This number is expectedly increasing in the following academic semester.

The availability of quality online courses accessible through ICE-I minimizes the constraint of shortage of experienced faculty and lecturers, and it can be addressed cost-effectively. Furthermore, many quality courses that are not offered in many HEIs due to the absence of qualified faculty will become available much faster than the traditional delivery methods. Topics on the 4th IR technologies are new developments that change the global landscape of human life. In ICE-I, online courses on those topics are instantly accessible sourced from international partners, thus allowing the transmission of new knowledge to be accelerated in Indonesian higher education institutions.

According to official statistics (Lembaga Layanan Dikti III 2020), it is targeted that ICE-I participates in providing access to online courses to more than 4 million students in Indonesia out of the 9,061,977 students population in higher education, to 1605 higher education institutions, and to 12,671 study programs that need quality learning experience.

In short, ICE-I facilitates the distribution of quality online courses from various higher education institutions to the Indonesian higher education community, especially those in remote areas, across time and space. Considering the wide geographic distribution of the population in the archipelago, ICE-I has the potential to provide access to quality education to all Indonesians.

Quality

ICE-I has been strategic in offering quality online courses across the country. Nevertheless, one major issue in online learning has been its quality. There is always some degree of comparison with conventional education. Online learning is not simply an electronic copy of traditional face-to-face education. The ultimate test of online learning—in any form—will be learning effectiveness (Garcia et al. 2021). Theoretically, there are minimum standards to be fulfilled to guarantee that the online learning process will be well-implemented.

At the start, contributed online courses have been curated based on the six domains, i.e., (1) instructional design, (2) content, (3) interaction and delivery process, (4) assessment and evaluation, (5) system and technology, and (6) human resources (Pannen 2019). The review was conducted on each course to be uploaded in ICE-I. The indicators have been provided in a self-evaluation form. This provides a space for the lecturer to reflect and revise their online course accordingly. Then, the lecturer can resubmit the online course for the verification process by the ICE-I team. When the course is regarded as lower than expected, training will be provided by ICE-I on strategies to improve the quality level of the online course.

Recently, the indicators have been modified into seven domains to include Course information, Instructor Information, Technology and Learning Tool, Learning Material and Activity, Interaction and Engagement, Assessment, and Evaluation. The measure on system and technology has been omitted due to the rapid development of technology in higher education institutions, especially during the Pandemic.

The increasing number of new online courses needs quality assurance mechanisms and tools. ICE-I facilitates higher education institutions and lecturers to ensure its online courses' quality through quality assurance service in ICE-I, including the indicators, measurement instrument, mechanism, and guidance and training.

Efficiency

The provision of online courses for the higher education community by ICE-I is perceived to be efficient. Students may enrol in the online courses available in ICE-I for free, including the opportunity to take the exams and obtain a certificate once they pass the exams.

The increasing number of contributed online courses by various institutions accessible through ICE-I provides a straightforward way for the students and institutions to access the marketplace of online courses.

A study done by several universities in Indonesia indicates that 76% of students and 91% of lecturers preferred to start their semester using the online or blended delivery mode (Kesiapan UI dalam Kegiatan Belajar Mengajar 2021; Lembaga Layanan Dikti III 2020). The resource sharing of online courses to higher education institutions within the ICE-I Consortium and beyond has decreased the financial burden of higher education institutions to carry out the traditional face-to-face courses and provide quality lecturers. As such, ICE-I introduces efficient measures to conduct higher education while maintaining quality.

In addition, while the capital investment for the provision of an online courses marketplace is relatively high to be managed by a single university, the emergence of ICE-I as a marketplace for various universities and institutions assists them in overcoming the constraint of high capital investment. Thus, ICE-I offers a marketplace system that all partners can use and share.

Conclusion and Implications

The rapid growth of information and communications technology has provided ways to the impressive growth of online higher education worldwide, including Indonesia. ICE-I has been established based on its aims to provide equity and access to quality education, increase access to learning opportunities and learning flexibilities for students, develop the skills and competencies needed in the twenty-first century, and improve the efficiency of higher operation education.

At present, ICE-I has gained popularity as a marketplace for online courses in Indonesia, mainly due to strong collaboration between ICE-I and its partners based on good intentions to improve the quality and equity of higher education in Indonesia. The number of partners and the number of contributed online courses collection are increasing significantly. Nevertheless, as a new effort, ICE-I still needs to be promoted widely and intensively as a marketplace for online courses in Indonesia to gain a wider market share in the Indonesian higher education community.

Furthermore, while ICE-I has been able to participate in facilitating the MBKM Policy, its operation needs to be improved continuously through concerted efforts in quality assurance, research, and innovation. According to Agarwal (2021), online learning will not subside during the post-COVID-19 Pandemic; thus, ICE-I provision of online courses will continue to flourish. Concerted efforts from the Government, the ICE-I Consortium as online course providers and also governing board, and the users are expected to maintain the operation and its quality. High-quality curated online course collections need to be increased to open a wider market, dissemination needs to be conducted to gain market share, participation needs to be pushed forward, and policy on recognition by academic institutions needs to be devised.

Thus far, ICE-I has had 22 partner institutions out of the 100 top-ranked Indonesian universities. Therefore, those universities have strong potential for becoming partners to provide quality online courses that can further lead to micro-credentials in various competencies, aligned with the industry demand from Indonesian and regional or global markets. Furthermore, collaboration with international institutions is highly potential in increasing ICE-I's collection of quality international online courses. With growing collections, ICE-I coverage can also be enlarged to serve Indonesian and other countries needing such a service.

In the future, ICE-I also opens to the workforce and the public. With the changing nature of jobs due to the industrial revolution, the workforce can access up-to-date and relevant knowledge to keep them abreast with new types of jobs, new skills, and competencies through ICE-I. ICE-I collections of quality online courses facilitate the reskilling and upskilling of the workforce and the public as lifelong learners, thus enabling them to fill in new jobs and professions. Furthermore, ICE-I services will also need to be diversified to cover the provision of online courses for flexible learning and micro-credentialing and a provision of online courses quality assurance system in Indonesia, provision of systems and technology for online courses offerings for use by higher education institutions.

The increased capacity of ICE-I needs to be combined with other essential factors that contribute to success: (a) policy and regulation, (b) empowerment, (c) public and private sector partnership and also empowered users in the higher education community in Indonesia. While there have been supporting policies from the government regarding online learning, freedom learning, and distance education that were issued before the pandemic, in the new normal, it is expected that those policies will be revised and renewed to facilitate more rapid digital transformation in higher education. For example, there is certainly a need for policy and regulation regarding the strategy for recognizing online course certificates and micro-credential certificates in the formal curriculum of a degree-granting program, and by the job market.

Furthermore, the digital transformation, especially in the education sector, has brought about new mindsets, new attitudes, and new ways of thinking digitally. Thus, empowerment of users to be active players in this digital transformation process needs to be done massively by the Government via MOECRT, ICE-I, individual HEIs, and collaboration with private sectors. The timing of massive users' empowerment could not be more strategic as at present in the time of the community entering the new normal where digital transformation is taking place at speed and at scale.

Private sectors involvement in the digital transformation has been immensely important, as technology providers, infrastructure providers, training providers, etc. ICE-I collaboration with private sectors in the future will also need to be upscaled to enable ICE-I's growth as an online course marketplace in Indonesia.

The landscape of education in Indonesia has been changed dramatically in the last couple of years. Concerted efforts are important to shape that landscape to achieve the nation's human development goals. ICE-I is taking its step to carry its mission as one of the drivers in digital transformation in higher education in Indonesia.

6.7 Case 6: Malaysia: The Alignment of Digitalisation and Management Strategies to Enhance the Use of ICT-Driven Teaching and Learning Innovations in the Higher Education Ecosystem[7]

Executive Summary

The alignment of Malaysian higher education institutions' (HEIs) digitalisation and management strategies involves the efforts to promote and enhance the use of ICT in higher education. The alignment poses critical questions for policy-makers responsible for implementing ICT-driven innovations in higher education according to five core areas of the higher education ecosystem. These five areas include: (1) policy measures, (2) enablers and platforms for collaboration, (3) institutional training providers, (4) youth and adult learners, and (5) strategic partnerships. The alignment will focus on the need to create future-ready ICT-driven policies to enhance the teaching and learning activities in HEIs. Stakeholders need to determine how the current policies are systematic enough to meet the need of diverse counterparts. Stakeholders also need to determine the necessary ICT-driven tools and technologies most suited to their educational contexts. The alignment is also important to help stakeholders to identify the most appropriate and effective training programs and providers for creating more systematic and sustainable training delivery mechanisms. In addition, the alignment helps stakeholders to connect ICT-driven innovation with the need to enhance educational opportunities for marginalized groups espoused in the SDGs and to leverage the strategic partnerships across sectors. The education system requires ingenuity, wisdom and kindness in planning, coordinating and managing resources. This Malaysian case illustrates how the alignment of Malaysian higher education institutions digitalisation and management strategies act as a catalyst for the sustainability of a learning and teaching ecosystem that meets the need of diverse stakeholders.

Introduction and Context

The rapid growth of digital transformation throughout Asia and the Pacific continues to challenge the role of Malaysian higher education systems. Although efforts to promote and enhance ICT use in higher education in Malaysia have increased rapidly in recent years, there is a need for appropriate alignment from all areas in the ecosystem. At the outset of 2020, the year Malaysia was set to welcome a fully developed nation status (The Eleventh Malaysia Plan 2016–2020), the world was struck with the first major global pandemic in a century. By February, the COVID-19 crisis had worsened dramatically, affecting the health and well-being of not only individuals but also the entire Malaysian higher education ecosystem. Almost overnight, new approaches to teaching and learning for students staying both on- and off-campus

---

[7] Authored by Paulina Pannen, Chairman, Indonesia Cyber Education Institute, Universitas Terbuka, Indonesia, ppanen@gmail.com, paulina@ecampus.ut.ac.id.

became a pressing need, one in which higher education institutions (HEIs) were ill-prepared for.

To meet this challenge, more rigorous and methodical efforts are needed to establish an ICT-enabled higher education ecosystem through digitalisation that supports efforts to achieve the Sustainable Development Goals (SDGs) 2030 and ensure equitable access to quality higher education and lifelong learning opportunities for all (i.e., SDG 4), especially to cater to the post-pandemic era. This case study puts forward potential strategies to align and strengthen institutional governance and partnerships to provide equal access to quality education through their digitalisation and management strategies which mainly involves the efforts to promote and enhance ICT-driven teaching and learning innovations in higher education.

This case study poses critical elements for policy-makers responsible for implementing ICT-driven innovations in higher education according to five core areas of the higher education ecosystem. These five areas include: (1) policy measures, (2) enablers and platforms for collaboration, (3) institutional training providers, (4) youth and adult learners, and (5) strategic partnerships.

This case study explores the alignment of digitalisation and management strategies in a top rank university in Malaysia by observing the university's efforts to promote and enhance the use of ICT in its ecosystem. Universiti Putra Malaysia (UPM) has recently launched 'UPM Strategic Plan 2021–2025' to drive the research university striving to become a smart campus. UPM will pay special attention to strengthening the crucial aspects of smart campus digitisation that involve teaching and learning, services, infrastructure and sustainability. Even though the plan is very new, it is important for UPM to evaluate the whole system to make sure that upcoming initiatives from the plan can be implemented successfully.

The implementation is spearheaded by the Centre for Academic Development (CADe) through the Innovative Teaching and Learning Delivery Transformation initiatives as follows:

Design and Implementation

Theoretical Framework Underpinning and Design

HEIs should determine assessment targets based on their missions, goals, and culture. Current literature, models, theories and research have suggested such relevant assessment targets (Lim and Wang 2016). Albeit untested for such purposes, we believe that the Performance Improvement (PI) Theory—a theory that can be applied to improve the performance of organisations, processes, and individuals (Rummler and Brache 1995)—could plausibly be applied to align current practices to specific targets. Concerned with determination and alignment of performance, the model (see Fig. 6.5) includes five interrelated components or characteristics: performance analysis; cause analysis; intervention selection design; implementation and change management; and evaluation (Fig. 6.6).

The five components were used to evaluate the current practices of ICT driven teaching and learning innovations among HEIs in Malaysia. These components also

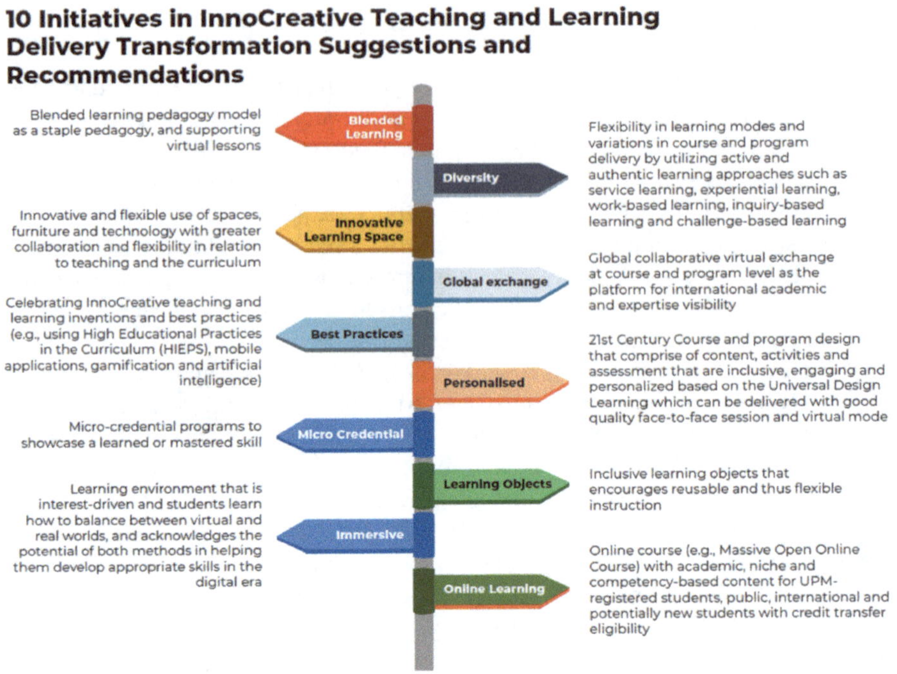

10 Initiatives in InnoCreative Teaching and Learning Delivery Transformation Suggestions and Recommendations

Blended learning pedagogy model as a staple pedagogy, and supporting virtual lessons

Blended Learning

Diversity

Flexibility in learning modes and variations in course and program delivery by utilizing active and authentic learning approaches such as service learning, experiential learning, work-based learning, inquiry-based learning and challenge-based learning

Innovative and flexible use of spaces, furniture and technology with greater collaboration and flexibility in relation to teaching and the curriculum

Innovative Learning Space

Global exchange

Global collaborative virtual exchange at course and program level as the platform for international academic and expertise visibility

Celebrating InnoCreative teaching and learning inventions and best practices (e.g., using High Educational Practices in the Curriculum (HIEPS), mobile applications, gamification and artificial intelligence)

Best Practices

Personalised

21st Century Course and program design that comprise of content, activities and assessment that are inclusive, engaging and personalized based on the Universal Design Learning which can be delivered with good quality face-to-face session and virtual mode

Micro-credential programs to showcase a learned or mastered skill

Micro Credential

Learning Objects

Inclusive learning objects that encourages reusable and thus flexible instruction

Learning environment that is interest-driven and students learn how to balance between virtual and real worlds, and acknowledges the potential of both methods in helping them develop appropriate skills in the digital era

Immersive

Online Learning

Online course (e.g., Massive Open Online Course) with academic, niche and competency-based content for UPM-registered students, public, international and potentially new students with credit transfer eligibility

Fig. 6.5 The 10 innovative teaching and learning delivery transformation initiatives

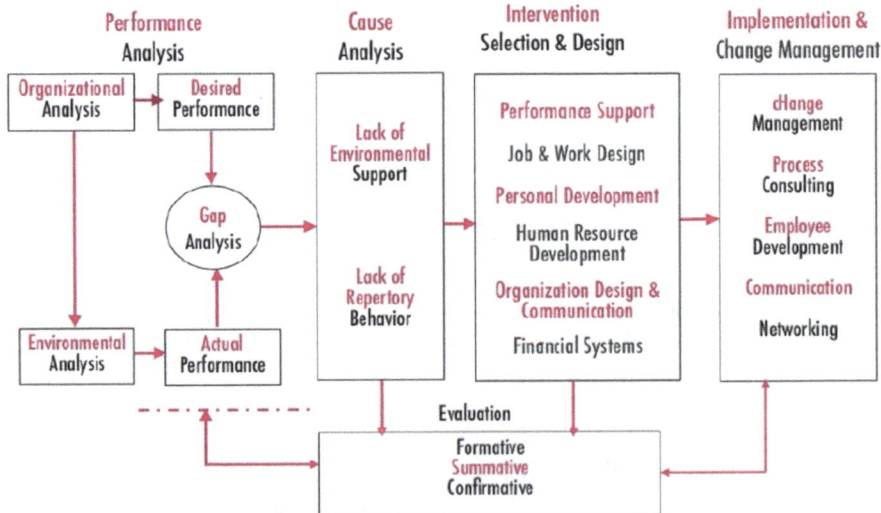

Fig. 6.6 A comprehensive model of performance improvement

are used by policy-makers to determine the most appropriate policies or strategies and, more importantly, to align the formulation of ICT-driven with actual practices.

To interpret the level of ICT implementation taken place, there is a need to set along a spectrum of stages that can reflect institutional strategies supporting technology integration practices. Therefore, the current study references the progression stages broadly defined by UNESCO (2005) as they are highly recognised in the Asia-Pacific region and proved useful to track where an institution is in supporting technology integration. To reflect different levels of ICT implementations in specifically higher education contexts, this case study further readapts UNESCO's (2005) work and sets the stages in its interpretation of the analysis. The UNESCO study identified four broad stages of ICT adoption and use in education. These stages, termed Emerging, Applying, Infusing and Transforming, are shown in Table 6.4.

UNESCO suggests a comprehensive approach to ICT in education policy implementation based on experiences in Asian nations. This approach considers crucial aspects such as ICT resources, curriculum, assessment, teacher professional development, and fund-raising for institutions' digitalisation and management strategies (UNESCO 2004).

Table 6.4 Stages of ICT adoption and use

Categories of implementation	Stages of technology usages	Description
Emerging	Becoming aware of technology	Educational institutions are still rooted in traditional, teacher-centred practice. Administrators and teachers are beginning to investigate the possibilities and consequences of using ICT for institutional management and incorporating ICT into the curriculum
Applying	Learning how to use technology	Administrators and teachers actively participated in integrating ICT to acquire specialised subject skills and knowledge, beginning to transform the classroom teaching approach by increasing the use of ICT in various subject areas with specific tools and software
Infusing	Understanding how and when to use technology	Educational institutions incorporate ICT into their curricula and use a range of computer-based technology in laboratories, classrooms, and administrative offices. Educators employ technology to manage both their own and their students' learning
Transforming	Specializing in the use of technology	ICT has become an essential aspect of personal productivity and professional activity. The curriculum's emphasis is now learner-centred, with academic areas integrated into real-world applications

Source (UNESCO 2010)

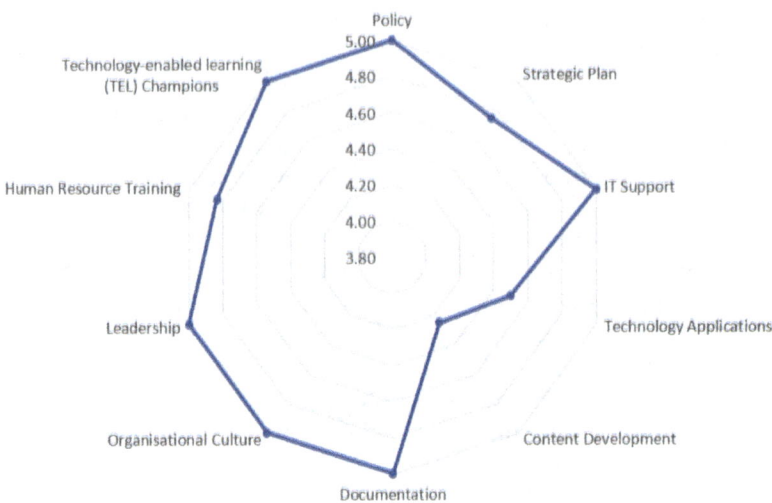

Fig. 6.7 Consolidated benchmarking scores from tactical managers

University's tactical managers who possess the criteria below were invited to validate the evaluation outcomes by giving scoring to ten aspects provided with discussion input in several workshops, which contributed to the findings for this case study report (Fig. 6.7). The criteria set for expert evaluation are:

(a) Active involvement in university strategic planning more than five years
(b) An academic who is also an expert in e-learning
(c) Active involvement in formulating and assessing national e-learning policy implementation.

Both inputs from the scoring and discussions held in the one-day workshop were evaluated and mapped as presented in the following section.

Malaysian higher education institutions' alignment of digitalisation and management strategies through the use of ICT

The following matrix was used to evaluate the alignment of digitalisation and management strategies through investigation of technology use from the aspects of policy, enablers, continuous development (training), learners' inclusion and partnerships. The outcomes of the components are mapped as follow. University Putra Malaysia (UPM), a public university, chose to use the matrix in order to align the holistic evaluation of technology in the running of teaching and learning of the university (Table 6.5).

Table 6.5 The evaluation matrix adapting from the model of performance improvement

Component	Performance	Cause	Intervention–selection and design	Implementation and change management	Evaluation (need of alignment)
Policy measures	Applying	Respond to ever-changing technology development	Involved as a player with top-down projects of innovations to enhance the policy	Systematic and enterprise-wide	Need of more dynamic policies in place
Enablers and platforms	Applying	External uses are more rapid than internal	Creating more channels for flexible teaching and learning	Depending on technology affordances for individuals or collectively	Critical for alignment on system integrations
Institutional training providers	Infusing	Highly aware of the future direction of knowledge and skills	A proper plan for training online to update teachers' knowledge and skills	Active at all levels	Need consistent alignment–updated internal and external changes
Youth and adult learners	Transforming	The youth and students are highly connected to new innovations	Organisation prepared to acknowledge programme/course delivery and completion	'Fluidity' is the key to improvement and experimentation	Need consistent alignment–updated internal and external changes
Strategic partnerships	Infusing	Both parties understand the shared value and visions	Incentives to all parties (grant, acknowledgement, collaboration, etc.)	Need of policy improvement and flexibility	Need attention

Impact on Equity, Quality and Efficiency

The model of performance improvement and the alignment of digitalisation and management strategies have made an impact on the equity, quality and efficiency of UPM. As the education sector is gearing towards complementing Industry Revolution 4.0, Society 5.0 and SDGs 2030, aspects of equity in education as well as quality and efficiency in the higher education delivery system are enhanced through the use of an appropriate model of performance improvement. Digitalisation and management strategies have synergised with the Malaysian Higher Education Framework 4.0 and the Malaysian Education Blueprint (Higher Education) by using the performance improvement model.

The Blueprint and the Framework are two shreds of evidence of how the performance improvement model of digitalisation and management strategies enhances the quality and efficiency of UPM. The implementation process of the Blueprint has been consistently assessed based on the institutional performance in the ten initiatives, which nurture digital literacy, critical thinking and problem solving to all learners to thrive in Industrial Revolution 4.0. A new learning ecosystem that makes use of future-driven curriculum, new technologies, new learning space and infrastructure are evident in the formulation of the Experiential Learning and Competency-Based Education Landscape (EXCEL) framework launched by the Higher Education Ministry in 2021 aiming at produce holistic and highly skilled graduates. The four new learning paradigms, namely Industry Driven Experiential Learning (IDEAL), Community Resilience Experiential Learning (CARE), Research Infused Experiential Learning (REAL), and Personalised Experiential Learning (POISE), will transform the curriculum and instruction in Malaysian HEIs to nurture forward-thinking lifelong learners, innovative entrepreneurs, creative practitioners and change-makers.

The new model of performance improvement also seemingly contributed to widening the networks of stakeholders involved in the HEI ecosystem and strengthening the quality assurance mechanism needed to facilitate and sustain the quality and efficiency in higher education delivery systems. Learners from different walks of life can now access quality education, enjoy lifelong learning opportunities, and experience flexible modes of learning methods. Massive Open Online Courses (MOOCs) and Micro-Credentials are now widely used to complement the blended learning initiatives adopted by HEIs, especially in the post-COVID-19 norm of work, live and study.

Last but not least, the model of performance improvement and the alignment of digitalisation and management strategies have also shaped the new curriculum that is both industry- and community-driven. Thus, greater collaboration between higher education, community and industry partners to support this new curriculum has gradually become a common practice in Malaysia. The smart campus initiatives in HEIs, which blend physical infrastructure and digital technologies in supporting the HEI management operation and delivery system, has transformed the way quality education is delivered to learners in Malaysia now and in the future.

Conclusion and Implications

This case study hopes to provide a guiding matrix to direct research and policy discussion around what ICT-driven innovations, curricula delivery, and learning ecosystems are necessary and relevant. This case study focuses on the alignment of digitalisation and management strategies through investigation of technology use from the aspects of policy, enablers, continuous development (training), learners' inclusion and partnerships. There is a need to create future-ready ICT-driven policies to enhance educators' and learners' participation in HEIs. The matrix aims to help stakeholders determine whether current policies are systematic and meet the diverse needs of stakeholders and contingencies. On the ground level, stakeholders might need to determine necessary ICT-driven tools and technologies most suited to their educational contexts.

Additionally, stakeholders are suggested to identify the most appropriate and effective training programs and providers for creating systematic and sustainable training delivery mechanisms. It would be helpful to consider the needs of youth and adults outside of the formal education system and how ICT-driven innovation can be used to enhance educational opportunities for marginalised or the 'lost generation' groups due to the pandemic. Stakeholders might need to consider the best ways of digitalising teaching and learning via leveraging strategic partnerships across sectors in the region to achieve the related SDGs.

Building on these core areas and the impacts of COVID-19, the findings of this case study report expand perspectives of digitalisation through ICT-driven innovation in light of emerging, disruptive technologies, which continue to impact educational systems. Given the technology affordances in all HEIs in Malaysia, evaluating the impact of digitalisation strategies on curriculum development, delivery and assessment could be crucial. The alignment may help stakeholders to connect ICT-driven innovation with the need to enhance educational opportunities for marginalised groups espoused in the SDGs and to leverage the strategic partnerships across sectors.

According to lessons learnt from UPM's practice, HEI administrators are suggested to ensure that the ICT governance structure enables them to effectively provide support to internal and external clients efficiently, with a high degree of accountability and transparency. HEI administrators can also maintain close collaboration with internal and external stakeholders to ensure that adequate resources related to ICT driven teaching and learning innovations are allocated, and that institutions have the appropriate cost model and capital efficiency to address the financial needs of the ICT-driven initiatives. Through the help of the industries, HEIs can enhance faculty's pedagogical knowledge and skills through offering online Continuing Professional Development (CPD) training and support programs for faculty on how to carry out remote and online teaching. Faculty may also use social media and online forums to share best practices of remote and online teaching with their colleagues. As cyber-attacks might dampen the continuity of ICT-driven teaching and learning innovations implementation in some HEIs, administrators can invest in cybersecurity defence systems at the HEI with the help from industries and develop resilient faculty and student to ensure efficient continuity of teaching and learning is in place. Ultimately, the education system may require ingenuity, wisdom and kindness in planning, coordinating and managing resources. This Malaysian case has illustrated how the alignment of Malaysian higher education institutions' digitalisation and management strategies act as a catalyst for the sustainability of an ICT driven learning and teaching innovation ecosystem that meets the need of diverse stakeholders in Malaysia.

Data-driven national monitoring and evaluation systems are crucial to enhance the management of education systems, ensure accountability, and help implementers understand the key roles that ICT-driven innovations play in the transmission of knowledge, the acquisition of new skills and competencies, and in the development of values and attitudes that are relevant to the building of sustainable and peaceful societies. Monitoring and evaluation of systems thus serve the needs of three different user communities—policy-makers, researchers and teachers. Effective policies should consider the level of centralisation and decentralisation of respective countries' education systems to ensure flexible policy translation and implementation. Zagami et al. (2018) propose four key areas that need to be addressed in order to measure the level and quality assurance of agencies and HEIs' ICT-driven innovation policies available in each country. The key drivers for a comprehensive ICT-driven innovation policy suggested in the paper include: (i) future-ready higher education visions, (ii) a systemic perspective, (iii) promotion of commitment to policy learning, and (iv) effective development and implementation of policy processes.

In this Malaysian case of UPM, the university found it crucial to cope and adapt to new technologies and practices; otherwise, they will be left behind. ICT-driven innovation in the university should not be limited to only MOOCs and blended learning, but also other ICT-driven innovations. Means and enablers of ICT-driven innovations should also consider integrations of Artificial Intelligence (AI), automation, mixed realities, learning analytics and Internet of Things, as well as openness to emerging technologies in the future.

ICT-driven innovations can enable vulnerable and underserved populations to improve and adapt their skills, with particular attention to the elimination of gender-based barriers, and to vulnerable groups such as those with disabilities and less privileged countries. Therefore, there is a need to provide UPM educators with adequate technical skills to address the challenges of special education. Instructors involved in curriculum design, the development of teaching materials and ICT-based education must undergo continuous professional development.

Finally, multi-sectorial engagement, including with educational technology providers, appears to be significant in terms of sustainability and innovation. Cross-sector partnerships between universities, universities and industry, universities and government, as well as universities with the community, create mutual benefit and goodwill that cut across formal, non-formal and informal education sectors at regional and national levels. More efforts are suggested to be made to link universities, government entities, communities and industries in supporting learning across formal, non-formal and informal sectors. Given different learning modes and the rapid expansion of digital credentials, fair recognition of qualifications will require close collaboration across sectors.

6.8 Case 7: Morocco: The Role of Smart Digital Platforms in Supporting Remote Practical Works in the Light of the Spread of the COVID-19 Crisis[8]

Executive Summary

The emergence of the COVID-19 pandemic and its rapid and unannounced spread in the world have had a significant impact on educational bodies and departments. All countries of the world have been forced to close down educational institutions; they have considered alternative education in parallel with the new phase. In this paper, we will highlight the role of the e-labs platform in supporting remote practical works and its activation under the COVID-19 spread to sustain education and reduce the spread of the pandemic. To test this platform, the analytical description curriculum was used to provide results with a questionnaire conducted on a group of professors and students who had used this platform designed at the Faculty of Sciences Semlalia, Cadi Ayyad University Marrakech, Morocco. The results of the study showed that the e-labs platform could play a significant role in supporting university education, contributing to maintaining the health of professors and students, and reducing the spread of the epidemic.

Introduction and Context

Regular education often suffers from finding appropriate solutions to many of the problems during the educational process, most recently the spread of COVID-19. The pandemic has led to the closure of universities and educational institutions throughout the world in general and the Kingdom of Morocco in particular. All this has quarantined learners in their homes, leading to serious thinking about new types of learning based on modern technologies (El Gourari et al. 2020), primarily the internet. Internet transcends the limits of time and can stand up to many educational problems, for example, reducing overcrowding in universities, as well as benefiting from asynchronous lessons that are developed by some professors. Thanks to the development of internet, e-learning and distance learning through digital educational platforms have become imperative. Educators, particularly those in higher education, are suggested to accelerate the adoption and application of e-learning. Considering the emergencies that we now live in, the digital transformation in higher education will enhance the competence of its students and teachers to prevent the disruption of the course of education and its activities. The e-learning platform to be introduced in this article is available at the expense of the Faculty of Sciences Semlalia, Cadi Ayyad University, The platform's role in supporting distance learning under current global health conditions and how it is designed and managed to support and sustain education will be analysed and evaluated. The focus of this paper is the impact on

---

[8] Authored by Abdelali El Gourari, Ph.D. student in the laboratory of physics the high energy and astrophysics at Cadi Ayyad University, Morocco; Professor Mustapha Raoufi and Professor Mohammed Skouri, Physics Department Faculty of Sciences Semlalia, Cadi Ayyad University Marrakech, Morocco.

education brought by the spread of the COVID-19 pandemic (Tria 2020) in general and higher education in particular. Under these difficult and urgent circumstances, Moroccan education officials had to seek for urgent alternatives to facilitate further higher education and finally decided to activate the role of distance learning and e-learning through digital platforms available, thereby ensuring the viability of learning (Addi et al. 2020)

This paper attempts to highlight a range of objectives, the most important of which are:

Demonstrate how the COVID-19 pandemic affects university-based education; Clarify what digital educational platforms are and how they help support e-learning in higher education.

Highlight the role of the e-labs platform available at the Faculty of Sciences Semlalia, Cadi Ayyad University, in the activation and application of distance learning based on the interaction between its teachers and their students through remote practical works under current global health conditions that have forced them to move away from the university and adapt to lockdown.

The aforementioned challenges also invite Cadi Ayyad University and the Faculty of Sciences Semlalia to think about whether the e-labs platform can play a role in supporting and sustaining distance learning and reducing the prevalence of the COVID-19 pandemic. Through the above, the research reviews the following question:

How does the e-labs platform contribute to the support and continuation of distance learning at the Faculty of Sciences Semlalia, Cadi Ayyad University for its students and professors, even amid the pandemic?

Design and Implementation

Our goal is to show how the e-labs platform contributes to the support and continuation of distance learning at the Faculty of Sciences Semlalia, Cadi Ayyad University by quickly and flexibly allowing students to conduct practical works remotely and in a passionate and eager-to-learn atmosphere. Figure 6.8 illustrates the fundamental mechanism of the e-labs platform (El Gourari et al. 2021)

Part One

In this phase, the professor shall be the manager of all completed and presented to students, whose work shall be as follows:

- To have an account on the e-labs platform in advance;
- Divide students into groups, after which a period of time is assigned to each group;
- Delete or add new students;

The process to be carried out by students is prepared by the LabVIEW environment as illustrated in Fig. 6.9 and coordinated with the NI ELVIS II+ card. This card enables us to complete and control operations through the LabVIEW program; in other words, any action done is simulated with the LabVIEW program and this card.

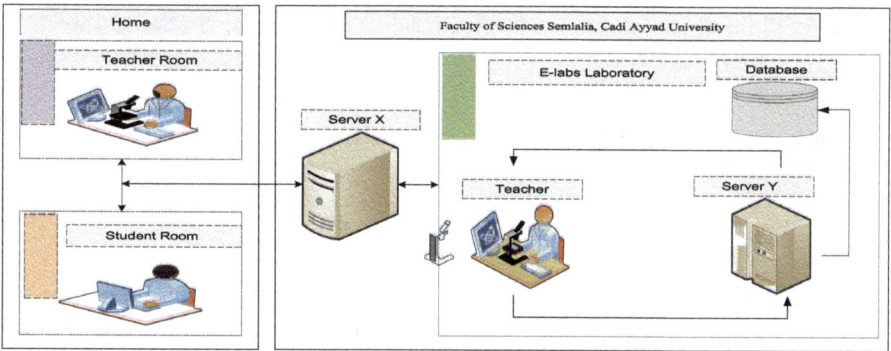

Fig. 6.8 The virtual architecture of the proposed work

Fig. 6.9 NI ELVIS II+
board with LabVIEW
environment

Recording all that the professor has done by clicking on the valid button in a particular file for use in other tasks such as changing the method of placement of experiments or the type of questions to the subject.

Part Two

The students who are required to perform the practical work submitted to them by the professor before the start of the remote practical work must go through the following stages:

- Register an account on the e-labs platform in advance;
- Be aware of the period in which the experiment was pre-developed by the professor and the group in which it was placed;
- Reserve the appropriate time from the professors' time limit;

- Wait until the reserved time and then check the operation submitted to them;
- Start work by answering theoretical questions, then moving to applied work and comparing it with hypothetical answers before concluding.

Upon completion, students press the right button, thus completing the process. All they have done during that period is stored in a particular location via the MySQL program to be processed after being used for student evaluation.

Part three

The laboratory is where most professor-designed operations are completed. It has NI ELVIS II+ , a high-quality process design computer that adapts to a virtual learning environment such as LabVIEW. NI ELVIS II+ (Figs. 6.9 and 6.10) can realistically perform professor-designed operations, link what has been done in reality to LabVIEW to implement operations virtually, and upload relevant data to the server to communicate externally through the Internet. The relay switches of NI ELVIS II+ play an essential role in controlling the passage of electricity between the elements of the circuit to be studied.

Digital educational platforms

The idea of an interactive educational platform was suggested by Feoktistov et al. (2020). These platforms employ web technology and combine features of electronic content management systems with social media platforms and communication networks. An interactive educational platform's main objectives include:

- Facilitate posting lessons on the web and developing online educational tasks and activities for students;
- Allow students to contact the professor directly through multiple techniques;
- Teamwork by splitting students into work regiments;

Fig. 6.10 NI ELVIS II+ board with relay switches

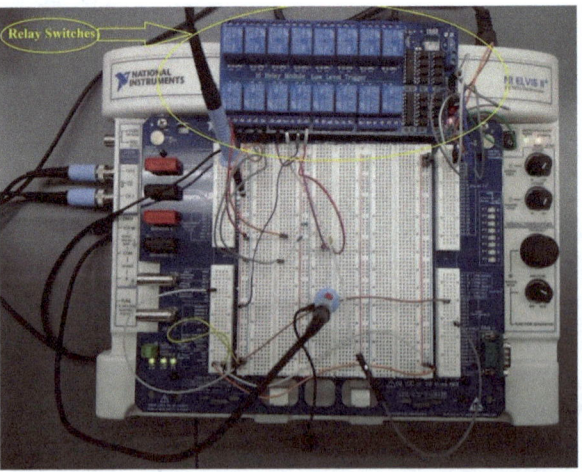

- Discussion of ideas and views and sharing of scientific content among professors and students will help to achieve high-quality educational output.

E-labs platform

The e-labs platform was first designed in 2017 (Ouatik et al. 2019) with software languages such as PHP, HTML, CSS, Python, JavaScript, LabVIEW, and MYSQL. Its main role was to perform remote practical works at any time and place. In 2019 (El Gourari et al. 2021), the platform became more versatile by adding some features and integrating artificial intelligence technologies. For example, theoretical lessons could be added to the platform to assess students before practical works start or after each course ends. What makes this platform significant is that it is open-source and can be used by any person or educational institution.

Faculty of Sciences Semlalia at Cadi Ayyad University is among the institutes in Morocco whose platform is designed to be a dynamic learning environment geared towards all categories of students enrolled in this platform and all levels. The e-labs platform is also designed on scientific rather than engineering or technical grounds to help learners provide e-learning tools capable of managing remote practical works delivery and tests based on artificial intelligence techniques (El Gourari et al. 2022). It is currently available at the faculty, as shown in Fig. 6.11, allowing the exchange of information between students and professors, by simultaneous communication mechanisms, icons, and asynchronous ones. The platform is one of the most accessible open-source online learning platforms that allow for the creation of many real-life lab experiments, and its content is accessible only to enrolled students. The e-labs platform can be classified as one of the systems:

- Educational content.
- Learning management system.
- Management of the education contents.

E-labs and E-learning

It is evident that e-labs can support e-learning through the positive impact of its use in learning outcomes and retention rates. For example, some e-labs features, including mentoring students and quickly providing them with feedback, are powerful to understand student orientation and effectively transmit information. It is, therefore, natural that e-learning produces better results at different levels of mindfulness in students. Also, quick knowledge entry and dissemination are key elements in the e-labs platform, improving the learning effectiveness and outcome. Also, given that an important purpose of higher education is to prepare job-ready talents, the e-labs platform was designed as an open and unfettered participatory learning environment that supports self-learning and helps to share and store experiences and ideas among learners in a way that makes them accessible to all.

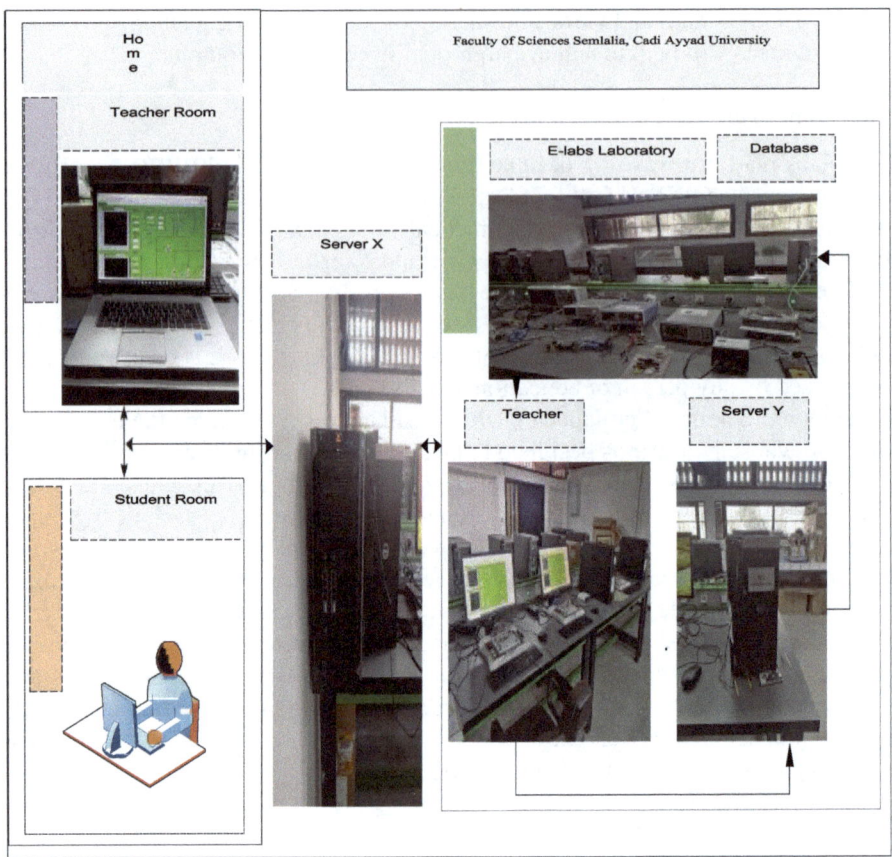

Fig. 6.11 The real architecture of the proposed work

Impact on Equity, Quality, and Efficiency

Evaluation Instrument

To evaluate the effectiveness of the e-labs platform, a questionnaire containing 14 closed questions was designed. The design process of this questionnaire consists of multiple phases as follows:

- Phase one: This phase consists of choosing the quality of the questionnaire either in a closed (unlimited), open (specific), or varied (non-specific) form. The choice was depended on the kind of information to gather, which was about group behavior. Also, simple information was identified regarding the questions in Tables 6.6 and 6.7, so the research team used both types (specific and non-specific questionnaires).

Table 6.6 Contribution of digital platforms to the promotion of distance learning in COVID-19

Questions	Response 1	Response 2	Discussions
Are digital platforms important in university learning?	50% yes	50% no	This convergence is since some professors and students are not important for digital learning and do not use digital platforms to learn much; in this case, we refer to the category who answers by no. However, technological development and health conditions dictate it
Are there any benefits to the pedigree of digital platforms?	80% yes	20% no	The majority of students and professors know that digital platforms are ancient, not modern. But the truth is they have been created for a long time; we mean the digital platforms in general
How do you feel about extending digital platforms to all university education systems?	90% yes	15% no	Acceptance of the presence of digital platforms within the university is evidence that they help solve many problems
Do you see that the students of the Faculty of Sciences Semlalia (FSSM) have favored the use of digital platforms in learning?	15% yes	70% no	This high percentage suggests that students need to be motivated to use the virtual learning environment and to form on how to use the digital platforms
How do you feel about the transmission of satisfaction when practical work is done through the platform to the web?	60% yes	40% no	The idea of the application of remote practical works is going in the right direction, so it must be further developed well
Do you see digital platforms as inevitable in a college education?	70% yes	32% no	The services provided by digital platforms facilitate many things for professors, students, and even administrators
How would you like to recreate each professor's application of the digital platforms?	85% yes	15% no	The necessity of training teachers and students before using digital platforms

- Phase two: This phase concerned the design of the questionnaire form, through the formulation of questions on the subject matter. It was clear, smooth, understood by the study sample, with the importance of using a polite method of asking questions. These high-end construction methods have motivated respondents to answer the questions asked honestly.
- Phase three: Then, the team decided on sampling methods.
- Phase four: This is a very important stage, a pilot of the questionnaire. The aim was to identify the extent to which there were deviations in the questions in the

Table 6.7 Contribution of the e-labs platform at Faculty of Sciences Semlalia to reducing the spread of the COVID-19

Questions	Response 1	Response 2	Discussions
Are digital platforms contributed to reducing the prevalence of the COVID-19 epidemic?	91% yes	9% no	This underscores the role of digital platforms in mitigating the spread of the COVID-19 pandemic
Do you consider the success of the e-labs platform to be contingent on the good training of professors and students?	95% yes	6% no	This is a very high proportion even though health conditions by decision of the Ministry of Higher Education are used in education
Is there any difficulty in composing on the platform for pre-preparation of practical work in the laboratory and taking it down on the platform?	55% yes	45% no	That confirms that the platform only needs a little focus to work on well
Is the e-labs platform quick and easy to learn?	60% yes	20% no	That ratio indicated that there was a need to reconsider how it was used, to increase the flow of the Internet, and to make it available to all
How much do you think the platform of E-labs continues to be carried out remotely beyond COVID- 19?	56% yes	44% no	This suggests to them that the operation is temporary and will cease to exist with the demise of COVID-19
Do you see that the appearance of the e-labs platform was caused by the COVID-19 pandemic or by manual reasons?	61% COVID-19	43% manual	COVID-19 played an important role in showing the background and importance of the e-labs platform
Are digital platforms one of the important ways to alleviate Corona's hunger?	95% yes	5% no	This means that these digital platforms, especially the e-labs platform, played a major role in alleviating the anticipation of the COVID-19 pandemic

questionnaire, and modify or replace current questions. The questionnaire was presented to a group of experts to evaluate its internal validity.

- Phase five: It is the application of the questionnaire form to the student respondents. Since the pandemic prevented us from directly meeting the study sample, we emailed the questionnaire. Currently, with the technological development and expansion of the use of computers, the questionnaire has also been launched through the website. In addition, social media sites such as Facebook and WhatsApp have also been used to spread it widely and access data quickly.

Participants

The questionnaire was distributed to 100 professors and 400 students from the Faculty of Sciences Semlalia and the Faculty of Science and Techniques through purposive sampling, and the response rate was 100%. The respondents were invited to share their perspective on the role of the e-labs platform at the Faculty of Sciences Semlalia, Cadi Ayyad University, in supporting distance university education and its contribution to reducing the spread of COVID-19.

Data preparation

The data were collected and further analysed through the following steps:

• Determining the objective of data analysis:

At this point, the research team sets the target for which we are going to analyse the data—The role of the e-labs platform in supporting remote practical works and its activation under the COVID-19 spread to sustain education and reduce the spread of the epidemic. The team also used descriptive and deductive analysis and adopted data visualisation tools and techniques.

• Data collection:

As described in the *Evaluation Instrument* section, during this phase, the research team collected data from the questionnaire and available data in the e-labs platform in advance for analysis. A record was also made to keep all the data and its sources.

• Data cleaning:

After collecting data, the research team also cleaned the data to mitigate potential errors during the data analysis process.

• Data analysis:

Having collected, refined, and processed the data, data analysis tools and programs were used to understand, interpret and draw conclusions based on pre-established objectives.

• Data interpretation:

At this important stage, results from the data analysis process through a detailed report are displayed in Tables 6.6 and 6.7.

• Data visualisation:

At this stage, the research team visualises data through the diagrams shown in Figs. 6.12, 6.13, 6.14, and 6.15 to monitor relationships and compare data sets, enabling us to discover new information that contributed to the success of the research.

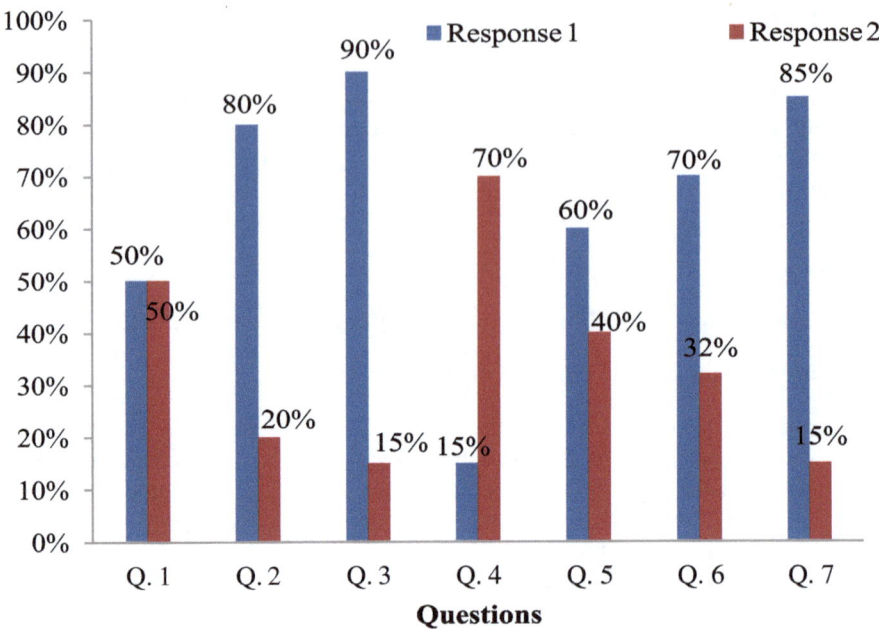

Fig. 6.12 Contribution of digital platforms to supporting university education according to each question

Fig. 6.13 Contribution of the platform to supporting university education by an average rate

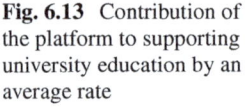

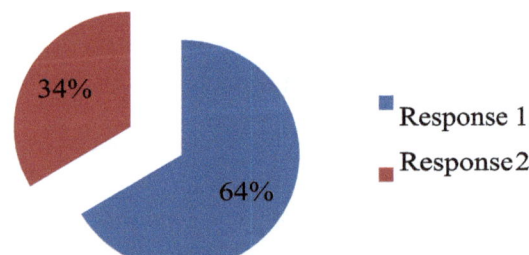

Results and discussion

Table 6.6 shows the discussion of the first focus on the contribution of digital platforms to the promotion and continuation of distance learning in the context of the COVID-19 pandemic.

Table 6.7 shows the presentation and discussion of the other focus on the contribution of the e-labs platform at the Faculty of Sciences Semlalia to reducing the spread of the COVID-19.

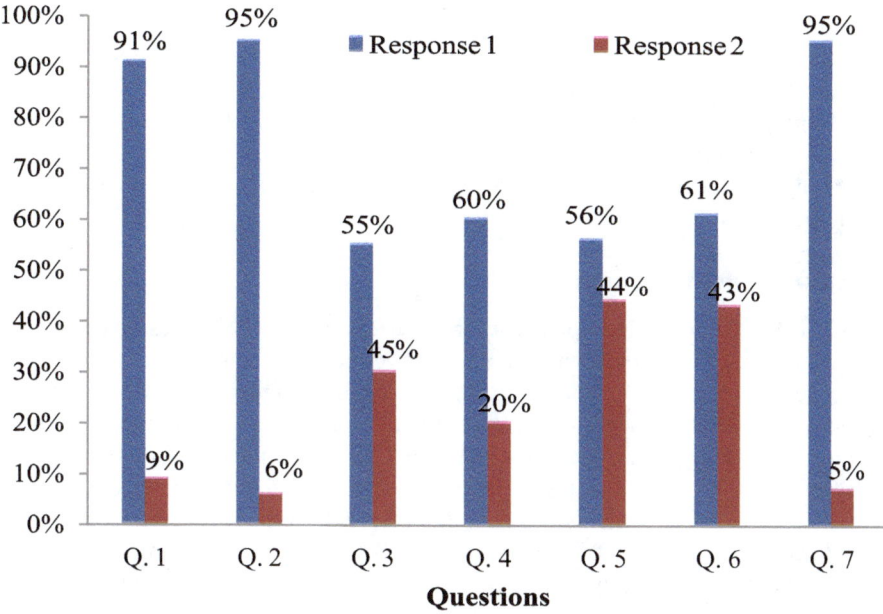

Fig. 6.14 Contribution of the E-labs platform at university to reducing the spread of the COVID-19 according to each question

Fig. 6.15 Contribution of the e-labs platform at university to reducing the spread of the COVID-19 by an average rate

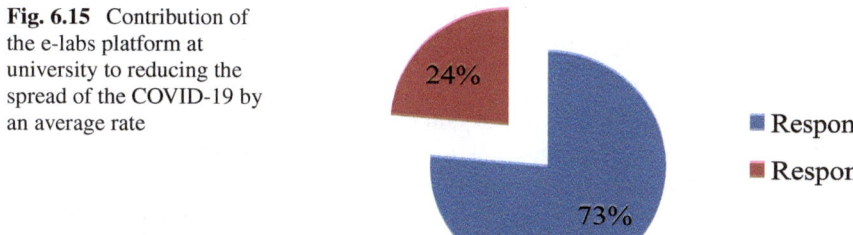

The questionnaire results confirmed the essential role that digital learning platforms play in the success of the educational process during all public times and this crisis. The results of the design and implementation of the e-labs also confirmed that e-learning and distance learning had resolved one of the biggest crises in education.

There are many benefits from the e-labs platform that reinforces quality education:

- Encouraging engagement in the educational process, to upgrade the competence of teachers, students, and anyone involved in the educational process;
- Improving the administrative system to be able to clarify the tasks and responsibilities of each party;

- Addressing complaints from parents and trying to satisfy them in such a way as to reduce the volume of such complaints. An atmosphere of cooperation and understanding among all parties;
- Solving problems in the right ways and methods away from those that might be more harmful than good.
- Raising the value of the university among other universities and making it competitive at both internal and external levels.

Conclusion and Implications

The COVID-19 pandemic imposed severe restrictions and challenges on education, and the closure of universities required urgent action to address the problem. One of the consequences of this pandemic is that the lockdown must be forced to curb the spread of this deadly epidemic and that educators should have recourse to distance learning. They chose open education platforms, primarily the e-labs platform.

Based on observations of this research, the browser at the Faculty of Sciences Semlalia, Cadi Ayyad University notes that efforts have been made in the field of distance learning in the COVID-19 pandemic. The platform needs more support to alleviate its difficulties for development and improvement. Hence, the investment of the smart e-labs platform at the Faculty of Sciences Semlalia, Cadi Ayyad University in distance learning still requires several modifications. Given the speed with which the e-labs platform is employed in this sensitive situation and their low composition in exploiting it, it is advised to start thinking about a post-COVID-19 strategy to further develop the platform. To achieve the desired effect of the e-labs platform or other similar smart digital platform, stakeholders or interested parties may consult the following notes:

- The lack of technology requirements and capabilities should be recognised and rapidly eliminated and improved, taking quality into account. The e-labs platform, which has enabled students and professors to continue their communication and to complete remote practical works, will be able to raise the technological capabilities of relevant stakeholders.
- A mechanism should be in place in the short, medium, and long term for the continuous training of professors in how to design real practical works and to raise them on a platform–for presentation to students. Despite the positive impact of the e-labs, efforts must be intensified to train these professors to keep up with each update of the platform.
- A short, medium and long-term mechanism for the continuous training of students should be in place to facilitate both remote and onsite usage of the e-labs (remote and presence practical work). Questionnaire responses also imply that the formation and training of students are necessary.
- Educational, digital, and applicable programs and content that are genuinely relevant to students' needs and facilitate the roles of professors are needed. The programs will help students and professors become more connected and motivated to use platform tools.

- Providing digital curricula capable of improving and enriching the educational level of students is also a necessity, along with developing their intellectual abilities, training them in research skills, and offering access to information. Students' development can also be tracked from the reports of the professor and students stored in the e-labs platform analysed by their supervisors.
- It is proposed to establish a commission on digital education at the institutional level with all educational institutions participating. The commission shall be responsible for the formation and training of professors and students in online higher education through a platform designed specifically for this purpose.

6.9 Case 8: Mongolia: Development of the Open Education Center Towards Accelerated Digital Transformation in Mongolian Higher Education Sector[9]

Executive Summary

Mongolia is a landlocked country with a vast territory (18th in the world) and a sparse population (about two people per square kilometer). The main challenge for the Mongolian higher education system is providing services in remote and rural areas. Within the context of ensuring inclusive and equitable quality education, e-learning has established itself as a promising and cost-effective education delivery method for Mongolia. Although Mongolia has made significant commitments to the design and deployment of ICT throughout the education sector, researchers have concluded that e-learning in higher education in Mongolia is in its early stages of development. Therefore, there is a need for trailblazing institutions that can act as a national benchmark for accelerating digital transformation in the higher education sector in line with global trends. The purpose of the current case study is to share our experiences of developing the Open Education Center established in 2019 that can act as a "leading light" in the digital transformation of Mongolian higher education. The study will provide information related to institutional policy and planning; provide a summary of nationwide activities within the context of online learning and blended learning, massive open online course development, professional development training organized before and after Covid-19 outbreak; demonstrate OEC's infrastructure capacity for online and blended learning; OEC international outreach and networking while also sharing the future development perspective and challenges. The lessons and knowledge learned from the Open Education Center development process, which is unique due to pandemic overlap, summarized in the current study is valuable information for higher education professionals and policymakers, especially in developing countries.

---

[9] Authored by Badarch Dendev, Director of Higher Education Research Development laboratory of OEC at MUST, badarch88@yahoo.com; Ganbat Danaa, Director of OEC at MUST, ganbatda@must.edu.mn; Tserenchimed Purevsuren, Senior specialist and researcher of Higher Education Research Development laboratory of OEC at MUST, tserenchimed.p@must.edu.mn.

Introduction and Context

To ensure inclusive, equitable, and quality education in Mongolia with its vast territory and sparse population, online learning is considered a promising and cost-effective education delivery method. Although the majority of Mongolian universities are located in the Ulaanbaatar city (the capital), a survey study revealed that Mongolian students in the higher education (HE) sector struggle most with their working and learning schedule and the distance between school and university, and the internet connectivity (Steinbeck et al. 2019). This indicated that appropriate development of e-learning and digital education by considering these constraints could be the solution.

Mongolia has a well-developed infrastructure for e-learning, which was developed based on the distance education national program 2002–2010 (Government of Mongolia 2002) and E-Mongolia National Program 2005–2012 (Government of Mongolia 2005). However, researchers concluded that e-learning in HE in Mongolia is in its early stages of development (Tuul et al. 2016). A recent policy review report outlined two main issues related to ICT infrastructure that further need to consider for ensuring the access to ICT devices and the sustainability of ICT Infrastructure (UNESCO 2021). For Mongolian higher education, the students are aware of the advantage of online learning and the chances provided by the digital transformation (Steinbeck et al. 2019). Students are confident about their ICT skills (Steinbeck et al. 2019). However, the main problems for online learning were the lack of teachers' ICT competency and limited opportunity for teachers to involve in advanced training (UNESCO 2021).

Digital contents or e-contents play a crucial role in developing online learning. "Vision-2050" long-term development policy of Mongolia ("Vision-2050" Long-term Development Policy of Mongolia n.d) and "Digital Nation" government initiative (Soyolmaa 2021) emphasized the importance of developing digital educational content to transfer all levels of education into e-learning program fully. At the policy level, it was also essential to develop and prepare e-learning content to overcome the economic and social difficulties caused by COVID-19 (Government Palace, Ulaanbaatar 2020). The global trend for developing e-content more accessible was the Open Educational Resource (OER) movement (Richter and McPherson 2012). For Mongolia, the OER concept was introduced in 2010 with a series of seminars and workshops on OER implementation in the K-12 sector. However, no such initiatives have been launched for the HE system, and OER awareness remains modest amongst HE educators and administrators (Hodgkinson-Williams and Arinto 2017). Recent policy change promoting the creation of digital content will benefit the education sector. However, there is a need for policy to establish quality assurance for digital content and resources (UNESCO 2021).

The use of ICT has been highlighted as an opportunity to innovate and increase the quality of the educational systems. It also promotes open education that can be defined as a learning experience that provides a great degree of flexibility in the choice of topic, place, speed, and method to the learner. The development and use of OERs and MOOCs proved useful in many ways, such as removing entry barriers to education, increasing access to knowledge, promoting personalized and self-directed learning, and supporting lifelong learning. Therefore, the promotion of open education is crucial to enhancing the quality of Mongolian HE, and it is an important strategy to achieve SDG4 (Beijing Declaration on MOOC Development 2020). The concept of MOOC is relatively new in the Mongolian HE system. Recently, there were several attempts to develop a limited number of MOOC courses at the Mongolian University of Science and Technology, National University of Mongolia and Erdenet Institute of Technology (Erdenet Institute of Technology n.d; Mongolian Open Online Course n.d). However, the majority of developed courses, which are basically video-lectures, are not open access MOOCs for all stakeholders and are only available for respective university students. Classical open MOOC developed in Mongolian HE is very limited and counted as less than ten (Erdenet Institute of Technology, n.d; МУИС-ийн цахим хичээл n.d). Therefore, there are lots of steps we need to consider to accelerate MOOC development in Mongolia.

While the Mongolian HE sector is struggling to implement traditional e-learning or ICT-enabled learning along with the above-mentioned problems, the global trends in online learning are rapidly changing due to the advancement of Artificial intelligence (AI), Machine learning (ML), Big Data, Augmented reality (AR) and virtual reality (VR) technologies in education (Keser and Semerci 2019). Moreover, the overall vision of HE is shifted towards a more open, inclusive, equitable and sustainable manner. Therefore, there is a need for trailblazing institutions that can act as a national benchmark for accelerating digital transformation in the higher education sector in line with global trends.

Design and Implementation of OEC

Mongolian University of Science and Technology (MUST), one of the leading universities in online learning in Mongolia, established the Open Education Center (OEC) in 2019 that can act as a "leading light" in the digital transformation of Mongolian higher education. OEC is a premier research and academic institute devoted to the academic study of education policy, educational technology, learning, open education through dialogue and exchange ideas, research and innovation, and engagement with national and international scholars, opinion makers, teachers, instructional designers and practitioners (Badarch 2019). Guided by the principles of academic excellence, forward-looking vision, the OEC mission covers five main goals:

To provide a forum of scholars and researchers on education strategy and policy;
To encourage an in-depth exchange of ideas on online education and digital transformation;
To foster thoughtful dialogue among scholars, students and practitioners on innovative ideas on learning and teaching;
To develop and promote OER, MOOC, open textbook and open education;
To engage in outreach activities with a wide range of local, regional and international partners.

The structure of OEC consisted of several sub-divisions (Fig. 6.16). The education development department, which includes a teaching and learning laboratory, was established to develop and strengthen existing educational programs and curriculums; to provide methodological and pedagogical guidelines for face-to-face, online and blended learning; and to conduct formal and non-formal professional development training for HE teachers. The innovation and education technology laboratory was organized to support MOOC, OER, and Open Textbook development. Its duty is to create digital educational content using advanced technologies such as 3D video, computer graphics, AR and VR. It was purposed the provided digital contents must be a benchmark for all Mongolian HE institutions. The system dynamics laboratory was established to conduct systematic research and model comprehensive systems, such as the Mongolian educational system, based on a system thinking approach. Such a dynamic model can be used as a tool for decision-makers, including the Ministry of Education and Science (MoES). Higher education research and development laboratory is also established under the umbrella of OEC. The primary function of the laboratory is to advance in research for the field of HE policy, governance, and management. All these laboratories of OEC had one vision that is to accelerate and promote teaching to learning paradigm shift, and the HE digital transformation in Mongolia. Therefore, all activities, including training, seminars, workshops, MOOCs, OERs, best practices of professional development programs, were open for all levels of stakeholders in the Mongolian HE sector. The OEC works closely and collaboratively with external institutions such as MoES, Institution of Teacher Professional Development (ITPD) of Mongolia, Mongolian Institute for Educational Research (MIER), Asian Development Bank (ADB), UNESCO, Mongolian national chamber of commerce and industry, and other higher educational institutions. Internally, OEC is a methodological center of MUST for online and blended learning, professional development, curriculum development, and HE leadership.

In the beginning, OEC was working on producing a series of policy briefs and its workshops (Fig. 6.17) covering important topics that can strengthen the foundation to enhance quality and increase the accessibility of Mongolian HE. The topics were research university, lifelong learning, corruption in education, outcome-based education, system thinking, HE & innovation, quality of HE, national qualification framework, Academic freedom, HE governance, and university & SDG etc.... It was also assumed such work could introduce OEC to the Mongolian HE sector. Furthermore, five distinct training, namely Open education, Open educational resource, Instructional design, Heutagogy, and MOOC, were conducted to increase awareness of the open education concept towards the Mongolian HE sector (Fig. 6.17). The OEC is the first institution in Mongolia that raises the concept of "Education 4.0".

Although OEC had few years of experience, the OEC could demonstrate several benchmark MOOCs (Fig. 6.17) for all stakeholders in the HE sector [14] thanks to the funding from ADB and MoES. For instance, "Higher Education Governance and Management" MOOC together with motivational webinar training could have delivered state-of-art knowledge to the decision-makers at MoES, management-level people at every HE institution in Mongolia.

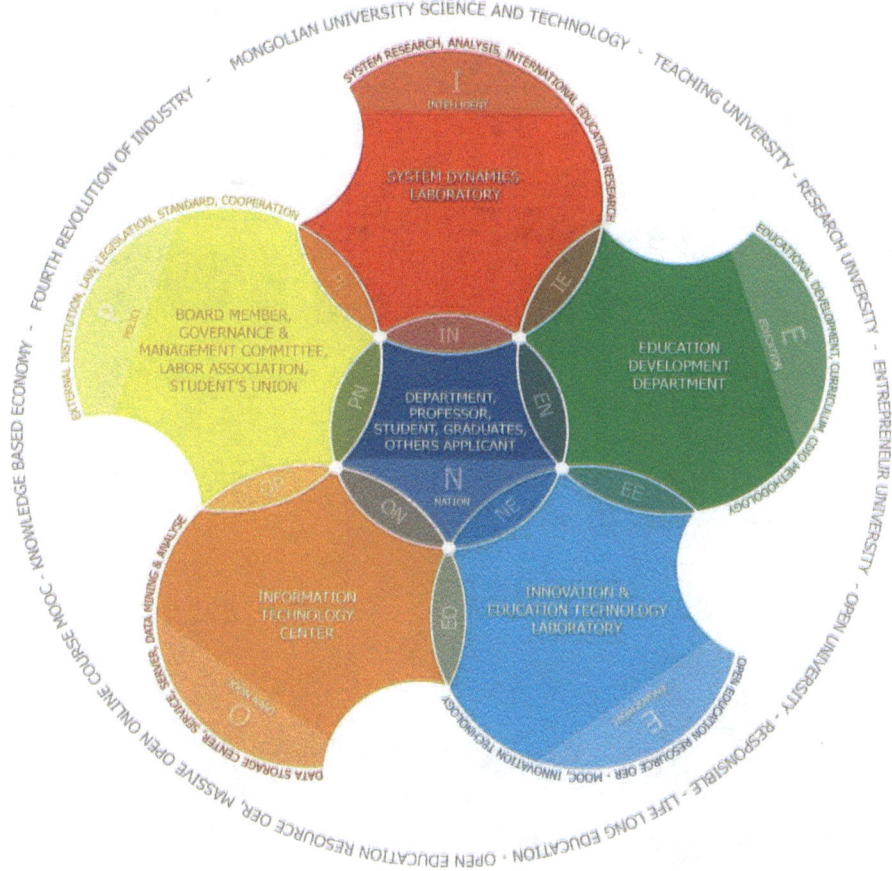

Fig. 6.16 Structure of the open education center at Mongolian University of Science and Technology

The establishing process of OEC is unique because the process was overlapped with the COVID-19 pandemic. COVID-19 was either a challenge or an opportunity for OEC. To overcome the pandemic successfully and to accelerate the rapid shift from face-to-face to online learning brought by the pandemic, OEC challenged itself to strengthen existing professional development by rapidly organizing and conducting online training for HE teachers. Specifically, in collaboration with ITPD at Mongolia, OEC had developed an "Online Professional Development Program" during the COVID-19 pandemic and implemented nationwide training for university teachers (Ganbat and Purevsuren 2021). The program was designed as a 2-week online webinar series accompanied by a professional development MOOC (Fig. 6.18).

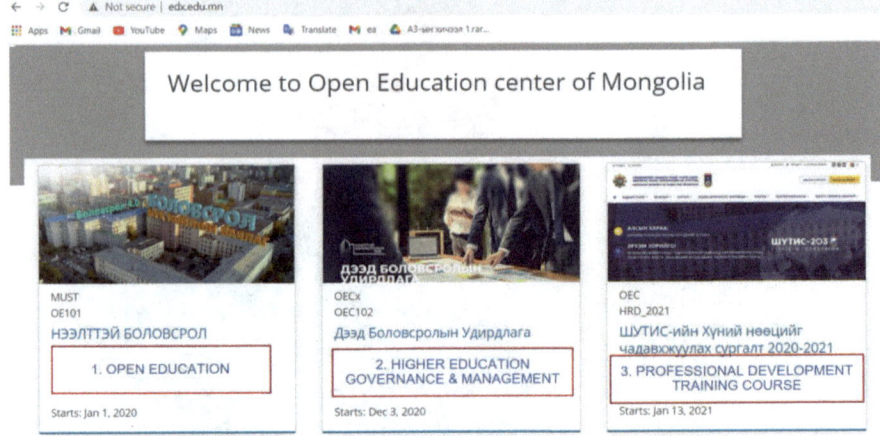

Fig. 6.17 MOOC development at OEC

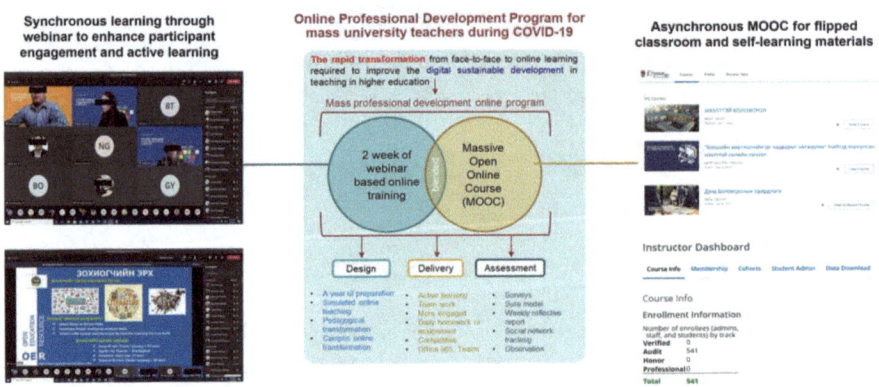

Fig. 6.18 Design and implementation of the online professional development program

Impact on Equity, Quality and Efficiency

OEC has raised the awareness of Open Education and the need to enhance higher education quality in Mongolia. First of all, OEC organized five main training ranging from OER to Instructional design. About 300 representatives from MoES, ITPD, MIER, and more than 15 universities located in Ulaanbaatar participated in all five series of training in a face-to-face format. The open education training series were then further organized in an online format for staff members from several local universities that have teacher education programs, including the distance learning center at Mongolian National University of Education, one of the biggest universities for teacher preparation in Mongolia. All trained individuals would organize

Fig. 6.19 Training materials and magazines to increase awareness of OEC as well as Open Education concept to Mongolian higher education

cascading training at their institution and thus create a sustainable teaching-learning cycle within each higher education institution. To increase the awareness of Open Education, a MOOC was developed based on the previous face-to-face and online training materials and received positive feedback (Fig. 6.19).

The implementation of such an online professional development program played a crucial role in adapting to the pandemic effectively and accelerating higher education digital transformation in Mongolia through re-educating teachers toward rapid shift. In collaboration with ITPD at Mongolia, the "Online Professional Development Program" implemented by OEC saw a nationwide influence in the higher education sector. At the end of 2021, more than 1500 higher education teachers have been directly trained by the program, taking up 20% population of HE educators in Mongolia, according to MoES statistics. Since its establishment in 2019, OEC has also developed and implemented a full online certified training program for pre-service teachers. A total number of 437 pre-service teachers had been trained by this certified program, which contributes to the enhancement of online and blended learning methodology and pedagogy in Mongolia.

At the policy level, OEC has also been a major player in the ground of national policymaking for higher education. OEC pushed forward the generation of the objective 2.1 of "Vision 2050", the long-term development policy of Mongolia, which states, "Provide equal opportunity to receive a quality education for all, establish education as a basis for personal development, family security, and the country's development and strengthen the life-long education system." In particular, OEC contributed to the interpretation of this object: "to develop an open education system and create an integrated online learning platform to be accessible to everyone for lifelong education in the field of their choice regardless of time and space" ("Vision-2050" Long-term Development Policy of Mongolia n.d). OEC also provided policy guidelines in developing the "Education sector mid-term development plan 2021–2030" of Mongolia (Ministry of Education and Science 2020). The concept of Open Education is now integrated into almost every sector of education to increase accessibility, quality, and equity in the future education system of Mongolia. There are also upcoming activities nationwide that are strongly linked to OEC's mission and perspectives, namely:

Upgrade and establish university-based open education centers in urban and rural areas.

Deliver capacity building training to education and industry leaders, experts, teachers, entrepreneurs and trainers focusing on the development of open, online and distance learning resources such as Massive, Online Open Courses (MOOC).

Establish recognition, validation and accreditation of prior learning (RPL) system at the open education centers.

Establish a credit transfer system among high schools, universities and technical colleges.

Such a planned program is purposed to scale OEC all over Mongolia, especially in the HE sector.

Another important work that has been initiated and implemented by OEC is the Quality assurance framework (QAF) for HE (Дээд боловсролын чанарын баталгаажуулалтын хөтөлбөрт Сингапуртай хамтран ажиллаж байна, 2021), laying critical foundations for the sustainable development of higher education in Mongolia. In 2020, MUST-OEC brought up the QAF project funded by the TEMASEK foundation that purposed to create a QAF in the Mongolian HE system based on Singapore Polytechnic's (SP) experience. Initially, a QAF introductory module was introduced to 130 selected HE teachers and quality managers from six top-ranking public universities. After strict review and selections, a group of master teachers received training from SP experts to outline the QAF and generated a guide-book. These teachers would also be responsible for organizing domestic cascading training to further develop QAF in Mongolia. Such a project has been highly appreciated and supported by MoES, and a unit of QA was established at MoES in 2021, with the idea of "QAF" to be included in the upcoming education law.

Conclusion and Implications

The current case study shares valuable experiences of the Open Education Center (OEC) at the Mongolian University of Science and Technology (MUST). The story of OEC can act as a "leading light" in the digital transformation of Mongolian higher education in line with international trends. Although OEC was only established in 2019, it has successfully provided key insights for policymakers and contributed to the future education of Mongolia based on the concept of Open Education. The center has also delivered a number of professional development training programs for HE teachers that leverages digital transformation, teaching to learning paradigm shift and help to alleviate the impact caused by COVID-19. A notable achievement could be that OEC increased nationwide awareness of the OER initiative and the idea of Open Education for the first time in the Mongolian HE system. MOOCs developed by OEC are now a benchmark for other HE institutions and support lifelong learning.

The establishment of OEC was challenging due to limited funding resources, lack of professional human resources and infrastructure, insufficient existing policy on online and blended learning, incomplete stakeholder's understanding of OER and MOOC, and the COVID-19 pandemic, among others. However, we could say that COVID-19 may act as an accelerator for OEC development by reinforcing HE stakeholders to fully utilize OEC and the Open Education concept with ambition and forward-looking vision. There are lots of things that we need to strengthen in the future, and establishing the foundation of QAF in the Mongolian HE system is one of them. Although OEC has spared some effort developing sample OER based on advanced technology such as AR, VR, and 360-degree video, the methodology and guidelines are not yet disseminated to the HE institutions in Mongolia. Furthermore, OEC strategically planned to adopt more advanced technology, including Big Data, AI, ML, and Block-Chain, though limited financial and human resources are being main obstacles.

At the early stage of development, OEC puts more attention on local engagement. Recently, the Center focused on international outreach and networking. The center could extend international collaboration with MIT J-WEL (Abdul Latif Jameel World Education Lab), International Centre for Higher Education Innovation under the auspices of UNESCO (UNESCO-ICHEI), Tsinghua University, Singapore polytechnic to enhance online and blended learning, OER and MOOC development, and professional development in HE. As a result, MUST-OEC is now one of the founding members of the International Institute of online Education (IIOE) and Global MOOC alliance. Our future vision is that the Center will be a hub for international networks in online and blended teaching and learning.

6.10   Case 9: Nepal: Enhancing Capacity of the Faculty Members for Online Teaching During the Pandemic in Tribhuvan University[10]

Executive Summary

As the government declared the nationwide lockdown in March 2020, things became a stand-still, and all the university classes had to be suspended. Tribhuvan University (TU) preponed its summer vacation to prevent the learning loss during the lockdown, hoping the pandemic would end in a short period so that classes could resume. As the

---

[10] Authored by Dr. Ganga Ram Gautam, Associate Professor of English Education and Director of Open and Distance Education center (ODEC), Tribhuvan University, Nepal.

situation worsened, TU followed the global practice and moved towards online education. However, many challenges needed to be addressed to ensure a smooth transition.
Technology infrastructure was very limited, and faculty members had hardly used
any technology in their teaching. Despite such a difficult situation, TU succeeded
in managing online classes during the pandemic thanks to the committed leadership
and faculty members' positive support. This success built a strong foundation for
blended learning beyond the pandemic. This case study presents the highlights on
how TU, as one of the largest universities in the world, was able to prepare faculty
members for online teaching and learning during the pandemic. The case study also
reports the key challenges and issues that emerged during the faculty development
process. Strategies adopted to address these challenges and issues are discussed. By
drawing upon key lessons learned from this experience, how they can be used as a
foundation for blended learning in TU beyond the pandemic are illustrated.

Introduction and Context

Tribhuvan University (TU) is the oldest and largest university of Nepal that serves
nearly 400,000 students annually through its 300 plus programs in 1100 campuses
across the country. Due to the mega-structure of the university, TU faced many
challenges in responding to COVID-19. One of the biggest challenges is how to
develop the capacity of about 8,000 teachers with a wide range of digital literacy so
that they can facilitate continued education online. There were also other system-
level obstacles such as a lack of policy documents for the online learning activities,
limited ICT infrastructure, technological anxiety among the faculty members, poor
internet connectivity, and high costs for the mobile data. Establishing communication
with teachers and students and connecting them to the online education network
was also challenging. This is because TU had not issued official email IDs for its
teachers, students and staff before the pandemic, making communication difficult to
stay connected during the lockdown.

In responding to these challenges, TU leadership came with their three-phase plan
and immediately disseminated it to the TU stakeholders; (a) immediate switch into
the online teaching to respond to COVID-19; (b) creating a groundwork for blended
learning to ensure quality learning in the online classes; and (c) online classes beyond
COVID-19 to provide access to those who cannot attend the face-to-face mode of
education (Gautam 2021). To implement this three-phase plan, TU immediately
deployed Microsoft Office 365 as the online class portal (Fig. 6.20), provided email
IDs for all the students, teachers and staff, and provided orientation to the faculty
members to run online classes using Microsoft Teams. TU simultaneously worked
for an extended plan to develop the ICT capacity of teachers and so that they could
start a blended mode of education beyond the pandemic.

TU has about 8000 teachers in its 124 constituent units. Teachers' digital literacy
varies, and most of them had not used technology for pedagogical purposes. Preparing
them for online teaching was significantly challenging for TU. Training teachers on
how to use technology was not easy. This situation is most severe among senior
professors–many of them had not even used emails regularly. We had to work on a
cautious approach to train them to use technology while respecting their academic

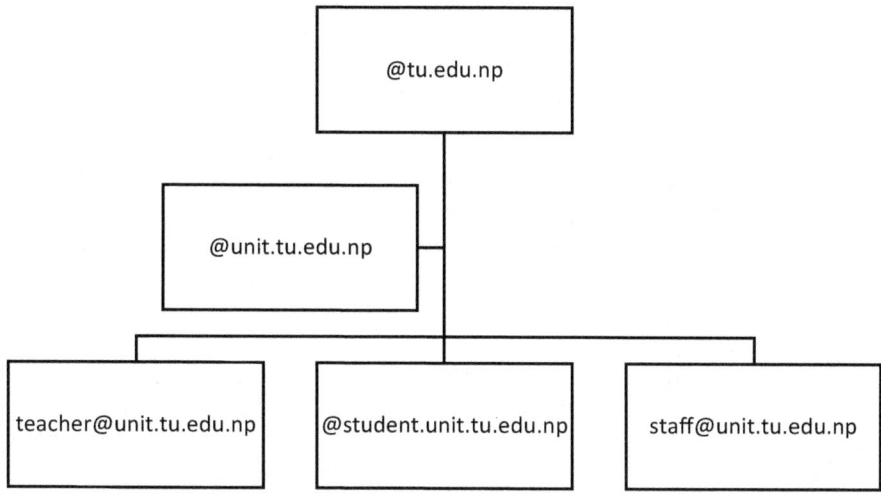

Fig. 6.20 Structure of microsoft office 365

profile and professional hierarchy in our cultural context. There was a great deal of reluctance to use technology, and there was a feeling among many of them that online teaching and learning was something they could not handle. To address such a diverse ICT competence of teachers, we decided to adopt a humble approach. We asked them to share their existing knowledge and skills of ICT in the first few sessions to create an accommodating environment and alleviate their disinclination. Then we gradually integrated necessary training in subsequent sessions. To facilitate this, TU trained a group of trainers by organizing a three-day training of trainers (ToT) program. This ToT group was instrumental in taking the faculty development program forward. There were two specific outcomes in mind when this ToT program was designed: (a) training the teachers of TU for virtual classes to respond to COVID-19, and (b) sensitizing the teachers to go for a blended mode of educational delivery in certain subjects as TU's regular program beyond the pandemic. The results have been positive; the initiative has created a good foundation for TU to move towards blended and online learning and teaching (OBLT) as the next level.

Design and Implementation

Open and Distance Education Center (ODEC) of TU took the lead in implementing the Faculty Development Program and adopted the ToT model to train teachers of its units. This model brought momentum among the faculty members to organize virtual classes during the pandemic. The faculty development training of TU had several elements that have positively reinforced the TU's move towards online classes in the short term and created a foundation for OBLT mode in the long term.

Firstly, TU efficiently mobilized and leveraged its human resources for faculty development on a large scale through the ToT program. A loose and informal network of a few hundred self-motivated teachers at TU collaborated with some alumni members who have been taught abroad to offer professional development activities at TU since 2016. They had been organizing webinars on various aspects of pedagogical reforms that include formative evaluation, student-centered pedagogy, use of ICT in teaching, academic writing for publication and research methods. Due to the previous exposure to the webinars series, they were digitally literate, and could swiftly understand the dynamics of online teaching and learning. TU leadership was well-aware of this voluntary initiative, and members of the network were also very keen to share their experience with the other teachers. TU invited the members of this network to join the ToT and included some faculty members from the ICT-related departments (Computer Science, Computer Engineering, ICT Education and Information Science) as well.

To attract competent candidates in the ToT program, a call for application was sent to the Deans' office and the Heads of the units; the leaders were requested to circulate the call to their faculty members and encourage the potential candidates to apply. The response was encouraging. Out of nearly 200 applications, we selected 120 participants based on several factors, namely the participants' interest in helping TU during the COVID-19 crisis, commitment to do a round of teacher training after the ToT, ICT literacy and their willingness to provide ongoing virtual support to the teachers as indicated in their application. The participants included teachers from all over Nepal, and about 20% were female. The contents of this training were the basics of Microsoft Office 365 with a focused discussion on the use of Microsoft Teams for virtual classes. At the end of the training, the cascading plan was developed through group discussion, and 30 groups were from with four members each.

With this group, a three-day ToT program was organized. Participants were taught to teach teachers how to make an immediate switch to online education so that students could attend their classes during the pandemic. The first day was spent on the basics of Office 365, its applications and how to log in to the portal. The second day covered topics that included creating channels, meeting links, uploading files, organizing groups, enrolling students, to name a few. Pedagogical features of the Teams were covered on the third day.

The second element that reinforces TU's adaptation to online classes turns out to be the official email ID, which was given to TU faculties for the first time to associate their job with TU; the TU email became a motivational tool for teachers to switch into the ToT and online classes. TU did not have a centralized system to provide email IDs to its teachers, students and staff. Some of the units did it in their own way, but most of the teachers, students, and staff used their personal emails run by commercial companies for e-communication. The creation of their official email IDs and the decision of TU for its mandatory use in their online classes contributed to strengthening their professional identity and attachment to their job, and this motivated teachers to continue online classes during the pandemic.

The third element worth mentioning is the accountability mechanism, as the unit chiefs were made responsible for training teachers of all teaching units of TU from different parts of Nepal. The Rector, head of the academic affairs of TU, organized a series of online meetings with the Chiefs of each teaching unit and shared the TU's plan to run the online classes. From these meetings, TU obtained the data of all the classes that were on hold, the availability of the teachers and their digital literacy situation. Once the data was obtained, a series of teacher training events were organized. Teachers who participated in the ToT were paired up, and each pair was assigned designated units to train their teachers for online classes. This strategy was helpful to train all teachers of TU as we were able to train nearly 6,000 teachers within three weeks, and disrupted classes that went online on the fourth week. In the TU system, such a quick move from face-to-face class to online class was possible due to the ToT model.

Fourthly, to motivate each unit to begin online classes, TU allocated an additional budget for each unit to support them for the online teaching and learning activities through the negotiation with the University Grants Commission (UGC) and the World Bank (Gautam 2021). The budget was pulled from the ongoing Higher Education Reform Project (HERP) funded by the World Bank. This additional budget was used to manage basic ICT infrastructure and create online resources at the unit level. Setting up the ICT systems and their use for online classes was also a part of the ToT program.

Fifthly, there was and still is a robust monitoring and follow-up mechanism on the progress of the online classes during the pandemic. Each week, every Friday evening, there is a virtual meeting of all the Deans, Directors and Heads of Divisions chaired by the Rector of TU in the presence of the Registrar and the Vice-Chancellor. All the Deans report the progress of their academic activities and share the difficulties faced by the units. Decisions are then made immediately to address the issues and any bottlenecks that affect the operations of the academic programs. There is also a technical team to address any technical issues in the program. If any capacity building events are required, ODEC is there to address them.

Finally, since the respective Dean's office manages all the academic programs in TU, Deans were made responsible throughout the process. Deans have been organizing virtual meetings with the unit chiefs and teachers to get regular updates on the academic activities. They then compile the information and report it in the weekly meeting. So, engaging the leadership meaningfully to monitor the progress of the faculty members and providing the required level of support for their professional development contribute to the enhanced results.

Impact on Equity, Quality and Efficiency

The ToT model of TU has already demonstrated some visible impacts. Firstly, a core group of trainers representing a diverse population has been identified, trained and developed. While selecting the participants for the ToT, efforts were made to make the group as inclusive as possible considering the gender, geographical location, teaching experience, ethnicity and age groups. Now, they are in the pool of resources for continuous professional development training of teachers at TU. Recently, TU recruited about 300 Lecturers, and ODEC organized 48-h job induction training for them. Six of the ToT participants were invited to facilitate some of the sessions in this training, and others have also shown their willingness to do similar training in the future.

Secondly, the ToT program successfully empowered many TU teachers with quality content and trainers. According to an internal survey, a ToT participant teaching in a campus outside the Kathmandu valley said she did not have her email address before the COVID-19. When TU provided her email ID and invited her to the teacher training program, she was inspired by a female facilitator. She conducted a teacher training event at the local level on her own initiative. Similarly, a ToT participant in a campus in Kathmandu is now coordinating a blended mode master's program and heavily engaged in developing the capacity of the teachers in his campus for online learning.

Thirdly, the ToT project and subsequent teacher training events integrated ICT into pedagogical activities and contributed to TU's sustainable development in online and blended teaching and learning. In a series of discussions with stakeholders, including trainers, teachers and students, a majority indicated that online classes could connect students and teachers in teaching and learning. This experience has been helpful to create an appetite for technology-based teaching and learning. Teachers also said that the COVID-19 crisis made them realize their agency as the instructor because they had to make most pedagogical decisions by themselves and navigate through the issues during the entire teaching, learning, and assessment process. One of the participants of ToT said that she learned the art of online pedagogy, and she has been trying to communicate this to her colleagues through teacher training events at the local level.

However, the most crucial element of teaching and learning, i.e., pedagogy, was still missing in the online classes. According to observations, current classes were mostly one-way traffic and lecture-based. There was not much interaction and discussion in the online classes. Students' engagement in learning and student-to-student sharing was minimum. Also, we have noticed that many of our teachers need to be oriented in using digital tools to create a learning environment in the online classes. Based on the feedback of the live class experience during the pandemic, TU has now adopted a two-pronged strategy to address the issue of digital pedagogical competence among the teachers. Led by the strategy, TU is working on ensuring the minimum ICT infrastructure in each unit to support the online classes and simultaneously developing the capacity of the teachers for blended and online learning with the help of the ToT participants using the same ToT model.

TU has already conducted a ToT on the Learning Management System (LMS), i.e. MOODLE training, that involved 69 participants of the previous ToT program. Since this was a more advanced program on the LMS, the participants who had demonstrated proficient ICT competence in the earlier training were included in this ToT. For LMS training TU has designed a modular teacher training package (6 Modules) to use LMS in TU's blended and online classes and trained 120 trainers (ToT) to cascade the training to the other teachers. The MOODLE training was a six-day training focused on digital pedagogy and e-assessment. Each module of the training/workshop was of three hours. Here is the list of the themes covered in those six modules of the MOODLE training.

Module 1: Introduction to Moodle
Module 2: Management of Course

Module 3: Management of Learning Resources
Module 4: Management of Learning Activities
Module 5: Monitoring, Feedback and Encouragement
Module 6: Learning Analytics.

To give hands-on experience to the teachers on the MOODLE, TU has deployed an online portal 'tuelearn.edu.np' and configured the MOODLE LMS on it. Five units of TU have started a blended mode of education in 15 different programs using this portal since the current semester. Respective subject teachers of those units have been trained on the MOODLE, and classes have started. Thus, the COVID-19 experience has also created a foundation for blended learning in TU. The ToT model has been adopted as the viable strategy to operationalize the program on the ground.

Conclusion and Implications

The proactive and swift initiation of the leadership, the collective efforts of the individuals in the different constituents of TU, and the teachers' motivation to switch to online learning made it possible to respond to the COVID-19 pandemic even in challenging circumstances. The learning loss of the pandemic has been estimated between 3 to 5 months only. During the first national lockdown in March 2020, some classes were resumed online in about three weeks first by using free online tools such as zoom, google meet, messenger. Once the Microsoft Office Suite was deployed, Microsoft Teams was used. All master-level classes were gradually resumed to full operation within two months. Teachers during the interaction mentioned that their desire to integrate technology has immensely increased, and they have been exploring ways of developing their ICT skills. Many of them have joined online classes on blended teaching and learning. They have requested the author to organize more capacity building training on ICT use in higher education. Also, social media such as live stream platforms have been used extensively for professional development purposes (Dam 2022) and pedagogical purposes. Fifteen units have organized additional teacher training events for online classes at the local level, and those who attended the ToT were invited to facilitate the sessions.

To offer quality education in the blended/online mode, faculty preparation is the key, given that TU has already decided to go for a dual-mode: face-to-face mode and blended/online mode. The more teachers are engaged in the instructional design, the more students are involved in the learning process. The motivation of the teachers in this context is very crucial. TU's experience of virtual teaching and learning during the pandemic has shown that it is not impossible to develop faculty capacity even on a large scale through the ToT model. But this requires serious planning, and it needs to be executed well right from the beginning. The role that ODEC played in the ToT model indicates that a designated center for faculty development is critical to implementing blended and online teaching and learning. Identifying the available human resources within the organization and making them responsible for the tasks that match their expertise is crucial to motivate them to the organization's goals and have them on board with their meaningful participation. This indicates that universities are not reluctant to change but ready to rapidly adapt during the crisis (Chan et al. 2022). However, a robust monitoring and follow-up mechanism with the involvement of the academic leaders, i.e. the Deans, is also crucial to ensure the successful implementation of the online and blended mode of education. Such a regular follow-up provides information on the status of the ongoing reform and contributes to identifying the areas to be addressed for the smooth implementation of the programs.

Though TU as a large organization has been able to make a quick transition to online learning during the pandemic, it is early to justify the effectiveness of the switch without generating evidence from the ground regarding the students' satisfaction, learning achievement and performance of the students. This indicates the need for continued research in the program to understand the intervention process and integrate the lessons learned. Also, due to the COVID-19 experience, there might be more demand for blended/online education and universities need to be prepared to assure quality in the blended/online education (Borasi et al. 2022). TU leadership has already outlined a research plan to study the effectiveness of the online education program implemented in TU during the COVID—19, and ODEC is taking the lead in that research. This study is expected to document the status and experience of online learning during COVID and identify the areas to be addressed for an effective online and blended mode of higher education in Nepal. Online and blended learning is a new initiative in Nepal, and it has been established as an alternative mode of higher education during the pandemic. Considering the growing demand for blended and online learning, TU needs to move on for OBLT through evidence-based planning.

6.11 Case 10 NIGERIA: Public–Private Partnership in ICT Capacity Building-The ABU Zaria-Huawei Academy Experience[11]

Executive Summary

Ahmadu Bello University, Zaria is Nigeria's largest University with 80,000 postgraduate, undergraduate, diploma and distance learning students, 3,038 academic and research staff (2,451 males and 587 females), and 8,838 support staff (7,065 males and 1,773 females). One of the critical challenges of the University has been the issue of enhancing information and communications technology (ICT) skills amongst staff and students to bridge the digital divide and improve the teaching and learning experiences. The efforts at addressing some of these issues led to the University becoming an African Centre of Excellence in New Pedagogies in Engineering Education (ACENPEE), setting up the Institute of ICT to develop an online and blended teaching and learning (OBTL) policy and enhance ICT capacity building among staff and students. However, the most promising effort with outstanding results is the university's public-private partnership to set up the Huawei Academy. The

---

[11] Authored by Muhammed Bashir Mu'azu, Professor and Head of the Department of Computer Engineering, Ahmadu Bello University, Zaria, Nigeria.

Huawei Academy is focused on accelerating skills transfer and creating a robust IT ecosystem via the development of IT industry certified talents which is in tandem with the University's vision. Since 2018, the University has enrolled over 1200 students in the Academy, many of which obtained HCIA, HCIP and HCIE certifications as a result. The talent pool out of the Academy has demonstrated the program's success— this is evidenced by the students' outstanding performances and instructors in the Huawei ICT Skills Competition. It has also justified the need to further hasten the integration of certifications into the University's existing curriculum to enhance the digital competencies and employability of the students.

Introduction

Ahmadu Bello University (ABU), Zaria, founded on October 4, 1962, is a federal government (public) University located in Zaria, Kaduna State, Northern Nigeria and is the largest and most cosmopolitan University in Nigeria. The student enrollment of the University's degree (undergraduate and postgraduate) and sub-degree programs is about 80,000. There are 3,038 academic and research staff and 8,838 support staff. The University has 106 Departments in 17 Faculties, 16 Research Institutes, and three Schools operating on its three campuses (Main campus (Samaru), Kongo campus and the Medical Complex). Three Colleges of Agriculture spread across Nigeria ABU also hosts three African Centres of Excellence (ACE): ACE for Neglected Tropical Diseases and Forensic Biotechnology (ACENTDFB), ACE on New Pedagogies in Engineering Education (ACENPEE), and ACE on Sustainable Procurement, Environment and Social Standards (ACESPESS).

The Directorate of Academic Planning and Monitoring is responsible for developing and monitoring the implementation of academic policies and quality assurance. It has four sub-units: Planning and Statistics, Quality Assurance, Affiliations, and Research and Innovation.

Improving the teaching and learning experiences via digital transformation is one of the critical challenges faced by the University. These challenges are largely related to capacity and finances. Many staff do not have the requisite skills to adopt technology in teaching and learning. Some staff are either unwilling to learn or do not have the right attitude or capacity to learn (especially among older professors) (OECD 2016). Others are hampered by the institution's inability to provide the requisite infrastructure to learn or actualize what they have learnt. This is due to the paucity of funds in public Universities in Nigeria, especially given the inadequate funding from the federal government (Faboyede et al. 2017).

Some of the initiatives adopted by the University include becoming an African Centre of Excellence on New Pedagogies in Engineering Education (ACENPEE), organizing ICT capacity building training and workshops, becoming a pioneer International Institute of Online Education (IIOE) partner higher education institution (HEI) (and as such benefitting from all the training and support for staff, students, and the Institution). However, the most promising effort with outstanding results is the public–private partnership for ICT capacity building between the University and Huawei to set up the Huawei ICT Academy, i.e., the ABU-HIA. Public–Private Partnership (PPP) is recognized as an innovative means for HEIs to effectively address constraints of financing and management of education (especially teaching and learning) (Helmy et al. 2020). The ABU-HIA is focused on accelerating skills transfer. It contributes to creating a robust IT ecosystem by nurturing more certified talents for the IT industry. This is in tandem with the University's vision of ensuring the employability of its students.

Design and Implementation

The philosophy of ABU is predicated upon the "cardinal principles of imparting knowledge and learning to men and women of all races without any distinction on the grounds of race, religious or political beliefs". The knowledge acquired and the learning process must be such that it produces people with the necessary skills and intellect to either be employable or employers themselves and contribute to national development. ICT is believed to be an important vehicle of teaching and learning in the twenty-first century (OECD 2016; van Laar et al. 2020). Therefore, ABU, desirous of such digital transformation, agreed to partner with Huawei Ltd. to establish a Huawei ICT Academy–the ABU-HIA. This is a PPP that is aimed at accelerating skills transfer through (1) the promotion of industry-standard IT certifications and enhancement of industry-level skills, exposure and experiences; and (2) bridging the digital skills gap (the gap between graduates' professional skills and industry standards) by the creation of a robust IT ecosystem and the development of IT industry talents (required for the digital development of the country). The attraction of the HIA program is because it focuses on ensuring students are exposed to the latest ICT technologies via the certifications, offering internship opportunities, and being able to integrate the certifications into the curriculum of existing programs (e.g., Computer Engineering). It is recognized that industry certifications like Huawei certificates can upgrade candidates' knowledge and technical skillsets to have a competitive edge in the employment market (Hitchcock 2007; Huawei TEDD 2022). The ABU-HIA model is structured as shown in Fig. 6.21.

The ABU-HIA agreement was signed between Huawei and the University in August 2018. This was quickly followed by the certification of the trainers under a train-the-trainer (TTT) model by Huawei. In this TTT model, a group of trainees are taught skills and knowledge required to become trainers themselves. They subsequently pass on what they have learnt to other staff and students. This model has proved to be an efficient and cost-effective way of upskilling the workforce (Mormina and Pinder 2018). In ABU's TTT, the training of interested students commenced with the Huawei Certified IT Associate (HCIA) certification in Routing and Switching, which, over time, has evolved to include others, as shown in Fig. 6.21. The HCIA certification was attractive for many students since Huawei was a dominant player in the Nigerian and global IT ecosystem. Upon the maturity of the HCIA certification program, ABU-HIA was granted the right to start training students on the Huawei Certified IT Professional (HCIP) level certifications; the instructors underwent another round of TTT. The ABU-HIA was supported by Huawei with the provision of lab equipment such as the Huawei AR6280 integrated chassis routers, Huawei S5731-H24T4XC switches, cables and other accessories, and access to the

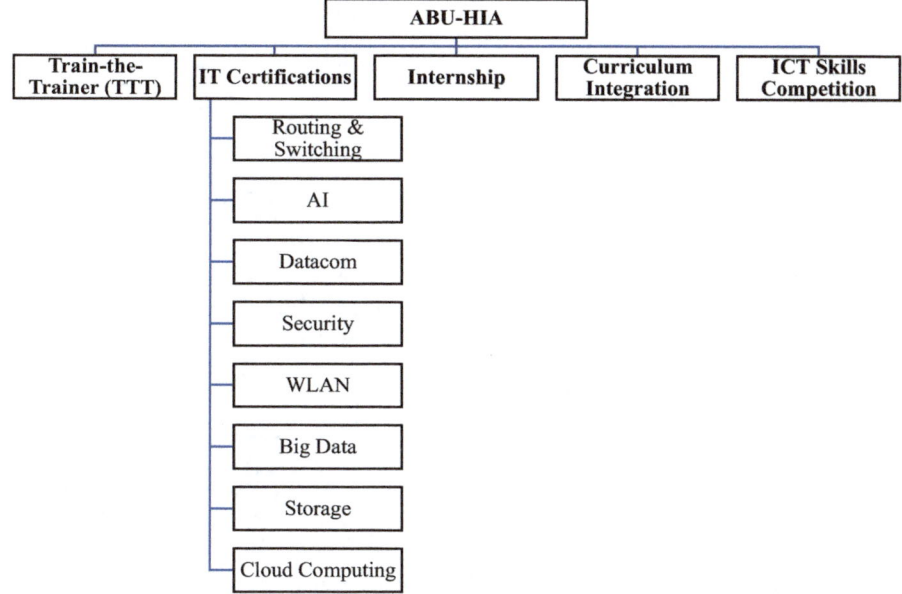

Fig. 6.21 ABU-HIA model

Huawei cloud services, virtual simulators. Vouchers were also provided to enable students to undertake the certification exams (waiver of $200).

Huawei has also made it possible for the students of the ABU-HIA to undertake internships with them or their partners where they attain the requisite industry environment exposure and experience and eventually employment opportunities via the Huawei job fair. The 2019 and 2021 job fairs took place at the University.

Integrating some certification courses into existing programs is another ABU-HIA focusing area. This has gradually been taking place in the Computer Engineering program, as seen in Fig. 6.22. The integration will become even more critical, especially now that the undergraduate program has been modularized into options such as AI, Computer Systems & Networks and Control & Intelligent Systems (starting from the 2021/2022 session). The current level of the integration is where the students are encouraged to take any of the certification courses available at the Academy and time allocated for such so that it does not conflict with their regular lecture times.

The next level of integration is targeted at incorporating the related contents of the certifications into those courses, such as Big Data Analytics, Cloud Computing, AI Fundamentals & AI Systems Development, Network Technology I & II, Network Security & Cryptography and Data & Digital Communication in Computer Engineering (as in Fig. 6.23), and in some instances, Telecommunications Engineering. This process involves discussions and deliberations between the ABU-HIA, related Departments, the Directorate of Academic Planning and the University Senate.

DEPARTMENT OF COMPUTER ENGINEERING, ABU ZARIA
SECOND SEMESTER B.ENG COMPUTER ENGINEERING TIMETABLE
2019/20 SESSION

DATE	LEVEL	8:00 - 8:55 am	9:00 - 9:55 am	10:00 -10:55 am	11:00 - 11:55am	12:00 - 12:55 pm 1 - 2pm	2:00 - 2:55 pm	3:00 - 3:55 pm	4:00 - 4:55 pm	5:00 - 5:55 pm
MONDAY	300	EEEN302 CIRCUIT THEORY AND SYSTEMS II (300L)			COEN308 OPERATING SYSTEMS ADA, RFA (300L)	BREAK			HCIA/HCIP TRAINING	
	500	COEN506 COMPUTER SYSTEM ARCHITECTURE THS, IJU, OA (500L)					COEN502 SOFTWARE ENGINEERING BY, BOS (500L)		HCIA/HCIP TRAINING	
TUESDAY	300	EEEN308 MEASUREMENTS AND INSTRUMENTATION (300L)			COEN306 NETWORK TECHNOLOGY EAA, BY, ADA (400L)		COEN314 LABORATORY PRACTICAL AND PROJECT II			
	500			COEN504 WEB-BASED DESIGN AND APPLICATIONS ZMA, ADA (500L)			COEN508 DIGITAL COMPUTATION HBS, EO (400L Class)			
WEDNESDAY	300	COEN304 OBJECT-ORIENTED PROGRAMMING BOS, SMX (300L)		COEN312 HUMAN COMPUTER INTERFACE ZMA, SMX, AU (400L)			COEN314 LABORATORY PRACTICAL AND PROJECT II		HCIA/HCIP TRAINING	
	500			FINAL YEAR PROJECT			FINAL YEAR PROJECT		HCIA/HCIP TRAINING	
THURSDAY	300	COEN318 COMPUTER ELECTRONICS II THS, IJU, HBS (400L)		COEN316 COMMUNICATION PRINCIPLES MBA, RFA (300L)			COEN314 LABORATORY PRACTICAL AND PROJECT II			
	500			COEN514 ROBOTICS AND AUTOMATION HZ, OA, UA (400L)			COEN516 NETWORK SECURITY AND CRYPTOGRAPHY EAA, MBA (500L)			
FRIDAY	300		COEN310 ACADEMIC WRITING VI, OA, NBN (300L)	COEN502 MICROCONTROLLER & APPLICATIONS ZMA, ZH (300L)			COEN314 LABORATORY PRACTICAL AND PROJECT II		HCIA/HCIP TRAINING	
	500		COEN512 ENGINEERING DESIGN AND SUSTAINABILITY STUDIES MBM, AU (500L)	COEN516 MECHATRONICS HZ, OA, NBN (400L)					HCIA/HCIP TRAINING	

Fig. 6.22 Integration of HCIA/HCIP training for computer engineering students

SECOND SEMESTER 300L COURSES

S/N	Code	Title	CU	Prerequisite	Status
1	COEN322	Laboratory Practical and Project II	2	-	Core
2	COEN332	Microcontrollers & Applications	2	-	Core
3	COEN334	Object-Oriented Programming	2	-	Core
4	COEN336	Network Technology I	2	-	Core
5	COEN338	Data Structure and Algorithms	2	-	Core
6	COEN340	Academic Writing	1	-	Core
7	COEN342	Communication Principles	2	-	Core
8	COEN344	Computer Electronics II	2	-	Core
9	COEN346	Fundamentals of Circuits II	2	-	Core
10	COEN348	Measurement and Instrumentation	2	-	Core
Total			19		

FIRST SEMESTER 400L COURSES (AI OPTION)

S/N	Code	Title	CU	Prerequisite	Status
1	COEN421	Laboratory Practical and Project III	2	COEN321	Core
2	COEN431	Agent Technology & Game Theory	2	-	Core
3	COEN433	Artificial Intelligence Fundamentals	2	-	Core
4	COEN435	Machine Learning Fundamentals	2	-	Core
5	COEN451	Digital Image Processing	2	-	Core
6	COEN453	Software Engineering & Applications I	2	-	Core
7	ENGG403	Law for Engineers	2	-	Cognate
8	MATH443	Numerical Analysis	3	-	Cognate
		Total	16		

FIRST SEMESTER 400L COURSES (COMPUTER SYSTEMS & NETWORK OPTION)

S/N	Code	Title	CU	Prerequisite	Status
1	COEN421	Laboratory Practical and Project III	2	-	Core
2	COEN435	Machine Learning Fundamentals	2	-	Core
3	COEN451	Digital Image Processing	2	-	Core
5	COEN453	Software Engineering & Applications I	2	-	Core
6	COEN455	Digital Communication	2	-	Core
7	COEN457	Network Technology II	2	COEN336	Core
8	ENGG403	Law for Engineers	3	-	Cognate
9	MATH443	Numerical Analysis	3	-	Cognate
		Total	16		

FIRST SEMESTER 500L COURSES (AI OPTION)

S/N	Code	Title	CU	Prerequisite	Status
1	COEN541	Natural Language Processing	2	-	Core
2	COEN543	Deep Learning Fundamentals	2	COEN435	Core
3	COEN545	Artificial Intelligence Applications	2	COEN433	Core
4	COEN551	Cloud Computing	2	-	Core
5	COEN553	Emerging Technologies	2	-	Core
6	ENGG597	Final Year Project	3	-	Core
		Total	13		

SECOND SEMESTER 500L COURSES (AI OPTION)

S/N	Code	Title	CU	Prerequisite	Status
1	COEN542	Big Data Analytics	2	COEN338	Core
2	COEN544	Cyberpreneurship and Cyberlaw	2	-	Core
3	COEN552	Computer Vision	2	-	Core
4	COEN554	Web Programming	2	-	Core
5	COEN562	Engineering Optimization	2	-	Core
6	ENGG598	Final Year Project	3	-	Core
Total			13		

SECOND SEMESTER 500L COURSES (COMPUTER SYSTEMS & NETWORKS OPTION)

S/N	Code	Title	CU	Prerequisite	Status
1	COEN544	Cyberpreneurship and Cyberlaw	2	-	Core
2	COEN552	Computer Vision	2	-	Core
3	COEN554	Web Programming	2	-	Core
4	COEN556	Network Security and Cryptography	2	-	Core
5	COEN558	Digital Systems Design	2	-	Core
6	ENGG598	Final Year Project	3	-	Core
		Total	13		

Fig. 6.23 Sample course outline for computer engineering for integration

The ICT Skills Competition, one of Huawei's ways of ensuring the development of competitive IT industry talents, is another key success of the ABU-HIA. The ICT Skills competition has three stages: National, Regional and Global, normally open for all in the Network and Cloud tracks. This implies that the students need a broad spectrum of certifications to compete in any tracks. The competition enables them to benchmark their capabilities and abilities with their peers on the latest IT technologies worldwide.

Selecting the students to represent the University starts with organizing a boot camp for the most promising students (usually about 20) from the ABU-HIA and preparing them for the National finals. Based on the outcome of the National finals, the teams (typically, teams of three representing an HIA) to represent Nigeria at the Regional finals are selected. Subsequently, those to represent the region at the Global finals in both tracks are selected. During the boot camps (organized by both the ABU-HIA and Huawei for the different stages of preparation), the University ensures that the students' daily academic work is not affected (as time lost is made up). The students are mentored during these processes by their instructors.

Impact on Equity, Quality and Efficiency

The PPP between ABU Zaria and Huawei that resulted in the ABU-HIA has been the most productive and result-oriented intervention in the effort at the digital transformation and capacity building. Before this partnership, IT capacity building and talent development have been seriously hampered by inadequate funding and investments, a lack of facilities, infrastructure, and clear path(s) into the IT industry for students. These challenges put the private–public partnership in IT capacity building, and certifications in an untenable position (Verger and Moschetti 2016) as the University was unable to purchase all required equipment by itself and the fact that the staff and students found it difficult to fund their certification exams.

The impact of this partnership in terms of opportunities it has provided for the students, staff and the University itself has been great with tremendous results. Since 2018, the University has enrolled over 1200 (staff and students) in the Academy, resulting in several of them acquiring HCIA, HCIP and HCIE certifications. Indeed, the ABU-HIA, in only its second appearance at the Huawei ICT Skills Competition, won both Cloud and Network tracks' Grand Prizes at the 2021/21 global finals. It has also proved effective; Huawei has granted the ABU-HIA an Academy Support Centre (ASC) status (the first of its kind in Nigeria), implying that it will be managing the HIA program in Nigeria on behalf of Huawei.

The ASC mandate includes, amongst others, such responsibilities as being the primary focus for the new and existing HIAs (as the partnership is scaled up to other institutions), developing strategies to encourage the integration of the certification programs into the conventional academic courses and adoption of the TTT model for staff and student capacity building. The TTT model (despite some of its challenges of sustainability, trainers' commitment, and cost (Brion and Cordeiro 2018)) has, however, proven successful to a large extent in the HIA program. It is evident from our experience at the ABU-HIA how this model has facilitated the scaling-up in IT capacity building and talent development within a short period of time and also how some of the staff (especially from the Computer Engineering Department) trained on the TTT model have found it easier to integrate some of the certification programs into the conventional curricula. Students from Computer Engineering represented the University in various competitions (two in Seeds for the future, two in the 2018/19 ICT Skills competition, two grand prize winners in the cloud track in 2019/

20, and four out of the six to represent Nigeria in both Network and Cloud tracks in the 2021/22 competition). Their performance exemplifies its capacity in cultivating students' digital competencies. In addition, it enables conditions in achieving education equality in terms of digital access and the improved quality of learning experience, which is also indicated by Laurillard et al. (2018).

With the setting up of the Huawei lab and upgrading of the ABU-HIA to an ASC status, it makes it imperative for the University to sustain the partnership and ensure that the integration practice extends to other relevant programs. This will ensure that ABU students have better employability chances with their knowledge, skills and experience. This claim is evidenced by the latest recruitment by Huawei and partners, where 13 students of the ABU-HIA who did their internship with them were recruited as IT Engineers in October 2021.

Some departments also desire to bridge the gap between degree programs and industry expectations by integrating the contents of some of the certification courses like AI, Big Data, Security, Cloud Computing, and Datacom into some of their courses. This is expected to enable the students to acquire the requisite knowledge, skills and experience based on contemporary twenty-first century IT technologies, which will allow them to graduate with industry-standard certification and, as such, enhance their employability.

Conclusion and Implications

ICT capacity building is critical to the digital transformation across all sectors to bridge the digital skills gap, enhance the acquisition of skills and experiences, and improve our schools' teaching and learning process. ABU Zaria has several initiatives targeted at improving its ICT capacity building, such as hosting the African Centre of Excellence in New Pedagogies in Engineering Education (ACENPEE), setting up the Institute of ICT develop an OBTL policy and enhancing ICT capacity building among staff and students via training courses and workshops, etc. However, the most evident and impactful has been the ABU-HIA (resulting from the public–private partnership with Huawei). This partnership has worked so far due to the commitment of both Huawei and ABU management, which is a critical element in the success of such engagements.

Before the PPP with Huawei, the staff were limited in practical exposure to cutting edge IT technologies and expert knowledge from an industry perspective. This situation was further exacerbated by the declining funding to the public universities from the federal government as various educational needs were competing for limited resources. This resulted in declining learning standards for the students coupled with teacher migration. The public–private partnership with the TTT model adopted has proven to be a quick-fix solution, evidenced by the success stories in certifications, internships, employment, and the ICT Skills competition. However, it is pertinent that measures be put in place to ensure the sustainability of the partnership's gains, even if the partnership ceases at some point in time.

One such way is the scaling up of the TTT model to ensure that more staff are trained on these contemporary technologies (with the aid of the Huawei course kits and laboratory equipment). This will ease the integration of the certification programs into the formal academic curricula. This is the model currently adopted in the Computer Engineering Department.

Way Forward

It will be helpful for the University to institutionalize all experiences gained from the partnership into a formal independent unit at the University. This Unit would be expected to manage such or similar partnerships and undertake regular assessments with a view to maximizing the benefits and mitigating the challenges both now and in the future. This is key as sustainability has been the bane of such arrangements.

6.12   Case 11: Pakistan: Measuring the Effectiveness of National OBTL Guidelines and Their Impact on Female Faculty During Covid-19 Lock Down[12]

Executive Summary

Sustainable Development Goals 2030 (SDG 2030) have been the top priority of many countries. Pakistan is also a signatory of the SDG 2030 agenda, aiming to progress in most sectors of human development and higher education is no exception. The sudden outbreak of COVID-19 and associated lockdown left educational institutes in a state of disarray due to the lack of a framework and policy that can support Online and Blended Teaching and Learning (OBTL). Therefore, the Higher Education Commission (HEC) in Pakistan issued particular guidelines for all higher education institutes (HEIs) to provide them with a unified framework for readiness and preparedness in the state of COVID-19 emergency. Though catching up quickly with the male enrollment, the female enrollment in HEIs in Pakistan has been traditionally low as the country ranks low on the gender equality scale. The COVID-19 pandemic and associated OBTL development under HEC guidelines posed unique challenges to female faculty and students in Pakistan. The purpose of this case study is to review and assess the experience of female faculty and students of this new paradigm. The study examines the female faculty's awareness and understanding of the HEC guidelines, their competency with respect to various technologies available for OBTL and assessment, any inequality they faced, support from family while working from home and other aspects. The female faculty have fared well in the majority of the aspects. However, improvements are needed in including female representatives in the policy and decision-making administrative bodies.

---

[12] Authored by Asma Khalid, Assistant Professor, Department of Product and Industrial Design University of Engineering and Technology, Lahore, Pakistan; Dr. Waqar Mahmood, Professor, Director, Al-Khwarizmi Institute of Computer Science (KICS) University of Engineering and Technology, Lahore, Pakistan.

Introduction and Context

Sustainable Development Goals (SDGs) as a collective call for action is opted by almost all countries of the world. Pakistan has also unanimously adopted SDGs after the approval from its National Assembly in 2016 and devised a strategy for planning, monitoring, and reporting the effort made to meet the agenda (United Nations n.d). Since then, the financial allocation of resources (2.3% of GDP) (Nations, 2018) and the best use of available technologies has been the prime focus to envisage a national vision in the higher education sector. As part of the effort, the three goals of "Quality Education, Gender Equality, and Decent Work and Economic Growth" are the priority areas to be addressed through Online and Blended Teaching and Learning (OBTL). The COVID-19 pandemic has forced the world to adopt a more resilient way of thinking, readiness, and preparedness for emergency situations. As part of global goals and efforts made by UNESCO, a large number of countries, including Pakistan, are thinking about recovery plans, best practices, and lessons learnt. There is a shift in the global paradigm from the traditional way of teaching and learning to the more digitalized way of communication, knowledge transferring and sharing. Developing nations worldwide faced more critical challenges at higher education institutions (HEIs). Pakistan faced challenges in Online Distance Learning (ODL) model due to lack of infrastructure, financial constraints and different social structures that initially led to a delay in transforming to online education (Ashraf et al. 2021; Bughio et al. 2014; Noreen and Hafeez 2016; Qureshi et al. 2012). The ODL model was not new, but implementation at a national scale with uniformity and smooth running of the education system in the state of global emergency was a challenge. The ODL framework also requires quality assurance as a key element in the implementation to disseminate knowledge in its true spirit, as a quality assurance mechanism helps to identify local institutions' needs and creates a sustainable feedback loop among stakeholders in a systemic and less-interruptive way (UNESCO-ICHEI 2021). In this regard, the Higher Education Commission (HEC), a regulatory body that streamlines higher education initiatives for all institutes in Pakistan, played a significant role by issuing guidelines to save the weakening education sector. The effort was to bring all academicians and institutes on one page to manage the new challenge of the distant learning model. The students and, in some cases, teachers were remotely participating in the classroom. Therefore, they faced several problems such as lack of internet and other facilities, copyrighted issues of lectures and class contents, learning of digital platforms as the medium of teaching and communication. According to HEC, there is a significant increase in the number of graduates having 16 years of education and above from universities campuses and affiliated colleges, including both on-campus and distant learning ways (HEC n.d-b). This requires a more rational approach for the future of higher education at national and global levels and developing a margin for continuous improvement to bridge the knowledge gap in OBTL.

Another issue in the OBTL also coming into forth is equitable education for all layers of society where women also take equal part in continuing the education. There was a need for a more inclusive approach for all female students and teachers to contribute to the best of their abilities and represent women in particular. In Pakistan, the ratio of female teachers is at par compared to the number of female students opting for higher education (Mehmood et al. 2018; Shah et al. 2018). Besides a rationalized approach for the online system and OBTL implementation, there was no single female representation in the Covid Response Oversight Committee formation of the HEC, Pakistan (HEC 2021). Although there are elements not as female-friendly as it is supposed to be, HEC has facilitated female students and teachers in general for their particular situation. One such example is the facilitation of expecting and lactating female faculty members (HEC 2020). This action was further in support of SDG target 3.2 at the global level to facilitate working females (Heymann et al. 2017; Robila 2016). Considering this, the case will look into the guidelines issued by HEC, Pakistan and will assess the policy implementation at the university level across Pakistan. This paper attempts to address the social constraints, gender equality, the role of women and their contribution in the education sector in the backdrop of the COVID-19 crisis.

Design and Implementation

HEC issued a set of eight guidelines at various times and allocated Rs.10 million for each public sector university (HEC 2020) for the adoption, implementation, and smooth running of OBTL. The guidelines started from raising faculty and students' awareness of COVID-19 to an action plan in the form of a working paper set forth for HEIs. The guidelines tried to address various key concerns of academicians regarding teachers' online readiness and preparedness, government directives, admissions policies, online classes, assessment policy, and reopening of universities campus life. The HEC, Pakistan facilitated the internet facility for students across Pakistan to attend online classes. The faculty and staff were trained for various digital platforms to make the best use of technologies. The guidelines also include information regarding audiovisual recordings, lab demonstrations and effective and efficient class interaction between teachers and students. Teachers were asked to submit the course information, reading materials, library resources, audiovisual material, PowerPoint presentations, and recorded lectures in advance for approval by the quality assurance before the start of the semester (HEC n.d-a). The courses were offered subject to the issue of ODL readiness certificate from the higher authorities of HEIs. Table 6.8 below is an identification of HEC guidelines in parallel with SDGs in achieving quality, equity and efficiency during the health crisis.

Research Design

A survey was designed and conducted with the female faculty to measure the effectiveness of ODL policy guidelines on female faculty during COVID-19. The questionnaire was designed based on the analysis of eight guideline documents issued by HEC. In contrast, the HEC guidelines were based on the best practices of OBTL to ensure HEI achieve targets in line with worldwide practices. Given that the policy response for COVID-19 introduced by HEC was of prime importance to measure, the questionnaire questions tried to contextualize and specify the understanding and implementation of these guidelines. Therefore, all items with measurable variables

Table 6.8 Sustainable development goals versus HEC targets

No	SDGs	HEC targets and achievements
1	3-Good health and well beings	COVID-19 awareness guidelines adapted from World Health Organization information
2	4-Quality education	HEC deputed Rs.10 million for each public sector university. Digital Platforms and faculty training Assessment approaches, e.g., open-book exams, reports the memo, research papers, reflection papers etc
3	5-Gender equality	Equal opportunity and contributions from women at the university level Work from home policies for pregnant and lactating staff
4	8-Decent work and economic growth	Work from home policies for teachers HEC deputed Rs.10 million for each public sector university. Freelancing for female students

were derived from the content analysis of HEC policy guidelines. The set of guidelines helped generate items relevant to the issue under investigation, "impact of national OBTL guidelines on female faculty", with a particular focus on the issues and challenges faced by female faculty and success in adoption. The content analysis helped make a reliable instrument and its phase-wise testing with a small pilot test to ensure questionnaire validity. This step was important because the findings will be assessing the national HEI policy of Pakistan introduced by HEC, which was being universally followed in all educational institutes of Pakistan. Therefore, very careful consideration was given to the design of the questionnaire so that variables make a sequence of information from guidelines, methodology and findings from Pakistan's scenario. The questionnaire was developed using the Likert scale to facilitate quick insight from the female faculty members. The questions were edged through the policy guidelines of HEC, Pakistan but focused on the female faculty members to value their perspective. A set of 20 questions using Google form was distributed to the participants for recording their responses for various key variables of the study. The female faculty members, both from the public and private sectors, were encouraged to participate. Initially, it was aimed to get representation from all universities of Pakistan, but due to the lack of time duration and constraints in approaching the target audience, the research team used convenient sampling. Overall, it was a good response collection of about 90% that ensured accurate representation of the target audience for response analysis and concluding results for the said case. The faculty members were asked about their demographics and university affiliation employee status, marital status, and their satisfaction with policies of HEC and Higher Education Department (HED), Government of Pakistan.

Impact on Equity, Quality and Efficiency

To measure the impact of equity, quality education and efficiency in the time of COVID-19 with regards to females in the education sector, the survey responses were analyzed and reported quantitatively and qualitatively. To test the measuring variables identified from the literature, the questionnaire was based on the demographic analysis. It measured the variables of equity, quality education and efficiency through a series of close- and open-ended questions. The mixed methodology helped identify quantitatively measuring the impact of various initiatives taken by HEC and qualitatively describing the reasoning of the occurrences. As mentioned earlier, due to time constraints and other limitations, a large sample size could not be collected. However, a sample size of more than 90 respondents was collected for the questionnaire.

Demographic of the survey population

A total of 16 universities participated in the survey and shared their opinion. Public sector universities have a stronger infrastructure, and it was easy for them to equip their teacher with training assessment tools and start implementing online education. It was observed from the response rate of public versus private universities of Pakistan that teachers at public universities have a higher engagement rate. To address the goals of equitable and quality education, there should be a good female representation, at least from the public sector universities in the policy development bodies that can help sensitize policy guide specific to females at the university platform. This will further ensure bridging the issues and communication gaps of female teachers at a higher level and to the HEC and HED (provincial Higher Education Department). We received responses from females representing various disciplines ranging from natural sciences social sciences to engineering and design fields. When participants were asked about their employment status, 77.6% of the individuals were regular employees of the university, and only a very few, 22.4%, were on a temporary contract. Most participants were married (66.9%), and only a few were single (28.2%) or had other status (5.9%).

Quality

In response to the question of familiarity with HEC-initiated guidelines and policy measures taken during the COVID-19 pandemic, there was a good response from the female faculty member, and 98.8% were familiar with policy information (Fig. 6.24). The result shows that the policies might have been well disseminated to all faculty members by the management of each institute and department. HEC also helped to ensure the guidelines were easily accessible by making guidelines available on HEC's website. However, there was a mixed response when female faculty members were asked about their satisfaction with these guidelines, probably because of the lack of involvement of female faculty members in developing HEC policy guidelines. But still, most participants found the guidelines satisfactory for carrying out their online teaching during COVID-19 (Fig. 6.25).

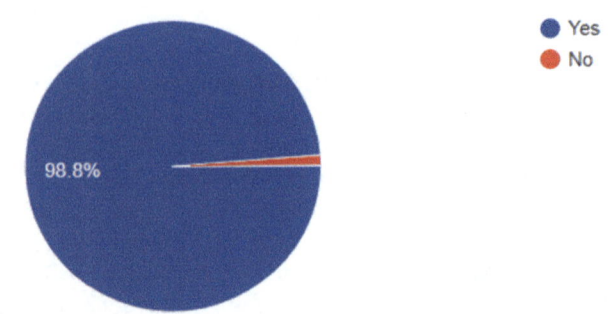

Fig. 6.24 Familiarity with HEC COVID guidelines

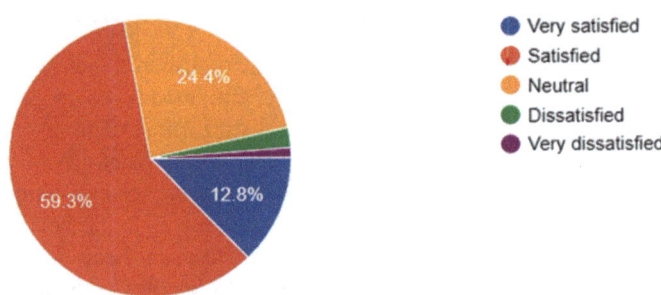

Fig. 6.25 Satisfaction with HEC COVID guidelines

In response to the question of experience in online teaching with their students, most female faculty members were either satisfied or neutral but not very satisfied (Fig. 6.26), probably due to the difficulty to keep students attentive during classes. Most students, especially female students, switch their cameras off during the class sessions creating ambiguity for teachers in engagement checking. Some faculty members arranged pop-up quizzes during regular class sessions that helped in attaining the participants' attention and interaction. Some female teachers used Google forms for quick analysis of their short lectures, and that ensured that students took the session more seriously in some cases. The female faculty member also shared that sometimes they had to call out students' name to encourage active participation. Therefore, there is a need to develop more technology-based solutions that may help students attend their classes more attentively as they used to do in the on-campus classes.

In terms of family support of the female faculty members, 48.8% of the female teachers reported they had highly favorable support (Fig. 6.27). They could manage their daily house chores and manage classes through online sessions. A very few participants, around 7%, found it difficult to gain support from their families for their online classes. The reason could be that while at home, these female teachers were blamed for not managing classes and daily household tasks simultaneously. The situation might get worst as some family members becoming COVID-19 patients.

Fig. 6.26 Experience of
online teaching

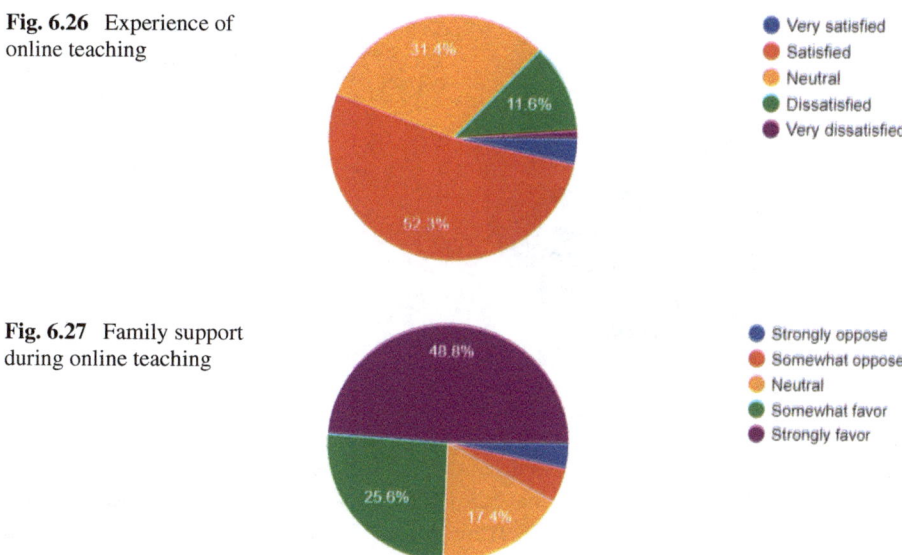

Fig. 6.27 Family support
during online teaching

Similarly, a significant percentage (30.6%) of students who faced difficulties in attending online classes from home (Fig. 6.28). It requires more in-depth analysis to know why female students faced difficulties in attending classes from home. Some of the general reasons reported are internet facilities, announced and unannounced load shedding, lack of computer and smart mobile facility, medical reasons of their own, and sometimes other family members because of COVID-19.

HEC and universities announced in their policy that all lecture contents, lab manuals, the courseware would be submitted in advance to get the course readiness certificates. In this way, the policy might have helped female teachers and students to achieve their required course learning outcomes. Besides some difficulties in continuing their online studies, the female students managed to get recorded

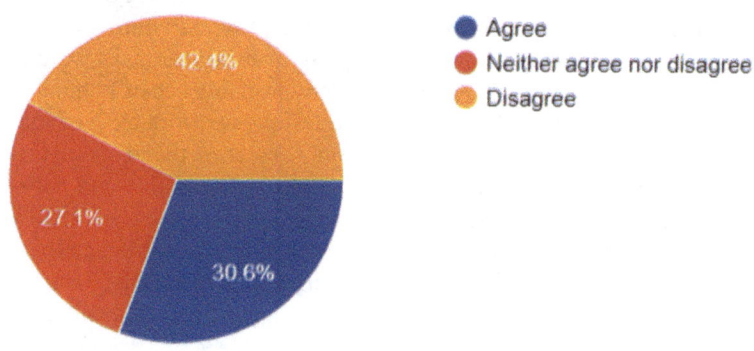

Fig. 6.28 Female students facing difficulties attending online classes

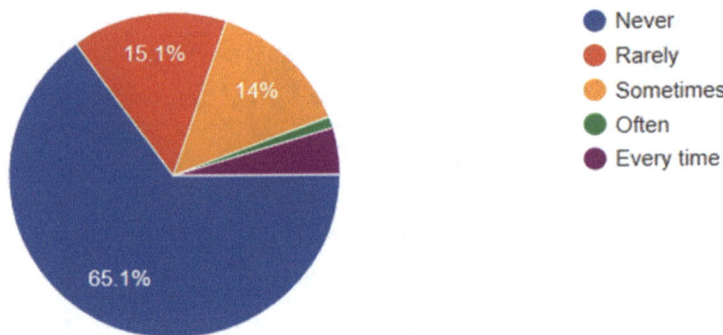

Fig. 6.29 Financial inequality for female teachers

lectures, tutorials, lab and design manuals for their classes. In some cases, instructors allowed them to submit assignments beyond the deadline to ensure proper learning of the subject. The recorded lectures were shared with the whole class, and students could view the lecture if they missed any point during the live stream. Students were given a chance to post questions later in Microsoft Teams and other communication platforms to ensure quality learning. Therefore, the consequent impact on female students was not much different than on male students, and female students were able to manage their tasks in the given time slots by instructors. Teachers also used more updated and flexible modes of communication and assessment to achieve quality learning with a uniform policy for all students.

Equality

To measure equality, female faculty members were asked about the financial inequality they faced from their institute due to the COVID-19 crisis. The most financial inequality was faced where female teachers were on contract. In some private universities, female faculty teachers were not given an extension of their job contracts, creating financial burdens for them in times of crisis. But most of the female faculty members did not face financial difficulty. There were very few women in the education sector who did not receive any support during the pandemic. However, the other social inequality in assigning institutional tasks were observed and shared by the female faculty members. This is probably because female workers face social constraints and gender bias in general. However, with the passage of time, there could be more females participating in all sectors of the economy, including education, to help them to create a more conducive, comfortable and participatory environment for fellow female workers (Figs. 6.29 and 6.30).

Despite the above inequalities, the learning opportunities were equally available to all teachers regardless of gender as most training were available free and accessible through online platforms. Various organizations helped the teachers generally and female teachers, in particular, to define and achieve the same learning outcomes as were implemented during on-campus sessions. Various international resources were made freely available to teachers to ensure quality learning that was once difficult

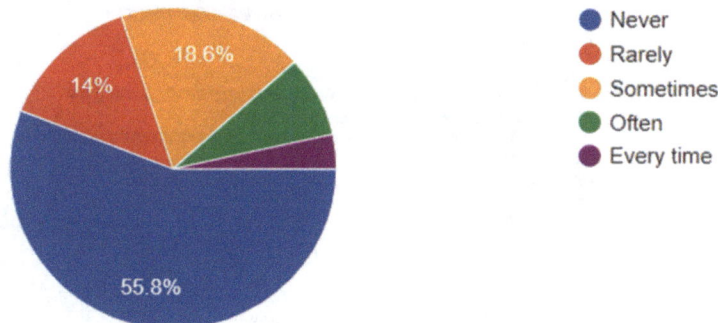

Fig. 6.30 Social inequality for female teachers

to acquire in the in-person training. Online platforms also helped to achieve equity for all and especially for females to attend these training online, which otherwise were limited due to many factors such as travel, and related costs involved. Hence, it could be said that international, national and regional online training has positively impacted equity in the higher education sector thanks to equal opportunities for female teachers. Such initiatives and training will have a lifelong impact on teacher experience of handling classes virtually and in on-campus classrooms. One of such successful examples is the series of training offered by the International Institute of Online Education of UNESCO-ICHEI that equipped teachers with smart virtual learning and practiced it in their classrooms (UNESCO-ICHEI 2021). HEC motivated universities, institutes and colleges to train their staff for online and virtual classes and made online tools and software available to teachers together with their tutorials as resources in the public domain.

Efficiency

Female faculty members may have been more proficient in using a range of tools and platforms utilization for carrying out their smooth teaching during online sessions. They make the best use of the various available tools like Rubric (16.5%), Kahoot (7%), Google form (55.3%), open book (36.5%), mind maps (1.2%), one-to-one quiz sessions (41.2%), short assignments (69.4%) and oral presentations (62.4%) as shown in Fig. 6.31. The quizzes developed by online tools generate a list at the end of the quiz that helps classify the quick and accurate identification of answers. It prioritizes the names of students who go through lecture content and assimilates the class content, helping them solve quizzes more quickly. Since the female teachers have used a range of devices and instruments for carrying out assessments, it proves that they were familiar with the various assessment approaches, got proper training of their effective use in teaching and implemented them successfully in their classes for carrying out the assessment. But overall, they were not satisfied with available technologies because the commonly used tools were not effective in bringing the outcome as they required strenuous efforts on the part of the teachers (Fig. 6.32). The reason for teacher dissatisfaction is probably because students were not quickly adaptable to

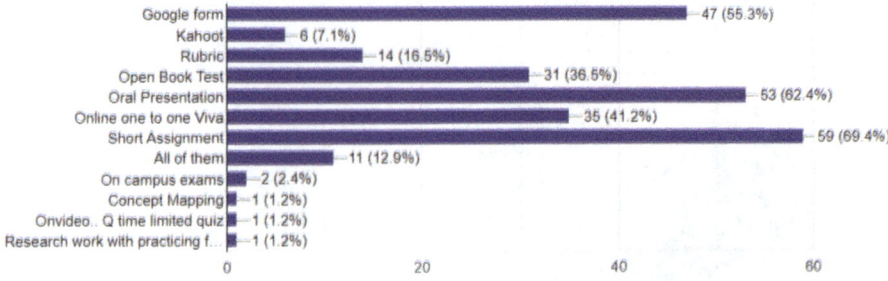

Fig. 6.31 Teachers' response to the HEC assessment approaches

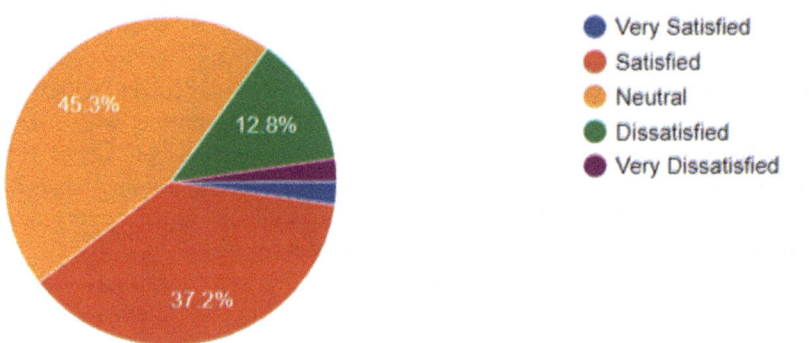

Fig. 6.32 Satisfaction with online assessment approaches

the new mode of examination, online study or completing quizzes through the digitally accessible platform. In addition, the predominant issues of the quality internet accessibility non-availability of electricity, especially in remote areas, were also major factors according to the survey.

The education sector provides skilled human resources to the industry, so it was important to measure the impact on female graduates specifically for this case. The teachers were asked to which extent female students could benefit from OBTL. About 50% of the teachers suggested it may work in providing education to female students who otherwise may not be able to attend a higher education institute (Fig. 6.33) because it is possible that female students would not be allowed to leave home due to family restrictions and other barriers of studying in co-education. Therefore, the online platform offers female students an opportunity to attend university education remotely and overcome societal barriers. For these students, some education is better than no education. Even if female students themselves choose to stay at home after graduation, they can still leave a big societal impact by educating future members of the society–their children–and creating a more educated and socially responsible world.

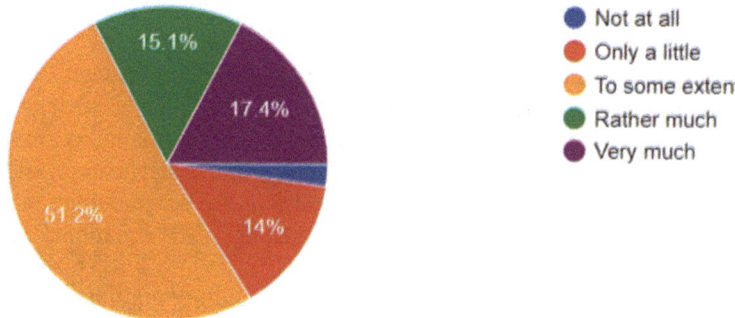

Fig. 6.33 Benefits of online education for female students

The female teachers were also asked to compare students graduating during COVID-19 with regular graduates in terms of securing jobs in industry or self-employment. The response was not very encouraging. A significant percentage (58.1%) classified them worst than regular graduates. This is probably because students lack quick adaptation to the online system of education (Fig. 6.34).

The students were not used to the online system, and it required more time for adaptation to a new mode of assessment compared to traditional ways of assessments. To alleviate the situation, these female teachers who responded often used quizzes with shuffled questions, one to one viva voce and oral presentation in online assessments, as well as open-book and numerical-based questions. However, tools like Kahoot were not freely accessible to all female teachers. The policy suggested by HEC for assessment emphasized the variety of methods in addition to quizzes and viva voce. Female teachers also reported on using open-book exams as suggested by HEC in its policy to achieve efficiency, but it was much different from the traditional mode of assessment. However, more recently, these assessment tools are being applied and used by female teachers in their regular on-campus classes, which shows the potential and their popularity in years to come.

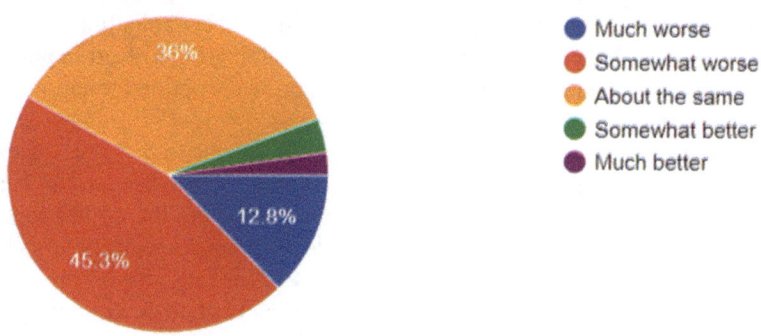

Fig. 6.34 The success rate of graduates during COVID-19

Conclusion and Implications

Overall, OBTL has great potential to be successful in the education sector, but there is a need of making inexpensive technologies available and equitable to teachers, which will help them in exercising authority during assessments. It is also considered to mandate all students to keep their cameras on during lectures and assessment sessions to increase engagement level. There may be a stricter set of guidelines, a separate set of requirements approved by the HEC for achieving SDGs at national and global levels.

HEC has taken good initiatives in preparing and handling the state of emergency for all HEIs at the national level in Pakistan. It was a considerable achievement made on the part of faculty members students, especially females who continue to support their profession through active participation. The roadmap shared by HEC, Pakistan, in the form of its guidelines, helped carry the OBTL in many public and private universities.

However, there is room for further improvement by adopting international best practices in the context of OBTL. The framework can be extended to normal situations for supporting the online distance learning model. It will expand the education network of universities in remote areas and help universities generate additional income through larger online enrollment. However, this education network may require the implementation of a stronger quality framework for OBTL programs and ICT capacity building of teachers and students.

There was no representation of female faculty in all committees of HEC. It is problematic that the formulated guidelines lack the involvement of females in decision making at the national level since there was no female member in the technology support and COVID-19 response committees of HEC, Pakistan. It is suggested that at least one female member may be added to such committees to include a female perspective.

A few lessons have been learned from the implementation of national OBTL guidelines, especially from the perspectives of female faculty, to ensure that introduction and familiarity of a unanimous policy was a success in most public and private sector universities. The information is suggested to make publicly available on the HEC website to access students, parents and teachers equally to be aware of information and policy adoption in the education sector. HEC's effort in publicizing information has resulted in the fair growth and adaption for opting for national OBTL in the state of global emergency.

However, a few difficulties and challenges emerged in the transformation to a new mode of digital communication compared to the on-site experience. The hands-on experience of lab experiments was not fully substituted with the digital experience of watching it from a camera's eye. Also, female teachers responding to the survey found it difficult to engage their students in remote learning due to the limitation of internet accessibility and power load shedding. Nevertheless, it seemed helpful that current HEC policies include recording lectures and activities that were made available for students to view later based on their convenience.

National OBTL policy guidelines introduced by HEC stems from previous best practices and has been successfully implemented in the higher education sector. The survey results reported a good and encouraging response for all the variables of quality and efficiency as core values to SDGs. These OBTL guidelines initiated by HEC can be further enhanced and enlightened through international partnerships such as those HEC has with UNESCO-ICHEI. Future challenges might also be addressed by incorporating three core dimensions of "OBTL & Education transformation, Higher Education Administration and Management and Smart ICT & Education Innovation" and its phased implementation of knowledge acquisition, application, creation and sharing. Last but not least, it is suggested that some internationally validated frameworks and toolkits be used for the policy refinement of the online education system, which may need adaptation to the socioeconomic condition of Pakistan with case-specific consideration.

6.13   Case 12: Peru: Design and Implementation Process of Online Teaching and Learning to Ensure Continuity and University Education Quality at Pontificia Universidad Católica del Perú[13]

Executive Summary

In the area of quality assurance and the improvement of online and blended teaching and learning (OBTL), practices developed by the Pontifical Catholic University of Peru (PUCP) comprise a set of actions responding to the COVID-19 pandemic, keeping our community healthy, and at the same time, ensuring continuity of education and academic quality as a right to higher education. Likewise, actions allowing the progressive return to a blended modality have begun to be developed.

This research aims to describe the process of leading, innovating and supporting OBTL to ensure its quality and to discuss strategies adopted to alleviate the pandemic. These strategies mainly focus on selecting courses and content in the online and blended modality, training for professors to provide online education, support for students, and guidelines to ensure quality and equity in online and blended academic education.

Introduction

The global health crisis has made it clear, now more than ever, that educational institutions must navigate an uncertain future. Universities need to permanently adapt to change in an agile and flexible manner and, at the same time, maintain their mission and core principles with a commitment to comprehensive education, the generation of scientific knowledge, and sustainable human and environmental development.

---

[13] Authored by Dr. Cristina Del Mastro Vecchione, Head Professor of the Department of Education and Academic Vice-president, Pontificia Universidad Católica del Perú.

This requires the design of strategies allowing universities to manage the crisis and guarantee equitable access to quality education within a framework of equal opportunities (UNESCO-IESALC 2020) while taking care of the wellness of their students, professors, and employees (PUCP educational model).

We had to implement distance education shows the importance of incorporating information and communication technologies (ICT) in higher education. It also revealed the need to place students at the center and clarify the role of professors in the optimal and creative design of teaching and learning processes.

Pontifical Catholic University of Peru (Pontificia Universidad Católica del Perú, PUCP), founded in 1917, has taken measures to ensure the quality of online teaching and learning in response to the COVID-19 pandemic since March 2020. This set of actions has sought to maintain the health of the community and ensure the continuity of quality training, a right in higher education. Likewise, since August 2021, PUCP has begun to plan actions that will allow the progressive return to a blended learning modality.

Before the pandemic, PUCP did not have undergraduate programs in the online modality but has offered graduate and continuing education programs through distance learning and more than 30 years of distance teacher training activities of the School of Education. With the support of the Department of Information Technology (DTI) and the experience in the field of Engineering, PUCP could respond in a collaborative and agile manner to the health emergency thanks to the experience of over 20 years of "PUCP virtual" (a unit in charge of adapting courses and programs to online learning modality).

In response to the social confinement measures enacted by the Peruvian Government in March 2020, Academic Vice-President's Office at PUCP immediately prepared and disseminated a series of guidelines that allowed collaborative work with the authorities of the Academic Departments and professors, aiming to develop a process of adaptation and training that would enable the continuity of education in the distance modality.

Shortly thereafter, the National Superintendence of University Higher Education (SUNEDU) adapted the criteria for the supervision of university quality and, on an exceptional basis, specified that the design and implementation of the adaptation to distance education should consider the principles of students' best interests and responsible authority. The design and implementation should not harm fundamental rights, particularly the right to education, and must ensure quality conditions in terms of accessibility, adaptability, quality availability, monitoring, relevance and coherence.

Universities in the country, as in the rest of the world (Torrecillas 2020), started to redesign, from one day to the next, their processes to provide all their students with online classes. This adaptation developed faster in private universities because they had greater access to technology and resources. To strengthen their capacities as well as technological and economic resources, a group of public universities received support from the Ministry of Education through a support program to ensure the quality of training, in which national and international entities participated

(PMESUT). Likewise, the Ministry created scholarships for permanence and other mechanisms to reduce the impact of the pandemic on dropouts.

In this context, under the coordination of the Academic Vice-President's Office together with the support of the areas involved (Department of Academic Affairs DAA, "PUCP Virtual", University Teaching Institute, Department of Information Technology), PUCP planned its first online semester during the three weeks before the start of classes, trained professors (Pardo Kuklinski and Cobo 2000; García Aretio 2000), and carried out permanent monitoring of the process that enabled the incorporation of adjustments and improvements.

The objectives of this case study are as the following:

To describe institutional policies and strategies that were developed to ensure the continuity of academic education through online and blended teaching.

To explain mechanisms implemented for development and quality assurance of online and blended teaching and learning (OBTL).

To analyze impacts and lessons learned from the online and blended modality implementation process at PUCP.

Design and Implementation

In response to the imminence of the pandemic and the forthcoming confinement measures enacted by the Peruvian government in March 2020, PUCP had to face pedagogical, technological, and organizational challenges in a very short time to ensure continuity and quality of the teaching and learning processes, such as the right to receive higher education and health care in the community during the pandemic of Covid-19.

In the initial context for institutional adaptation to the OBTL, the main challenges that had to be met were: moving the education process to an institutional online environment; continuously offering most undergraduate and graduate courses through OBTL; training professors to prepare and develop their courses on the online platform and to use technological resources; ensuring connectivity and access to technology for students and professors.

Firstly, PUCP decided to postpone the start of the first semester (originally scheduled on March 16th) to organize and plan the first actions to ensure that students could continue their studies in the OBTL remotely.

Likewise, Presidency immediately took a series of measures communicated and coordinated periodically to the academic authorities, who had to lead the preparation and implementation of this adaptation process to the OBTL distance learning modality in their departments and curriculums.

It is important to point out that before the pandemic, PUCP only had 16 blended learning graduate programs and some continuing education activities. There was little experience in the undergraduate programs with OBTL, and only 7% of the courses use the institutional LMS (Moodle). However, the University had personnel who were specialists and had successful experiences in this modality. PUCP virtual, the department in charge of the online education process for over 20 years, performed an important task of developing programs inside and outside the university. Besides, the School of Education, which had worked for over 30 years together with teachers majoring in continual education in the online modality with the support of the Department of Information Technology (DTI), allowed the technological support and pedagogical training to prepare both students and professors for the online modality.

Design of the learning and teaching process, both online and blended

– First measures and academic planning

During the plan identification process and organization in the online modality, in order to unify criteria and to direct the adaptation work of the academic departments and professors' training, the Vice-President's Office established and communicated the following institutional guidelines.

Selection of the institutional platform Paideia (Moodle), as an institutional online learning environment, was able to gather the learning environment and monitor its implementation used by professors and students. Based on this decision, the teacher training process was prepared to focus on the use of this environment and the follow-up actions of this implementation.

Initial and imperative assistance to the undergraduate programs. During the first week, the institutional resources focused on this level since it covers 78.61% of all students. Graduate programs were addressed during the second week, and later, it was continuing educational activities.

Schools had to analyze their curriculum map and select those courses that, due to their nature (mostly theoretical), could be taught in the online environment to prioritize its implementation in OBTL.

Courses that required physical resources, such as workshops and laboratories, and those practical ones had to ensure theoretical content and possible remote practical activities, leaving the essential face-to-face sessions pending for the following semesters.

Departments were requested to identify those professors who had used Paideia in order to let them cooperate with their peers in the training process.

For each school to be able to carry out the analysis process identifying the features of their academic offer, courses are categorized into three classifications: Courses that could be taught entirely online (100%); Courses that could NOT be taught online; and Blended Courses.

The implementation of these first measures was taken during weekly online meetings held among the President's team, technical teams and the group of academic authorities. These meetings led to reaching agreements and having common institutional criteria to be applied by every department according to their contexts. Periodical meetings were held with the technical teams, as well as biweekly meetings of the Academic Vice-President's office; the latter were to inform them about the progress and the development quality of teaching and learning activities of OTL, thus making changes and enhancing their implementation.

To draw lessons from the first semester and the needs to improve for planning and to organize the second semester 2020, the Academic Vice-President's office created a committee integrated by Heads of academic support offices, two representatives of deans, two heads of departments and two study directors. This Committee systematized the prior experience and created a guiding document to prepare and organize the academic activities of the second semester.

As of 2021–2, thanks to the health situation and national regulations, face-to-face activities of blended learning courses (laboratories, workshops and fieldwork) started to take place. Currently, the university, which is getting ready to return to a blended learning modality, has already developed a guiding document for the departments to choose and organize their blended courses to be taught in 2022.

– Professor Training

Training professors played a central role in the adaptation process to the online modality in terms of knowledge and use of the online learning environment Paideia PUCP (Moodle). In this regard, a self-instructional online course was offered with the following objectives:

To sensitize teachers to the distance learning modality.

To know and use the Paideia platform and its activities.

To prepare the design and implementation of learning activities for the distance learning modality in four progressive and complementary levels. These levels were organized to cover every essential aspect of the learning process and to optimize the very short time to get prepared for online courses.

To develop this online training course and ensure the preparation and quality of online courses, a total of 41 groups of professors were formed, accompanied by a tutor who performed the following duties throughout the semester:

To monitor the course adaptation progress made by professors.

To have constant communication with professors to identify problems or doubts.

To hold Zoom meetings in groups to address any concerns and model the use of the tool.

To elaborate a checklist for professors to verify the minimum elements needed to achieve qualified teaching.

This course was offered again to new teachers before the beginning of each semester (2020–2, 2021–1 and 2021–2).

Furthermore, the web called "Recursos para la virtualización" (Resources for online learning) was developed and made available for teachers to search and use.

Additionally, a help desk was made available for technological support in coordination with DTI (Department of Information Technology), which can address any potential needs or problems.

Finally, professors who had classes with over 40 students (without Professor assistants) could request a teaching assistant to be in charge of providing technical support and monitoring students during the development of the course.

– Digital resources and technological access

The institutional platform Paideia provides tools and activities for content presentation development of individual and group activities and allows to get reports on access to activities and interactions. PUCP has bought videoconference software licenses, ZOOM, and integrated it with Paideia to develop synchronous teaching and learning activities. In addition to this, the use of other free online tools was promoted, and specialized software licenses were bought for specific programs to complement and ensure the quality of learning in specific disciplines.

Moreover, the library service offered several digital resources for professors and students to access essential academic sources of information for the teaching and learning processes. It offered access to databases, electronic journals and books, subject guides and online repositories; service of online document provision; videos, and subject guides promoting research. It also offered online training in database management, bibliographic management, etc.

The Administrative Vice-President's Office offered the Connectivity Fund PUCP, which consisted of a 20 GB modem free of charge a month. This ensured that every student and professor had access to the platform and scheduled online activities. Likewise, a program to lend digital devices was offered to students in vulnerable situations.

Implementation of online learning and teaching activities

– Professor training and support during the development of the semesters

During the development of the four semesters from 2020 to 2021, several needs arose since professors needed to reinforce pedagogical aspects, as well as teaching and learning activities in the online modality. Also, they had to create an environment of trust and better interaction with students and among themselves.

For this reason, the University Teaching Institute (IDU) held a series of open workshops and micro-workshops aiming to improve and reinforce the implementation of resources, communication and pedagogical strategies of the learning and assessment activities in the distance learning modality.

Likewise, "Guía del docente PUCP para la modalidad no presencial" (Teacher's guide for the distance learning modality) was elaborated, offering information on guidelines and providing support to prepare and develop teaching, learning and assessment activities of OBTL.

Two Conferences of Teaching experiences were held to help identify and share good teaching practices. These conferences enabled PUCP to systematize experiences and create a space for reflection and dialogue among colleagues to enrich the teaching quality. As a complement, the Academic Office of Faculty offered a psychological support program to help those professors affected physically and emotionally due to the health crisis and its consequences.

At present, the university is preparing training activities and guiding documents to return, mainly guiding teachers in the design of blended-learning courses and the use of hybrid classes in 2022.

– Assistance to students and their wellness:

The week before classes started, "induction activities" took place in specific courses of each school. Students could interact with the platform, the professor and their classmates. Likewise, informational videos and guidelines were offered for a better understanding of this modality.

Due to the economic crisis caused by the lockdown period, exceptional economic support was given to students who were going through difficult times, which enabled them to continue with their studies. Besides, immediate assistance was given to students infected with COVID 19 and orphan scholarships to those experiencing an unfortunate parental loss.

Regarding psychological wellness and mental health, the Academic Office of Student Affairs (DAES) offered various services such as online psychological support, psycho-pedagogical counselling, training and classes of 16 types of sports on Facebook.

– Actions to ensure quality:

Three mechanisms were selected to monitor and ensure teaching quality:

PAIDEIA Reports

The Department of Academic Affairs (DAA), together with the support of DTI, organized and presented weekly reports about the access and types of activities developed in every online course to each academic department.

The indicators reported by the platform in 2020 and 2021 were the following ones:
% of course-schedule identified to be taught online according to the curriculum of each department.
% of course-schedule on Paideia having a timeline for the registered distance learning modality.
% of students who join in their course-schedule.
% of students who make use of resources, such as "file"; "questionnaires"; "forums"; and "tasks" on Paideia.
Number of meetings held on Zoom by course-schedule.
Number of students enrolled by course schedule on Paideia.
Number of withdrawn students by program.

Thanks to this information, each school could identify possible problems in courses. Professors or students can also make decisions as well as take actions to improve.

(b) Minimum required Documents on PAIDEIA

To inform SUNEDU about the academic offer at an institutional level, minimum required documents of each course on Paideia were established: syllabus, weekly schedule of the synchronous activities within the course time (no less than 50% of regular face-to-face classes) and other asynchronous; recordings of the synchronous classes; basic materials of the course: digital bibliography, web links, videos, among others.

(c) Satisfaction survey on the online modality

At the end of the first semester of each year (2020–1 and 2021–1), satisfaction surveys were conducted among students and professors of undergraduate and graduate programs. Surveys were divided into three dimensions:

General experience (access to online resources, user-friendliness).

Perception of online modality (interaction, course organization, personal organization and communication, support given by university services).

Open questions to gather comments and experiences regarding the main weaknesses and strengths of the online modality experience.

These survey results were presented to the school and department authorities in order to identify possibilities of improvement when organizing and implementing upcoming semesters.

Impact on Equity, Quality and Efficiency

Academic offer, access to the platform and support for the continuity of studies.

Together with the participation of departments and professors, PUCP made a major institutional effort to ensure equity in students' access to most courses and to guarantee the continuity of the academic education. As Table 6.9 shows, the percentage of the academic offer in the distance modality during the first semester almost surpassed 85% of the total and improved substantially, reaching 98.8% in the academic semester 2021–2. In the semester 2021–2, blended learning courses were firstly offered in undergraduate programs (4.19%). These involved laboratories, workshops and fieldwork to maintain the learning quality, demanding for face-to-face experiences, were allowed by the current regulations.

The continuity of education and the enrollment rate during this phase show positive results regarding the access and satisfaction with the teaching quality (Table 6.10). During the semester 2020–1, in addition to the lack of confidence in the quality of distance education, a higher number of students withdrew due to the initial impact of the health and economic crisis caused by the pandemic and its consequences on families. However, the institutional effort to provide conditions to have access, equity and quality in education witnessed a significant increase in the number of students who re-enrolled in the following semester. This reveals that the technological and economic support provided by PUCP was efficient and that reliability in the quality of the modality improved substantially.

Table 6.9 Courses that could be taught entirely online, courses that could not be taught entirely online and blended courses by semester (undergraduate and graduate programs)

Courses	2020–1 (%)	2020–2 (%)	2021–1 (%)	2021–2 (%)
Courses that could be taught entirely online	84.8	95.8	98.8	95.81
Courses that could not be taught entirely online	12.8	3	0	0
Blended	2.33	1.2	1.2	4.19

Table 6.10 Students enrolled, re-enrolled and withdrawn by semester (undergraduate and graduate programs)

	Semester 1		Semester 2	
	2020–1	2021–1	2020–2	2021–2
Total students enrolled	26,494	29,719	27,831	28,363
Re-enrolled students	1142	1597	3057	1533
Withdrawn students	6296	3843	3428	4127

Additionally, periodical reports on access to the Paideia platform enabled each school to monitor efficiently the percentage of students accessing different courses and resources (documents, forums, activities and questionnaires). This information helped people detect difficulties in some courses, groups and professors, investigate their causes and propose improvements, ensure access and quality of teaching and learning.

Thanks to the monitoring system, planning and development of training actions, student engagement level also achieved a satisfactory result. As shown in Table 6.11, there is a high percentage (98%) of access and participation of undergraduate and graduate students in their courses, activities and resources on PAIDEIA. It should be noted that in the case of activities of some thesis seminars, other synchronous and asynchronous alternatives were used in order to carry out personalized counselling, which could explain why such access did not reach 100%.

During these two years, a series of supportive measures were implemented to guarantee equity and continuity in online teaching and learning activities. The connectivity fund provided support for more than 8000 beneficiaries, including students and professors (Table 6.12). In addition, the number of orphan scholarships caused by parental loss from COVID-19 increased in the last two years, reaching a total of 940 (Table 6.13).

As the health crisis continuously affects the socioemotional aspect of the university community, PUCP accordingly developed a series of Wellness and Mental Health activities through psychological care and other actions. During the year 2020, a total

Table 6.11 Percentage of students accessing the PAIDEIA platform

	2020–1	2020–2	2021–1	2021–2
% of students accessing their course-schedule	98%	96%	98%	(In process)

Table 6.12 Beneficiaries of the connectivity fund by semester

Semester	Quantity
2020–1	5000 beneficiaries
2020–2	6400 beneficiaries
2021–1	7500 beneficiaries
2021–2	8000 beneficiaries

Table 6.13 Number of orphan scholarships by semester

	2021–2	2021–1	2020–2	2020–1	2019–2	2019–1	2018–2
Orphan scholarships (law no. 23585)	341	306	188	105	52	48	51

of 7653 students were assisted; and during the year 2021, 3799 students were assisted. These actions contributed to ensuring the permanence and the learning process of those affected students.

Professors trained for quality teaching and online learning

Thanks to the variety of training actions and pedagogical and technological support, professors are reported to have built their capacity for distance teaching on the institutional platform and their use of OBTL tools. These competencies have contributed to improving the quality of OBTL. A total of 71.5% of active professors successfully completed the self-instructional course "Organize your PAIDEIA" offered at the start of the Pandemic in the semester 2020–1 (Table 6.14). And during the following semesters, new professors and those who wanted to design new courses using the online modality also took part in it.

While the initial focus of these training sessions was the use of online tools and the assurance of information transmission, training also started to incorporate elements to encourage professors' greater interaction and communication with students to contribute to improving the comprehensive education of students.

Student Satisfaction

The student satisfaction was evaluated through an annual survey (2020 and 2021) and a qualitative study before the start of the second year of OBTL (March 2021). Assessing the satisfaction in several aspects was a measure to evaluate the quality of OBTL and identify achievements and difficulties which led to improving the teaching and learning experience.

The satisfaction survey on the distance modality addressed to students was responded to by 55% of the population in 2020 and by 24% in 2021 and had a scale from 0 to 5.

General experience (access to online resources, user-friendliness).

Table 6.14 Professors enrolled and certified in the self-instructional course "Organize your PAIDEIA" by semester

Semester	Enrolled and certified professors
2020–1	1997 (71.5% of the total number of active professors)
2020–2	378
2021–0	121
2021–1	309
2021–2	751

Perception of the online modality OBTL (interaction, course organization, personal organization and communication, support given by university services).

Open questions to gather comments and experiences regarding the main weaknesses and strengths of the online modality experience.

At the beginning of 2021, based on 20 focus groups with students from different careers, a qualitative study was developed by focusing on online modality and learning assessment.

Students have become more adapted to the online learning platforms as OBTL implementation continues. The survey results show a gradual increase in the students' satisfaction regarding the access to resources on Paideia and its user-friendliness. The percentage of very high and high satisfaction (scale 4 and 5) increased to 75% in 2021 compared to 52.5% in 2020. This positive result may have been caused by the improvement in the adaptation and learning curve in the use of the online classroom, but also by measures taken by the institutions or families based on their possibilities to improve online access. The usefulness of learning tools/activities on Paideia showed positive results above 50% except for forums, which reached only 25%. Based on these results, workshops were carried out with foreign specialists to advise on the best use of those tools.

The OBTL approach at PUCP was of high quality, according to the survey. Students showed a very high and high level of satisfaction with the courses' overall quality. Over 60% were satisfied with the quality of the contents developed in the courses, increasing from 62.8% (in 2020) in the satisfaction level to 78% (in 2021). Similarly, tools considered as the most useful (with a high and very high level of satisfaction of 70%) were those in which professors presented content such as video-conferences (synchronously) and videos (asynchronously). Also, reading resources containing learning materials and exercises related to more practical activities showed high satisfaction (60%) as well.

The OBTL approach adapted by PUCP also encourages communications and enhances professor-student relationships. With respect to the communication and willingness of professors to resolve doubts, 56% of students expressed a high level of satisfaction in the first year, and this percentage increased by 67% in the second semester.

These results are analyzed in more detail with the qualitative study, where students value positively various online elements such as class recordings and greater access to online material. Since they can be reviewed at any time as a study resource or as a way to catch up, they can certainly contribute to greater equity and quality in students' learning. Besides, this equity has been reinforced since the OBTL has allowed shortening the distance for students who live far from the campus and working people who have made faster progress in their careers, for the latter became able to study and work at the same time.

There are also downsides of the current OBTL approach worth considering. While the valuation of the online learning quality focuses mainly on the acquisition of content and exercises, students show lower satisfaction levels regarding their participation and interaction with classmates and organization of study time. These aspects were improved in the second year but still did not exceed 43% of high or very high satisfaction. These results indicate that students are more satisfied with the course, contents, materials and professors than with their own level of participation, interaction and organization showing in the learning process.

The effectiveness of online teaching seems to be greater in theoretical learning than in practical one. Professors have been able to transmit quality content through videoconferences in synchronous sessions, recordings, and reading materials. But they had greater difficulty designing experiences that promote practical and on-hand learning, as well as the interaction with and among students.

Professor Satisfaction Surveys

The satisfaction survey on the distance modality addressed to professors was answered by 53% of the population during the first year and by 28% during the second year, with a scale from 0 to 5. Generally speaking, professors at PUCP who responded to the survey have realized the strengths of OBTL and gradually become accustomed to the OBTL approach.

Professors showed high and very high satisfaction (scale 4 and 5) regarding the institutional training for OBTL. 76% of professors expressed satisfaction with the support provided by the University through the self-instructional course "Organize your PAIDEIA"; 68% with the support provided by the University through the assigned tutor; and 75% were satisfied with the training and micro-workshops offered by IDU. These results show the effectiveness of the training provided to professors to plan and develop their online teaching and learning activities.

These levels of satisfaction with the PAIDEIA platform resources are very high in both years. Professors were also satisfied with their own process of preparation and organization of their courses, which included the adaptation of the contents and activities proposed in the syllabus to the distance modality and their organization of time to address students' doubts and queries.

It also shows high levels of satisfaction with their level of interaction with students in synchronous activities and with their level of interaction in asynchronous activities even though rates dropped slightly in the second year with an average of 10 percentage points, which may take place due to the perception of lower student participation.

The evaluation team sees the need for more reflection spaces on their teaching practice when dealing with students' communication needs to address their doubts and queries. This last element presents a difference from the qualitative students' opinions in which they express difficulties in this interaction, despite having a positive result in the survey.

Conclusion and Implications

With participative work among the Academic Vice-President's office, the academic authorities and professors, it becomes feasible for PUCP to initiate its institutional adaptation process to OBTL and to face the challenges of the pandemic. Thanks to constant communication and coordination, the authorities of each department have participated in the decision-making and implementation of institutional policies, which guide academic planning and management, and in turn, meet the particular needs of each discipline to ensure academic quality.

Significant efforts have been made to support professors in the development of technological and pedagogical competencies, as well as to offer them resources and tools for OBTL. This training, together with the LMS support and resources provided by the library, led us to redesign 100% of the courses in the OB modality with a high level of satisfaction from both professors and students.

There is recognition of quality in the contents provided in OBTL, especially those theoretical ones, as well as resources allowing the transmission/ acquisition of information such as videoconferences, recordings, and readings. These digital or digitalized contents reinforce the academic quality of the acquired knowledge. Meanwhile, it also shows a weakness regarding the development of knowledge and competencies, which need to be put into practice and demand greater pedagogical challenges in OBTL, and need to be developed in a face-to-face or blended modality considering the nature of each discipline.

Communication and interaction between professors and students are aspects that need to be analyzed in detail since they express contradictory valuations regarding the satisfaction level in the survey and in the focus group. Since the quality of face-to-face communication has been affected, professors and students require a higher level of synchronous interactivity that promotes immediate feedback on the progress in the learning and teaching process. The communication aspect in the online classroom has been developed during the training for professors, which can also be improved from the pedagogical point of view with the possibilities provided by OBTL.

The health crisis and the impact on families and people have shown the importance of considering the care and prevention of mental health as part of the quality of education. Besides, the wellness of the community is also suggested to become an aspect that universities must guarantee beyond the pandemic.

Greater qualitative follow-up might be necessary regarding teaching and assessment practices to identify difficulties and good practices in practical courses, communication and evaluation in OBTL in different disciplines. According to PUCP's experience, it could also be meaningful to unify criteria with institutional standards to guide the didactic design and assessment systems of courses in different modalities, taking into account the diversity of disciplines and the nature of courses.

Improving the monitoring indicators of quality parameters that allow compliance with the necessary process of continuous improvement might help the OBTL development—providing necessary information to be accountable from an internal quality system of the online and blended modality.

Due to changes experienced since September 2020, a participatory process of revision and updating of the PUCP Educational Model has been carried out to incorporate the technological and pedagogical changes to develop programs in blended and online modalities. The generic competencies of students and teaching roles in these modalities have been reviewed and updated, together with teaching and learning models, online resources and media, and the support that needs to be available and operational.

Appendix

See Tables 6.15, 6.16, 6.17 and 6.18.

Table 6.15 Number of professors participating in micro-workshops and workshops offered by IDU per semester

Training line	Name of activity	2020–1	2020–2	2021–1	2021–2
Use of online tools	Zoom videoconferencing	390			
	Group activities using zoom	545			
	Online forum moderation	723			
	Interactive video design with edpuzzle	532			
	Preparing powerpoint presentations during online learning modality 2020-01	40			
	Training activities using padlet and mentimeter	499			
	Pedagogical use of digital whiteboards: liveboard and jamboard	345			
	Guidelines for effective presentations	323			
	Creation of videos with loom and screencast		133	79	
	Content generation with google tools: slides and jamboard		148		
	Collaborative work using google tools: drive and chat		110	103	
	Learning activities using miro			120	
	Designing digital resources with genially			124	
	Creating Digital Learning Materials				35
Planning learning activities	Development of learning outcomes			120	
	Organization of teaching–learning activities in distance modality			162	
Communication and interaction	Communication skills in online environments	318			
	Emotional regulation in online teaching	130			
	Assertive communication in online teaching		115	193	64
	Care and wellness in the classroom			57	
	Professor's oral and communication skills in synchronous classes				189
	Creative use of voice and body in distance teaching				60
	Motivation in the teaching–learning process				95
Assessment for learning	Guidelines for designing assessments consistent with learning outcomes	152			

(continued)

Table 6.15 (continued)

Training line	Name of activity	2020–1	2020–2	2021–1	2021–2
	Effective feedback through online means	440	85	41	
	Using the questionnaire tool to design assessments	956			
	Developing online tests with socrative and kahoot	526		100	
	Using the homework tool for assessment	397	62	37	
	Grading instruments: checklists and rating scales	171			
	Designing rubrics: holistic and analytical	171		52	109
	Advanced use of the questionnaire tool: development of the question bank	149	64		
	Student monitoring with paideia tools		116		
	Creation of portfolios and wikis with google sites		89		
	Characteristics of distance assessment			209	
	Portfolio and logbook as self-assessment strategies			63	
	Communication in the assessment process			40	
	Designing written assessments with google forms			87	
	Strategies and instruments for performance assessment			163	38
	Implementing and assessing teamwork				47
	Planning a course assessment system				73
Others	Professor's role and the grieving process			45	
	Teaching and learning within diversity			78	
	Characteristics of education modalities				55
	Teaching and learning process as an opportunity for the inclusion of students with special needs				33
	University social responsibility approach in the teaching and learning process			76	91
	Guidelines for returning to classes				43
	Promoting academic integrity in the online classroom				91

Table 6.16 Gathering of teaching experiences in 2020: 72 experiences from 13 departments

Subject area	# Experiences
Course planning and organization	18
Communication and interaction in the classroom	14
Collaborative learning	16
Assessment for learning and feedback	13
Online workshops and laboratories	11

Table 6.17 Gathering of teaching experiences in 2021: 67 experiences from 15 departments

Subject area	# Experiences
Course design and planning	24
Communication and interaction in the classroom	11
Collaborative learning	12
Assessment for learning and feedback	13
Online workshops and laboratories	7

Table 6.18 Teachers attended for psychological support by year

	2020	2021
Full-time	32	23
Part-time	152	108
Total number of consultations	**184**	**131**

6.14   Case 13: Papua New Guinea: COVID-19 Pandemic and the Abrupt Pivot to Online and Blended Learning at Papua New Guinea University of Technology[14]

Executive Summary

As part of the expanding effect of the COVID-19 pandemic, the educational systems in most countries around the world have been adversely affected, with most universities cancelling physical classes and abruptly shifting to the online and blended mode of lesson delivery and assessment as they seek to reduce COVID-19 spread. Papua New Guinea University of Technology (PNGUoT) has not been left out in this pivot. With the intent of identifying gaps and formulating strategies through the lens of a Quality Assurance framework, this report delves into the large-scale transformation of online learning that occurred at PNGUoT in the wake of the COVID-19 pandemic. It reports on the interventions taken by the university to ensure a seamless transition

---

[14] Authored by Dr. Tindi Seje Nuru, Associate Professor and Director of the Teaching and Learning, Papua New Guinea University of Technology, Email: tindiseje@yahoo.com /tindi.nuru@pnguot. ac.pg.

into this mode of learning that was considered the second class for so long and now suddenly deemed worthy of interest in an unprecedented way. Specific measures taken to ensure the quality of online and blended teaching and learning at PNGUoT are highlighted in this report and further how related guidelines were operationalized at various levels. On the brighter side of the pandemic, this paper also reports on the agile creativity and nimble adaptability that is also a characteristic of life in 'the land of the unexpected'. As institutions seek to lead, innovate, and support online and blended teaching and learning, the report concludes with the impact achieved from the interventions and lessons learned from the entire experience that would foster quality assurance and make this pivot less brutal but more sustainable.

Introduction and Context

COVID-19 has ripped apart the comfortable assumptions about the world and how we as communities and societies should operate within it. Practices have been disrupted, such as students attending school in face-to-face settings, or groups of people chatting together in comfortable physical proximity. United Nations (2020) notes that this pandemic has occasioned the largest disruption of the education systems in recent history. Rosales (2021) argues that amid higher education's seismic shift, colleges and universities are following the retail and service sectors in deploying technology to make the entire learner experience seamless—from recruitment and teaching to student and alumni interactions. While the pandemic has caused massive upheavals, it has also forced universities to use technology to bring much-needed change and innovations, making them more innovative and inventive (Champagne and Granja 2021). With COVID-19, many of these technologies and innovations have now been widely adopted across campus, a leap overnight that otherwise would have taken a generation or more to adopt (Flanagan 2021).

In the face of the worldwide social experiment where people were inventing, adapting and creating new practices of human sociality in academia, many instructors and learners, including those in Papua New Guinea (PNG), are frontline workers in this social experiment. In the context of PNG, the education of nearly 2.4 million students was abruptly disrupted by school closures following the government's COVID-19 mitigation measures (Khan and Molendijk 2020), as reported in an article by Nuru et al. (2021). The higher education (HE) sector in PNG, like in most developing economies, needs to rethink and embrace innovative solutions that limit in-person class attendance, especially in the wake of COVID-19. Khan and Molendijk (2020) corroborate this unfortunate situation as they report on the obtaining conditions in PNG, arguing that instructors are vital to implementing education response to COVID-19 and need to be equipped with the knowledge, skills, and resources to support remote learning. The PNG Department of Higher Education Science and Technology urges educational institutions to consider widening opportunities for educational services through digital avenues.

According to UNESCO (2013), it is imperative that higher education institutions have an ongoing, continuous process of evaluating, assessing, monitoring, guaranteeing, maintaining, and improving the quality of higher education provided. The Quality Assurance framework, as interpreted within the context of the existing quality management model at PNGUoT, is undergirded by the Academic Quality Assurance Team (AQAT). AQAT is under the umbrella of the University's Academic Board Committee with a responsibility to foster quality teaching and learning across all Academic Departments in light of accreditation requirements. The AQAT also takes care of increasing graduates' core competencies to meet employer expectations. During the pivot to online learning, AQAT worked with other academic departments in a cooperative spirit to achieve a culture of continuous improvement in course offerings across all instructional modes so that student learning is enhanced, and pedagogical standards upheld-this is now institutionalized as a routine practice within the university.

While deciding on the incorporation of online learning into current practices, Papua New Guinea University of Technology (PNGUoT) was cognizant of Sing and Hardaker's (2014), that the decision-making process must be all-inclusive with a buy-in from all parties involved; a clear strategic vision should guide the entire effort and should be made known to all stakeholders. Coincidentally, shortly before the emergence of the COVID-19 pandemic, the University had prioritized online learning in Domains 2 and 7 of its strategic plan 2020–2024 (PNGUoT 2022). An internal education policy document of PNGUoT was also developed to socialize the concept of online learning to relevant stakeholders across the university (Renagi 2021). It was, therefore, relatively easy for the University to activate its processes, systems and procedures so to address the challenges associated with the abrupt transfer to online teaching in the wake of COVID-19.

Against the backdrop of challenges occasioned by COVID-19, PNGUoT remained aware of the opportunities that online education could contribute to its mission to "grow world-class technocrats through high-quality experiential teaching, research and ardent application of scientific and technological knowledge and innovation." Therefore, the University is committed to developing systems that would support high-quality online and blended education opportunities for its students.

Design and Implementation

Hinged on its 2020–2024 strategic plan, PNGUoT made impressive emphatic progress towards activating and implementing online learning in the wake of COVID-19. Over the past few years, the university has been using Google Classroom as its main Learning Management System (LMS). However, the university was also considering migrating into a site-wide adoption of Moodle platform that is well customized to improve online learning with content-driven concepts and data that backs it up (PNGUoT 2021). This is in line with Divine Word University (DWU, another university in PNG), which opines that social distancing restrictions are increasing the use of Moodle and also reinvigorating attention on the capabilities needed to support effective blended and online learning. In 2020, PNGUoT made a huge investment in online teaching infrastructure: paying for a site license for the Zoom app to enable seamless online interaction between academics and students, and subscription for a site license for Camtasia software helps in high-quality lecture video production and editing. All the academic departments were provided with Wacom Tablets with stylus pens that allow faculty to input graphical data online. Specifically, staff could now demonstrate how to derive an equation while using these stylus pens to write on screens for students who are attending the lectures virtually. Onboarding technology-mediated teaching and learning was relatively easy because PNGUoT also has a policy of giving laptops to every student on admission at the university. To ensure sustainable optimization of these efforts, the University also partnered with Digicel Telecommunication Company to provide all students with 20 GB of internet data plan per month, assigned to the students' SIM cards and MiFi devices (PNGUoT 2021). The University also audited its ICT infrastructure and planned a major upgrade of its LAN and other infrastructures that support ICT. This resonates with a proposition by DWU's experience (2020) that an important yet currently untapped idea to reduce internet expenses is to partner with internet service providers and relevant industries with a strong presence in PNG to support online learning.

To help staff take lessons from how other universities around the world were dealing with teaching continuity in the time of COVID-19, TLMU organized several in-house webinars and three international webinars. One under the title 'Shifting Teaching and Learning online during COVID-19; Lessons learnt through research and practice' was facilitated by an internationally renowned educational technologist, Ben Daniel, Ph.D., who is the Head of Higher Education Development Centre, University of Otago, New Zealand. The second international webinar was facilitated by Dr. Michele Dale, a senior Academic Developer from James Cook University-Australia. The webinar focused on 'Student-Centred Teaching in the era of Online Teaching; great online engagement for optimum learning outcomes. The third international webinar was preceded by a survey 'thriving in the face of a global pandemic: Options for students and young adults', and targeted students and addressed relevant survey findings. This particular webinar was facilitated by Ms. Ruby Quantson Davis, an international learning and impact specialist (PNGUoT 2021).

To ensure inclusion and sustainability, the University also rethought its programs that were being offered on a face-to-face basis and made them fully adaptable to an online environment. PNGUoT continued repositioning itself to expand its pedagogical potency by taking remote learning to the next level since it ensured that staff who were undertaking their postgraduate course in student-centred teaching also balanced a blended model of in-person and online instruction as part of their orientation to online teaching (PNGUoT II 2020). The Teaching–Learning Methods Unit (TLMU), and Department of Distance Learning (DODL), of the University, extensively capacitated staff on the best ways to make online learning experiences coherent, educationally meaningful, and attractive to students. TLMU provides ongoing instructional support to staff in teaching online, redesigning course offerings, and determining which experiences to be done in person and those that can be done remotely. Whereas institutions may not want to remain online forever, they must prepare for moving towards blended learning as the "new normal" by embracing some of the tried and tested practices that PNGUoT adopted. The new shape of learning is will gradually be in the virtual space, and PNGUoT has robustly invested in making the online learning experience more human, enabling students to form bonds with one another, and better translate the campus experience to the computer screen. It is hoped that the future of online learning cannot be better enough for PNGUoT.

Impact on Equity, Quality and Efficiency

The introduction of blended/online learning initiatives at PNGUoT to a greater extent allowed more equitable and inclusive access to quality higher education at the University. Learning outcomes and students' learning experiences were greatly enhanced with the advent of these digital approaches. It is also evident that efficiency also increased in the education space given the automation of some routine tasks, flexible work arrangements, and the ability to benefit from analytics generated by the LMS that spurred data-driven decisions.

To help consolidate its experiences and put into perspective its opportunities for improvement, a survey was designed to get instructors' and students' individual experiences with Online Teaching that took place in Semester 1, 2020 at PNGUoT. In the second half of 2020, the University further hosted virtual seminars on online teaching experiences. It compared notes with other overseas universities regarding how they handled teaching–learning business continuity in the wake of COVID-19. The findings from the survey informed the content of the plenary discussion in these virtual conferences.

The survey noted that in the transition to the online learning systems, most students and instructors had a high percentage of laptop use (63.6%), probably because the university provides laptops to all first-year undergraduate students and new staff. Subsequently, this was closely followed by using desktops (34.1%), then finally mobile phones by students with very few opting to use tablets. These figures for students are not surprising given that most teenagers are often very handy with mobile phones than other devices. For the instructors, the predominant device usage was the laptop and desktop with a combined total of approximately 98% see Fig. 6.35. Furthermore, while most students confirmed their ability to utilize their primary devices in completing their studies, it is not the case for most instructors, as represented in Table 6.19. This is largely due to internet problems. The University thus must move with speed to resolve internet lethargy that bedevils the institution.

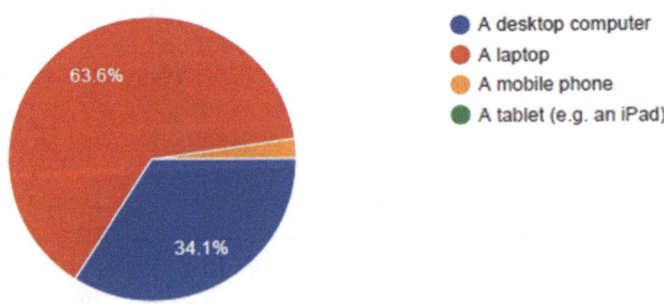

Fig. 6.35 Devices used in assessing online classes (a) Student (b) Staffs

Table 6.19 Summary of the quantitative dataset

S/N	Question set	Student		Staff	
		Yes (%)	No (%)	Yes (%)	No (%)
1	Is the internet connection you use to access your online learning adequate for your needs?	25.40	74.60	22.70	77.30
2	Can you complete your course using your primary device (tablets, computer etc.)	74.00	26.00	47.70	52.30
3	Do you have any recorded lectures as part of your course?	60.40	39.60	63.30	36.40
4	Does your course include live lectures delivered through video conferencing?	65.70	34.30	50.00	50.00
5	Do you have assessment tasks that you need to complete online?	55.90	44.10	46.70	53.30

Additionally, data extracted from the questionnaire showed that an average of 75% of both instructors and the student population have issues with internet connection. One respondent reported that "I'm disturbed about our internet connection. When doing an online quiz or downloading materials from Google class and my internet plays up, that's the end for me. But the majority of instructors have been incredibly helpful on these technical issues." This represents a serious concern given that it is the foundation on which the online system is being deployed and can severely impact studies. The University, therefore, should invest in providing a more reliable internet plan. The bureaucracy around sim card issuance to students should also be lessened, and more sim cards made available to the students and staff in time.

Part of the online education system employed in PNGUoT at this time was based on pre-recorded videos that were uploaded to Google Classrooms together with lecture notes. This then left little room for an interactive synchronous and synchronous interaction between instructors and students, hence a considerable strain. While the recorded lectures were averagely between 10 to 30 min, few instructors uploaded videos of over an hour, and 17% of all instructors uploaded 10 min videos, probably due to limited technical competencies of video editing. Given that most PNGUoT students are used to long lectures, instructors might need new skills and knowledge to capture new education priorities and means of delivery.

When asked to contrast online/blended versus in-person experiences, qualitative responses reveal respondents' paranoia around online teaching. While they appreciate its benefits, they also are quick to add that it just can never replace in-person classes "I'm already tired of studying in my lodging. The pain of physical distance remains strong. With Zoom, we're doing everything we ought to do in a physical classroom; however, it's impossible to replace a situation of getting close with instructors, schoolmates and other people (Fig. 6.36)."

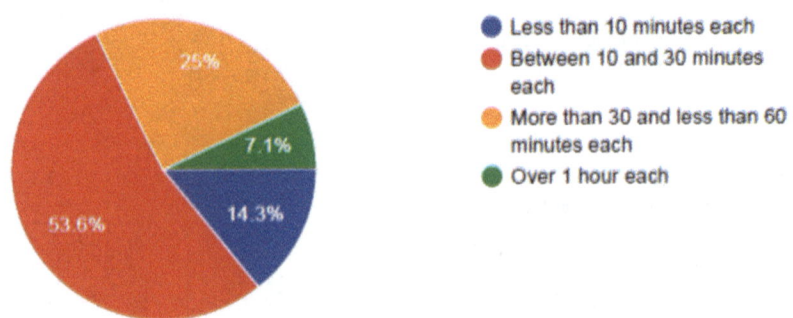

Fig. 6.36 The average time frame of recorded videos

Conclusion and Implications

The survey results show that through the implementation of online and blended teaching and learning at PNGUoT, various devices are leveraged, among which laptops and desktops are most frequently used. However, the internet infrastructure needs to be updated to ensure the quality of teaching and learning. Also, interactions between the lecturers and students of online education remain to be improved.

According to PNGUoT's experience, the video quality of recorded lectures would affect the online learning platform's user experience and impact students' learning effectiveness. Thinking of ways to upload High Definition (HD) video lectures or providing alternatives might help to facilitate the university-wide willingness to participate in online and blended teaching and learning. That being said, a draw-back of HD videos is often the final output size. For the instructors, uploading a video larger than 500 Megabytes on the Google Classroom platform already takes time due to the internet structure in the region, so people are being reluctant to use high-quality videos though it enhances the user experience. Simultaneously, the instructors seemed to struggle with work completion, given that 47% of the instructors found it quite difficult. Furthermore, instructors found it quite stressful to prepare lecture content on the online system. While these corroborate the that "disruption to education systems during the COVID-19 has disproportionately affected the most vulnerable learners, exacerbating pre-existing inequalities with potentially dramatic and long-lasting implications. This requires urgent action to address learning gaps and ensure smooth and continued educational pathways for all learners of new technologies, including instructors.

Fortunately, the aforementioned dilemma at PNGUoT has now been remedied by using Zoom live sessions, which can be recorded and made available to students. Most students currently report satisfactorily completing their required courses and assessment using the online platform. As OECD (2020) suggests, urgent actions are now required "to address learning gaps and ensure smooth and continued educational pathways for all learners", and that "over the longer term, systems will need to strengthen learner resilience, fostering environments in which every individual has the competencies required to reach their full potential". It points towards the need for further skilling instructors in the areas of developing instructional materials for the online environment, technological development and the use of a mix of technologies for online learning, strategies for evaluation of the process and outcomes of online learning, education about specific technical processes such as integrating multimedia applications, working knowledge of the range of students support services as outlined by USAID (2014). Pieces of training in this regard have been planned for in the ongoing in-house capacity-building programs, which will also help educational actors to nurture resilient mindsets that value people and processes over classroom devices. For example, collected data have shown that most instructors chose to use the software (Camtasia). PNGUoT purchased a university-wise license and provided training for lecture preparation, despite the existence of other available popular software.

Another issue of PNGUoT's online and blended education worthwhile for future consideration is the attendance rate. Instructors also noted in their evaluation report that there was a sharp decline in the attendance rate after the switch to the online system, with 73% of the instructors stating that less than 25% of the total students attended live lectures and only 13% accounted for over 75% of class attendance. This was largely blamed on lack of devices by some students, lack of know-how on how to on-board online classes, and general fear and anxiety emanating from COVID-19, among many other excuses. The University needs to develop approaches to incentivizing students to attend online classes.

The online/blended system has also changed how students are being assessed. The online feature currently in vogue mostly favours written exams and multiple-choice questions rather than the traditional group projects and term papers, quizzes and tests in Mathematics and other technical exams. Online tools that convert mathematical equations into digital format and 'workarounds' such as uploading complex formatting as pictures have been part of the solution. But educators have to be able to identify technical solutions to challenges of teaching and assessing technical graphical concepts online. Whereas the university had invested in Camtasia software, it seemingly benefited instructors rather than students when it comes to assessments because students equally needed an interactive board where they could graphically present their calculations virtually. The qualitative responses reflect the challenges associated with online assessments: "While in Zoom we see people's faces on the screen, it's hard to reach out and build rapport with them. I'm missing a walk to the library or playing sports and even hanging out with our colleagues. Besides, I don't seem to understand the entire online assessment processes since they leave a lot to be desired". Quantitative responses reveal that blended learning experiences might remedy students' struggles. 36% of instructors use rubric cube methods for assessing answers which involve a lengthy write-up, and 28.6% of instructors do not even bother to set this kind of question in their assessments of the students. Furthermore, rather than implementing the regular assessment of students based on a point-based marking or other formatted structure, most instructors (28.6%) preferred to use a pass or fail method for student assessment which might have disadvantaged some students. The results indicate a need to train instructors on assessments.

On the general experience gained from the usage of the online system, another set of data showed that an average number of students were satisfactorily able to utilize the new method in adjusting to the new educational system. At the same time, most instructors were not sufficiently able to manage this shift. It is clear that addressing online learning gaps (for both students and teachers) now will minimize disruptions in students' education journeys and enable them to have high-quality teaching–learning experiences.

Last but not least, logistical and administrative support for instructors in preparing and conducting high-quality online programs might also significantly contribute to the overall effectiveness of OBTL. As posited by Fetzner (2003), technology is crucial, but it's the provision of enabling support that allows people to collaborate, be creative and thrive with the right technology without losing connections between teams. Premised on the work of Abdulrahman (2015), the learning institutions need to provide logistical support that involves adequate access to contemporary technology and related paraphernalia: both hardware and software. Combining with PNGUoT's experience, institutions are supposed to implement a framework for the provision of sustainable ongoing professional support in the use of ICT for their workforce. There should be targeted training that is informed by a needs analysis, and instructors should be incentivized to attend these capacity-building initiatives.

The post-pandemic era demands new models for higher education, and OBTL has proven itself an adaptable approach to teaching and learning. Universities are suggested to make strategic investments in ICT adoption and diffusion, as well as provide support to enable the campus community to benefit meaningfully from the availed technology through online and blended forms of education.

6.15 Case 14: The Right Time to Receive a Helping Hand: A Story of Blended Learning Practices at the University of Colombo[15]

Executive Summary

Technology-enhanced education has proven benefits for higher education. Having understood that, the University of Colombo has been using online learning technologies for their distance learning programmes, such as postgraduate and external bachelor's degree programmes. However, until 2017, the adoption of e-learning technologies in internal undergraduate programmes was minimal. With the support of the SFIT-blended learning project of UNESCO-ICHEI, Shenzhen, China, during 2017–2019, the University of Colombo could introduce blended learning practises in their internal undergraduate programmes.

---

[15] Authored by Thushani Alwis Weerasinghe, Senior Lecturer, University of Colombo School of Computing (UCSC), Sir Lanka. e-mail: taw@ucsc.cmb.ac.lk.

This project motivated all the lecturers to convert their courses to blended learning courses. During the project, the academic staff were trained on designing and developing blended learning content, activities, and e-assessments. By then, the faculties who did not have learning management systems (LMS) implemented Moodle LMS, and others upgraded their LMS. The lecturers researched blended learning practices and evaluated the effectiveness of their interventions. Their findings were presented at a blended learning symposium. At the end of the project, there were 50 blended learning courses, and 20 staff members qualified to train others on developing blended learning courses.

As a result, the university could face the pandemic more confidently. Blended learning policy drafted during the project was considered for improving teaching–learning quality frameworks and assessment criteria to improve online and blended teaching–learning practices in the university. Based on the experience, a checklist has been developed to ensure the quality of online learning courses in undergraduate and postgraduate degree programmes. The distance learning centre of the University of Colombo was renamed as Cyber Campus and broadened its vision to introduce international collaborations and expand its capabilities and services.

Today almost all the teaching–learning activities at the university are carried out online using the new blended learning approach of synchronous and asynchronous teaching–learning. All lectures conducted online are recorded and made accessible via LMS or Youtube. Therefore, most lecturers have already recorded video lectures that can be reused after editing if required. They can use these video lectures for developing other courses. Also, they can upload the videos to the LMS before the online class and practice the flipped-classroom approach to make their online sessions more interactive.

Introduction and Context

The University of Colombo is located in the heart of the commercial capital in Sri Lanka. It is the oldest and the best university in Sri Lanka (Cybermetrics Lab 2021). Currently, it has ten faculties, eight institutes, and one campus conducting internal undergraduate programmes.

Having understood that technology-enhanced education has proven benefits for higher education, the University of Colombo has been making a tremendous effort to adopt online learning technologies to their study programmes. Mainly, the student following distance learning programmes, such as postgraduate and external bachelor's degree programmes, received OBTL (Online and Blended Teaching and Learning) benefits. Some programmes had their own Learning Management Systems (LMS) and delivered courses online. For example, the Bachelor of Information Technology programme of the University of Colombo School of Computing introduced their LMS in 2006 with interactive learning content, activities, and quizzes. The students found this learning content very useful and effective. The research carried out at the university implies that blended learning practices can improve the effectiveness of teaching and learning activities at the university (e.g., Hewagamage et al. 2007; Someratna and Weerasinghe 2016). However, developing such highly interactive learning content needed skilled and dedicated staff. It was not feasible to keep such a staff team by many other faculties who depended totally on the government's financial support. As a result, the adoption of e-learning technologies in internal undergraduate programmes was minimal. Even though several faculty-level projects were conducted to introduce OBTL, adopting such practices to undergraduate programmes was not considered mandatory.

The staff had barriers such as a lack of information technology infrastructure and technical experts to support practising OBTL. Therefore, even the compulsory staff training programmes such as the Certificate in Teaching in Higher Education (CTHE) did not include OBTL in their curricula. Also, when designing curricula and courses, OBTL was not considered an essential component. However, the administration appreciated the lecturers who practised OBTL and created online course environments.

The Network Operating Centre introduced Moodle LMS to all the faculties and provided technical support to administer the systems. But the lecturers did not have the required knowledge and skills to develop online or blended learning content. In this needful situation, the university received tremendous support from its kind friend, UNESCO-ICHEI, Shenzhen, China. With the support of their blended learning project of UNESCO-ICHEI, which was titled "Shenzhen Funds-In-Trust (SFIT) Project on Seizing Digital Opportunities in Higher Education: Building staff capacity for ICT-driven innovation in Cambodia and Sri Lanka" and was conducted from 2017 to 2019, the University of Colombo could introduce blended learning practises to their internal undergraduate programmes.

The project could bring positive change to the teaching–learning practices. This paper discusses how the University of Colombo faced the challenge of introducing OBTL to their undergraduate courses.

Design and Implementation

The project was conducted in two phases: Phase I to train the staff to develop blended learning activities and Phase 2 to initiate faculty-level projects and introduce blended learning to internal undergraduate courses (See Fig. 6.37).

Each phase of the project was started by signing an agreement between the UNESCO-ICHEI and the University of Colombo. Planning was done collaboratively, involving all stakeholders of the project. The Bangkok Office of UNESCO supported the project administration by providing necessary budget lines, keeping track of the progress and sending review comments. The university appointed a

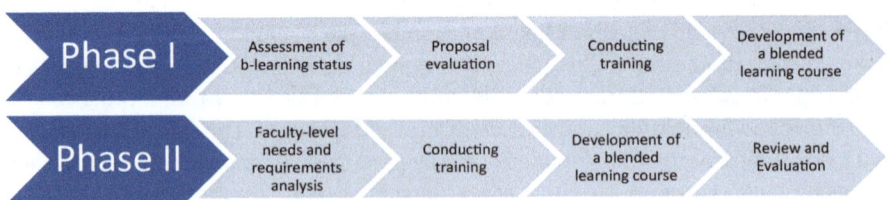

Fig. 6.37 Project phases

project coordinator and a steering committee to manage the project. The author of this paper played the coordinator's role. The steering committee consisted of the Rector of the campus, Deans of the faculties and the institute Directors. The Vice-Chancellor played the role of Project Director, and to advise the project coordinator and the team, two advisors were also appointed. This structure supported conducting all project activities very smoothly. The steering committee had meetings at least once a month to discuss the progress and solve the issues.

Phase I

It was started by assessing the status of blended learning practices using the self-assessment framework and tool of Lim and Wang (2016) and the possibility of practising blended learning at the university. By that time, the university had only 18 entities which consisted of faculties, institutes, a campus and a school. Each entity conducted the self-assessment and prepared a list of objectives and key performance indicators to measure and determine the achievement of objectives. As the second step of Phase I, each entity was requested to submit a proposal to improve their blended learning practices. By examining all proposals, the UNESCO-ICHEI identified one entity to develop an online course to practice blended learning.

The next step in Phase I was to conduct a capacity development programme for all university academic staff. This activity aimed to make "blended learning champions" who could take initiatives to introduce blended learning activities to curricula at their faculties or institutes of the university and lead their fellow academic staff members to implement policies and strategies required to practice blended learning activities. For this purpose, this activity attempted to achieve the following set of objectives;

develop positive attitudes towards blended learning in the academic staff,
increase the number of courses using blended learning practices,
develop action plans to carry out blended learning practices, and.
encourage a culture of sharing best practices of blended learning.

The responsibility for conducting these programmes was borne by the Staff Development Centre (SDC) and the University of Colombo School of Computing (UCSC). The programme conducted by the SDC discussed adult learner charac-teristics, learning theories and the difference between physical and virtual learning environments. Thereby, the SDC helped their programme participants determine the best practices and decide what learning activities should better be conducted in a blended learning approach. At the end of this programme, the participants had to present their improved syllabi incorporating blended learning activities.

The UCSC supported the programme participants in developing their blended learning activity development skills. The participants of the UCSC programme engaged in designing, developing and implementing sample online learning activi-ties.

Phase II

After successfully completing Phase I, Phase II of the project was launched in September 2018 in the presence of the Vice-Chancellor and with the participation of the steering committee. Five entities were selected to conduct mini-projects considering the number of students they have and the nature of the subject content they cover in their programmes. The five entities were Faculty of Arts, Faculty of Law, Faculty of Management and Finance, Institute of Agro-Technology and Rural Sciences and Sri Palee Campus. The overall purpose of this project was to increase access to quality higher education in Sri Lanka through technology and strategic partnerships that advance teaching and learning and promote effective institutional governance. To achieve this goal, the project aimed to achieve the following set of objectives.

Improve curricula and course syllabi based on the blended learning model at five academic entities of the University of Colombo.

Conduct applied research on effective and sustainable governance of blended learning at the University of Colombo.

Launch a pilot visiting faculty/partnerships scheme for sustaining blended learning.

At the initial stage of Phase II, the selected faculties improved curricula and course syllabi incorporating blended learning activities. All blended learning implementations were planned and conducted as action research (see Fig. 6.38).

Accordingly, the staff gathered data from the students and administration to determine the feasibility of conducting blended learning as curricular activities. They analysed the collected data and designed blended learning activities for selected sections in their course syllabi. The blended learning activities were designed and developed following the blended learning development process (see Fig. 6.39).

Since the blended learning process steps could be mapped easily with the steps in the action research process, the staff found their work interesting and got motivated to report and discuss their findings. The blended learning courses were evaluated by a panel appointed by the respective entity (faculty/institute/campus). The developers/lecturers of the best courses were invited to submit an abstract reporting their findings.

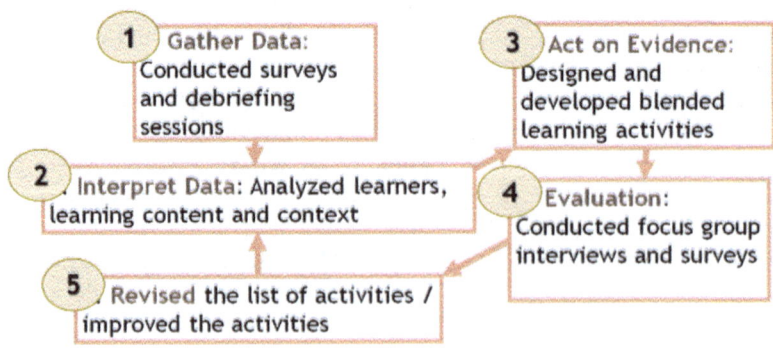

Fig. 6.38 Action research design

Fig. 6.39 Blended learning development process

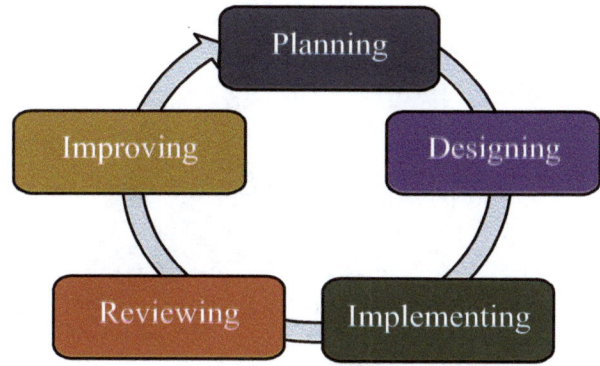

Also, they were allowed to present their findings at a blended learning symposium. The abstracts were collected and prepared a book of abstracts (University of Colombo 2018).

Results and Findings

The results of the self-assessment conducted at the beginning of the project were prepared considering only the seven faculties, four institutes and one campus as other entities failed to do and submit the analysis on time. The results are presented on a Radar Chart (see Fig. 6.40). It revealed that none of the dimensions had reached its topmost level (level 3). Also, six dimensions: (1) Curriculum, (2) Professional Development, (3) Infrastructure, Facilities, Resources and Support, (4) Policy and institutional structure, (5) Partnership and (6) Research and Evaluation- need more attention than the other two. Since the curriculum cannot be changed in the middle of a semester, the university decided to address the five other dimensions that required immediate attention (2–6) during the project. However, during the workshops conducted in Phase II of the project, the staff discussed how the curriculum could also be improved to accommodate blended learning practices.

Each entity's key performance indicator (KPI)s submitted were categorised and prioritised to prepare the following set of KPIs.
Number of staff using the LMS.

Number of Technical Staff recruitment and their availability.
Number of staff training workshops or discussions/year.
Stakeholder engagements.
Students' attendance percentage.
Number of publications related to O.B.T.L./year.
Students' satisfaction rate.
Students' performance evaluation marks.
Number of national and international partnerships.
Number of projects related to blended learning.
Number of new courses using blended or online learning technologies.
Number of courses receiving above 75% positive feedback from students.

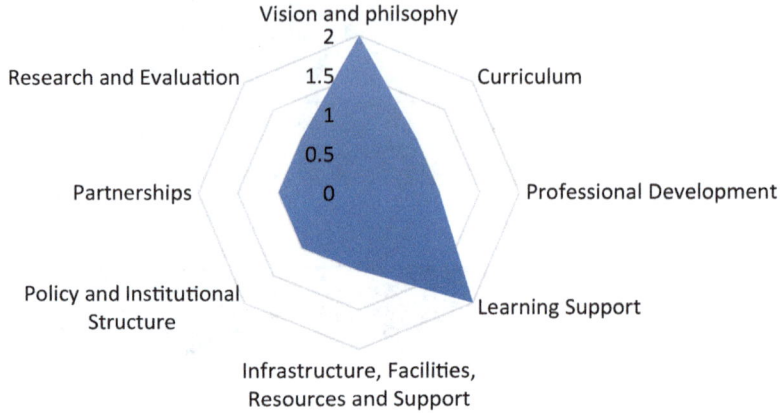

Fig. 6.40 Status of blended learning practices: areas that need particular concern

Number of IT-based teaching and assignment methods introduced.
Number of video courses developed.

Phase II of the project was conducted with five entities: Faculty of Arts, Faculty of Law, Faculty of Management and Finance, Institute of Agro- Technology and Rural Sciences and Sri Palee Campus of the university. Each faculty improved the syllabus of a selected course in one of their undergraduate programmes. The syllabi were evaluated using a checklist. The results of the evaluation are presented in Table 6.20.

The findings shown in Table 6.20 informed the requirement of preparing a blended learning policy, netiquette and a set of procedures and guidelines to support the students. This requirement was partly met by a resource person from the UCSC who shared all her resources with the other entities and explained how they could be customised to meet the entity requirements.

There were lecturers who had prior experience in practising blended learning (Weerasinghe 2018), and they were identified as resource persons to conduct training for other lecturers for the sake of efficiency. Accordingly, each entity conducted train-the-trainer programmes with the support of resource persons. Each programme consisted of four or five workshops. Participants of these workshops worked in teams to develop online courses to practice blended learning. Outcomes and findings of the activities and the current practices are summarised below with respect to the blended learning dimensions: (1) Professional development, (2) Learning support, (3) Research and evaluation, (4) Infrastructure, facilities, resources and support, (5) Internal partnership and collaboration and (6) Policy and institutional structure, which were aimed to enhance during Phase II of the project.

Professional development

Fifteen to forty staff members were trained with the support of blended learning champions at the entity and resources persons. The resource persons and the coordinators of train-the-Trainer workshops prepared online courses (see Fig. 6.41 for an

Table 6.20 Evaluation of blended learning syllabi

Evaluation of blended learning syllabi

Section A	Course outline	FoA	FoL	FoM	SP	IARS
1	Course Code	✓	✓	✓	✓	✓
2	Course title	✓	✓	✓	✓	✓
3	Semester, year	✓	✓	✓	✓	✓
4	Graduate/undergraduate credits	✓	✓	✓	✓	✓
5	Modality (online, in-class)	✓	✓	✓	✓	✓
6	Percentage of online and off-line (in-class) work	✓	✓	×	×	✓
7	Location for online work (lab, classroom, home etc.)	✓	✓	×	✓	✓
Section B	Course Information					
1	Course description and goal	✓	✓	✓	✓	✓
2	Course intended learning outcomes	✓	✓	✓	✓	✓
3	Prerequisite requirements clearly stated (technology and students' proficiency)	✓	✓	✓	✓	×
Section C	Instructional and Technological Information					
1	Required and recommended textbooks or ebooks.	✓	✓	✓	✓	✓
2	Online communication plan	×	×	✓	✓	✓
3	Help and support for students with special needs	×	×	×	×	×
Section D	Course Assignments and Assessments					
1	Asessment plan	✓	✓	✓	✓	✓
2	Asessment policy	×	×	✓	✓	✓
3	Feedback procedure	✓	✓	✓	✓	✓
4	Technical support during online assessments	×	×	×	×	×
Section E	Course Policies					
1	Expected behaviour of the students	✓	✓	✓	✓	×
2	Lecturer's role in the online learning enviornment	×	×	×	×	×
3	Attendance requirements	×	✓	×	×	✓
4	Netiquette	×	×	×	×	×
5	Deadline policy	×	×	×	✓	×
6	Copyright and intellectual property of online and shared materials	×	×	×	×	×
Section F	Weekly Content/Lesson Plan					
1	Intended Learning Outcomes	✓	✓	✓	✓	✓
2	Weekly topics	✓	✓	✓	✓	✓
3	Weekly schedule of readings and Activities	✓	✓	✓	✓	✓
4	Assignments and tests	✓	✓	✓	✓	✓
Section G	Course Administration					
1	Name, preferred title	✓	✓	✓	✓	✓
2	Contact information: phone, email	✓	✓	✓	✓	✓
3	Teaching Assistant	✓	✓	×	×	✓
4	Assistant's Contact information: phone, email	✓	✓	×	×	✓
	Count of ticks	22	23	20	22	23
	Done and OK.	✓				
	Done. But needs improvement	✓				
	Not done	×				

Faculty of Arts -	FoA
Faculty of Law -	FoL
Faculty of Management and Finnance -	FoM
Sri Palee Campus -	SP
Institute for Agro-technology and Rural Sciences -	IARS

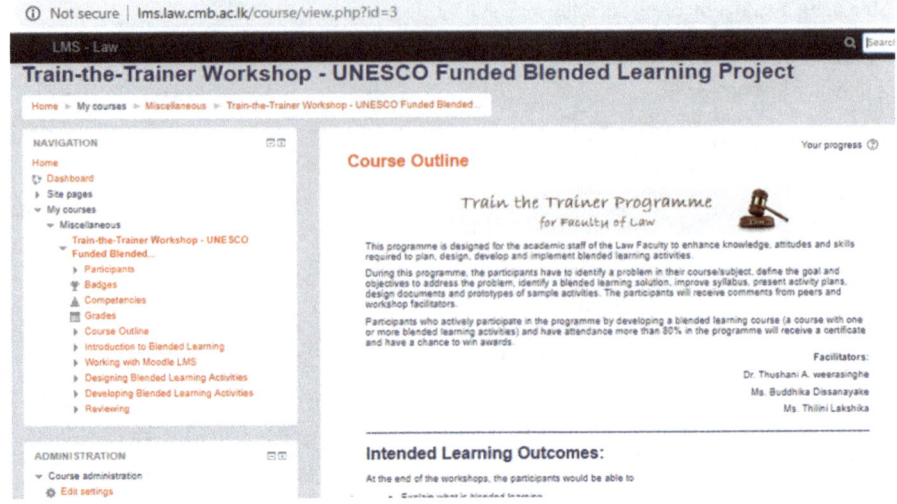

Fig. 6.41 Online course environment of blended learning programme at the law faculty

example) to share resources related to the workshops. These online courses shared tools and step-wise guides to develop blended learning activities.

The participants were trained to use tools such as H5P, Articulate and iSpring to develop interactive learning content that can be used before or after the lecture. Also, they used online tools such as Mentimeter (from www.mentimeter.com), Kahoot (from kahoot.com and kahoot.it) and Zeetings (from www.zeeting.com) to develop blended learning activities that can be conducted during lectures.

Training Outcomes

At the end of the training programmes, the participants could improve their knowledge and develop skills related to blended-learning activity development. They could design attractive online courses (An example is shown in Fig. 6.42). Also, there was a clear indication of enhancing positive attitudes towards e-learning and b-learning. Those who had negative attitudes towards e-learning and blended learning could at least share positive thoughts and ideas and appreciate the other's work.

Blended learning activities developed by the trainees:

The participants could develop different types of learning content. There were interactive online learning activities that could be attempted off-class/at home (See Fig. 6.43), blended learning activities that could be conducted during lectures (See Fig. 6.44) and Moodle LMS-based online quizzes to evaluate students' learning achievements.

The blended learning activities and online courses were evaluated using paper-based or online questionnaires (see Fig. 6.45) and interviews. The evaluation results informed that most students were delighted with the new learning method. For instance, a student at Management Faculty reported: "interactive contents enable

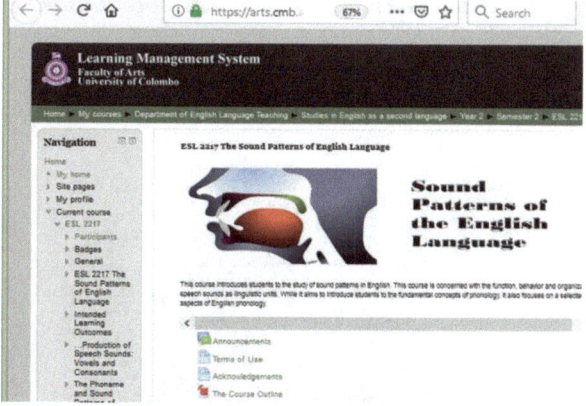

Fig. 6.42 An online course developed by art faculty

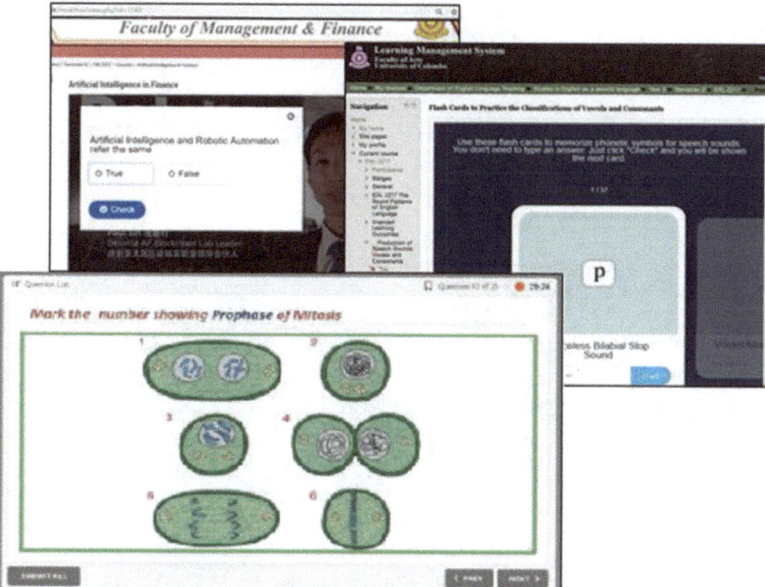

Fig. 6.43 Different types of activities developed by the entities

to overcome the boredom and enhance the understanding of the concepts" covered in the lesson. Online feedback received from a student at the Law Faculty revealed that the online activity helped them understand the lesson's key points, and practising blended learning in the classroom supported them to clarify doubts by engaging in discussions.

Fig. 6.44 A blended learning activities conducted during in-class lecture sessions

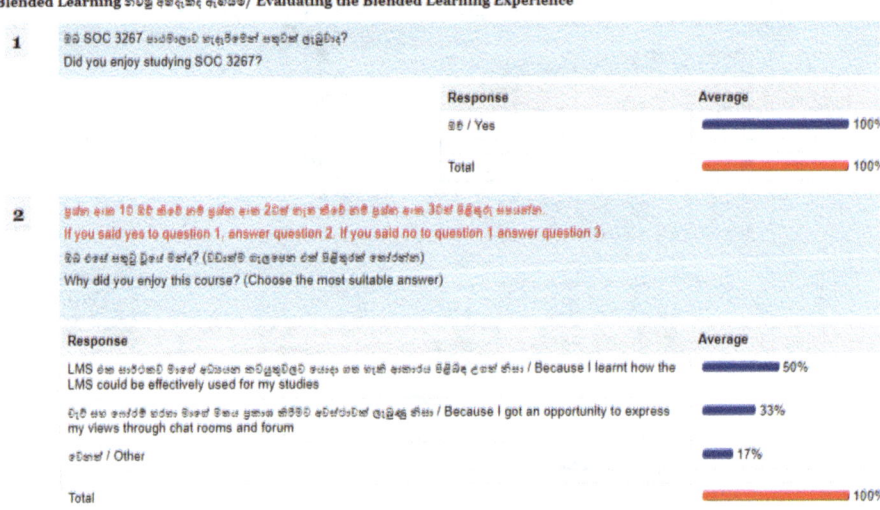

Fig. 6.45 A course evaluation questionnaire from art faculty

Learning support

Some lecturers had to develop course content in Sinhala medium too to support the students studying in the blended learning environment. The students were supported with online learning content, activities and assessments. All learning components were designed following instructional design guidelines such as Merrill's First Principles of Instruction (Merrill 2009), Gagne's Nine Events of Instruction (Gagne et al. 2005) and design principles and guidelines to promote individual and collaborative learning (Weerasinghe 2015). Therefore, lecturers could easily support the students' learning via online courses designed for blended learning. The students were facilitated through discussion forums and in-class face-to-face instructions during online activities. Also, LMS administrators and instructors of the relevant courses shared their contact information to support the students to solve their technical problems. The LMS administrators got motivated to upgrade their servers and keep monitoring system activities. Some entities organised special workshops for students to learn how to use the LMS.

Both lecturers and students highly appreciated this new approach and provided comments and suggestions to further improve the blended learning practices. For instance, lecturers suggested the importance of preparing a blended learning policy and incorporating blended learning into the programme evaluation criteria. A student reported that it is better to use forums for discussions than chat rooms as the forums are well organised and easy to follow.

Research and evaluation

Each entity developed 3 to 10 courses and selected the best courses for presenting at the symposium. Altogether there were 49 well designed online courses (Table 6.21). The results of their course evaluations and experience were reported in the book of abstract (University of Colombo 2018).

The entities had a common set of problems, such as lack of time to do learning activities during lecture hours, students' poor attention and attendance to lectures and poor or no interaction among the students and between the lecturer and the students. Blended learning activities were designed to address these problems as described in Sects. 2.2 and 3.1.2. Research studies were designed following the steps in Action Research (Elliot 1991) (See Fig. 6.38).

The findings informed that students were highly satisfied with the new approach and could learn effectively using it. For example, feedback received by Arts Faculty can be seen in Fig. 6.45.

The students' and lecturers' feedback and comments can be used to improve the blended learning practices in the future. For example, a student reported the importance of setting deadlines for forum discussions. It can be easily implemented with the forum settings in the Moodle LMS.

The students and the lecturers encountered several issues in developing and delivering blended learning activities and courses due to their lack of technical skills and infrastructure. More than 50% of the students have used their mobile phones to access the LMS resources and even attempt the quizzes. ITo address these kinds of issues, the university can invite the industry to provide a cheap and best solution for the students and lecturers. Also, many banks have already introduced loan schemes to support students in purchasing laptops.

Table 6.21 Number of online/blended learning courses developed

Entity	UCIARS	Sri Palee	Mgt	Law	Arts	Total
No. of courses	10	9	9	8	13	49

Infrastructure, facilities, resources and support

Most of the issues that the lecturers and students faced were related to the poor quality of the network connection, outdated software and lack of computers and required software to develop blended learning content. Also, the entities selected for the present study emphasised the importance of continuous support from the university's management, the Network Operating Centre and the UCSC for the sustainability of the blended learning practices at their entities.

Further, the entities insisted that their staff and the students need to have at least computers and an internet connection to practise blended learning at their entities. Since some students were having financial difficulties, they could not afford computers or the internet. Most of these students were from rural areas, and they stayed in university hostels. Therefore, one suggestion was to provide some computers and internet connection to the hostels and open more computer laboratories at the university.

Later, during the COVID-19 pandemic, this issue was addressed by offering computer loans through the University Grant Commission of Sri Lanka and the scholarships and donations provided by the external parties connected with the university. The Alumni Association of the university played a major role in this endeavour. With their support, the infrastructure issue could be solved to a greater extent. However, due to the geographical challenges and lack of landline connections to the internet, many students used mobile networks and often encountered connection drops.

Therefore, lecturers have to record all lectures, upload them to live stream platforms or Cloud services and share their links via the LMS. But students prefer to access all resources via LMS as it costs less, considering that the internet service providers introduce special rates for accessing data from school and university networks, and that it is easier to download from LMS than from commercial platforms. Since the university does not have adequate space in their servers to keep all video recordings, the lecturers are advised to delete the video files after keeping them accessible for one or two weeks. This strategy of recording, editing, uploading and deleting has increased the lecturers' workload drastically. Therefore, as a solution and with the consent from UNESCO-ICHEI, the university purchased data storage, spending the unutilised funds of the SFIT project. However, due to the increasing number of study programmes, courses, and students, the servers' storage space needs to be used carefully. A policy, guidelines and procedures should be prepared to support all users.

Internal partnership and collaboration

University of Colombo School of Computing (UCSC) has experience in teaching and developing blended learning courses. Therefore, UCSC supported the five selected entities to conduct Train-the-Trainer workshops during this project phase.

Also, the Network Operating Centre of the university provided constant support during the project by providing necessary instructions and guidance to solve network issues at the entities. Some faculties had old versions of LMS. As lecturers were not interested in online learning or blended learning, the faculty did not make any effort to improve their LMS. For instance, the Faculty of Law had an old version (Moodle 3.1) of Moodle, and there were several issues with their LMS. The staff were reluctant to use the system as it was too slow to respond. With the provision of the project, Law faculty could get support from the Network Operating Centre and the UCSC to solve their network and LMS issues. Thereby, they could get a new version of Moodle LMS (version 3.5) and transfer all the courses to the new LMS. The new system worked fast, and the staff were excited to work.

Policy and institutional structure: Policies and guidelines for faculty governance.

The applied research work at the entities informed that there should be sets of policies and guidelines to best practice blended learning at the entity and the university. The sets of policies and procedures identified by the entities are as follows.

Policies:

Faculty/entity level decisions should be taken by engaging with the curriculum review committee and quality assurance cell to promote the integration of blended learning.

All academic staff should undergo professional development programmes on blended learning.

IT infrastructure acquisition plans should be incorporated into the faculty strategic plans by periodically identifying infrastructure needs at the faculty/entity for promoting blended learning.

Rules and regulations of the faculty/entity should be revised to enable blended learning integrations.

All curricula of degree programmes should be improved to include blended learning activities.

All courses should have blended learning activities.

Conduct staff and student training programmes at the beginning of each academic year.

Strengthen internal as well as external partnerships for the sustainability of blended learning.

Promote research studies on blended learning.

Guidelines:

Entities informed that there should be guidelines to design syllabi for blended learning, preparing netiquettes, technical and service support, evaluation of blended learning courses, obtaining students' feedback and analysis for improvement, archiving of a digital repository for future resource sharing and management and applying for innovative teaching and research awards. Further, they identified the following guidelines.

Plan and design blended learning modules with the support of the pedagogical experts/subject matter experts and content developers and take into account resources available at the faculty/entity.

Get approval from the Quality Cell and Review committee at the faculty for faculty level consistency.

Organise and sequence teaching–learning activities in line with the faculty level academic calendar.

Provide required prior training for students and encourage student collaboration. Support students during the process.

Ensure that all the students have access to necessary technology before conducting specific blended learning activities such as online quizzes and assignments.

Monitor the status of the technology regularly and take necessary steps to rectify any issues.

Conduct staff training programmes to train the staff to use new technologies.

Introduce external partnerships to enhance the quality of blended learning practices.

Further, the faculties, campus and institute emphasised the importance of having a tool to assess the quality of online courses. Therefore, a checklist was prepared (See Annexe) based on our experience and referring to Weerasinghe et al. (2009) and Hill (n.d). The checklist was shared among the UCSC's academic staff and the Director, Centre for Quality Assurance (https://cqa.cmb.ac.lk/) for their comments and feedback.

Impact on Equity, Quality and Efficiency

During Phase I of the SFIT-Blended Learning project, the lecturers were trained on designing and developing blended learning content, activities, and e-assessments. By then, the faculties previously not having LMS implemented such a system, and others received expert support to upgrade their outdated versions. Since all entities used Moodle LMS software, it was easy to instruct how to design and develop the LMS-based online courses. At the end of Phase I of the project, 20 staff members qualified to train others on developing blended learning courses. They were the champions to promote online and blended learning practices at their faculties, institutes and the campus.

Phase II of the project motivated the lecturers to conduct research studies with their blended learning practices and evaluated the effectiveness of their interventions. Their findings were presented at a blended learning symposium organised by the project. At the end of the project, 50 courses used blended learning practises. The re-assessment of blended learning status conducted by the five entities that contributed to Phase II of the project revealed that the project supported improving all the dimensions (See Fig. 6.46).

The university could learn about its resources persons who can provide support to others. All entities of the university could strengthen their friendly ties with other entities. Thereby, they could be empowered with the knowledge and skills required to practice blended learning.

The project motivated the lecturers to convert their courses to blended learning courses. As a result, the university could face the COVID-19 pandemic more confidently. The students and the lecturers were ready to conduct teaching–learning activities online. According to Fig. 6.47, the students and the lecturers in the University of Colombo could use the LMS more than the other state universities in the country.

Since all lectures were recorded and shared online, the students who failed to be online during synchronous online sessions also could learn effectively. There was no

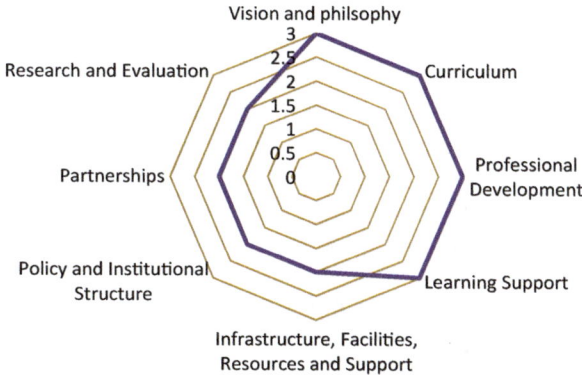

Fig. 6.46 Status of blended learning at the end-of-the project

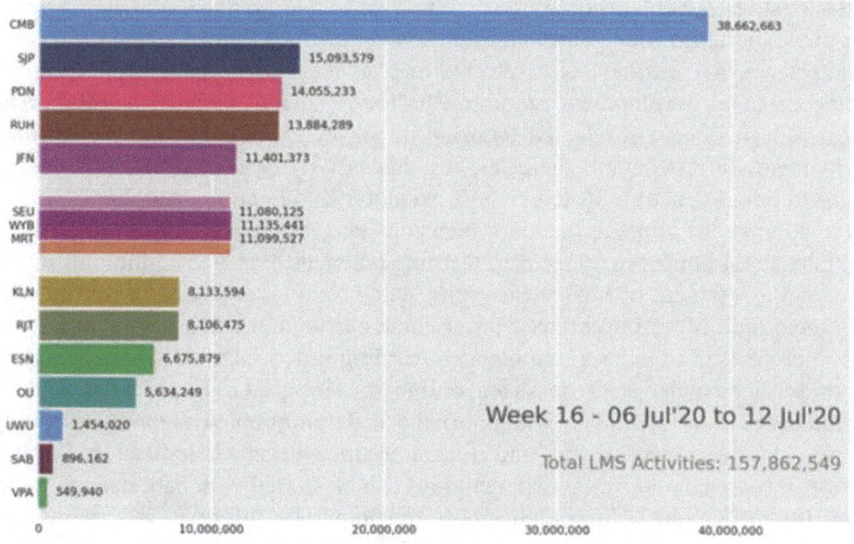

Fig. 6.47 A screen image from https://learnaclk.wordpress.com/

significant difference between the students' examination marks and pass rates before and during the pandemic.

Today almost all the teaching–learning activities at the university are carried out online using the new blended learning approach of synchronous and asynchronous teaching–learning. The distance learning centre of the University of Colombo was renamed as Cyber Campus and broadened its vision to introduce international collaborations and expand its capabilities and services.

Strengthening our friendship with the UNESCO-ICHEI, the university of Colombo has become a direct counterpart/partner of their project on the International Institute of Online Education (IIOE). As a major activity of its main platform, IIOE, UNESCO-ICHEI offered a new project to the university to co-develop a video course titled Video-based Learning Content Development for e-Learning and b-Learning, and the course will be delivered via IIOE. This course will support the academic staff of the University of Colombo and the universities in South Asia and African countries to design and develop video courses for the IIOE. It will be an excellent opportunity to share knowledge and experience in the regions and support each university to increase the efficiency of their study programmes.

Conclusion and Implications

The blended learning self-assessment conducted at Phase I revealed the status of blended learning practices and supported identifying the areas to be considered to promote blended learning practices at the university. Also, we could identify blended and online learning champions in each faculty. With that finding, the university entities could conduct staff training sessions further to disseminate the new knowledge and experience they gained during the project. Additionally, during Phase II of the project, five entities were selected to conduct mini-projects supporting the specific capacity development requirements for practising blended learning. The project activities were conducted focusing on six major dimensions: Professional development, Infrastructure, facilities, resources and support, Partnership, Policy and institutional structure, Research and evaluation and Learning support.

The attempts to improve the six dimensions and the findings informed that the university should improve its blended learning practices. For that, continuous monitoring and assessment of blended learning status can be conducted using the self-assessment tool. More importantly, programme curriculum and assessment criteria need to be revised to incorporate blended learning practices. Additionally, student support services such as help desks and online libraries need to be provided. Special consideration must be made to support the differently-abled students currently supported by the respective staff and student groups with much dedication. For this purpose, research and development activities can be started with national and international contributions to developing new and improved information systems and special devices.

The experience of the academic staff directly involved in the project and the students who participated in the blended learning activities informed that blended learning could make the learning more interesting and compelling. Based on the research findings conducted at the entities, the university attempted to prepare a set of policies and guidelines to practice blended learning. This draft set of policies and procedures needs to be improved based on the experience gained during the COVID-19 pandemic. Also, the checklist prepared to assess the quality of online courses (see Annexe) needs to be used to improve the existing course assessment rubrics and programme review criteria.

The university well appreciated the support received from the international partnership as it supported the university to get ready to face the pandemic competently.

With the new project on co-development of video courses and future projects, the university will work with the UNESCO-ICHEI more collaboratively, benefiting both parties and the world. Furthermore, the University of Colombo seeks international partnerships to collaborate with research studies. Thereby, the University of Colombo plans to make its' vision of blended learning to be realised.

Acknowledgement:

The former Vice-Chancellor of the University of Colombo, Senior Professor Lakshman Dissanayake, the Deans, Directors, Rector, entity-level project coordinators and the other university staff who supported conducting the SFIT-Blended Learning project during 2017–2019 are acknowledged for their dedicated contributions. Especially the lecturers who practised blended learning in their courses and submitted reports on their experience and students' feedback are highly appreciated. Moreover, the present Vice-Chancellor, Senior Professor Chandrika N. Wijerathna, who motivated all the staff to continue improving blended learning practices, is also acknowledged.

Annexe:

General information		√/X
1.	Course title: This should be clear and come on the top of the course home page	
2.	Course description: Brief description of the course describing the goal, major topics, activities, and assessments and what kind of learning behaviour is expected	
3.	Course outcomes: A list of course-level intended outcomes addressing higher-level thinking skills. All the outcomes (competencies) should be written from the learners' perspective. These competencies can be defined in the online course and linked with the course activities and assessments	
4.	Facilitators' information: Names and the contact information (emails) of the lecturers and the academic support staff members assigned to the course for delivering the course	
5.	Netiquettes: A link to read the netiquettes is provided	
6.	Terms of use and acknowledgement (if required) page: A page providing the copyright information and describing how students should use the content in the online course	
7.	Syllabus and schedule: Syllabus is prepared using the template shared by the faculty/department. An online course syllabus should provide the list of topics, time allocated for each major topic, schedule of continuous assessments, and the rubric for the final grade	

Quality Assurance Checklist for Blended/Online Learning Courses

Course structure		√/X
1.	Organise the course content in the order of the syllabus	
2.	Maintain consistency and use standard terminology to quickly identify different types of course components such as activities, notes, manual, section, sub-section, and assessments. E.g., Sect. 1: Introduction to programming	
3.	Easy to identify the main sections and sub-sections	
4.	Maintained consistency in designing section headings -considered font size, colour, and style	
5.	Content in each section has been organised in the same order (e.g., each section lists the teacher's note on the top)	
Lesson content		√/X
1.	All the content contributes to achieving the stated intended learning outcomes or competencies	
2.	Audio/video contents are audible enough and free of noise, and graphical content should be clear enough for understanding	
3.	Downloadable materials are cited where appropriate, and copyright information is provided	
4.	Links to supplementary content are updated and active	
5.	Content is current/updated	
6.	Tools/software needed to study/view the lesson content are readily available	
Activities		√/X
1.	They help the students to achieve the intended learning outcomes	
2.	Activities are well designed for authentic learning	
3.	Different types of activities have been designed to create interest	
4.	All activities encourage learners to engage in the learning process actively	
5.	Collaborative learning activities–encourage peer interaction and co-construction of knowledge	
6.	Instructions are clear	
7.	Deadlines are set and communicated to the students	
8.	The feedback procedure is planned and informed	
9.	Tools/software needed to do the activities are readily available	
10.	An adequate amount of time is allocated	
11.	Students' workload in the course has been considered	
Assessments		√/X/NA

(continued)

(continued)

Course structure		√/X
1.	Assignments have been aligned with the intended learning outcomes to measure the attainment of outcomes/competencies	
2.	Instructions are clear	
3.	The number of marks allocated for each assessment component is provided	
4.	The time allocated for the assessment is adequate	
5.	Assessments have been designed following the assessment preparation guidelines	
6.	Problem-solving/issue handling processes are identified, and relevant information has been provided to the students	
7.	Alternative methods of submissions have been identified and informed	
8.	All required devices and software to do the assessment and submit the answers are clearly stated	
9.	Tools/software needed to do the assessments are readily available	
10.	Ample time is allocated to do the pilot assessment	
11.	Marking and feedback processes have been defined	
12.	The grade book has been set up	
Course delivery		√/X
1.	Announcements–send announcements to pass messages to all the students–e.g. Welcome to the course and regarding zoom sessions, assignment deadlines and online assessments	
2.	Send private messages to address issues of individual students–send messages to the students who do not attend online sessions, not complete activities and assignments	
3.	At least once in two weeks, check the activity reports and students' participation in the course activities	
4.	Send reminders to the students who do not access the course for more than two weeks	
5.	Check all links and verify they are valid and active	
6.	Hide the links of overdue assignments or add restrictions to make them inactive automatically	
7.	Delete the irrelevant/old content that you need not have in the course	

If lecturers design their course evaluations, they can refer to the following checklist to ensure they have designed it appropriately.

Course evaluation checks		√/X
1.	Whether the design of each course component (lesson content, activities and assessments) is good	
2.	Whether the structure of the course is clear	
3.	Easiness to navigate and find the required content	
4.	Clarity of the instructions	
5.	Relevancy of the content	
6.	Readability of the downloadable material	
7.	Quality of the multimedia (audio, video and graphic content)	
8.	Adequacy of the time allocated for each assignment component and activity	
9.	Adequacy of the learner support during assessments	
10.	The usefulness of the feedback	

6.16 Case 15: The Philippines: Post-COVID Educational Innovations from Practices and Challenges of Teacher Education Institutions During the Pandemic[16]

Executive Summary

The emergence of the COVID-19 global outbreak brought unprecedented disruptions in people's daily lives worldwide. Community quarantines were imposed as the only measure to limit the spread of the virus. As regular face-to-face interaction became restricted, in-person classes were inevitably suspended. In the Philippines, millions of learners were affected by this educational crisis; thus, learning continuity amidst the pandemic emerged as a major concern. The situation demands an immediate transition from traditional to online or alternative learning modes.

At the tertiary level, the Commission on Higher Education (CHED) in the Philippines formulated the guidelines for flexible learning implementation or CHED Memorandum Order No. 4, series of 2020 (CMO 4, s2020). Although flexible learning is derived as the best possible solution, it requires a major transformation of the higher education landscape. Consequently, higher education institutions (HEIs) were challenged to make immediate preparations and drastic adjustments to keep up with the rapid paradigm shift in education and technology.

Meanwhile, most teacher education institutions (TEIs) in the country took the lead in flexible learning implementation. Hence, this study examined the responses of select TEIs regarding their flexible learning implementation as constituted in

---

[16] Authored by Jerome T. Buenviaje, Ph.D., Dean, College of Education, University of the Philippines Diliman.

CMO 4, s2020. Data were analyzed through various components of flexible learning modalities, which are also the theoretical lenses of this article. Through the responses of these seven (7) TEIs from the three major islands of the Philippines, valuable practices, challenges, and innovations emerged. These are later presented as key lessons and opportunities from the pandemic that can serve as a reference for future practices and research.

Introduction and Context

The Philippine government imposed a total lockdown in mid-March 2020 as a primary measure to prevent the widespread of COVID-19 disease (Presidential Proclamation 922). This historical event disrupted the usual activities and has brought crises in different sectors such as business, manufacturing, tourism, education, performing arts, agriculture, and other industries. According to Yu et al. (2020), the prolonged community quarantines or lockdowns in the Philippines had a consequential impact on the nation's economy. Specifically, it affected the national economy and resulted in a 16.5% decrease in the second quarter of the 2020 national GDP (Philippine Statistics Authority 2020).

The education sector likewise has been greatly affected by the prolonged lockdowns in the country. UNESCO (2020) identified over 28 million Filipino learners at the basic and higher education institutions who have been affected by the strict quarantine measures imposed by the government. Since the Philippines has a trifocalized education system, respective policies were crafted by the Department of Education (DepEd) for the basic education, Technical Education and Skills Development Authority (TESDA) for the technical-vocational programs, and Commission on Higher Education (CHED) for the tertiary education and graduate studies. However, the unifying objective is to provide guidelines for the continuity of learning in this time of emergency.

The issuance of a CHED Memorandum Order (CMO) was an imperative response to the never-before-seen challenges in the Philippine higher education sector during the pandemic. Particularly, CMO No. 04, series of 2020 or the Guidelines on the Implementation of Flexible Learning for public and private Higher Education Institutions serves as a guide to more than 2000 higher education institutions (HEIs) across the 17 regions of the country. Anchored on Republic Act (RA) 7722 or Higher Education Act of 1994 and RA 11,469 or Bayanihan to Heal as One Act, the core purpose of this policy is to ensure the continuity of providing quality, inclusive, and accessible education in times of crisis, where traditional teaching modalities are no longer possible. Its full implementation began in Academic Year 2020–2021.

CMO 4, s2020 describes flexible learning as a learner-centered, pedagogical approach that complements outcomes-based education. It allows learners and teachers to customize learning experiences depending on the unique needs of learners, such as the place, process, pace, and products of learning. The delivery mode of learning can be face-to-face, in-person learning, out-of-classroom, or a combination of these. "The main objective should be to provide learners with the most flexibility on the learning content, schedules, access, and innovative assessment, making use of digital and non-digital tools" (Republic of the Philippines Office of the President 2020, p. 3).

Facing inevitable drastic transitions with limited preparation time, all HEIs were challenged to immediately transform the entire education system by adopting flexible learning and making whatever necessary adjustments and innovations to achieve learning continuity for all students amidst the pandemic. Looking on the bright side, this policy has promoted collaborative culture, facilitated innovations, solidified learner-centeredness, and expanded learning opportunities. Likewise, this policy has served as a catalyst because it compelled different stakeholders to rethink alternative ways to challenge the status quo. It has become instrumental for expediting the long-overdue transformations that consider different contexts and possibilities.

In particular, the role of teacher education institutions (TEIs) in this time of crisis is crucial to the higher education sector where it operates and the basic education system for which it serves. Therefore, this case study presents the policy implementation of select TEIs in line with CMO 4, s2020 using the components of various learning modalities as the analysis lens. The participants comprise public and private universities representing the three major islands of the Philippines (three from Luzon, two from Visayas, and two from Mindanao) and elaborate their valuable experiences that gave birth to creativity and innovation in their contexts.

Design and Implementation

The implementing guidelines of CMO 4, s2020 were formulated and adopted by all HEIs in the country as an immediate response to the need for learning continuity during the pandemic. Through flexible learning, the education sector can thrive in times of national emergencies when face-to-face learning delivery is not viable. The fundamental principle of flexible learning is to address the diverse situation of learners where they experience many contextual challenges and limitations. It also facilitates customizable learning environments, thus allowing learners to have more control over the educational process (Isaias et al. 2020). In this approach, learners have the freedom to manage the place, process, pace, and products of learning.

According to CMO 4, s2020, all HEIs should implement flexible learning by integrating it as a complementary approach to the outcomes-based education approach (Tyler 2013). They should continue to observe the applicable existing policies, standards, and guidelines (PSGs) to assure teaching and learning quality. However, HEIs must make their autonomous judgment regarding the deployment of alternative modes of delivery, given that the decision must be "reasonable, transparent, and outcomes-based validated" (CHED COVID-19 Advisory No. 6). This means that HEIs can maximize the flexibility in delivery modes and assessment as long as each course's essential learning outcomes are achieved. Hence, flexible learning serves as the best option to ensure the continuity of providing inclusive, accessible, and quality education.

Furthermore, the policy mandates all CHED Regional Offices to require all HEIs to develop and submit their Learning Continuity Plan (LCP) at the beginning of the Academic Year 2020–2021 as a mechanism for monitoring and sustainability. Through this plan, articulation of readiness and responsiveness to the needs for undisrupted learning and resilient learning continuity can be observed. With the bulk of changes in the content, system, and procedures, the policy necessitates HEIs to implement or promote capacity-building programs for staff and administrators on the transition to flexible learning. HEIs are also required to develop their learning content by reviewing and adjusting curricular offerings to deliver learning whether offline, blended, or online (Republic of the Philippines Office of the President 2020).

Specifically, this case study looked at how TEIs implemented the various components of flexible learning modalities as follows:

Policies

The importance of policy at the institutional level operationalizes CMO 4, s2021 in consideration of the unique context of the TEIs covered in this study. Based on the gathered data, planning and policy designs were crafted based on their resources and capabilities. For instance, De La Salle University shared:

"We have the Academic Support for Instructional Services and Technology (ASIST) unit, which provides training in curriculum design, pedagogical techniques, and educational technologies. It also supports users of the university's Learning Management System."

This shows the importance of a context-based policy to implement flexible learning successfully. It includes the enhancement of the design, content, and delivery of instruction in different programs, regular review and recalibration of the curriculum, and management of innovative teaching. Specifically, developed modules and course files are covered by a copyright policy. This manifests adequate attention to copyright laws, especially when building online courses that require many resources (Nilson and Goodson 2021).

Overview and Orientation Guide for Students and Teachers

Information dissemination is crucial in conducting flexible learning among TEI participants. In this way, teachers and students are given opportunities and tools to participate in the program effectively. The Table 6.22 shows some guidelines and strategies employed by the University of the Philippines Diliman (UPD) to prepare its faculty and students for remote learning.

Technology

The use of technology has become a necessity more than ever in the time of education emergency. CMO 4, s2020 provided an opportunity for most of the TEIs to improve their technological infrastructure directly utilized for teaching and learning. Specifically, participating HEIs in this study ensured the quality of connectivity in their campuses. They acquired or developed necessary learning management systems (LMSs) and applications that have enabled them to conduct synchronous and asynchronous classes. This is a major development for these TEI; according to Sistek-Chandler (2020), the development of standard LMSs supports an inclusive learning environment. The balanced combination of synchronous and asynchronous modes help address both convenience and social interaction needs.

Table 6.22 Some UPD activities in preparation for remote learning

Faculty	Students
Online teaching readiness consultation Taking stock and gearing up webinar-workshop Gear UP for remote learning and innovation workshop (OVPAA* 2020–75) Program redesigning Faculty survey on availment of interest-free computer loans to enhance teaching in the time of Covoid-19 (OVPAA 2020–83) Guidelines for the submission of resource requirements for remote learning (OVPAA 2020-68B) Guidelines on using or incorporating copyrighted works into course packs; FAQs regarding faculty copyright over course packs (OVPAA 2020–91) Logistical support for printing and distribution of course packs (OVPAA 2022–93) Course pack preparation and incentives (OVPAA 2020–92)	Survey on internet access and preferred flexible learning modality Special program of the office of vice chancellor for student affairs on devices/ gadgets and other forms of assistance Infographics and online manual on remote learning FAQs for remote learning UP academic and student affairs roadmap (OVPAA 2020–100) Facilitation of enlistment of students (OVPAA 2020–101)
Academic plans for AY 2020–2021 and timetable for dialogues with faculty, students, staff, and concerned parents (OVPAA 2020–68) Webinar on the use of University Virtual Learning Environment (UVLE)	

* Office of the Vice President for Academic Affairs

Content and Learning Materials

The most common learning materials adopted by TEIs in their flexible learning consist of electronic modules, digital tools subscription, and LMS when internet connection and devices are available for the students. However, for those with limited internet access, materials include learning packets and printed modules that can be distributed or picked up from the campus. In both modalities, TEIs develop instructional materials following step-by-step guidelines. Using a re-calibrated syllabus, learning plan, or task analysis blueprint, instructional materials were developed, reviewed, uploaded, or printed for distribution This shows that providing a well-crafted guide or exemplar is crucial to coherent content development, especially when faculty create course content without professional assistance (Hillman et al. 2021).

Evaluation and Assessment

Despite the challenges presented by flexible learning on evaluation and assessment of students' learning, TEI participants ensured that this is not neglected in the re-calibrated course syllabi. The development of content and learning materials should include appropriate evaluation and assessment that aligns with the intended learning outcomes. In the case of Bukidnon State University, a review of rubrics for online performance tasks was conducted alongside their content and learning materials preparations. On the other hand, Mariano Marcos State University required the faculty to upload their modules with corresponding summative examinations through their virtual learning environment. These are just proof that some LMS platforms are effective for summative assessment (Hillman et al. 2020) and formative assessment in the form of feedback that is pivotal to support student learning during the pandemic (Guskey 2020). However, designing assessments can be very challenging because they threaten the academic integrity of the learning process (Khan et al. 2021).

Support Services

This study also identified three essential support services that TEIs need to effectively implement flexible learning: learner support, professional support, teaching and learning support, and ICT support. Appropriate learner support should stem from learners' actual needs and contexts, such as their capacity-building needs, student workload, and student preference of learning modality. Professional support provides staff with incentives, technical aid and service, and essential pedagogy and educational technology training. Meanwhile, teaching and learning support encompasses mechanisms that encourage instructional innovation, develop a conducive learning environment, ensure quality education, and promote continuous student improvement. ICT support also includes the provision of technological devices and continuous support to online learning platforms such as LMS. Toquero (2020) considered these as strengthening student support and staff training on instructional online teaching that are crucial responses of HEIs in the Philippines.

Impact on Equity, Quality, and Efficiency

In the time of the COVID-19 pandemic, CMO 4, s2020 has served as a unifying policy for more than 2000 HEIs in the Philippines. Based on the most recent record of CHED (2020), the overall HE enrollment is 3,408,425, while the total TEI enrollment is 671,421 in Academic Year 2019–2020. Specifically, data presented in this study apply to the faculty and students of the seven teacher education institutions as shown below (Table 6.23).

From these select TEIs, valuable practices on flexible learning were explored in line with the contextual implementation of CMO 4, s2020. Since these TEIs play a vital role in their respective universities, the study looked at the challenges of flexible learning, key lessons from their practices, and how these served as a model to other degree programs.

Challenges of Flexible Learning

There are four main challenges that TEIs encounter in their flexible learning implementation. The primary challenge deals with resources such as the stability and reliability of internet connectivity and the availability of devices or gadgets that should be used for teaching and learning. In addition, TEIs experience the limitations of some learning activities and assessments that need to be conducted with social interactions and the use of campus amenities and facilities. The learning environment also emerged as one of the challenges, given that some learners or faculty cannot avoid distractions at home. The finding of Barrot et al. (2021) revealed that

Table 6.23 Number of faculty and student enrollment of select TEIs in the Philippines

Higher education institution	Teacher education undergraduate program enrollment	College of education faculty	
		Full-time/ regular	Part-time
1. Bukidnon State University	1323	94	8
2. Capitol University	536	13	9
3. Cebu Normal University	3263	260	100
4. De La Salle University	365	40	106
5. Mariano Marcos State University	2441	74	0
6. University of the Philippines Diliman	370	53	15
7. University of San Agustin	338	113	40

the learning environment (e.g., noise, limited space) is the most difficult problem to address. Lastly, staff's integrity and capacity to deal with human emotions are also considered a challenge for stakeholders who lack ICT training and are hesitant to embrace change. Similarly, Chan et al. (2022) highlighted human factors as one of the challenges to online teaching and learning in higher education. This also concerns addressing health risks when necessary to go to the campus and ensuring that proper work and life balance is considered. In the research of Dayagbil et al. (2021), Pawilen (2021), and Rotas and Chapay (2020) identified similar challenges that Filipino higher education students face in the remote learning setup. Therefore, these challenges can be used as rich sources of information on how to possibly address the gaps presented in this education emergency.

Key Lessons Learned from Flexible Learning Practices

Even at this unfortunate time, the "gifts of the pandemic" have brought innovations and creativity among the TEIs participating in this study. The primary key lesson brought by flexible learning policies and implementation is directed to the importance of considering the context of every learner and what the institution can do about it. Specifically, the available resources and mechanisms can be utilized to ensure that all students are given equitable opportunities to study during the pandemic. Below is a simplified model about this resilient action (Fig. 6.48).

Another important element for successful flexible learning is having systematic communication between teachers and learners. This study shows the importance of effective communication to policy success through creative and accessible means such as social media messaging, discussions or forums in the LMS, and the most common email threads. In addition, the feedback mechanism through these communication platforms is not solely about academic activities but also about fostering student–teacher engagement and looking after the well-being of the students. Finally, despite high-stake investment and limited resources, improvement of technological

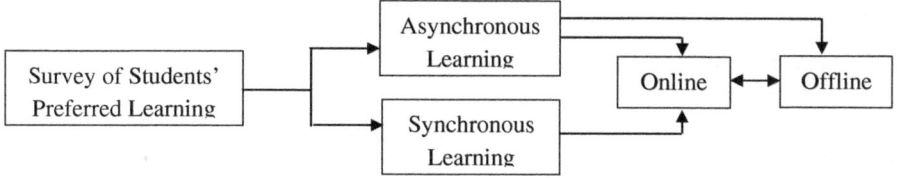

Fig. 6.48 Pathways of flexible learning

infrastructures and upskilling of teachers on ICT must be maintained. These are important prerequisites of flexible learning that higher education systems must take as a valuable lesson. In terms of teachers' capacity building, this study highlights the significance of regular training on utilizing educational technology, which should be central to the professional development programs of every university.

All these meaningful lessons in the implementation of flexible learning during the pandemic must be foundational to the revitalized higher education system immediately after the pandemic and in creating a sustainable future. Beyond these challenging times, HEIs should search for the silver lining, such as taking the opportunity to upscale online teaching capacity (Hillman et al. 2020), integrate 21st-century skills in online learning design (Munday 2021), develop new knowledge and pedagogy (Pawilen 2021), and strengthen research effort to improve student learning amid another educational crisis (Toquero 2020).

Flexible learning practices that serve as a model to other degree programs

Teacher educators' significant role and contribution have become evident in the higher education sector because of the need to upscale flexible learning that they practiced even before the pandemic. For instance, most of them spearheaded the pedagogy committee of their universities to train faculty members from other disciplines. In particular, re-designing courses and learning delivery strategies were imparted by TEIs based on their research publications, innovative practices, and pre-pandemic experiences.

With CMO 4, s2020 serving as a national framework, there are many initiatives contributing to the equity, quality, and efficiency of different HEIs. For instance, the flexible learning practices of TEIs were imparted to other HEI faculty members through a series of webinars. Many teacher educators became resource speakers and facilitators in the course pack preparation, effective teaching–learning approaches, and appropriate assessment strategies. All these are manifestations that well-developed courses in terms of design and teaching practices based on best practices give the most satisfaction to learners and faculty (Lederman 2020). Moreover, the research findings of Ashraf and colleagues (2021) revealed that course design is a significant predictor of online learning effectiveness. In this case, other faculty members benefit from teaching and learning centers and instructional designers, thus speeding up the preparations for remote teaching (Greene 2020) and therefore making these TEIs at the forefront of flexible learning implementation.

Conclusion and Implications

This case study presents the contextual implementation of CMO 4, s2020 among the select TEIs in the Philippines. Using the various components of flexible learning modalities as a theoretical lens, the study revealed the fundamental significance of institutional policy on flexible learning that must be based on the institution's contexts, resources, and capabilities. This institutional policy anchored on CHED policy must be well disseminated to the teachers, students, and other stakeholders to ensure positive reception and participation. Since effective communication is one of the key elements to policy success, there should be an established and strong line of communication between teachers and learners through available and appropriate means to promote healthy student–teacher engagement, relevant mentoring, and feedback mechanisms. The integration of technology in flexible learning during the pandemic has brought major progress in the digital transformation of the Philippine higher education system. Through the transformation process, content and learning materials development and evaluation and assessment have been digitized (becoming print-based to cater to the needs of students that do not have technological resources) and digitalized (improving equity, quality and efficiency through digital means). Finally, flexible learning during education emergencies requires strong support services, specifically on logistics, training, and well-being.

The flexible learning experiences of the TEI participants presented challenges and opportunities that can be a reference for further practice and scholarship. The challenges of flexible learning in this study focus on the lack of resources to deliver equitable higher education. This suggests that the government must allocate funds to improve the necessary technological infrastructures further so that education can propel in the direction that it should take. HEIs can establish partnerships with industries such as telecommunication companies, professional or civil society organizations, and international or local agencies to address the challenges on internet connectivity and other concerns. HEIs must also prioritize ICT training and upskilling of faculty to align with the agile education environment that the pandemic has highlighted. Sharing of resources through consortia, coalition, or networking can be put together to optimize capacity-building programs across different organizations.

There are also valuable lessons that higher education institutions can learn from the flexible learning practices during this pandemic. These can be the way forward for future practices and research. Some of the practices that can be beneficial even after the pandemic primarily include maintaining the virtual learning environment or LMSs and other digital tools. This is to maximize opportunities and time management in the proper integration of traditional and blended learning. Likewise, it is important to consider a schedule that integrates in-campus and work-from-home arrangements to promote work and life balance among education professionals.

Finally, based on the challenges of blended learning implementation, some recommendations for future research can be on (1) discovering effective learning activities and assessment techniques, (2) managing change that involves staff quality in terms of capacity and human behaviour, (3) exploring the concept of learner-centeredness in higher education, and (4) developing 21st-century learning skills through hybrid learning.

References

Abdulrahman, M. A. (2015). Enriching professional practice with digital technologies: faculty performance indicators and training needs in Saudi higher Education. International Journal of Instructional Technology and Distance Learning, 12 (1): 44–57.

About Unitech I PNG University of Technology. (n.d.). Retrieved March 7, 2022, from https://www.unitech.ac.pg/About_Unitech.

Addi, R. A., Benksim, A., Amine, M., & Cherkaoui, M. (2020). Covid-19 outbreak and perspective in morocco. *Electronic Journal of General Medicine*, *17*(4), 19–20.

Agarwal, A. (2021). The new normal of education. Presented at the 4th Cyber Education Forum Webinar, ICE Institute, 29 July, 2021.

Ajadi, T. O., Salawu, I. O., & Adeoye, F. A. (2008). E-learning and distance education in Nigeria. *Turkish Online Journal of Educational Technology*, *7*(4), 61–70.

Ali, W. (2020). Online and remote learning in higher education institutes: A necessity in light of COVID-19 Pandemic. *Higher Education Journal, 10*(3), 16–25.

Amin, M.E. (2005). Social science research: Conception, methodology and analysis. Kampala, Makerere University, Uganda.

Ashraf, M., Ashraf, S., Ahmed, S., & Ullah, A. (2021). Challenges of online learning during the COVID-19 pandemic encountered by students in Pakistan. *Journal of Pedagogical Sociology and Psychology*, 3(1), 36–44.

Badarch D. (2019, October 17) Open Education "Delivering Open Education for All". Fliphtml 5. Retrieved March 5, 2022, from: https://fliphtml5.com/wvtme/iltr/basic.

Barrot, J. S., Llenares, I. I., & Del Rosario, L. S. (2021). Students' online learning challenges during the pandemic and how they cope with them: The case of the Philippines. *Education and information technologies*, 26(6), 7321–7338.

Bazeley, P. (2009). Analyzing qualitative data: more than 'identifying themes'. *The Malaysian Journal of Qualitative Research, 2*, 1–18.

Beijing Declaration on MOOC Development (2020, December 11). Retrieved March 5, 2022, from: https://mooc.global/gmc/beijing-declaration-on-mooc-development/.

Belawati, I. T., Nizam, I., Letak, P., Darmanto, B. A., Des, S., Kover, P., ... & Belawati, I. T. (2020). Potret pendidikan tinggi di masa covid-19.

Boddy, C. R. (2016). Sample size for qualitative research. *Qualitative Market Research: An International Journal, 19*(4), 426–432.

Borasi, R., DeMartino, R., Harris, N. & Miller, D. (2022). Could COVID – 19 be a catalyst for disruption in higher education?. In Chan, R. Y., K. Bista, & R. M. Allen (Eds.), Online teaching and learning in higher education during COVID - 19. *International Perspectives and Experiences* (pp.153–166). London: Routledge.

Brion, C., & Cordeiro, P. A. (2018). Lessons learned from a training of tTrainers model in Africa. *Journal of Educational Leadership and Policy Studies*, 2(1), 1–10.

Brooks, D.C., Grajek, S. & Lang, L. (2020, 9 April). Institutional readiness to adopt fully remote learning. Why IT Matters to Higher Education, EDUCAUSE Review. https://er.educause.edu/blogs/2020/4/institutional-readiness-to-adopt-fully-remote-learning.

Bughio, I. A., Abro, Q. M. M., & Rashdi, P. R. S. (2014). Effective online distance learning in Pakistan and challenges. *International Journal of Management Sciences*, 2(6), 274–279.

Champagne, E., & Granja, A. D. (2021). How the COVID-19 pandemic may have changed university teaching and testing for good. *The Conversation, 6.*

Chan, R. Y., Bista, K., & Allen, R. M. (Ed.). (2022). Online teaching and learning in higher education during COVID-19. *International Perspectives and Experiences*. London: Routledge.

Chan, R. Y., Bista, K., & Allen, R. M. (Eds.). (2021). *Online teaching and learning in higher education during COVID-19: International perspectives and experiences*. Routledge.

CHED. (2020). *Higher Education Graduates by Discipline Group AY 2010–11 to 2018–19*. https://ched.gov.ph/wp-content/uploads/Higher-Education-Graduates-by-Discipline-Group-AY-2010-11-to-2018-19.pdf.

Cheng, Y. C. (2003). Quality assurance in education: Internal, interface, and future. *Quality Assurance in Education, 11*(4), 202–213.

Cuaton, G. P. (2020). Philippines higher education institutions in the time of COVID-19 pandemic. *Revista Românească pentru Educaţie Multidimensională, 12*(1 Sup2), 61–70.

Cybermetrics Lab (2021, December 02). Ranking web of universities. Webometrics. Retrieved from: https://www.webometrics.info/en/asia/sri%20lanka%20.

Czuba, J. (2020). Future-proofing access, quality and delivery in Papua New Guinea's Higher Education sector. *DHERST Quarterly Newsletter, 3*(1), 10.

Dam, L. (2022). Pandemic Pedagogy. Disparity in university remote teaching. In R. Y. Chan, K. Bista, & R. M. Allen (Eds.), Online teaching and learning in higher education during COVID - 19. *International Perspectives and Experiences* (pp.28–38). London: Routledge.

Dayagbil, F. T., Palompon, D. R., Garcia, L. L., & Olvido, M. M. J. (2021, July). Teaching and learning continuity amid and beyond the pandemic. In *Frontiers in Education* (Vol. 6, p. 678692). Frontiers Media SA.

Dhawan, S. (2020). Online learning: A panacea in the time of COVID-19 crisis. *Journal of educational technology systems, 49*(1), 5–22.

El Gourari, A., Raoufi, M., Skouri, M., & Ouatik, F. (2021). The implementation of deep reinforcement learning in E-learning and distance learning: Remote practical work. *Mobile Information Systems, 2021*, 1–11.

Elliot, J. (1991). *Action research for educational change*. McGraw-Hill Education (UK).

El Gourari, A., Skouri, M., Raoufi, M., & Ouatik, F. (2020). The future of the transition to e-learning and distance learning using artificial intelligence. *Proceedings of the International Conference on E-Learning, ICEL, 2020-Decem*, 279–284.

El Gourari, A., Raoufi, M., & Skouri, M. (2022). *Formulating Quizzes Questions Using Artificial Intelligent Techniques* (Ben Ahmed M., Teodorescu HN.L., Mazri T., Subashini P., Boudhir A.A. (eds); pp. 535–547). Springer, Singapore.

Erdenet Institute of Technology. Erdenet Institute of Technology. (n.d.). Retrieved March 7, 2022, from https://edx.eit.edu.mn/.

Espino-Díaz, L., Fernandez-Caminero, G., Hernandez-Lloret, C. M., Gonzalez-Gonzalez, H., & Alvarez-Castillo, J. L. (2020). Analyzing the impact of COVID-19 on education professionals. Toward a paradigm shift: ICT and neuroeducation as a binomial of action. *Sustainability, 12*(14), 5646.

Faboyede, S. O., Faboyede, A. O., & Fakile, S. A. (2017). Funding of University education in Nigeria: challenges and prospects. *European Journal of Social Sciences Studies, 2*(8), 221–238.

Feoktistov, A. V., Trofimenko, O. N., Ognev, S. P., Lyakhovets, M. V., & Koynov, R. S. (2020). Digital educational platform as a personnel management tool. Journal of Physics: Conference Series, 1691(1).

Fetzner, M. J. (2003). Institutional support for online faculty: Expanding the model. *Elements of quality online education: Practice and direction, 4*(229–241).

Fiji Bureau of Statistics. (2017). 2017 Census Report. Retrieved March 7, 2022, from: https://www.fiji.gov.fj/Media-Centre/News/Fiji-Bureau-of-Statistics-Releases-2017-Census-Res.

Flanagan, B. (2021, March 26). Covid-19 silver linings: Technology has helped universities be more innovative and inventive. University Affairs. https://www.universityaffairs.ca/opinion/in-my-opinion/covid-19-silver-linings-technology-has-helped-universities-be-more-innovative-and-inventive/.

Gagne, R., Wager, W. W., Golas, K. C., & Keller, J. M. (2005). *Principles of instructional design*. Belmont, CA: Thomson Wadsworth.

Ganbat D. & Purevsuren, T. (2021, December 6). Implementation of the online professional development program during COVID-19 Pandemic: Case study for Mongolian University of Science and Technology (MUST). *Global MOOC and Online Education conference*. Retrieved March 5, 2022, from: https://www.xuetangx.com/live/live20211201m001/live20211201m001/10117562/16350647.

García Aretio, L. (2020). *Los saberes y competencias docentes en educación a distancia y digital. Una reflexión para la formación* [Teachers' knowledge and competences in distance and digital education. A reflection for teaching]. RIED. *Revista Iberoamericana de Educación a Distancia*, 23(2), pp. 09–30.

Garcia, M., Perez, L. D., Hayashi, R. (2021). Accreditation of online courses in higher education—Early adopters in the European Union, India, Indonesia, and Malaysia . Asian Development Bank.

Gautam, G. R. (2021). Digitization efforts of Tribhuvan University: Responding to COVID – 19 and Beyond. *TU Bulletin Special Issue* 2021. TU. Nepal.

Government of Mongolia (2002, January 25). Distance Education National Program 2002–2010. *Unified Legal Information System*. Retrieved March 5, 2022, from https://legalinfo.mn/mn/det ail/2825/2/201090.

Government of Mongolia (2005). E-Mongolia National Program.

Government of Mongolia. (n.d.). "Vision-2050" long-term development policy of Mongolia. Retrieved March 5, 2022, from https://cabinet.gov.mn/wp-content/uploads/2050_VISION_LONG-TERM-DEVELOPMENT-POLICY.pdf.

Government Palace, Ulaanbaatar (2020, August 28). Resolution of the State Great Khural of Mongolia #24 Approval of the Action Plan of the Government of Mongolia for 2020–2024. *Cabinet Secretariat of Government of Mongolia*. Retrieved March 5, 2022, from: https://cab inet.gov.mn/wp-content/uploads/2020-2024_-ActionPlan_GOM_Eng_Edited_OE-2.pdf.

Greene, J. (2020, March 17). Keep calm and keep teaching: Shifting unexpectedly to remote instruction requires as many human solutions as technology solutions. *Inside Higher Ed*. https://www.insidehighered.com/advice/2020/03/17/shifting-unexpectedly-remote-instruction-requires-many-human-solutions-tech.

Gullapalli, S &Ren, P. (2019). ICE institute and digital education in Indonesia. Official Presentation to the MORTHE by Darden School of Business, University of Virginia, Jakarta.

Guskey, T. R. (2020). Assessments and grading in the midst of a pandemic. *Education Week*.

Haris, A. (2021, April 19). Kesiapan UI dalam Kegiatan Belajar Mengajar (KBM) Tatap Muka [Readiness of UI in Face-to-Face Teaching and Learning Activities]. Universitas Indonesia.

HEC. (2020). Work from home policy template Faculty Guidelines. *In Backstage at workable*. https://resources.workable.com/work-from-home-company-policy.

HEC, P. (n.d.-b). Graduates having 16 years of Education and above from Universities Campuses and Affiliated Colleges including Distance Learning (Provisional). Retrieved December 5, 2021, from https://hec.gov.pk/english/universities/Pages/AJK/Graduates-16-years.aspx.

HEC. (n.d.-a). COVID-19 Technology Support Committee. Retrieved from https://www.hec.gov.pk/english/HECAnnouncements/Documents/nCoVirus/Approved-Working-Paper.pdf.

Helmy, R., Khourshed, N., Wahba, M. & Abd El Bary, A. (2020). Exploring critical success factors for public private partnership case study: The educational sector in Egypt. *Journal of Open Innovation: Technology, Market, and Complexity*, 6(142), 1–27.

Hewagamage, K. P., Premaratne, S. C., & Peiris, K. H. R. A. (2007). Design and development of blended learning through LMS. *Blended Learning*, 15, 279–291.

Heymann, J., Sprague, A. R., Nandi, A., Earle, A., Batra, P., Schickedanz, A., Chung, P. J., & Raub, A. (2017). Paid parental leave and family wellbeing in the sustainable development era. *Public Health Reviews*, 38(1), 1–16.

Hill, L. (n.d.) Online course development pack. Welch Centre For Graduate and Professional Studies, Goucher College. https://www.goucher.edu/learn/graduate-programs/distance-learning-resour ces/documents/ONLINE_COURSE_DEVELOPMENT_PACKET_ONL_050819.pdf.

Hillman, D., Schudy, R., & Temkin, A. (2020). *Best practices for administering online programs.* Routledge.

Hitchcock, L. (2007). Industry certification and academic degrees: Complementary, or poles apart? *Proceedings of the 2007 ACM SIGMIS CPR Conference on Computer Personnel Research 2007,* April 19–21, 2007, St. Louis, Missouri, USA.

Hodges, C., Moore, S., Lockee, B., Trust, T., & Bond, A. (2020). The difference between emergency remote teaching and online learning. *Educause.* Retrieved March 7, 2022, from https://er.educause.edu/articles/2020/3/the-difference-between-emergency-remote-teaching-and-online-learning.

Hodgkinson-Williams, C., & Arinto, P. (2017). Adoption and impact of OER in the Global South (p. 610). African Minds.

https://e.huawei.com/en/publications/global/ict_insights/201907041409/talent-cosystem/huawei-ict-academy.

Huawei TEDD (2022). Huawei ICT academy: Building a talent ecosystem and boosting the ICT industry's development. Retrieved from:

Isaias, P., Sampson, D. G., & Ifenthaler, D. (Eds.). (2020). *Online teaching and learning in higher education.* Berlin/Heidelberg, Germany: Springer International Publishing.

Joaquin, J. J. B., Biana, H. T., & Dacela, M. A. (2020, October). The Philippine higher education sector in the time of COVID-19. In *Frontiers in Education* (Vol. 5, p. 208). Frontiers.

Keser, H., & Semerci, A. (2019). Technology trends, Education 4.0 and beyond. *Contemporary Educational Researches Journal,* 9(3), 39–49.

Khan, Z. R., Sivasubramaniam, S., Anand, P., & Hysaj, A. (2021). 'e'-thinking teaching and assessment to uphold academic integrity: lessons learned from emergency distance learning. *International Journal for Educational Integrity,* 17, 1–27.

Khan, M. T. & Molendijk, S. (2020, June 29). Papua New Guinea: Reinventing learning in the time of corona. GPE Transforming Education. Global Partnership for Education and UNICEF Papua New Guinea. https://www.globalpartnership.org/blog/papua-new-guinea-reinventing-learning-time-coronavirus.

Laurillard, D., Kennedy, E., & Wang, T. (2018) How could digital learning at scale address the issue of equity in education? In C. P. Lim & V. L. Tinio (Eds.), *Learning at scale for the global south* (pp. 1–31). Quezon City, Philippines: Foundation for Information Technology Education and Development.

Lederman, D. (2020, July 8). What worked this spring? Well-designed and -delivered courses. *Inside Higher Ed.* http://www.insidehighered.com/digital-learning/article/2020/07/08/what-kept-stu dents-studying-remotely-satisfied-spring-well.

Lembaga Layanan Dikti III. (2020). Sinergi Perguruan Tinggi di Tengah Pandemi[University Synergy in the Midst of the Pandemic]. Jakarta: LLDikti III.

Lim, C. P., & Wang, T. (2016). A framework and self-assessment tool for building the capacity of higher education institutions for blended learning. *Blended learning for quality higher education: Selected case studies on implementation from Asia-Pacific,* 1–38.

Lincoln, Y. S., & Guba, E. G. (1985). *Naturalistic Inquiry.* Newbury Park, CA: Sage Publications.

Lion, R. & Stark, G. (2010, Sept 22). A glance at institutional Support for faculty teaching in an online learning environment, Why IT Matters to Higher Education, EDUCAUSE Review. https://er.educause.edu/articles/2010/9/a-glance-at-institutional-support-for-faculty-teaching-in-an-online-learning-environment.

Mehmood, S., Chong, L., & Hussain, M. (2018). Females higher education in Pakistan: an analysis of socio-economic and cultural challenges. *Advances in Social Sciences* Research Journal, June. https://doi.org/10.14738/assrj.56.4658.

Merrill, M. D. (2009). First principles of instruction. In C. M. Reigeluth & A. Carr (Eds.), *Instructional design theories and models: Building a common knowledge base (Vol. III)*. New York: Routledge Publishers.

Mgaiwa, S. J. & Poncian, J. (2016). Public–Private partnership in higher education provision in Tanzania: Implications for access to and quality of Education. Bandung: *Journal of the Global South*, 3(6), 1–21.

Ministry of Education and Science of Mongolia. (2021, April 24). Дээд боловсролын чанарын баталгаажуулалтын хөтөлбөрт Сингапуртай хамтран ажиллаж байна. Retrieved March 5, 2022, from https://www.meds.gov.mn/post/65998.

Modelo Educativo PUCP [PUCP Educational Model]. (2021). Lima: Pontificia Universidad Católica del Perú.

Mongolian open online courses - index. *Mongolian Open Online Courses. (n.d.)*. Retrieved March 7, 2022, from http://www.mooc.edu.mn/.

Moore, J. L., Dickson-Deane, C., & Galyen, K. (2011). E-Learning, online learning, and distance learning environments: Are they the same? *Internet and Higher Education*, 14(2), 129–135.

Moorhouse, B. L. (2020). Adaptations to a face-to-face initial teacher education course 'forced' online due to the COVID-19 pandemic. *Journal of Education for Teaching*, 1–3.

Mormina, M. & Pinder, S. (2018). A conceptual framework for training of trainers (ToT) interventions in global health. *Globalization and Health*, 14(100), 1–11.

Morocho, M., Instituto Latinoamericano y del Caribe de Calidad en Educación Superior a Distancia (CALED), Universidad Técnica Particular de Loja (UTPL-Ecuador) (Editores). (2021). El Aseguramiento de la Calidad de la Educación Superior en Latinoamérica y el Caribe, en tiempos de COVID-19: visión de las Instituciones de Educación Superior.

Nargis, A. R. A. (2012). Gender discrimination in education–a barrier in development of female education at higher secondary level. *DEZBATERI SOCIAL ECONOMICE nr. 2/2012.*

National University of Mongolia. (n.d.). 'МУИС-ийн цахим хичээл'. Retrieved March 7, 2022, from https://online.num.edu.mn/.

Nations, U. (2018). United nations sustainable development framework for Pakistan. In Pakistan One United Nations Programme III (OP III). https://pakistan.un.org/en/44136-un-sustainable-development-framework-2018-2022.

Nilson, L. B., & Goodson, L. A. (2021). *Online teaching at its best: Merging instructional design with teaching and learning research*. John Wiley & Sons.

Noreen, S., & Hafeez, A. (2016). Challenges of digital learning for distance universities of Pakistan. *Gomal University Journal of Research*, 32(1), 69–80.

Nuru, S. T., Fred, S., Oyekola, P., & Ngene, C. T. (2021). Resourcing as an antecedent of effective online learning adaptation in the face of COVID-19: The case of papua new guinea university of technology (PNGUoT). *Journal of Education, Society and Behavioural Science*, 34(2), 80–89.

OECD. (2016). *Innovating Education and Educating for Innovation: The Power of Digital Technologies and Skills*. OECD Publishing, Paris.

OECD. (2020). *Lessons for Education from COVID-19 A Policy Maker's Handbook for More Resilient Systems*. OECD Publishing.

Ouatik, F., Raoufi, M., Mohadab, M. El, Ouatik, F., Bouikhalene, B., & Skouri, M. (2019). Modeling collaborative practical work processes in an e-learning context of engineering electric education. *Indonesian Journal of Electrical Engineering and Computer Science*, 16(3), 1464–1473.

Oyo, B., Maiga, G., & Muyinda, P. B. (2019). Online courseware development in public universities in Uganda: The precepts of active, passive and exclusive participation. In *e-Infrastructure and e-Services for Developing Countries: 10th EAI International Conference, AFRICOMM 2018, Dakar, Senegal, November 29–30, 2019, Proceedings 10* (pp. 12–23). Springer International Publishing.

Pannen, P. (2019). Indonesia online education and quality assurance. *Higher Education Dialogue on the ASEAN Vision*, 2025, 29–30.

Papua New Guinea University of Technology (PNGUoT). (2021). Heads of Departments' Annual Report. (Unpublished).

Pardo Kuklinski, H.& Cobo, C. (2020). *Expandir la universidad más allá de la enseñanza remota de emergencia. Ideas hacia un modelo híbrido post-pandemia* [Expanding the university beyond emergency remote teaching. Ideas towards a post-pandemic hybrid model]. Outliers School. Barcelona.

Parentela, G., & Vargas, D. (2021). Pandemic Era (COVID-19) and higher education in the Philippines against the world perspective: A literature survey analysis. *Available at SSRN 3786765.*

Pawilen, G. T. (2021). Preparing Philippine higher education institutions for flexible learning during the period of COVID-19 Pandemic: Curricular and instructional adjustments, challenges, and issues. *International Journal of Curriculum and Instruction, 13*(3), 2150–2166.

Pedro, N. S., & Kumar, S. (2020). Institutional support for online teaching in quality assurance frameworks. *Online Learning, 24*(3), 50–66.

Philippine Statistics Authority. (2020). GDP drops by 16.5 percent in the second quarter of 2020; the lowest starting 1981 series. Retrieved from http://www.psa.gov.ph/national-accounts/sector3/Gross%20Domestic%20Product.

Pond, W., K. (2002). Twenty-first century education and training Implications for quality assurance. *Internet and Higher Education, 4*, 185–192.

Presidential Proclamation 922. (2020). Declaring a state of health emergency throughout the Philippines. Manila, Philippines: Malacañang Palace. Retrieved from https://www.officialgazette.gov.ph/downloads/2020/02feb/20200308-PROC-922-RRD-1.pdf.

Qureshi, I. A., Ilyas, K., Yasmin, R., & Whitty, M. (2012). Challenges of implementing e-learning in a Pakistani university. *Knowledge Management and E-Learning, 4*(3), 310–324. https://doi.org/10.34105/j.kmel.2012.04.025.

Renagi, O. (2021, January 20). *Welcome to the papua new guinea university of technology.* Papua New Guinea University of Technology. https://www.unitech.ac.pg/unitech/welcome.

Republic of the Philippines Office of the President. (2020). Guidelines on the Implementation of Flexible Learning. (CHED Memorandum Order No. 4. Series of 2020). Retrieved from: https://ched.gov.ph/wp-content/uploads/CMO-No.-4-s.-2020-Guidelines-on-the-Implementation-of-Flexible-Learning.pdf.

Richter, T., & McPherson, M. (2012). Open educational resources: education for the world?. *Distance education, 33*(2), 201–219.

Robila, M. (2016). Families, mental health and well being: pursuing sustainable development goal 3. *In United Nations Expert Group Meeting.* https://www.un.org/esa/socdev/family/docs/egm16/MihaelaRobila.pdf.

Rosales, R. (2021, March 12). *Online learning in the post pandemic world.* University Affairs. https://www.universityaffairs.ca/opinion/in-my-opinion/online-learning-in-the-post-pandemic-world/.

Rotas, E., & Cahapay, M. (2020). Difficulties in remote learning: Voices of Philippine university students in the wake of COVID-19 crisis. *Asian Journal of Distance Education, 15*(2), 147–158.

Rummler, G. A., & Brache, A. P. (1995). *Improving Performance: How To Manage the White Space on the Organization Chart. The Jossey-Bass Management Series.* Jossey-Bass, Inc., 350 Sansome Street, San Francisco, CA 94104.

Schmid, R. F., Bernard, R. M., Borokhovski, E., Tamim, R. M., Abrami, P. C., Surkes, M. A., ... & Woods, J. (2014). The effects of technology use in postsecondary education: A meta-analysis of classroom applications. *Computers & Education, 72*, 271–291.

Sethi, G. K., & Saini, N. K. (2020). COVID-19: opinions and challenges of school teachers on work from home. *Asian Journal of Nursing Education and Research, 10*(4), 532–536.

Shah, D., Amin, N., Kakli, M. B., Piracha, Z. F., & Zia, M. A. (2018). Pakistan education statistics 2016–17. *In National Education Management Information System (NEMIS) Academy of Educational Planning and Management (AEPAM),* Pakistan (Issue 25).

Siemens, G. (2015). Preparing for the digital university: A review of the history and current state of distance, blended, and online learning.

Simbulan, N. P. (2020). The Philippines–COVID-19 and its impact on higher education in the Philippines. The Head Foundation.

Singh, G., & Hardaker, G. (2014). Barriers and enablers to adoption and diffusion of eLearning: A systematic review of the literature–a need for an integrative approach. *Education+ Training*.

Sistek-Chandler, C. M. (2020). Exploring online learning through synchronous and asynchronous instructional methods. Advances in Mobile and Distance Learning (AMDL) Book Series. *IGI Global*.

Someratna, P. & Weerasinghe, T. (2016). Exploring student interactions through classroom and computer-supported collaborative learning, In *EDULEARN16 Proceedings* (pp. 2194–2200). Valencia, Spain: IATED.

Soyolmaa, D. (2021, April 14). UN explores opportunities to accelerate Mongolia's digitalization agenda. *United Nations Mongolia*. Retrieved March 5, 2022, from https://mongolia.un.org/en/124798-un-explores-opportunities-accelerate-mongolias-digitalization-agenda.

Staff, D. T. (2020). Increasing blended and online learning in PNG universities: The DWU experience. *Devpolicy Blog*.

Steinbeck, H., Matthiessen, J., & Vladova, G. (2019). Student learning behaviour in the digital age. *ICIS 2019 Proceedings. 7*.

Sustainable Development Goals (SDGs). Retrieved from https://sdgs.un.org/goals.

Susilo, D. (2020). Revealing the effect of Work-From-Home on job performance during the Covid-19 crisis: empirical evidence from indonesia. *The Journal of Contemporary Issues in Business and Government, 26*(1), 23-40.

Swanson, A. C. (2010). Establishing the best practices for social interaction and e-connectivity in online higher education classes.

Tallent-Runnels, M. K., Thomas, J. A., Lan, W. Y., Cooper, S., Ahern, T. C., Shaw, S. M., & Liu, X. (2006). Teaching courses online: A review of the research. *Review of educational research, 76*(1), 93–135.

Toquero, C. M. (2020). Challenges and opportunities for higher education amid the COVID-19 pandemic: The Philippine context. *Pedagogical Research, 5*(4).

Torrecillas, C. (2020) *El reto de la docencia online para las universidades públicas españolas ante la pandemia del Covid-19*. [The challenge of online teaching for Spanish public universities in the face of the COVID-19 pandemic]. ICEI Papers COVID. Instituto Complutense de Estudios Internacionales. Retrieved from: https://www.ucm.es/icei/file/iceipapercovid16.

Tria, J. Z. (2020). The COVID-19 Pandemic through the lens of education in the Philippines: The New Normal. *International Journal of Pedagogical Development and Lifelong Learning, 1*(1), ep2001.

Tuul, S., Banzragch, O., & Saizmaa, T. (2016). E-learning in Mongolian higher education. *International Review of Research in Open and Distributed Learning, 17*(2), 181–197.

UNESCO IESALC International Institute for Higher Education in Latin America and the Caribbean. (2020). *COVID-19 y Educación Superior: De los efectos inmediatos al día después, análisis de impactos, respuestas políticas y recomendaciones* [COVID-19 and Higher Education: From the Immediate Effects to the Day After, Analysis of Impacts, Political Responses and Recommendations].

UNESCO (2004). *Integrating ICTs into education: lessons learned: a collective case study of six Asian countries*. UNESCO Office Bangkok and Regional Bureau for Education in Asia and the Pacific.

UNESCO. (2005). *Regional guidelines on teacher development for pedagogy-technology integration*. Bangkok, Thailand: UNESCO Asia and Pacific Regional Bureau for Education.

UNESCO. (2013, June). *Quality Assurance in Higher Education*, Education sector technical notes. https://unesdoc.unesco.org/ark:/48223/pf0000222126.

UNESCO. (2016a). *Curriculum*. Retrieved from http://www.unesco.org/new/en/education/themes/strengthening-education-systems/quality-framework/core-resources/curriculum/.

UNESCO (2016b). *Blended learning for quality higher education: Selected case studies on implementation from Asia-Pacific*. UNESCO Bangkok Office.

UNESCO. (2020). National education responses to COVID-19 summary report of UNESCO's online survey. Retrieved March 7, 2022, from https://unesdoc.unesco.org/ark:/48223/pf0000 373322.

UNESCO (2021). ICT in Education Policy Review Report Mongolia.

UNESCO, G. (2020). Education: From disruption to recovery. *UNESCO Building peace in the minds of men and women. https://en. unesco. org/news/covid-19-educational-disruption-and-response, Accessed on, 3,* 2020.

UNESCO, ICHEI, I. (2021). IIOE Quality Assurance 2.0: Framework and Toolkit for Driving and Supporting online and Blended Teaching and Learning (Vol. 2). https://ichei.org/Uploads/Dow nload/2021-11-19/61975ec315b6e.pdf.

UNESCO-ICHEI. (2021). IIOE competency framework for the higher education workforce (IIOE-CFHEW). In Suggestions on IIOE-CFHEW from the pre-consultation meetings on 15 July 2021 & Exective summary of IIOE-CFHEW (Vol. 1). https://ichei.org/Uploads/Download/2021-08-26/61274c28ee5f6.pdf.

United Nations. (2020). *Policy Brief: Education during COVID-19 and beyond.* https://www.un.org/development/desa/dspd/wp-content/uploads/sites/22/2020/08/sg_policy_brief_covid-19_and_education_august_2020.pdf.

United Nations. (n.d.). Sustainable Development Goals | United Nations in Pakistan. Retrieved December 5, 2021, from https://pakistan.un.org/en/sdg.

United States Agency for International Development (USAID). (2014). African higher education: Opportunities for transformative change for sustainable development.

University of Colombo (2018, December 13). *Book of Abstracts: Symposium on Blended Learning for Quality Higher Education*, University of Colombo, Sri Lanka. [Unpublished e-Book]

UPM Strategic Plan 2021–2025. Retrieved from https://pspk.upm.edu.my/upm_strategic_plan_2 021_2025-2998.

van Laar, E., van Deursen, A. J. A. M., van Dijk, J. A. G. M. & de Haan, J. (2020). Determinants of 21st-Century skills and 21st-Century digital skills for workers: A systematic literature review. *SAGE Open, 10*(1), 1-14.

Van Tiem, D. M., Moseley, J. L., Dessinger, J. C., Hartke, G., & Phillips-Hudson, Y. (2001). Fundamentals of performance technology: A guide to improving people, process, and performance. *Performance Improvement, 40*(3), 60–63.

Verger, A., & Moschetti, M. (2016). Public-Private partnerships as an education policy aApproach: Multiple meanings, Risks and Challenges. *Education Research and Foresight Series*, No. 19. Paris, UNESCO. Retrieved from: https://en.unesco.org/node/268820.

Weerasinghe, T. A., Ramberg, R., & Hewagamage, K. P. (2009). *Designing online learning environments for distance learning. Instructional Technology*, 21 [Online]. http://itdl.org/journal/mar_09/article03.htm.

Weerasinghe, T. (2015). *Designing online courses for individual and collaborative learning: A study of a virtual learning environment based in Sri Lanka* (Doctoral dissertation, Department of Computer and Systems Sciences, Stockholm Univeristy).

Weerasinghe, T. A. (2018, July). An evaluation of different types of blended learning activities in higher education. In *2018 IEEE 18th International Conference on Advanced Learning Technologies (ICALT)* (pp. 42–45). IEEE.

Weller, M. (2020, 12 March). *The COVID-19 online pivot: The student perspective.* LSE Blog. Retrieved from https://blogs.lse.ac.uk/impactofsocialsciences/2020/03/12/the-covid-19-online-pivot-adapting-university-teaching-to-social-distancing/.

Yarrow, N. & Afkar, R. (2021, September 17). Rewrite the future: How Indonesia can overcome the student learning losses from the pandemic and increase learning outcomes for all. World Bank Blogs. https://blogs.worldbank.org/eastasiapacific/rewrite-future-how-indonesia-can-ove rcome-student-learning-losses-from-the-pandemic.

Young, J. R. (2002). The 24-hour professor: online teaching redefines faculty members' schedules, duties, and relationships with students. *The Chronicle of Higher Education*, A31-A33. Retrieved from https://www.chronicle.com/article/the-24-hour-professor/.

Yu, K. D. S., Aviso, K. B., Santos, J. R., & Tan, R. R. (2020). The economic impact of lockdowns: A persistent inoperability input-output approach. *Economies, 8*(4), 109.

Zhang, W., Wang, Y., Yang, L., & Wang, C. (2020). Suspending classes without stopping learning: China's education emergency management policy in the COVID-19 outbreak. *Journal of Risk and Financial Management, 13*(55), 1–6.

Chapter 7
Trends of Future Development

Shuyu Yu, Li Chen, and Zhuli Wang

The rapid development of Information and Communication Technology (ICT) has and will continue to shape and transform the development of education. Blended learning, as an important educational innovation, has brought about profound changes in teaching and learning. The design of blended learning environments will be an important area for researchers and practitioners in preparing students for future learning. Influenced by the initiatives of openness, digitization and sharing of resources, Open Education Resources (OER) have become an important area in blended learning. Blended learning has become the new normal in higher education. Ubiquitous learning is well supported by blended learning. Emerging technologies are changing the way we think about the nature of education, education reform, and the structure of the higher education ecosystem.

This chapter explores the future development of blended learning from various aspects, such as blended learning space, OERs, ubiquitous learning, change of educational philosophy, and design of educational ecosystem. Section one discusses the definition of blended learning and the affordances of technology for blended learning space design, the trend of future development of blended learning space, and its impact on teaching and learning. Section two provides a systematic review of OERs, identifies the future development of OERs, and suggests the strategies to promote the application of OERs for blended learning. Section three discusses the concepts of ubiquitous learning, strategies for promoting ubiquitous learning, and the future development of ubiquitous learning. Section four deals with the recent development of educational philosophies and learning theories, and the reform of the educational

S. Yu (✉)
School of Educational Technology, Northwest Normal University, Lanzhou, China
e-mail: yu_shuyu@163.com

L. Chen
School of Educational Technology, Beijing Normal University, Beijing, China

Z. Wang
Center for Faculty Development, Sun Yat-Sen University, Guangzhou, China

© The Author(s) 2024
M. Li et al. (eds.), *Handbook of Educational Reform Through Blended Learning*,
https://doi.org/10.1007/978-981-99-6269-3_7

ecosystem. This chapter discusses the connection between theories and practices to ensure a realistic yet forward-looking perspective. The target audience of the chapter includes administrators, teachers, and researchers at various levels of higher education and vocational education institutions.

7.1 Space for Blended Learning

With the development of the Internet, big data, cloud computing, artificial intelligence, and other emerging technologies, the teaching and learning space is undergoing significant changes. The integration of various learning spaces is an important trend of the future development of blended learning. The integrated blended learning space, allowing future teaching and learning to occur, is an important basis for systematic reform through blended learning.

7.1.1 Blended Learning Space

Pan (2018) pointed out that human society is moving from a traditional physical-social dual space to a ternary space of physical-social-information. All aspects of human work and life, including teaching and learning, are carried out in these three spaces. Compared with the physical and social spaces, information space demonstrates characteristics such as spatio-temporal flexibility, resource sharing, digitalized behaviors, networked relationship, and system connectivity (Chen et al. 2019). The information space not only breaks through the limitations of physical and social spaces, but also helps bridge other two spaces and creates a brand new blended learning space through blending the virtual and physical learning environment.

The traditional teacher-centered perspectives called the places where teaching activities occurred as "teaching spaces" (Qi 2011), one of which is the traditional classroom. With the shift from teacher-centered to learner-centered perspectives and with the development of educational technologies, concepts such as "learning space", "online learning space" and "virtual learning community" have emerged. This *Manual* refers all places where either teaching or learning activities occur as "learning spaces". Given that a traditional teaching space is mainly physical whereas an online learning space is mainly virtual, many scholars adopted the term "blended learning space" meaning a combination of the offline physical space represented by classrooms, libraries, laboratories, etc. and the online virtual information space supported by ICT. In blended learning space, the real time multi-facet data related to the learning activities in the physical and virtual learning environment could be collected and analyzed through various sensors (Li et al. 2013). In a blended learning space, the definition of learning and the role of learners and technologies may change (Wu 2017). The blended learning space allows learners to engage in learning activities continuously and ubiquitously with any devices, enabling learners to learn anytime, anywhere. Through in-depth data mining and analysis about learners' learning and context, evidence-based learning analytic and assessment could be conducted to understand and monitor learners' learning, and recommend high-quality learning resources, suggest suitable learning tasks which are appropriate for the individual learners, so as to help learners make informed decisions, and promote the creative and inventive thinking, character building, competency development (Zhu 2016a, b). The blended learning spaces, with the combined advantages from physical learning space and virtual learning space, has become an important learning place for future learning to occur.

7.1.2 Affordances of Technologies for the Design of Blended Learning Space

The meaningful blended learning cannot be achieved without the support of various technologies in the information age, such as the Internet, big data, 5G, artificial intelligence, virtual reality/augmented reality, etc.

(1) The Internet. There are huge number of educational resources on the Internet, promoting the sharing of high-quality educational resources. Similar to the case that grassroots can open stores on Taobao, in the Internet age, large amount of valuable educational resources are created and shared by various stakeholders in the society. Almost everybody, including authoritative experts, teachers, enterprises, and grass-root individuals can develop educational resources and share them online. Teachers are no longer the only authoritative sources of knowledge. The "knowledge wall" in higher education institutions is collapsing (Chen 2016). The knowledge dissemination is much more convenient than before. The depth, breadth and speed of such dissemination can be enjoyed by everyone with Internet access (Chen and Qi 2014). The openness, resources sharing and digitalization initiatives are changing the traditional mode of resource development in higher education institutions. Mobilizing various stakeholders to co-develop education resources together does not only help solve the problem of repetitive effort of resource creation, but also helps break the bottleneck created by "information island" in higher education institutions. Therefore, it can effectively address the gap between what education provides and what society demands (Chen et al. 2017). In the future, Internet technology will continue support the development of spatio-temporally flexible, multi-modal, and interconnected blended learning spaces, providing new opportunities for the development of blended learning.

(2) Big data and educational data mining. The rapid development of big data technology facilitates the digitization of behaviors and provides strong support for more accurate and customized information push and selection in the online environment (Chen et al. 2019). In the future, all behaviors of digital learners can be collected and analyzed real-time. The learning analytics of online teaching and

learning behaviors could inform educators and learners about the teaching and learning processes and outcomes, which inform them the next step of action for teaching and learning. The learning analytics could help us understand learners' strength and areas of improvement much better.'The learning resources can be more accurately recommended to learners, thereby improving their learning efficiency and effectiveness. Teaching analytics based on the online data'also reflect teachers' teaching behaviors, which facilitate evidence based decision making for teaching and educational management. In the future, the teaching and learning, and educational management will be transformed into a much more refined mode with educational data mining. Data science will be pervasively applied in various aspects of teaching and learning, which will promote the development of future educational research paradigms.

(3) 5G technology. 5G technology has the characteristics of broad bandwidth, wide connection, and low latency. 5G technology has a profound impact on the construction of learning spaces, and in turn affect other elements of teaching and learning, and their relationships. In particular, the learning spaces supported by 5G technology are more conducive for skill- or competency-based learning. Such a learning space can provide richer teaching resources during the learning process, which will promote structural changes in physical learning spaces. Physical learning spaces and virtual learning spaces, and in and out of school learning spaces can be well connected. Broad bandwidth and low-latency network connection not only facilitates the integration of classroom learning and workplace learning, but more importantly, it supports students to interact in real time with the virtual or virtual-real learning contexts. The big data on students' learning behaviors recorded during the learning process can be used for diagnostic assessment which support evidence-based decision making for future improvement in teaching and learning. In the future, 5G technology, together with other emerging technologies, will promote the advancement of educational hardware and software, facilitate the integration of physical and virtual learning environments, and make personalized, contextualized, and data-driven learning a norm (Zhuang et al. 2020).

(4) Artificial intelligence (AI). The development and application of AI technology, including machine learning, knowledge graph, natural language processing, robotics and intelligent control, are increasingly applied in education. The AI will affect the education in the future in the following aspects. First, machine learning can be used to predict learners' academic performance, analyze learning challenges and obstacles, and identify the risk of dropout. Second, natural language processing technology can be used to realize automatic assessment of essays and spoken language. Third, knowledge graphs can be applied to automatically answer knowledge-based questions, and accurately recommend customized learning resources to learners. Fourth, robotics and intelligent control technology make it possible to develop robots for educational purposes such as learning companion to help with knowledge transfer and emotional companionship.

Another important future direction is AI (such as perceptual intelligence and computational intelligence) empowered differentiated and personalized learning. First, learning context data can be analyzed to provide information on personalized and differentiated learner profiles. Second, appropriate teaching context can be provided to personalize teaching and learning. Third, multi-facet automated assessment can be conducted and personalized learning and development paths can be formulated and recommended to students. By doing so, the individualized and personalized learning can be achieved.

(5) Virtual Reality (VR)/Augmented Reality (AR). VR/AR technology can be embedded in physical learning space. They can replicate the virtual scenes that do not exist in physical space (Yang et al. 2021). For example, a virtual library built based on VR/AR technology can simulate the precious or obsolete books in the library and present them in a dynamic three-dimensional manner, allowing readers to read the books in the virtual space. A team led by Professor Hwang Gwo-Jen of National Taiwan University of Science and Technology used VR/AR technology in ubiquitous learning of context awareness, where authentic scenes that learners cannot perceive in physical space were represented in virtual space, realizing the integration of physical and virtual space (Yang et al. 2021). The virtual reality and augmented reality technology will impact future education in the following aspects. First, it helps students learn course content in a richer context that is closer to the real world. Second, it breaks the constraints of traditional physical classrooms, allowing students to explore and interact with environments and characters that are difficult to access in reality. Third, it facilitates students' experiential learning, helping them overcome their challenge of over-reliance on theory and lack of practical inquiry.

On top of the above technologies, other emerging technologies such as the Internet of Things, cloud computing, and block chain technology will also play a supportive role in the construction and application of future blended learning spaces, supporting the design and implementation of various teaching and learning activities in blended learning spaces.

7.1.3 The Future of Blended Learning Spaces

Supporting smart seamless learning

The blended learning spaces supports the free and orderly switching of different learning scenarios such as online and offline, formal and informal, and providing learners with a complete set of integrated learning support. The blended learning spaces accommodate diverse learning strategies such as class lecture, group collaboration, self-directed learning, and improves learners' adaptability and comfortableness. It is an environment that facilitates students' collaboration, their access to the

Internet, promotes authentic learning, and respects the individual needs of students (Yang et al. 2013).

Seamless learning occurs in different contexts at any time, where fast and easy switch between learning contexts is realized with the support of mobile devices. It helps bridge of the in-class and out-of-class learning, synchronous and asynchronous communication, formal and informal learning, and the integration of various pedagogies and learning activities (Zhu and Sun 2015), providing students with a complete and continuous learning experience. The blended learning space is highly flexible. By addressing the constraints of traditional physical learning spaces, it provides learners with diverse learning support, allowing them to flexibly choose from online or offline, or from synchronous or asynchronous learning methods according to their time, space and learning resource preferences. In this way, students are no longer passive learners, but are empowered to flexibly select appropriate learning methods according to their own learning needs. Therefore, blended learning space opens up a new opportunity to realize seamless learning (Xiao et al. 2021).

Adaptive learning space based on big data

Adaptive learning space refers to a learning space with adaptive learning function. To construct an adaptive learning space, it is necessary to pay attention to different variables that affect the learning outcomes and their relationships, so as to establish an optimized learning path. This requires an investigation into the learning styles and cognitive processes of different profiles of learners, and then builds a "learning model". A "mathematical model" is built based on the complex learning model. This "mathematical model" needs to match human cognition when constructing of the adaptive learning spaces (Shen 2020).

Students' learning behaviors in authentic learning contexts are often complex and diverse. Traditional assessment methods emphasize on the level of knowledge acquisition. The formative and diversified assessment requires the support of technology and the collection of big data. Learning analysis based on big data can describe and explain the past learning behaviors, inform or intervene ongoing learning, and infer and predict future development trends. These allow learners to understand their own learning process and outcomes much better. They can be guided with optimized development path. In a blended learning space, conducting in-depth mining and analysis of big data can enrich the assessment indicators, strengthen the formative assessment and improve learners' self-assessment and peer assessment (Qian and Wang 2013).

A learning environment of virtual-physical integration

The development of technologies such as artificial intelligence, human–computer interaction, and the Internet of Things in education have impact in constructing a blended learning environment that integrates virtual and physical learning spaces. A virtual-real fusion environment relies on sensors to connect the physical world and the virtual one through the Internet. As an important part of the Internet of Things, sensors which identify and acquire information in the real world can be directly used by learners after digital processing. The Internet and multimedia technology support the acquisition of resources related to their learning topics in a personalized learning environment (Zhang et al. 2013). Digital Twin (DT) technology, which emerges with modeling simulation and sensing, makes it possible to build multi-dimensional, multi-scale, multi-disciplinary, and multi-physical dynamic digital virtual models of physical objects in the virtual space. It effectively connects physical space and virtual space, to provide learners with more real-time, efficient and intelligent educational services (Wang and Zhou 2021). The diverse experiences brought by different spaces in the virtual-real integration environment provides learners with various learning experiences ranging from concrete to abstract, and to experience multi-modal perceptual learning, embodied cognitive learning and connected learning (Yang and Zhang 2021).

7.1.4   The Impact of the Development of Learning Spaces on Blended Learning

A learning space is important for teaching and learning to occur. Its development profoundly affects the area of blended learning. Since the Internet began to be applied in education, it has had a huge impact on teaching and learning in schools. Internet technology is increasingly widely used by teachers in various learning contexts, and more and more students start to engage in online learning. As teachers' online teaching and students' online learning is increasing, a blend of online and offline learning has become a rising. There are two forms of blended learning, namely, blended learning supported by traditional physical spaces and blended learning supported by blended learning spaces.

In the early stage of blended learning, learning and teaching was largely happening in physical spaces supported by technologies, such as multimedia classrooms, laboratories, simulation training places, libraries, network interactive places, etc. The technologies provided teaching or learning resources, and teaching aids, etc., and yet they were not able to generate a learning space that was to be integrated with the offline physical spaces. The role of technology in limited without exerting a deep impact on learning. This kid of blended learning space could not meet the requirements of integrated learning scenarios, full coverage of learning processes, intelligent learning activities, customized learning progress, and personalized learning interventions. The proportion of face-to-face teaching in the classroom was relatively high where students had less opportunities to engaged in active learning.

With the rapid development of technology the form of blended learning has shifted from blended learning supported by traditional physical spaces to that supported by blended learning spaces. Blended learning spaces integrate offline physical space and online virtual, forming a virtual-real integrated learning environment that supports the blended teaching needs of teachers and students (Han 2022). Technologies such as the Internet, big data, artificial intelligence, virtual reality/augmented reality (VR/

AR) not only provide teaching or learning resources and teaching aids, but effectively constitutes an information space that is integrated with the offline physical space to form a new learning or teaching space. This role of technology in this blended learning space goes beyond mere "assistance". Instead, it begins to exert a deep influence on teaching and learning. Moreover, it realizes the integration of learning scenarios, comprehensive coverage of the learning process, intelligent learning activities, customized learning progress, and personalized learning interventions (Han 2022). For blended learning supported by the blended learning space, the proportion of face-to-face teaching in the classroom is getting lower and lower, while that of self-directed learning supported by online learning spaces is getting increasingly higher. Thus, a transformation of teachers' pedagogy and of students' learning strategies is truly realized.

7.2 Open Educational Resources: Important Learning Resources for Promoting Blended Learning

Since the launch of the Open Course Ware Initiative (OCW) at The Massachusetts Institute of Technology (MIT) in 2001, the Open Educational Resources Movement has flourished around the world. Open educational resources (OERs) have promoted educational equity, co-construction and sharing of resources, and transformation of higher education, which are bound to be an important form of learning resources that supports the development and reform of blended learning.

The concept of OERs was first proposed and defined by the United Nations Educational, Scientific and Cultural Organization (UNESCO) at the Forum on the Impact of Open Courseware for Higher Education in Developing Countries held in 2002 (UNESCO 2017). Since then, OERs have been continuously endowed with richer connotations. In the "Recommendation Concerning Open Educational Resources" approved by UNESCO in 2019, OERs are defined as " any form of learning, teaching and research materials in a variety of media that are available in the public domain or in the form of open licenses that allow others to access, reuse, repurpose, adapt and redistribute them free of charge" (UNESCO 2019). An open license refers to "a license that provides permission for the public to access, reuse, repurpose, adapt, and redistribute educational materials while respecting the intellectual property rights of the copyright owner" (UNESCO 2019).

7.2.1 Types of Open Educational Resources

The Organization for Economic Cooperation and Development (OECD) classified OERs into three categories: a. learning content including courses, courseware, modules, learning objects, collections, and journals etc.; b. tools which refer to software supporting the development, use, reuse and delivery of learning content, including tools for searching, developing, and organizing content, learning management systems, and online learning communities. c. implementation resources which refer to learning intellectual property licensing of learning content and tools, strategies for promoting public distribution of materials, optimized practice design principles and localization of content (Hylén 2006). Some commonly used OERs are listed below.

Open Courseware (OCW)

Open Courseware (OCW) is the earliest developed and most mature form of OERs. Open Courseware Consortium (OCWC) defines open courseware as a. digital resources with free public licenses, which can be accessed by anyone at any time through the Internet; b. high-quality curriculum-level educational resources for higher education institutions; (3) course-based which include course plans, assessment tools, and subject content. MIT initiated the OCW movement. As of 2017, MIT has made more than 2,400 courses available to the public, nearly half of which are available in translated versions. Its open courseware covers 36 majors of its 5 colleges, with more than 2 million monthly visits and a total of more than 250 million visits.

"iCourse" is the official website of the "High-quality Open Courses in Chinese Higher Education Institutions" program launched by China's Ministry of Education. It displays open courses in video format and share resource of higher education institutions in China, with 329 partner universities and 2,882 online courses. Upon voluntary application and sharing by higher education institutions and teachers, high-quality open courses based on recommendation, evaluation and selection are displayed on the website.

Open access repositories

Open access (OA) archives or repositories are equivalent to online interactive document sharing platforms, providing access to teaching materials, exam question banks, professional development resources and other materials. Generally, materials are uploaded by authors using a specific format, and released after going through official review, whereas users can read and download the documents online (Cai 2007). For example, Baidu Wenku (https://wenku.baidu.com) was launched on November 12, 2009. To date its content has covered 53 subject areas including basic education, qualification exams, humanities and social sciences, IT, natural sciences, etc., with more than 2,600 organization users, and a daily visit of 40 million. More than 8 million teacher users, that is, nearly 60% teachers in China, shared educational resources through Baidu Wenku. Moreover, it has been integrated with existing information platforms of many provinces, cities and schools.

Massive Open Online Courses (MOOC)

MOOC (Massive Open Online Course) are online courses featuring with large-scale student interaction and network-based open access. It has the characteristics of large scale, openness, networking, personalization and participation. Typical

MOOC platforms include: Udacity (http://www.udacity.com), Coursera (http://www.coursera.org), and edX (http://www.edx.org) in the United States, Future Learn (http://www.futurelearn.com/courses) in the United Kingdom, Open2Study (http://www.open2study.com) in Australia and NetEase Cloud Classroom (http://study.163.com), Chinese University MOOC (http://www.icourse163.org), and Xuetangx Online (http://v1-www.xuetangx.com) in China, etc.

Massive Open Online Experiments (MOOE)

MOOE (Massive Open Online Experiments) is a brand-new mode of experiment. Using technologies such as virtualization and Software Defined Network (SDN), MOOE can quickly build various experimental environments with high complexity and strong isolation that addresses the limitations of traditional laboratories in terms of time, space and experimental content (Zhu 2016a, b). MOOEs can be applied in various scenarios. For example, as of February 28, 2022, China's national virtual simulation experiment teaching course sharing platform (http://www.ilab-x.com/) has included a total of 3,250 experimental projects, covering 61 disciplines including management, chemistry, and mechanics.

Open textbooks

Open textbooks are an important form of open digital books which are under an open copyright license that is available online for free use by students, teachers, and the public. It is published in print, e-book, or audio formats. Under the license, anyone is free to use, adapt or redistribute the content of the textbooks (Zhao et al. 2019). College Open Textbooks, an online community established in 2008, aimed to promote public awareness and the use of open textbooks. It served more than 200 community colleges, promoted the use of open textbooks to more than 2,000 communities and some other two-year colleges, and offered nearly 800 textbooks covering 24 subject areas. It conducts peer review on the content of open textbooks to ensure the quality of the content (Zhao et al. 2019).

Digital venues

Using VR, AR, Mixed Reality (MR) and other technologies, digital venues use the Internet as the basic platform to display exhibits including those that cannot be displayed in physical venues. It has the characteristics of digitization, networking, distribution and sharing, which, to a large extent, makes up for the imbalance caused by geographical distances. Digital venues include digital museums, digital science and technology museums. For example, Digital Exhibition Hall of the National Museum of China (http://www.chnmuseum.cn/portals/0/web/vr/) hosts more than 50 exhibitions, covering the themes of historical relics, art treasures, cultural relics from various countries, etc. Metropolitan Museum of Art, New York (https://www.metmuseum.org/) launched "The Met Unframed" program in January 2021, bringing visitors an immersive virtual art and gaming experience. China Digital Science and Technology Museum (https://www.cdstm.cn/museum/) used virtual reality technology to provide 3D models, virtual assemblies, panoramas and other content in its "Aviation" and "Aerospace" expo halls, where 3D models of aircraft of spacecraft on exhibition can be freely rotated and zoomed. In "Earth Dinosaur" exhibition of the Virtual Science and Technology Museum of Japan (https://www.miraikan.jst.go.jp/zh/), more than 10 dinosaur simulation models were used. The dinosaurs roared from time to time, with their limbs slowly swinging, which was very real during the simulation (Zeng 2010).

7.2.2 Future Direction of OERs

Since the beginning of the twenty-first century, OERs have spread out to the world, bring impact to education and other areas in the whole society. Many countries and region have exploring OER projects that are suitable to their specific context. Although the development of OERs faces many challenges, with its open concept, technology and collaboration platforms, many areas of OERs can be continuously explored.

The role of OERS has shifted from supporting to innovating education

OERs have been developed rapidly. The role of OERs is shifting from merely supporting education toward innovating education. With the increasing depth and breadth of openness, OERs continuously expand the learning space, enhance the quality of educational services, promote the creation, dissemination and application of knowledge and information, and brings about innovation in various aspects of teaching and learning.

The educational innovations brought by OERs include the depth and the breadth of innovation and openness. OERs help transform open school educational resources to open lifelong educational resources. Since MIT launched the OCW in 2001, OERs gradually changed from static materials to dynamic teaching, and then to dynamic learning, all of which, in essence, are important elements of school education. Providing services to support lifelong learning is an important trend for the development of OERs. For example, the Open Learning Project of Open University of the United Kingdom, the National Digital Learning Resource Center project led by National Open University of China, and the Shanghai Education Resource Bank Project undertaken by the Shanghai Distance Education Group are all large-scale projects that support lifelong learning. These large-scale high-quality OERs take the advantages of distance education and the experience of constructing high-quality resources.

In terms of the breadth of innovation and openness, the target groups of OERs have expanded from the general population to the groups that need special education. This is to address the problem that despite the increasing availability of OERs, few resources are available for learners with special needs. Aiming to increasing educational opportunities and equity, OERs benefit learners, especially those with special needs. Meeting the needs of special learning groups will be a direction of the development of OERs in the future. In fact, ICT with multimedia affordances not only offset the constraints of the physical learning space by reducing the learning barriers to some extent, but also help with personalized learning. One example was using VR game prototype developed by Nicoletta for teaching mathematics to deaf children in kindergartens.

OERs are transforming higher education system in that many courses offered by different universities are parked in a single website. Nathan Harden (in press) pointed out that network technology and new educational models will contribute to the collapse of the traditional higher education system, and a considerable number of universities will disappear. In fact, this is happening. For example, as a new type of distance education university, Western Governors University in Utah does not offer any course but do accreditation only. Learners are awarded a certificate once they pass a test organized by the school. In recent years, with the promotion of MOOC and other OERs, programs such as credit certification, degree certification, and project certification emerged, which have transformed the higher education system.

From open digital educational resources to intellectual educational resources

Digital educational resources are educational resources in digital form that are specially designed for teaching and learning purposes. The examples are various teaching material libraries, test question banks, etc. Compared with physical resources, digital resources are easily to be created, replicated, disseminated, and openly shared across regions and schools. The digital educational resources still exist in a static form.

Intellectual education resources often include skills, knowledge, experience, know-how, learning ability, creativity developed by teachers and researchers. The resources also include values, insights, perceptions, interpersonal synergy, emotional control, responsibility and loyalty that can be identified in individual minds. Intellectual education resources are developed gradually. Compared with static digital education resources, intellectual education resources are more dynamic. The creators of intellectual education resources include outstanding researchers and practitioners in higher education institutions, who are able to effectively use ICT for collaboration and sharing, so as to quickly organize knowledge resources, design and develop online learning environment, and provide comprehensive valuable educational services to others.

Since the outbreak of COVID-19 epidemic, the trend of opening up intellectual education resources to the public has been accelerated. Higher education institutions in China have begun to explore the ways to realize "suspending classes without stopping learning", exploring more online education, blended learning and other teaching and strategies. Online teaching and learning are promoted by taking the advantages such as synchronous and asynchronous learning, inquiry-based learning, learning at anytime and anywhere etc. It is predicted that, the abovementioned learning models will become a new normal in the post-epidemic era. The sharing of intellectual education resources has become a trend, with more and more college learners benefiting from it.

Integrating emerging technology into OERs

The emerging technologies represented by artificial intelligence, big data, VR etc. are deeply integrated in education. These technologies have lent great support to the development of OERs. Many OERs have transformed from one-dimension into three-dimensions. For example, VR technology can be used to develop immersive experiential digital educational resources, 5G technology can be used to develop high-definition reality-based digital educational resources, and artificial intelligence technology can be adopted to create digital educational resources featuring human–computer collaboration.

In terms of application of OERs, 5G + VR/AR technology can support high-speed transmission and processing of complex interactive resources on various intelligent learning terminals. Artificial intelligence technology can support ontology feature recognition and adaptive recommendation of various multi-modal resources (Ke et al. 2021). Some other promising applications include the multi-modal learning analytics in the resource learning system, machine learning in the digital resource content supervision, and blockchain technology in the management of digital education resource circulation. At present, ICT integration in teaching, learning and educational management supports the knowledge creation, dissemination, and processing, and thus help creates a new ecology of richer and more scientific open education resources supported by ICT.

7.2.3 Strategies for Promoting OERs

The previous sections discussed the characteristics of OERs and identified the future directions of OERs. The following section will propose strategies for promoting OERs.

Promoting quality certification system and high-quality development of OERs

Since 2013, OERs have sprung up in China. However, in the early years the quality certification system was relatively loosely controlled. As a result, the quality of resources on the OER platforms such as Chinese University MOOC, XuetangX, and NetEase Cloud Classroom has been uneven. The volume of China's OERs has become very large nowadays. It is time to emphasize on the quality instead of quantity of OERs. A quality assurance framework with a clear set of criteria and standards could help ensure the healthy development of OERs. Policymakers shall take the lead in this by forming a committee of experts and stakeholders from various fields to work. At present, the Ministry of Education of China is actively researching and formulating national standards for OERs. In the future, the accreditation of OERs of universities will be explored deeper with collaboration among various stakeholders. Effort need to be made to improve the reputation and gain social trust. Moreover, requirements for access and permission of OERs should be improved, and recognition from education authorities and universities should be implemented.

Promoting the integration of MOOE and MOOC, and opening of experimental platforms

With the development of OERs, especially the MOOCs, the walls between universities have been broken. Cross-university learning has been realized. Taping on MOOC platforms, learners from all over the world can learn courses offered by prestigious universities and institutions colleges around the world very easily. Learners from various geographical locations with different profiles can form learning communities online.

China's MOOCs, such as courses offered on Chinese University MOOC, XuetangX and other platforms, also have their limitations. Most of the courses are theoretical courses, with less practice and experimental courses offered. In this regard, the emergence of MOOE can address the disadvantages of MOOC by emphasizing on practical teaching and cross-school learning. With the help of the experimental environment built by virtual platforms, experimental tasks are no longer limited to classrooms on campus, but can be completed anytime and anywhere. Students conduct experiments, exchange learning experiences and learning habits, evaluate courses, and experiments together on MOOE platforms. It is necessary to integrate MOOE and MOOC for courses which are practice driven. MOOE and MOOC complement with each other by achieving optimized teaching and learning effect (Wang 2019).

Promoting the integration of digital twin and venues, and advancing the open digital venues

Multi-modal digital venues is one of the trendy OERs. Venues has great potential to enhance school education. The existing venues have some limitations such as poor information service efficiency, poor data sharing, and low level of learning support services. Research shows that the integration of big data, artificial intelligence, VR, digital twin and other technologies can make the venues smarter to meet the personalized learning needs. It is beneficial to build a digital twin of physical entities in the virtual space to connect the data of the virtual space and that of the physical space of the venues, and optimize the presentation and configuration of resources in the venues. With more convenient acquisition and use of resources, more accurate learning analytics, and diversified learning strategies, the goal of opening the venue is achieved.

Any object in the physical space of digital twin has its corresponding "twin" in the virtual space. Such a "twin" spontaneously aggregates data from different spaces and to form a unique mapping of the physical object in the virtual space. Learning that takes place in such venue mostly takes the form of a trigger interaction. After the digital "twin" joins, the interaction in the venue is not only limited to the interaction between the learner and the exhibits, the learner and the environment, and the learner with other learners, but also in between the learner and the digital twin, and between different digital twins (Wang and Zhou 2021).

7.3   Ubiquitous Learning to Support Blended Learning

With the advent of the information age and the rapid development of science and technology, modern information technology, especially the new generation, continues to evolve and permeate all areas of society, including education; the teaching and learning styles of humans have also been deeply influenced and have undergone profound changes. In the information age, blended teaching and learning have become normalized methods in higher education, and ubiquitous learning will also become an important form of learning that adapts to this normal teaching or learning mode.

7.3.1   The Basic Idea of Ubiquitous Learning

As early as the twelfth century, in the Southern Song Dynasty of China, Zhu Xi had put forward the concept of "Learning in everything, every moment and everywhere". In the seventeenth century, Comenius introduced the pansophic idea of "to teach all the things to all people" in his book *Didactica Magna*, which is the earliest Western exposition related to the concept of ubiquitous learning (Liu and Nong 2020). Ubiquitous learning is derived from the concept "Ubiquitous Computing", which was pioneered by the American scientist Mark Weiser in 1988. As Weiser puts it in *The computer for the twenty-first century*, "The most profound technologies are those that disappear. They weave themselves into the fabric of everyday life until they are indistinguishable from it" (Weiser 1991). Scholars in Japan, South Korea, Europe and North America have successively put forward similar concepts, arguing that ubiquitous learning is as naturally integrated into the daily social life of human beings as air and water. Jones and Jo (2004) suggested that the assimilation of ubiquitous computing technologies in education marks a great advancement— the emergence of ubiquitous learning through the concept of ubiquitous computing. Bomsdorf (2005) argued that ubiquitous computing has led to ubiquitous learning, which embeds individual learning activities in everyday life.

Since its emergence, the concept of ubiquitous learning has taken a relatively short period of time to develop from 3A (Anywhere, Anytime, Any Device) to 4A (Anyone, Anytime, Anywhere, Any Device), then to 5A (Anyone, Anytime, Anywhere, Any Device, Anyway) and 7A (Anyone, Anytime, Anywhere, Any Device, Anyway, Any contents, Any learning support). Therefore ubiquitous learning is also known as universal learning, seamless learning, learning everywhere and so on.

The understanding of the connotation of ubiquitous learning varies, mainly in the broad and narrow senses. In the narrow sense, ubiquitous learning is primarily defined in terms of the supporting environment and technology; with the support of ubiquitous technology and pervasive computing, learners actively use easily accessible resources to carry out a variety of learning activities according to their learning content and cognitive goals. In the broad sense, ubiquitous learning is defined more at a conceptual level, as a type of learning that can be done everywhere and pervade everywhere. Learners can access information and resources in a timely manner with appropriate tools and environments, as long as they are willing to. Ubiquitous learning is characterized by its ubiquity, accessibility, interactivity, contextuality and personalization.

7.3.2 Strategies for Promoting Ubiquitous Learning

Ubiquitous learning requires ubiquitous networks, computing power, learning resources, and learning services. Li and Zheng (2006) believed that the research on ubiquitous learning should be conducted in three aspects: technical environment, learning resources, and learning concepts. Yang et al (2013) argued that the realization of a harmonious ubiquitous learning environment needs to address three key problems: hard technical problems, soft technical problems, and pedagogical problems. Informed by these, we believe that the realization of ubiquitous learning requires attention to the construction of technical environment (i.e., issues related to the basic supportive environment and learning terminals), the construction of learning resources, the construction of the support service system, and the construction of the learning community (i.e., issues related to learners, facilitators, and pedagogy).

Building a ubiquitous learning technology environment

The construction of a ubiquitous learning environment is the foundation and guarantee for the successful implementation of ubiquitous learning. In order to effectively support ubiquitous learning, it is necessary to build a technical environment for learners to use any terminal device for learning anytime, anywhere, and to provide learners with various technical means, mainly including a basic ubiquitous environment and ubiquitous learning terminal equipment (Chen and Zhang 2011).

The basic environment provides basic technical support including network, computing, storage, platform, etc. for ubiquitous learning. It is the basic element that constitutes the ubiquitous learning environment. The ubiquitous Internet, with the help of new-generation information technologies such as the Internet of Things, education cloud, big data, blockchain, artificial intelligence, and 5G, etc., together with satellite mobile communication network and ground mobile communication network, forms a comprehensive network environment with three-dimensional communication and seamless global coverage, which extends the network to all spaces where people live and learn. At the same time, learning resources and learning support services adopt the cloud storage mode and are together stored in the "Cloud". This can provide learners with a technical environment that allows them to use any terminal device for learning anytime and anywhere to support their ubiquitous learning needs. Therefore, in the wave of rapidly developing information technology, the relevant departments need to accelerate the construction of a network support environment that enables high-speed access and multi-network interoperability, so that the ubiquitous Internet and cloud technology can be extended to people's living and learning spaces, and the development and implementation of ubiquitous learning can be promoted.

At the same time, ubiquitous learning depends on the support of various learning terminal devices. With the development of technologies such as computers, mobile networks, and sensors, various learning terminals like smartphones, tablet computers, notebook computers, mobile TVs, and flat TVs appeared. In the ubiquitous learning environment, the learning terminal is responsible for communicating with the cloud computing center, invoking various learning services needed, connecting and sharing information with each other, receiving response data, and adaptively presenting learning resources. It is a tool used by learners to learn and interact which is easy to access, various in nature, and simple to apply. Therefore, relevant departments need to accelerate the development and upgrade of intelligent mobile terminals that support learning interaction, so that mobile terminals can intelligently identify the environmental information of the learner, the physical status information of the learner, and the introductory information of real objects, etc., so as to better meet their learning requirements, provide learners with seamless learning opportunities, enable them to access resources and interact at any time, extend their learning time, and enhance their learning effect.

Building up ubiquitous learning resources

In the ubiquitous learning environment, learning resources are the bridge connecting learners and learning behaviors. It should be able to perceive different learning situations, to analyze, construct, and recommend services for social knowledge networks, and to perceive and record the evolution of knowledge. And it can be dynamically and adaptively aggregated according to the needs of learners (Yu et al. 2021). The learning resources with openness and adaptability should be jointly built and shared to meet the diverse and bite-sized learning needs of ubiquitous learners.

New information technology has profoundly changed the way human learn. The emergence of learning styles also brings about massive needs for learning. Thus, more diversified high-quality learning resources should be built to meet the massive and diversified learning needs of learners. At the same time, it's also a new learning mode by which learners conduct bite-sized learning according to their own needs with the help of the Internet. This requires the construction of learning resources that can meet the learner's needs of personalized learning content and using a fragmented learning time. On the one hand, the construction of learning resources should be more bite-sized, video-based, networked, and mobile to meet the personalized learning needs of learners from all walks of life and different fields. On the other hand, in order to gradually make ubiquitous learning the mainstream learning mode, miniaturized learning resources that are suitable for mobile terminals need to be built to adapt to the learner's bite-sized learning time and personalized learning needs.

Providing ubiquitous learning support services

Ubiquitous learning is a kind of self-directed learning which largely relies on students' learning motivation, self-awareness, and self-control to monitor and manage the entire learning process. An important factor for the success of ubiquitous learning is to build a support network for learners and provide comprehensive, sufficient, effective, and personalized support services (Chen 2011).

The learner is the core element in the learning support service system. Services such as technical environment services, learning resource services, intelligent tutoring services, and learning community services all exist because of students' self-learning. Therefore, appropriate learning support services should be provided according to the specific context of learners to meet the different learning needs of different learners in different periods. In terms of technical environment services, artificial intelligence technology should be used to improve the learning environment and change the standardized support services so that data can be used by learners through the two-way or multi-way communication to enhance learners' learning. In terms of learning resource services, learning support should be provided that is suitable for learners according to their learning needs and content, provide personalized learning content services, flexible information resource services, and a network environment that supports high-speed retrieval to meet the diverse learning needs of students. In terms of intelligent tutoring services, in order to provide learners with the most helpful services, context-aware devices can be used to perceive and analyze some information about the learner or the surrounding environment, can automatically recommend suitable learning objectives, as well as provide the optimized path to the learner according to internal factors such as learning ability and learning style. In terms of learning community services, in order to strengthen learners' common progress in cooperation, collaborative learning can be carried out, namely, helping learners to find learning partners or someone who is willing to interact, or by creating learning communities according to the learners' learning style, learning ability, knowledge level, and other factors.

Build a ubiquitous learning community

In the ubiquitous learning environment, the construction of the technical environment and learning resources ensures the physical aspects of education technology for the development of ubiquitous learning and lays the foundation for the establishment of a social mechanism for learning. The construction of the learning community and the transformation of its concepts are also particularly important (Chen and Zhang 2011).

The learner is the subject. The intelligent space constructed by the information space and the physical space is the object, and the learning procedure is the interaction between the subject and the object. First of all, learners should fully realize their own learning subject status, change their approach from passive learning to active learning, choose learning content independently and formulate suitable study plans according to their own cognitive level, personality characteristics and learning ability, self-learning needs, multiple learning resources and other conditions. Secondly, learners should improve their own abilities, such as the ability to identify and process information, the ability to think about problems, the ability to actively explore and analyze problems from multiple perspectives, and improve self-directness and openness.

The establishment of the ubiquitous learning community also depends on the guidance of the facilitators. On the one hand, in the ubiquitous learning environment, facilitators need to re-examine their roles, play the role of building learning resources, guide and supervise students' learning. According to the learners' cognitive level and learning needs, facilitators should guide learners to actively and effectively use learning resources, actively construct knowledge, and provide timely support and help through reasonable guidance to learners. On the other hand, facilitators are supposed to establish a lifelong learning awareness, make full use of modern information communication technology, and continuously explore new pedagogies such as collaborative learning and online learning by participating in relevant skills training, so as to improve their professional skills, transform theoretical achievements into practical applications, and form a virtuous circle. Learners and facilitators integrate into the community through sharing, communication, negotiation, active participation, and collaboration, etc. They gradually form common goals, consciousness, identities and a sense of meaning, and finally obtain learning results through a sense of belonging, and achieve excellence in collaboration in the learning community.

7.3.3 The Trend of Future Development of Ubiquitous Learning

With the development of ubiquitous computing and wireless communication technology, the use of portable mobile devices has become more and more frequent and pervasive, which has made ubiquitous learning more appealing to learners.

Intelligent and ubiquitous learning environment

In recent years, the construction of ubiquitous learning environments has become more intelligent due to the strong technical support from artificial intelligence technologies such as big data, semantic analysis, and cloud computing etc. The intelligent ubiquitous learning environment, with the main purpose of acquiring knowledge, is the direct interface for learners to learn through the ubiquitous network. It has various forms, rich functions, and has characteristics of intelligence, simplicity and connectivity.

The ubiquitous learning environment supported by big data, artificial intelligence and VR environments will become a learning environment in line with "Internet+". Breaking away from traditional classrooms, learners can use mobile devices to master content knowledge, and learn at any time any place in any situation. Ubiquitous learning can not only help learners solve problems in any terminal-supported learning environment, but also enable learners to reflect on the learning process, which is very conducive for personalized development of learners.

Diversified and ecological learning resources

As a link between learners and learning behaviors, learning resources are the key species for building an educational ecosystem. They are living organisms that can continuously evolve and develop themselves, with ecological attributes such as adaptability, integrity, openness, and evolution. In the future, the construction of learning resources tend to be more ecological and agile, so that they can actively adapt to the development and changes of other species (learners, learning tools or platforms), and highlight their dynamic connections and interactions with another key species (learners) to promote its evolution and development (Yang and Yu 2013).

In the ubiquitous learning environment, learners come from different industries and fields, and their needs for learning resources are also diverse. Many learners use their fragmented time to engage in bite-sized learning, which makes learning resources adapt to learners' customized learning needs. In the face of massive and scattered learning needs, the construction of learning resources is also progressing towards diversification, and at the same time, it increasingly reflects its ecological attributes.

Specifically, the content of ecological learning resources should be open and evolvable, allowing more people to create and edit them to generate dynamic learning resources. In addition, the future learning resource aggregation model should also develop in a dynamic and adaptive direction, which requires that the most suitable learning resources can be dynamically aggregated according to the needs of learners to solve problems in a specific learning context to promote personalized learning. The learning resources develop in the direction towards progressing multi-adaptation and dynamic structure attributes. Moreover, ubiquitous learning is the process of sharing and building individual cognitive networks and social cognitive networks. In the future, the construction of learning resources should maximally integrate the cognitive intelligence of the learner community, and then form a cognitive network that includes physical and human resources that can dynamically evolve and self-develop (Yu and Chen 2011).

Personalized and contextualized learning support

Ubiquitous learning meets the diverse needs of learners. Therefore, effort should be made to provide learners with timely, efficient, effective, and human-centered learning support to improve their learning and meet their personalized needs. This requires the design of ubiquitous learning support to be personalized and contextualized (Dong et al. 2015). The personalization and contextualization of ubiquitous learning support are mainly reflected in three aspects. First, in terms of service content, learning support is evolving towards learner-centered personalized learning with the deepening of the "human-centered" concept and the development of intelligent technology. Since ubiquitous learning is essentially a kind of on-demand learning (just in case), we need to provide different learning services according to different learning contexts to enhance their learning experiences. Second, in terms of support services, the focus shifts from asynchronous support and further extends to include both synchronous and asynchronous support. With the development of the

'Internet + education' and artificial intelligence education in recent years, more forms of interaction have emerged. Real-time synchronous support services can achieve point-to-point online Q&A and instant feedback, and are also conducive to the formation of significant teacher-student and student–student interactions. With the addition of emerging technologies, their interactions will become more personalized and contextualized in the future (Sun and Chen 2021).

The learning support service is an organic system with many elements coexisting. The optimal function of the system can be brought into play only by the integration and coordination among the elements. The intelligent and ubiquitous learning environment demands more advanced learning support services. Therefore, the ubiquitous learning support service will turn out to be more completer and more comprehensive in the future. Not only do student guidance, learning resources, and learning strategies require personalized and contextualized services, but their technical and emotional supports should also be more comprehensive.

More open and social ubiquitous learning community

A learning community is a learning team composed of learners, facilitators, and other people with a clear sense of team belonging, common aspirations and extensive communication opportunities. This learning team shares common goals, communicate and engaged in activities with each other (Shi and Liu 2008). Technologies provide new opportunities for the ubiquitous learning community by making it more open and social.

The open nature of a ubiquitous learning community is manifested in the openness of objects, resources, and learning methods. First of all, the participant of the ubiquitous learning community are not only students but also adult learners with different profile. Any people can use mobile devices at hand to learn anytime anywhere. Additionally, in the open ubiquitous learning community, various learning resources are integrated to meet the diverse needs of learners who use the fragmented time for learning, and thereby realize the opening and sharing of high-quality learning resources. The openness, personalization, and interaction of community are further strengthened by the open learning resources. Learners can customize their own learning path according to their individual needs. Ultimately, the learning model has shifted from the traditional "teacher-centric" to a "learner-centered" open blended learning style. The open ubiquitous learning community has shaped the original closed school structure by enabling an open learning approach for learners. learners can quickly access various resources they need on various platforms.

The social nature of the ubiquitous learning community is reflected in two aspects: the formation of the social cognitive network, and the wide application of various social software. With its open objects and resources, the ubiquitous learning community can better promote the formation of individual an social cognitive networks of learners. In the process of human–human and human–computer interaction, the interactive network between knowledge and human is formed. The essence of social platform is participation and sharing with everyone's voice to be heard. Therefore, social software plays a positive role in promoting the expansion of interpersonal communication in the real world. The social software augment learners' participation in the ubiquitous learning communities.

7.4 Rethinking Education and Building Educational Ecosystem

The emerging technologies centered on the Internet not only change the teaching space, learning resources and learning strategies, but also make researchers and practitioners rethink about the nature education and how to reconfigure the higher education ecosystem to respond to the changing education landscape. For example, researchers and practitioners are rethinking what to teach and learn in the digital era, and how to teach and learn better empowered by technologies. The education system need to change to respond better to the society need. In 2022, the main work of the Ministry of Education of China is to implement the strategic initiative of education digitalization, to actively develop "Internet Plus Education", and to accelerate digital transformation and the intelligent upgrading of education. Strategic initiatives of implementing education digitization are a national response to these changes and development.

7.4.1 Knowledge: From Elaborative Symbolic Information to Human Intelligence of the Whole Society

The most important thing brought by emerging technologies is that the connotation of knowledge has changed—from refined symbolic information to human intelligence of the whole society (Chen et al. 2019).

Knowledge in school education is a refined human intelligence. In order to better disseminate knowledge through schools, human beings abstract, structure, logicalize and characterize intelligence and wisdom, and solidify it in books. The knowledge at this point is explanatory and constructive. The Internet assembles and shares various types of human intelligence and wisdom. In the digital era, the connotation of knowledge, as well as its form, creation, and modes of transmission, has changed. And a new type of knowledge—growth knowledge, has been generated. Relying solely on explanatory and constructive knowledge can no longer adapt to aid social development, especially as technology changes rapidly. And thus, growth knowledge emerged. The Internet has enriched the connotation and types of knowledge. It not only includes the traditional knowledge perspectives which is based on linear static knowledge, abstract knowledge about principles, disciplinary system knowledge, and prescribed common knowledge, but also covers dynamic network knowledge, situational operation knowledge, comprehensive fragmented knowledge, and networked knowledge (Chen 2020). As UNESCO redefines knowledge in its report "Rethinking Education: A Conceptual Shift Towards a 'Global Common Good': "Knowledge can be understood broadly as information, understanding, skills, values, and attitudes acquired through learning" (UNESCO 2017). At the same time, knowledge creation shows respect towards individual values and attention towards the individual experience of practitioners; knowledge selection put an emphasis on meeting individual needs and promoting individual development. The smaller the granularity of knowledge is, the more flexible the combined application will be, and also the stronger the targeted problem-solving ability will be (Wang and Chen 2020).

The storage of knowledge is networked and multimodal. Knowledge exists in multimodal carriers in various forms, and it has stronger capabilities of absorption, integration, storage, and application. Therefore, it can support a faster dissemination speed, has stronger communication, a wider audience, and a more personalized expression (Chen et al. 2019). Knowledge is no longer a static phenomenon, but a network phenomenon. The creation of knowledge is no longer at the individual level, but at collective community level. In the past, human beings first crated knowledge and then disseminated it; today, knowledge production and dissemination are used in the same process in the Internet environment. In the past, creators and disseminators were not the same group; today, producers are communicators and beneficiaries at the same time. This is a unique phenomenon that occurs in the Internet environment. The way of appreciating personal knowledge has changed accordingly (Chen 2020).

7.4.2   Learning Theory: Learning is a Process of Connecting Specialized Nodes and Information Sources

How should students be facilitated to face and adapt to the changes that have occurred in the connotation, creation and dissemination of knowledge, and what kind of learning is valuable? A learning theory called connectivism is proposed to explain the open and complex digital era. It is a new and noteworthy theory which considers learning as a process of establishing connections between the internal neural network of human beings, the conceptual network of human society, and the external social network (Siemens 2005), and connectivity is an important way of learning. Learning is not only about learning from the experience of others and digesting knowledge, but also a process of creating knowledge and connecting specialized nodes or information sources, as shown in the figure below. Learning may also exist in non-human applications, and the ability to learn is more important than the knowledge that has been currently acquired. The goal of learning is to grow knowledge based on creation and to achieve a flow of knowledge. The process of learning is no longer unidirectional and linear, but rather a continuous process of building pipelines and maintaining information flowing smoothly within them (Siemens 2012; Downes 2012). Significant learning takes place when a person establishes connection with valuable sources of information and shares information on an ongoing basis.

The learning theories are evolving with the development of digital learning. The purpose of teaching is to help students establish connections with valuable information sources, and build an ecological network that promotes connectivity. In this process, individuals, organizations and the external world interact and develop together. As topics are constantly being generated, core concepts gradually emerge, giving a polycentric character to the social network relationship of the course, and active learners gradually acquire new competencies, such as communication, interaction, integration, and decision making. In addition to the traditional face-to-face learning and lecture-based learning, there is a need for more diverse, flexible and open learning formats and also more effective and customized pedagogies, so as to achieve connectivity for students and respond to the society need. For example, "Internet Plus Education", a group collaborative online community-based course was developed by the National Engineering Laboratory for Cyberlearning and Intelligent Technology in Beijing Normal University. Aiming of the nexus between theory and practice, the course is based on open and cutting-edge learning themes, designed with socialized and interactive learning activities, provides guided and generative learning resources, and offers personalized and processive learning support. It helps students achieve knowledge creation and supports the development of connectivity, and cultivates their higher-level competencies such as collaboration, critical innovation, integration, and decision making.

7.4.3 Education Systems: From Linear to Open and Complex Dynamic Systems

In the past, education was understood to involve a linear relationship, while the new type of education supported by technologies has become a complex system, with the relationship in teaching changing from a simple linear one to a nonlinear one (Xu and Chen 2021). The relationship also presents the characteristics of a complex network: self-organization, emergence and uncertainty (Guo et al. 2020). The complex system refers to a dynamic nonlinear system with a hierarchical structure which composes of components or subjects that follow basic operating rules and have interactive relationships. This kind of complex system is a new research perspective and approach to understand the world (Chen and Xu 2021). With the development of the technologies and the emergence of more open, equal and interconnected learning spaces, great changes can be witnessed in the education system, various teaching elements, as well as the interaction between them. The simple linear interaction of "one-to-one, one-to-many" in the original teaching and learning process has been transformed into a complex interaction of "many-to-many", which intensifies uncertainty, disorder, and multi-level approaches to teaching and learning behavior. The interaction between components and agents will lead to the generation of complex systems, and the relationship between teaching and learning will be more complex.

The complexity of the system is reflected in two aspects: collective and individual, i.e., the complexity of collective behavior (symbolic representations, formal systems, and sociocultural practices) and the complexity of the interactive behavior of individuals or subjects in the system. The collective complexity of the entire system involves five aspects: components and agents, system level, self-organization, initial value sensitivity and nonlinearity, and emergence. The complexity of independent agents in the system is reflected in three aspects: parallelism, conditional triggering, adaptation and evolution (Jacobson et al. 2018). From the complex perspective of online teaching and learning, Chen et al., (2021) explored the complexity under the new knowledge concept of "Internet Plus Education"—online learning based on student–student interaction. As a result, ten characteristics were identified: seven characteristics can be observed from the perspective of the complexity of collective behavior, namely the diversification and heterogeneity of participating subjects, a polycentric network structure formed by self-organization, the formation of network status and identity through dialogue, the connection between the level and quality of initial interactions with later learning effects, the emergence of collective knowledge and wisdom, nonlinear interaction between within and between the groups, and the continuous exchange of elements with the external environment. Three characteristics can be observed at the individual level, namely parallel processing of interactive information, a positive correlation between network status and learning effects, continuous adaptation, and the evolution of individual and collective networks.

The characteristics of the complexity shows that new education supported by the Internet is different from traditional school education (Chen 2018). Researchers and practitioners need to shift from traditional linear thinking perspectives to nonlinear thinking in order to understand the nature education in the new era. The technology can record the behavior of teaching and learning processes in the form of data, which makes it possible for humans to understand teaching and learning from Science of Learning perspectives. It is necessary to transform and update the educational research paradigm and develop technology enhanced pedagogy.

7.4.4 New Forms of Education: Future Schools and Beyond

Many new educational forms and educational service providers emerged in the past decade. In the era of "Internet+", a new form of university that does not adhere to the traditional concept of education has emerged. It uses Internet thinking and technologies to transform the organizational system and service model of higher education.

As a university innovation in the digital age, Minerva University is "a world university without walls" (Wang and Wang 2015), with four-year undergraduate studies distributed in seven major cities around the world, including San Francisco, Hong Kong, Mumbai, London, etc., the whole city is their campus. By collaborating with local universities, research institutes, and companies, schools are no longer the only place for students to acquire knowledge. Students can have access to the world-class libraries and laboratories, etc. The university makes use of all excellent social resources to run schools openly and focus on curriculum development and attracting quality faculty members (Shang et al. 2017). The structural innovation of the university organizational system has been realized. At present, residential education is the mainstream education model for higher education which relies on on-campus resources, adopts standardized content, extensive supply units, and face-to-face teaching as the main mode of learning. This learning model is difficult to meet the needs of students for high-quality, flexible and personalized education. The new mode of learning supported by technologies provides a solution for tackling current problems in colleges and universities to meet the diverse learning needs of students, and to cultivate talents who adapt to the information society.

In the "Internet+" era, the provider of educational resources and services for a university will no longer be one university but will move towards a new pattern of coordinated provider by multiple entities such as governments, universities, and enterprises. On the one hand, universities can collaborate to exchange high-quality resources across campuses, schools, and regions, providing students with more choices, meeting students' diverse educational needs, and providing support for the growth of interdisciplinary innovative talents. On the other hand, colleges and universities can actively explore an education model which break down the barriers between knowledge, technology, and industries by allowing or even encouraging enterprises and alumni entering the schools, and promoting the integrated research and development in educational innovations. Various stakeholders such as the government and enterprises can be involved in providing educational services, enhancing students' practical and innovation competencies through diversified and open practical activities, and building universities into scientific and technological innovative clusters (Liu 2021).

Therefore, the emergence of new forms of education inform us the following: we should build an open educational organization system and pay attention to the integration of education and society since the public education system of schools and the whole society can provide services for human development. Not only the existing self-built resources, but also the whole society contains rich educational resources, and a new mechanism for co-construction and sharing can be built, so that various stakeholders have the opportunity to participate in creation, sharing, selection, and recommendation. It is necessary to shift from supplier-driven education services to user-driven education services by connect various providers and users and realizing cross-border "co-creation, sharing, and co-governance". The educational organization system should create a new connected ecology through continuous reconstruction, development, iteration and evolution, so that higher education can serve the needs of students and society.

7.4.5 Learning System: Building a Flexible Lifelong Learning System

With the development of new-generation technologies, the needs for lifelong learning and the evolution of educational service systems have expanded from the classroom and school scenarios to the entire society (Chen 2018). Schools and society will also be deeply integrated, which demands a complete system to consolidate social resources, collaborate with the society and serve the human development.

The faculty and the resource are insufficient to meet the needs of talent training in the traditional higher education system. In fact, the society contains much more resources. At present, there have been many practical explorations on resource integration platforms. Even though the models of these platforms are different, they all organize and integrate the development and application of instructional and teaching resources generated by the society. There is an urgent need to coordinate these resources and make them available openly to the community and society so that all learners can have access to the high-quality instructional resources. In the long run, it is necessary to establish a quality assurance system to identify the level of social resources, which facilitates the schools to make better choices. As traditional higher education does not yet recognize certificates and diplomas of adult education, and employers to some extent discriminate against adult education certificates and diplomas. It is difficult for students to get recognition on their personal learning experiences and outcomes, such as taking off-campus online courses, vocational certificates, competition awards etc.

We should build an institutional mechanism for flexible lifelong learning: Firstly, we need to establish a lifelong learning credential framework which recognizes the learner's learning experiences and outcomes obtained through formal and informal education, such as degrees, diplomas, industry training certificates, skill level certificates, professional qualifications and certificates, MOOC Certificates, and various achievements (innovation and entrepreneurship, scientific research, cultural heritage, and professional awards, etc.). Secondly, we need to establish the education quality assurance system which can formulate national criteria and standards for various types of education at all levels which. In addition, it is necessary to explore and establish an operation mechanism to clearly figure out the relationship among state power, academic authority, and market power, to actively exert and aptly restrain the role boundaries of different entities, to clarify rules and procedures to facilitate labor division, collaboration, and liaison among them, and to pay special attention to strengthen and optimize the role of third-party institutions. Thirdly, we need to establish learners' personal learning portfolio to record, and store their learning experience and achievements. In this system, learning experiences and outcomes can be tracked, queried, transferred, and monitored.

John Dewey (1916) stated a hundred years ago about the educational reform in the United States: "If we teach today as we taught yesterday, we rob our children of tomorrow". To borrow his sentence, "If we still use yesterday's educational ideas and concepts to educate today's students, even if we apply the new Internet-centered technology very well, skillfully, and dazzlingly, we will not be able to cultivate future-ready innovative talents" (Chen 2020). The impact of the emerging technologies on education is not only about the pedagogical innovation supported by technology, but also amount the renewal of educational philosophy and theories, and the reconstruction of the educational ecosystem.

The higher education system is transforming in various aspects, including educational philosophy and theories, approaches and methods, educational forms and systems. It brings the integration of on-campus and off-campus, face-to-face and online education, and formal and informal education. It's a highly open and interconnected new educational ecosystem that is greatly integrated with society. At present, the purpose of China's strategic implementation of education digitization actions and the development of "Internet Plus Education" is to build a new higher education system that is compatible with the information age.

References

Bomsdorf, B. (2005). Adaptation of learning spaces: Supporting ubiquitous learning in higher distance education. In *Dagstuhl Seminar Proceedings*. Schloss Dagstuhl-Leibniz-Zentrum fr Informatik.

Cai, C. (2007). *On open educational resources development model and operation: A comparative study of MIT OCW and Beijing quality OCW* (in Chinese). Master's thesis, Xiamen University.

Chen, K., & Zhang, K. (2011). The integration of learning science and pervasive computing: The option to build ubiquitous learning environments for university students (in Chinese). *Journal of Distance Education, 5,* 50–57.

Chen, L. (2011). *Distance Education* (in Chinese). Beijing: Higher Education Press.

Chen, L. (2016). The innovation essence and reforming trend of "Internet+Education" (in Chinese). *Journal of Distance Education, 34*(4), 3–8.

Chen, L. (2018). ICT in Education 2.0: Trends and directions of Internet-facilitated educational transformation (in Chinese). *Distance Education in China, 07,* 9.

Chen, L. (2020). "Internet + Education": Innovation and development of knowledge view and ontology (in Chinese). *E-Learning, 11,* 44–46.

Chen, L., Lu, X., & Zheng, Q. (2019). Conceptualizing knowledge in "Internet + education" : the nature of knowledge and knowledge evolution (in Chinese). *Distance Education in China (7),* 10–18+92.

Chen, L., Wang, H., Sun, H., & Liu, C. (2017). The return of MOOCs in China and the reform direction of teaching service model in higher eEducation (in Chinese). *China Educational Technology, 8,* 7.

Chen, L., & Xu, Y. (2021). Ten new academic propositions of "Internet + Education" research. *e-Education Research, 11,* 5–12.

Chen, T., & Qi, M. (2014). Movement of Open Education Resources: Changes and challenges facing higher education (in Chinese). *Tsinghua Journal of Education, 5,* 9.

Dewey, J. (1916). *Democracy and Education: An Introduction to the Philosophy of Education.* NY: Macmillan.

Dong, Z. Li, P., & Li, W. (2015). Research on the Construction of New Learning Support Service System in the "Internet Plus" Era (in Chinese). *Journal of Distance Education, 6,* 93–98.

Downes, S. (2012). *Connectivism and Connective Knowledge: essays on meaning and learning networks.* National Research Council Canada. Retrieved on June 9, 2014 from http://www.downes.ca/files/books/Connective_Knowledge-19May2012.Pdf.

Guo, Y., Chen, L., Xu L., & Gao, X. (2020). Social network characteristics of learners in connectivist learning (in Chinese). *Distance Education In China, 02,* 32–39+67+76–77.

Han, X. (2022). *Blended Teaching Research and Practice (in Chinese).* Beijing: Tsinghua University Press.

Hylén, J. (2006). Open educational resources: Opportunities and challenges. *Proceedings of Open Education,* 49–63.

Jacobson, M., Kapur, M., Reimann, P., Zhang, J., Wang, Y., & Cao, L. (2018). Conceptualizing Debates in Learning and Educational Research: Toward a Complex Systems Conceptual Framework of Learning (in Chinese). *Journal of Open Learning, 2,* 1–8.

Jones, V., & Jo, J. H. (2004, December). Ubiquitous learning environment: An adaptive teaching system using ubiquitous technology. In *Beyond the comfort zone: Proceedings of the 21st ASCILITE Conference,* 468–474.

Ke, Q., Lin, J., Ma, X., & Bao, T. (2021). Construction direction and development path of digital education resources in the era of new infrastructure for education (in Chinese). *e-Education Research, 11,* 48–54.

Li, L., & Zheng, Y. (2006). Conceptual model of ubiquitous learning environment (in Chinese). *China Educational Technology, 12,* 9–12.

Li, H., Xu, W., & Zhang, J. (2013). Learning activities and their design in the context of virtual-reality integration (in Chinese). *China Educational Technology, 01,* 23–29.

Liu, G. (2021). The new development pattern and high-quality development of higher education (in Chinese). *Tsinghua Journal of Education, 1,* 25–32.

Liu, G., & Nong, L. (2020). From "pansophism" to ubiquitous learning to smart learning: On the intrinsic relevance and value implication of "Pan" educational thought (in Chinese). *e-Education Research, 6,* 27–32+67.

Pan, Y. (2018). Artificial intelligence 2.0 and education development (in Chinese). *Distance Education in China, 05,* 5–8.

Qi, J. (2011). On the connotation of teaching space and its relationship with neighboring concept (in Chinese). *Journal of Shanghai Educational Research, 04,* 12–14.

Qian, M., & Wang, X. (2013). Course-embedded assessment of general education in American public universities (in Chinese). *Modern Education Management, 11,* 6.

Shang, J., Wang., & Cao, P. (2017). "Internet +" and the reform of higher education: A preliminary study on the development strategy of higher education informationization in China (in Chinese). *Peking University Education Review, 1,* 173–182.

Shen, S. (2020). An adaptation to the new normal: Constructing adaptive learning space (in Chinese). *Journal of Guangxi Normal University (Philosophy and Social Sciences Edition), 56*(5), 9.

Shi, C., & Liu, Y. (2008). Significance and construction of learning community in classroom (in Chinese). *Research in Educational Development, 24,* 26–30.

Siemens, G. (2005). Connectivism: A learning theory for the digital age. *International Journal of Instructional Technology and Distance Learning.* Obtained through the Internet: http://www.idtl.org/Journal/Jam_05/article01.htm. [Accessed Sept. 2008].

Siemens, G. (2012). *Orientation: Sensemaking and wayfinding in complex distributed online information environments* (Doctoral dissertation, University of Aberdeen).

Sun, Z., & Chen, D. (2021). A review on learning support services in modern distance education (in Chinese). *Journal of Vocational Education, 10,* 113–120.

UNESCO. (2017, November 12). *Final report of Forum on the Impact of Open Course Ware for Higher Education in Developing Countries.* Retrieved from http://unesdoc.unesco.org/images/0012/001285/128515e.pdf.

UNESCO. (2019, November 25). Recommendation concerning Open Educational Resources.

United Nations Educational, Scientific and Cultural Organization. (2017). Rethinking education: Shifting to the idea of a "global common good"? (in Chinese). Beijing: Education Science Press.

Wang, H., & Chen, L. (2020). Conceptualizing networked knowledge and constructing its representation model (in Chinese). *Distance Education in China, 5,* 10–17+76.

Wang, R. (2019). Research on the construction and use of resource pool combined with MOOC and MOOE (in Chinese). *China Computer & Communication, 17,* 250–252.

Wang, X., & Zhou, Q. (2021). Twin museum: The virtual-real symbiosis learning space integrated with digital twin (in Chinese). *Modern Educational Technology, 31*(7), 7, 5–11.

Wang, Y., Bao, X., & Wang, X. (2015). Minerva school: An explorer of innovative universities in the Era of MOOCs (in Chinese). Journal of Distance Education, 2, 3–10.

Weiser, M. (1991). The computing for the twenty-first century. *Scientific American,* 94–104.

Wu, N. (2017). Blended Learning Space: Connotations, Utility Representation and Formation Mechanism (in Chinese). *e-Education Research, 8*(1), 7.

Xiao, J., Liang, X., Hwang, L., & Pan, Z. (2021). Focus and trends of seamless learning: Academic highlights from 18th mLearn conference (in Chinese). *Distance Education in China, 2,*10.

Xu, Y., & Chen, L. (2021). Exploring complexity patterns of online learning featuring student-student interaction (in Chinese). *Distance Education In China, 10,* 12–18+38.

Yang, J., Huang, R., & Liu, B. (2013). Review of study on study space abroad (in Chinese). *China Educational Technology, 6,* 6.

Yang, X., Li, Y., Wang, D., & Xing, B. (2021). Integration of learning spaces in the intelligent age: pattern and path (in Chinese). *Distance Education in China, 1,* 46–53.

Yang, X., & Yu, S. (2013). The design of ubiquitous learning environment from the perspective of ecology (in Chinese). *Educational Research, 3,* 98–105.

Yang, Y., & Zhang, J. (2021). The design framework of embodied learning activity in immersive virtual-reality fusion environment (in Chinese). *Modern Distance Education Research, 04,* 63–73.

Yu, S., & Chen, M. (2011). The characteristics and the trend of ubiquitous learning resources construction: Exemplified by the "learning Cell resource model" (in Chinese). *Modern Distance Education Research, 6,* 14–22.

Yu, S., Wang, Q., Wang, F., & Wan, H. (2021). Designing an organization and description framework for ubiquitous learning resources: A study of international standards for Learning Cell (in Chinese). *Distance Education in China, 7,* 1–9+76.

Zeng, M. (2010). *A comparative study of digital science and technology museums at home and abroad* (In Chinese). Information Center of Beijing Association of Science and Technology, Beijing Association for Digital Science and Technology.

Zhu, J. (2016). First exploration on Massive Open Online Experiment: Taking network security as the Eexample (in Chinese). *Journal of Henan Radio & TV University, 1,* 13–16.

Zhang, J., Xu, W., Yang, J., & Li, H. (2013). Learning environment of virtual-actual fusion: Concept, characteristics and its applications (in Chinese). *Journal of Distance Education, 31*(3), 7.

Zhao, Y., Xiao, M., Zhang, X., & Li, X. (2019). The sustainable development of Open Educational Resources: A study of the current status and challenges (in Chinese). *Library Tribune, 03,* 42–50.

Zhu, Z. (2016b). New developments of smarter education: From flipped classroom to smart classroom and smart learning space (in Chinese). *Open Education Research 22*(1),10.

Zhu, Z., & Sun, Y. (2015). Seamless learning as a new normal learning form in digital age (in Chinese). *Open Education Research, 21*(1), 6.

Zhuang, R., Yang, J., & Huang, R. (2020). New opportunities and challenges for education in the 5G Era (in Chinese). *China Educational Technology, 12,* 1–8.

Appendix
Glossary of Terms

Ubiquitous learning: refers to that, with the support of ubiquitous computing and technology, learners actively engage in a variety of learning activities according to their own learning goals, by taking advantage of resources available anytime, anywhere.

Flipped classroom (Inverted classroom): refers to that events that have traditionally taken place inside the classroom now take place outside the classroom and vice versa. The learning belief behind flipped classroom is active learning.

Lage, M. J., Platt, G. J., & Treglia, M. Inverting the Classroom: A Gateway to Creating an Inclusive Learning Environment [J]. The Journal of Economic Education, 2000, 31(1): 30–43.

Simulation training software: refers to the computer software used for vocational skills training. It is based on the process of modeling a real phenomenon with a set of mathematical formulas. Simulation software is the creation of a true-to-life learning environment that mirrors real-life work and scenarios.

Woofresh. The 9 Best Simulation Software [DB/OL]. [2022–08-06]. https://woofresh.com/simulation-software/#:~:text=The%209%20Best%20Simulation%20Software%201%20AUTODESK.%20Autodesk,...%207%20SIMULATION%20X.%20...%20More%20items...%20.

Distributed learning: refers to the instructional model that allows instructor, students, and content to be located in different, non-centralized locations so that instruction and learning occur independently of time and place. The model can be used in combination with traditional classroom-based courses, with traditional distance learning courses, or can be used to create wholly virtual classrooms.

Blended learning: refers to an instructional model that combines online learning with face-to-face teaching. Its deeper connotation: blended learning is a new instructional form formed by reconstructing the core elements of teaching, including learning

M. Li et al. (eds.), *Handbook of Educational Reform Through Blended Learning*, https://doi.org/10.1007/978-981-99-6269-3

objectives, content (resources), activities, evaluation, and teaching team, in the environment of physical and virtual binary integration, aiming to achieve the optimal learning effect under specific conditions.

Blended instructional design: refers to the systemic process of arranging a series of instructional activities and corresponding instructional strategies so as to form the instructional plan with a hybrid of multi-variables in order to fulfill the specific learning objectives, by taking advantages of both face-to-face teaching and online learning.

Blended learning environments: refers to the technology-enhanced classroom environment and learning cyberspace, for supporting both online and face-to-face learning, meanwhile supplying learning resources.

Johnson, M. C., & Graham, C. R. Current Status and Future Directions of Blended Learning Models. In M. Khosrow-Pour, D.B.A. (Ed.), Encyclopedia of Information Science and Technology (Third Edition)[M]. IGI Global, 2015: 2470–2480.

Blended course: is defined as having course contents delivered both online and face-to-face and having the instructional model reconfigured.

Instructional design (ID): refers to the systematic process of designing and creating a high-quality instructional blueprint (including learning objectives, content, activities, evaluation, etc.) based on teaching and learning theories.

Curriculum development: refers to a dynamic process of identifying curriculum goals, selecting and organizing curriculum content, and implementing and evaluating the curriculum.

Curriculum development models: refers to the process of curriculum development utilizing sets of concepts to achieve both quantity and quality education through a guided learning experience.

Modebelu, M. N. Curriculum Development Models for Quality Educational System. In N. Ololube, P. Kpolovie, & Makewa, L. (Eds.), Handbook of Research on Enhancing Teacher Education with Advanced Instructional Technologies [M]. IGI Global, 2015: 259–276.

Problem-based learning (PBL): refers to the active learning method that involves learners working together to understand and solve complex, ill-structured problems. In PBL, students learn by solving authentic real-world problems. Teachers guide student reflection on these experiences, facilitating learning of the cognitive skills needed for problem-solving, the skills needed for collaboration and articulation, and the principles behind those skills.

Hmelo, C. E. F. The problem- based learning tutorial: Cultivating higher order thinking skills [J]. Journal of the education of the gifted, 1997, 20 (4): 401–422.

Project-based learning: refers to the instructional model carried out through the implementation of a complete project, which aims to combine theory learning and its application together, improve students' ability of comprehensively applying knowledge to solve practical problems. The model often requires students to think across disciplines to integrate and solve complex problems in authentic contexts, driven by projects.

Resources-based learning model: refers to the learning model in which learners learn by interacting with various types of learning resources. Learning resources are all print and non-print media that are available, involving books and articles, audio and video materials, electronic databases and other computer-based, computer multimedia and computer network resources, etc.

Textbooks: are compiled according to the curriculum standard and reflect the subject content systematically, used for teaching and learning.

Instructional strategies: refers to the ways, approaches, and the knowledge of operational principles and procedures followed by the teachers for effective instructional problem-solving.

Akdeniz, C. Instructional strategies. In Instructional Process and Concepts in Theory and Practice: Improving the Teaching Process [M]. Springer, 2016: 61.

Instructional environment: refers to the material and non-material conditions for teaching activities to be carried out, made up of multiple, inter-related facets that can either support or inhibit learning.

Instructional model: refers to the relatively stable interactions between the elements of teaching designed and gradually formed through practice under the guidance of certain educational theories to accomplish specific teaching objectives, including the combination of the teaching elements, procedures and their corresponding strategies and evaluation methods, etc.

Instructional design models: are simplified overviews of instructional design procedures. They are typically visual representations, such as process flowcharts, that prescribe the steps that should be followed in a design project. All models are the representation of instructional design theory and they typically describe the process of instructional design.

Richey, R.C., Klein, J. D., & Tracey, M.W. The instructional design knowledge base: Theory, research, and practice [M]. New York: Routledge, 2011.

Teaching support services: are provide by educational institutions (colleges) to support teachers in carrying out blended learning, such as support service for preparation for teaching, instructional design, implementation and evaluation, etc.

Wray, M. Additional support services and the utilisation of teaching assistants in university settings: dissuading inclusive practice or improving academic outcomes? [J]. Support for Learning, 2021, 36(1): 102–115.

Mmny, A. M., Ellis, J. R., & Abrams, P. In- service Education in American Senior Colleges and Universities: A Status Report [DB/OL]. (1969) [2022–08–06]. https:// files.eric.ed.gov/fulltext/ED057731.pdf.

Educational communication: refers to a special form of human communication, which is an activity of transmitting knowledge, skills, ideas, concepts, etc. to specific educational targets by educators in accordance with certain purposes and selected appropriate contents through effective media channels, and is a communication activity between educators and educated people.

Educational communication model: refers to a theoretical and simplified form of reproducing the reality of educational communication. It is a general and concise representation of the phenomenon of educational communication, a simplified form of the composition and relationship of the elements of the educational communication process, and reflects the essential characteristics of the phenomenon of educational communication.

Educational evaluation: refers to the continuous inspection of all available information concerning the student, teacher, educational program, and the teaching–learning process to ascertain the degree of change in students and form a valid judgment about the students and the effectiveness of the program.

OA archives or repositories: refer to online interactive documents or sharing platforms of documents, including teaching materials, exam question banks, resources, etc. In general, the author uploads the data to a document server in a specific format, which is officially reviewed and then released, and users can read and download the documents online.

Open textbooks: are available online for free use by students, teachers and the general public, in print, e-book or audio format that are licensed under open access licenses.

Open educational resources (OER): refer to teaching, learning, and research resources that reside in the creative commons and/or public domain or have been released under an intellectual property license that permits their use and repurposing by others. OER may include full courses, course materials, modules, textbooks, streaming videos, tests, etc. used to support access to knowledge.

UNESCO. Recommendation concerning Open Educational Resources [EB/OL]. (2019–11–25) [2022–08–06]. http://portal.unesco.org/en/ev.php-URL_ID=49556& URL_DO=DO_TOPIC&URL_SECTION=201.html.

Open Course Ware (OCW): refers to an online free publication of course materials from courses, freely sharing knowledge with learners and educators over the Internet. Each OCW includes a syllabus, some instructional material (such as lecture notes or a reading list), and some learning activities (such as assignments or exams).

Curriculum: refers to all the instructional contents and plans required in order to achieve educational objectives.

Courseware: refers to a multimedia material or software that presents one or several knowledge units. According to the difference of the purpose of use, it can be divided into teaching-assisted courseware (such as PPT lecture notes used by teachers, etc.) and learning-assisted courseware (such as courseware for students to learn, etc.).

Curriculum objectives: Objectives are statements that describe the end-points or desired outcomes of the curriculum, a unit, a lesson plan, or learning activity.

Kridel, C. Objectives in curriculum planning [EB/OL]. [2022–08-06]. https://dx.doi. org/10.4135/9781412958806.n331.

Course evaluation: refers to the process of systematically examining and refining the fit between the course activities and what students should know at the end of the course. Conducting a course-level evaluation involves considering whether all aspects of the course align with each other and whether they guide students to achieve the desired learning outcomes.

Curriculum design: is the art and science of designing curricula. Its inputs are information about reality and creative thought. Its output is curriculum. Its functions are information processing and decision making. Curriculum design is systematic to the extent that its processes are coherent and interactive, and unified by a common purpose. The same is true of the instructional system (or program) into which the curriculum is an input.

Face to face course: Course content is delivered face to face, with no use of online learning.

Allen, I.E., & Seaman, J., Sizing the opportunity: The quality and extent of online education in the United States, 2002 and 2003[J]. Sloan Consortium (NJ1), 2003, 36(23): 659–673.

MOOC: refers to the Massive Open Online Course, online courses that involves large-scale student interaction and open source to web-based resources.

Massive open online course. (2013–04-16). http://en.wikipedia.org/wiki/Mas sive_ open_ online_ course.

Assessment standards: The criterion and scale for value judgment on the quantity and quality of the efficacy of the evaluated object. Two elements are required: index system and evaluation benchmark. The evaluation index system is the embodiment of the evaluation objectives, and the evaluation benchmark is the critical point to distinguish the different performance levels of the evaluated objects.

Assessment instrument: refers to the specific tools for collecting information and feedback data in evaluation activities. Usually, the appropriate tools are selected according to the purpose, object, and stage of the evaluation.

Evaluating indicator: a marker of accomplishment/progress. It is a specific, observable, and measurable accomplishment or change that shows the progress made toward achieving a specific output or outcome in your logic model or work plan.

CDC. Developing Evaluation Indicators [DB/OL]. [2022–08-06] https://www. cdc.gov/std/Program/pupestd/Developing%20Evaluation%20Indicators.pdf.

Cognitive apprenticeship instruction: "Apprenticeship" shows its inheritance relationship or similarity with traditional apprenticeship, that is, it emphasizes that learning should take place in the context of its application, and knowledge and skills should be acquired through the combination of expert work and practical operation. Cognition, on the other hand, reflects a strong realistic significance, emphasizing that the learning of general knowledge takes place in the application scene and promoting the application of knowledge in various situations. The main purpose of cognitive apprenticeship is to develop learners' advanced cognitive skills, such as ability of problem solving and ability of reflection.

Collins, A. O. Cognitive apprenticeship: teaching the craft of reading, writing, and mathematics [J]. Knowing Learning & Instruction, 1987, 453–494.

Test papers: refer to a typical set of test questions used to conduct various types of tests, usually used after the study of a course unit or after the study of the entire subject, and is a tool for teachers and students to make summative evaluations.

Digital educational resources: belong to the category of curriculum resources, are all kinds of resources that exist and are used in digital form, which are specially designed for teaching purposes or can serve education.

Random access learning: refers to the instructional model that teaches complex (or advanced) knowledge and skills. Learners can enter the same teaching content multiple times through different channels, different aspects and different ways, so as to obtain knowledge and understanding of the same thing or the same problem in many aspects.

Spiro, R. J., Feltovich, P. J., Jacobson, M. J., & Coulson, R. L. Cognitive flexibility, constructivism, and hypertext: Random access instruction for advanced knowledge acquisition in ill-structured domains. In L. P. Steffe, & J. E. Gale (Eds.), Construc-tivism in education; Constructivism in education [M]. Lawrence Erlbaum Associates, Inc, Hillsdale, NJ. 1995, 85–107.

Web-facilitated course: Course which uses web-based technology to facilitate what is essentially a face-to-face course, following the traditional teaching model.

Allen, I.E., & Seaman, J., Sizing the opportunity: The quality and extent of online education in the United States, 2002 and 2003[J]. Sloan Consortium (NJ1), 2003, 36(23): 659–673.

Learning management system (LMS): is an e-learning platform and a supportive environment for the whole process of online learning and teaching, which can carry out online courses and support teaching and learning in the network environment.

Cyberspace for learning: refers to the virtual computer world, and more specifically, an electronic medium that is used to facilitate online communication. Cyberspace typically involves a large computer network made up of many worldwide computer subnetworks that employ TCP/IP protocol to aid in communication and data exchange activities. Cyberspace's core feature is an interactive and virtual environment for a broad range of participants.

Weller M. Virtual learning environments: Using, choosing and developing your VLE [M]. London: Routledge, 2007.

Seamless Learning: refers to learning that takes place in different contexts at any time, can be quickly and easily switched between different learning contexts with the aid of mobile devices, and integrates in-class and out-of-class, instant and non-instant communication, formal and informal learning, multiple pedagogies and teaching activities.

Disciplinary: is related to a specific field of academic study. Such as Physics, Chemistry in natural sciences, and history, linguistics in humanities and social sciences.

Learning motivation: is usually defined as an internal psychological state that stimulates, directs and maintains a certain behavior.

Learning styles: refers to the concept that individuals differ in regard to what mode of instruction or study is most effective for them.

Pashler, H., McDaniel, M., Rohrer, D., & Bjork, R. Learning Styles: Concepts and Evidence [J]. Psychological Science in the Public Interest: a Journal of the American Psychological Society, 2008, 9(3): 105–119.

Learning community: is a learning team composed of learners, facilitators, and other people with a clear sense of team belonging, common aspirations and extensive communication opportunities, with common goals, common sharing, communication, common activities, and mutual promotion.

Learning activities: refers to the sum of operations performed by learners and their related learning groups (including learning partners and teachers) to accomplish specific learning objectives. It includes at least four aspects: activity tasks and themes, basic procedure and steps of activities, activity rules, and evaluation rules of activity.

Learning objectives: are statements that clearly describe students' behaviors change after completing a prescribed unit of instruction.

Kibler R.J., Cegala, D.J., Barker, L.L. & Miles, D.T. Objectives for instruction and evaluation [M]. Boston, MA: Allyn and Bacon, Inc, 1974.

Learning ability: refers to learner's ability formed and developed in learning activities to seek knowledge, do things and seek development under the formal or informal learning environment.

Learning assessment: is defined as the deliberate process of collecting information about students' learning, using any of a number of different formats, to evaluate their learning and to make instruction-related decisions.

Richey, R. C. Encyclopedia of Terminology for Educational Communications and Technology [M]. Springer New York, 2013: 12.

Learning attitude: refers to a relatively stable psychological tendency formed by individuals in learning process, including cognitive, emotional and behavioral tendencies.

Learning interest: refers to the individuals' attention and investment in certain specific events and learning contents, is usually divided into two categories: individual interest and situational interest. Individual interest has the characteristics of persistence and stability while Situational interest is the immediate, short-lived psychological state.

Zhang, J. Learning Interest: A Review of Studies and Implications for Future Research Directions in Second Language Acquisition [J]. Teacher Education and Curriculum Studies, 2022, 7(1):15–22.

Learning needs: refers to the gap between the current learning development level of learners and the expected learning development level of learners.

Early warning systems (EWSs): By analyzing multiple sources of educational data, Early Warning Systems (EWSs) identify students who might undertake risk of academic failure and provide academic interventions to students and other stakeholders.

Learning support services: refers to various types of services provided by educational institutions to guide and help students to carry out blended learning and achieve learning goals, including learning planning and guidance, learning diagnosis and tutoring, learning monitoring and intervention, learning evaluation and feedback, etc.

Distance education: refers to the teaching and planned learning where the teaching occurs in a different place from learning, requiring effective communication supported by technologies and special institutional organizations.

Online course: is defined as having at least 80% of the course content delivered online. Typically has no face-to-face meetings.

Allen, I.E., & Seaman, J., Sizing the opportunity: The quality and extent of online education in the United States,2002 and 2003[J]. Sloan Consortium (NJ1), 2003, 36(23): 659–673.

Online learning: is a form of distance education where technology mediates the learning process, teaching is delivered completely using the internet, and students and instructors are not required to be available at the same time and place. It does not include more traditional distance education instruction methods, such as print-based correspondence education, broadcast television or radio, videoconferencing in its traditional form, videocassettes/DVDs and stand-alone educational software programs.

Gasevic, D., Siemens, G., & Dawson, S. Preparing for the digital university: a review of the history and current state of distance, blended, and online learning [M]. Arlington: Link Research Lab, 2015: 100.

Academic program: is a professional category divided by colleges and universities. comprising the required and elective courses that lead to a degree or certificate.

Knowledge: is broadly understood as information, understanding, skills, values and attitudes acquired through learning.

UNESCO. Rethinking education: towards a global common good? [DB/OL]. (2015) [2022–08–06]. https://unesdoc.unesco.org/ark:/48223/pf0000232555.

Self-efficacy: One's beliefs that he/she can be successful when carrying out a particular task. Perceived self-efficacy refers to people's beliefs about their capabilities to exercise control over their own activities.

Bandura, A. Social foundations of thought and action: A social cognitive theory [M]. Englewood Cliffs, NJ: Prentice-Hall. 1986.